THE BIBLE ON HUMAN SUFFERING

JOHN McDERMOTT

THE BIBLE
ON HUMAN SUFFERING

 St Paul Publications

St Paul Publications
Middlegreen, Slough SL3 6BT, United Kingdom

Copyright © St Paul Publications, United Kingdom 1990
Printed by The Guernsey Press Co Ltd, Guernsey, C.I.
ISBN 085439 363 3

St Paul Publications is an activity of the priests and brothers
of the Society of St Paul who proclaim the Gospel through the
media of social communication

Contents

Preface

The Bible on human suffering was originally intended to accompany and supplement my course lectures, *The theology of the Cross*, offered regularly at the Pontifical Gregorian University in Rome. I have slightly expanded the original text and added some footnotes in an attempt to clarify some technical terms and notions for the non-specialist.

Heartfelt words of gratitude are owed to many: to Ugo Vanni SJ, Professor of New Testament Exegesis at the Gregorian, who kindly wrote the Foreword; to my students at the English, Scots and North American Colleges in Rome, who spared me many hours of labour by checking the numerous biblical references in this work; and to Liza Palmer, a former student, who contributed to the book's clarity by reading the manuscript and noting obscure and technical phrases in need of further explanation. Needless to say, after all that help, the author bears the responsibility for the final version.

Foreword

The subject which J. M. McDermott tackles in this book, as already indicated in its very title, shows itself to be simultaneously difficult and fascinating. Suffering has always interested men and women and drawn their attention to itself on many different levels. On one level, easily identifiable, we find a disclosure of suffering and an attempt to let others participate in it. It manifests itself every time a human being seeks to express his or her own suffering: suffering exists, it is a daily reality, and we become aware of the need to talk about it, to describe it and to confide it to others. Many of the most beautiful pages in all the great literatures can be identified as belonging to this category.

Nonetheless we are not content just to speak about pain. The level of phenomenological description and of participation shared by other human beings in solidarity with us does not satisfy us. We would like to understand, and for that reason we ask, sometimes with great persistence, why suffering happens and especially what was the original cause of suffering. Inevitably at this point the question of suffering knocks at the door of God and becomes a problem particularly difficult; its answer seems to escape us every time we seem to be on the verge of attaining it. There remains Augustine's distressing question: if God is good, what is the source of evil?

With that question we arrive at the disconcerting aspect of suffering. Fr McDermott has noted the import and range of the problem which he tackles, and already in his introduction he exposes it with an almost crude clarity such as we find in the documents of the Mediterranean cultural basin that are roughly parallel to the biblical texts. Nonetheless, the author's principal interest and the more relevant part of his study – that part which is actually the most suggestive – moves in another direction. God, though he permits suffering, does not abandon us. Rather he accompanies us with his word which, developing around that theme of suffering through the centuries and in response to the most varied events and situations, finally comes together in a mighty synthesis and attains its culmination in Christ.

All the biblical material concerning this problem, from the Old Testament on, is taken into consideration, analysed and situated in its proper context within the total vision that *Dei Verbum*, Vatican II's Dogmatic Constitution on Revelation, wished to be typical of Catholic exegesis. In that way it becomes a message. The person who suffers, the person who concerns himself with his own suffering and that of others, seeing it as a true problem, is carried ultimately to the school of God's word.

That school is a demanding one. The author possesses the capacity to express himself in a style at once concise, clear and pleasant to read. Yet he never falls into the snare of rendering banal or of playing superficially with either the message which he conveys or the reader who is following his exposition. Besides a vast store of information and an assured biblical competence, the author enjoys an exceptional speculative talent. he reflects and he makes others reflect. Here the reader feels that he is taken seriously and willingly undertakes a journey that sometimes mounts to the heights, yet at the end comes to a conclusion.

There is in fact a progressive development from the Old to the New Testament, from Job to Christ, if we may mention the two most characteristic protagonists. Whoever has undergone the troubling experience of Job will be happy to be able to live it again and to understand it within the luminous framework that Christ provides.

The problem discussed recalls for me the famous novel of Mario Pomilio, *Natale 1833 (Christmas 1833)*. Its hero, the great Italian writer, Alessandro Manzoni, author of *I Promessi Sposi (The Betrothed)*, lost his wife, Enrichetta Blondel, on Christmas Day itself, and several days later his first-born daughter was also taken from him. Struggling with the problem of suffering, he finds himself immersed in spiritual exaltations and depressions, overwhelmed by flashes of light as well as by dramatic experiences of interior darkness. In Pomilio's imaginative reconstruction of those spiritual movements, Manzoni thought frequently of Job and desired to rewrite that experience, but at the end he found a satisfying response to his questions only in Christ.

The journey which Pomilio suggested to us in his rich poetic creation, Fr McDermott proposes in a reasoned and systematic manner. It is not, however, a dry and dusty journey. Even if the discussion is maintained rigorously within the limits of harkening to the biblical texts and of interpretative reasoning about them, on every page the reader is aware of the convinced tone of a fellow human being who has personally lived what he presents for the consideration of others. One has the encouraging impression that the author himself has successfully completed the complex itinerary that he proposes here. For that reason his book is a persuasive invitation to journey along the same path.

Ugo Vanni SJ

Introduction

The following pages represent an attempt to come to grips with the problem of suffering, especially apparently unmerited suffering, within the horizon of biblical revelation. Taking the biblical witness in both Old and New Testaments, we extract this one theme and try to organize somewhat systematically what God's word has said. There are certainly dangers in this attempt. God's word stands and speaks as a whole in its intricacies and directness. Isolating any one theme and considering it, if not as the principal theme of revelation, at least as the presently absorbing theme, risks forgetting the more vast perspective of God's word. "We murder to dissect," a particularly heinous crime when minor minds would carve up God's revelation. Moreover, organizing God's word as if he could not speak clearly enough to us himself might seem arrogant of any theologian. Nevertheless we should remember that such isolation is often necessary for us limited creatures who cannot capture the universe in a single glance but must make do with the limping, discursive reason at our disposal. Furthermore, God, recognizing our limitations, speaks to us in every generation as we are so that we might understand him better. This obvious truth about God's gracious consideration applies as well to the inspired authors of the Bible as it does to us moderns or post-moderns. Indeed, the Bible itself is meant not to be absolutized in itself and isolated from the history of the Church but to be read within a living tradition. Every age then has to act as the prudent scribe, returning to the biblical treasure chest, in order to discover in it things both new and old. It is the unique prerogative of the inspired authors as *inspired* to remain the permanently valid source and measure of later theological interpretation and application. While the theological confabulations are most often consigned by the succeeding generation to the closet of outmoded garments which the moth consumes, God's word challenges us again and again through history, renewing the Church and the hearts of individual believers.

Well aware of our limitations, we undertake this presumptuous task of searching the Scriptures to let it speak to the current generation, who is often too caught up in the pursuit of material satisfactions to think of God; yet, when suffering interrupts and frustrates our worldly endeavours, we become terribly sensitive and readily disposed to blame God for our woes. God's word must have something to say to us today so that our situation may be illuminated and our faith quickened.

The method employed in the following pages is a strange hybrid, neither painstakingly analytical exegesis nor straightforward speculation. We attempt to let God's word in the Old Testament enter into dialogue, not primarily with ourselves, but with itself, in order to bring to clarity the conundrum which suffering presents to believers. At times we have gone beyond the formulation of the Bible to highlight difficulties experienced by the modern age, whose sensibilities have been sharpened by excessive individualism, in order to show later how the New Testament witness has anticipated even the most trenchant modern critiques.

Already in the formulation of affirmation and question, thesis and antithesis, theological speculation may rightly be suspected. Our presupposition is that the Old Testament finds its fulfilment in the Christ, whom the New Testament proclaims to us as mankind's redeemer and saviour. Then even in our understanding of the New Testament we must confess further speculative presuppositions. We have attempted to give indications of our metaphysical standpoint elsewhere and we hope sometime in the future to find time to complete a speculative justification of the truth of the

14

Christian message. That metaphysical understanding admittedly guides our interpretation of Christ and the New Testament. Yet, lest the introduction of metaphysics into the interpretation of God's word seem an arbitrary infringement on the priority of God's revelation over human response, it should be noted that our metaphysics grew out of both a listening to modern philosophy with all its conundrums and complaints and a contemplative pondering of the New Testament message, especially the Pauline paradoxes of grace and freedom, indicative and imperative, universal and particular.

A brief Introduction to a consideration of human suffering cannot lay the entire groundwork of theological method, a task reserved to some future book. The method of these pages must justify itself, persuading the readers by a certain cogency of presentation that it remains faithful to the Christian message while addressing their problem and offering a more comprehensive solution than can be found outside the Bible. Love is man's beginning, love is his end, love must guide his every step along the paths of this world, even through the disappointments and woes of existence. That is the truth revealed in Christ, and we only pray that the following pages make this fundamental truth more intelligible to the readers.

Two final methodological remarks should be added. First, a great deal has been written about the problem and meaning of suffering in the Old Testament, and we have tried to take into consideration as much of the secondary literature as possible. Aside from remarks made at the end of the Old Testament studies, relatively little has been written specifically about the significance of suffering in the New Testament. Perhaps this is due not to a lack of interest but to the fullness of considerations which suffuses the New Testament. Many studies have been undertaken about the meaning of redemption, salvation, the Church, Christ, providence freedom and predestination. All of these deal implicitly with the topic of suffering, which reveals most existentially our desperate need of a saviour. Instead of citing all the secondary works read over the years, an employment of citations that would weary the reader, we have limited ourselves to a minimum of secondary references and let the New Testament texts speak for themselves.

Second, in our treatment of the New Testament we employ a certain liberty in citing various texts from different authors. Today many exegetes, in agreement with the fragmentary and fragmenting spirit of the age, distrust leaps of exegetical intuitions from one author to another. Each author, they think, must be treated for himself, since his presuppositions may be very different from those of the other authors. While admitting the necessity of clearly distinguishing theological positions and even having recourse to those distinctions within the corpus of inspired writings, nonetheless our present study considers that the basic unity of the New Testament revelation can and must be presupposed in and through all the diversity. Since the authors are inspired by the one God, who speaks to us in human terms and does not contradict himself, a theologian is challenged to see the New Testament and the Bible as a whole. Moreover, we have elsewhere argued that there is a fundamental consistency of intellectual structure that shapes the thought of the major authors of the New Testament, a structure rooted in the teachings of Jesus himself. Nevertheless, in order to satisfy to some degree the methodological demands of current scholarship as well as to indicate the rich fullness of the New Testament witness, we have often given many references from various authors and levels of the New Testament witness to Christ. Certainly from the density and complexity of divine revelation itself and due to our own intellectual limitations no claim can be raised that the following treatment of the biblical revelation about human suffering is exhaustive. At most we hope that our formulations of the problematic and of the biblical response will encourage others to go further and shed more light, under the guidance of Scripture, upon one of the central concerns of human existence.

Besides the scholarly interest and primary to it, we pray that these pages will bring hope, consolation and a strengthening of faith and love to their readers. Ultimately the author, who has bothered himself for years with the problem of suffering, would be very content if his reflections upon the message of Scripture coincide with the truth of the prayer, the Morning Offering addressed to the Sacred Heart, that initiates his day:

O Jesus, through the immaculate heart of Mary, I offer you all my prayers, works, joys and sufferings of this day for all the intentions of your Sacred Heart, in union with the Holy Sacrifice of the Mass throughout the world, in reparation for my sins, for the intentions of all our associates, and in particular for the special intention of this month.

Part I

Man's perennial problem and the Old Testament response

Perhaps the most poignant and comprehensible reason for modern atheism concerns its protest against the suffering in the world, especially the suffering of the innocent. Our present century has certainly witnessed acts of barbarism unparalleled in extent, efficiency and intensity during the whole of previous human history. Modernism's rejection of God in favour of humanity has too often led to horrendous atrocities against men. Yet suffering was not born in the present age, and it is really unjustified to speak of an ever increasing "amount" or "sum" of human misery, as if the global abstraction "humanity" somehow suffered. Pain touches the individual in his uniqueness, and each individual has to bear his own sorrow in order to discover the sense of suffering.[1] Apparently from the earliest days of our history we have been forced to face and grapple with the meaning both of suffering and of our lives, so filled with grief. Not surprisingly the Bible contains many reflections upon human suffering. For if it was not primarily concerned, as Milton was, with justifying the ways of God to man, it at least tried to describe them and explain them. Certainly the Old Testament offers many reasons for human suffering in order to preserve untainted the justice and majesty of God. The New Testament in turn takes over all those diverse explanations and radically adapts them to the new fact of Jesus Christ. Tracing that Christocentric adaptation of major Old Testament themes not only illuminates the relation of opposition, preservation and sublation of the Old into the New but also gives the Christian some insights into the existential concern of God for human suffering and his redemptive response.[2] But before proceeding to that contrast it would be worthwhile to put the biblical witness into a wider context by examining briefly some ancient, non-biblical witnesses to the problem of suffering.

Non-biblical testimony [3]

Early Mesopotamian epics about Gilgamesh, a man with a restless heart, recount this original hero's quest for lasting glory, his friendship with Enkidu, the jealousy aroused among the gods by their heroic accomplishments, and the resultant death of Enkidu.[4] Though his life was spared by the chief god Enlil, Gilgamesh was shattered by the death of his friend and mourned him for six days and seven nights. Thereafter, in fear of death he wandered, seeking the immortality which the gods had reserved for themselves; his lament was keen:

How can I be silent? How can I be still?
My friend, whom I loved, has turned to clay!
Must I, too, like him, lay me down,
Not to rise again for ever and ever?[5]

Pity moved the deified human Utnapishtim to reveal the location of the plant of new life, or of rejuvenation. Plunging into the depth of the sea Gilgamesh plucked out the plant, returned to shore and set off home with it. Stopping by a well to bathe himself, Gilgamesh left the plant untended; a serpent stole it away and in his flight shed its skin, signifying its own rejuvenation and Gilgamesh's definitive loss. The mortal Gilgamesh wept for his fate. A Sumerian version of the tale, later translated into Addadian, reported Gilgamesh's further attempt to communicate with the shade of Enkidu. When Enkidu appeared, he finally revealed, after Gilgamesh's pleading and against his better judgment, the "order of the nether world":

"My body..., which thou didst touch as thy heart
   rejoiced.
Vermin devour as though an old garment.
My body..., which thou didst touch as thy heart
   rejoiced... is filled with dust."
He cried: "Woe!" and threw himself in the dust.
Gilgamesh cried: "Woe!" and threw himself in the
   dust. ... "Hast thou seen?" "I have seen."[6]

Some have seen a decided influence of Mesopotamian
culture, even the Gilgamesh epic, upon Homer.[7] However
scholars ultimately decide such a moot question, the story of
Achilles certainly manifested striking similarities with the
early Mesopotamian tales of Gilgamesh: Achilles' quest for
immortal glory, his deep friendship with Patroclus, the rivalry
of the gods who caused the Trojan War and its tragedies, the
death of Patroclus, and the prolonged grief of Achilles. Both
epics doubtless indicated the common glory, tragedy and
dilemma of man. In Homer's telling, however, his deeper
humanity emerged very clearly when Priam went as a suppliant
to Achilles, kissing the hands that killed his sons, and Achilles
recognized in the Trojan's king's grief the image of his dear
father, doomed to lose in the near future his own son. Their
common grief and wonder showed the deep human solidarity
in suffering – Virgil's later *sunt lacrimae rerum"* – yet they
had to part and the war continued to its brutal end. "No good
comes of icy weeping. For so the gods assigned as fate to
miserable mortals, to live in grief; but they themselves are
without cares" (XXIV, 524-526). No matter how much glory
Achilles accumulated by his heroic death, the *Odyssey*
informed hearers that he much preferred to live on the earth
as the vilest serf than to reign as king among the dead
(XI, 488-491). This tragic view of life was woven like a dark
thread through all of Greek civilization. Even Anacreon,
renowned for his scorn of martial glory and his preference
for the vine, the lyre and love, recognized that death alone

brought liberating resolution of all life's griefs.[8] The sage Solon maintained that no man should be considered fortunate before his death.[9] But Theognis formulated more fiercely the insight into human fragility taken up later by Herodotus and Sophocles:

> But best of all for earth-dwellers is not to have been
> born,
> Not to have gazed upon the rays of the sharp sun,
> But, if born, to pass through Hades' gates as quickly
> as possible
> And to lie still under a great heap of earth.[10]

Though the glory of the Periclean Age could guild the valiant death of soldiers for the fatherland, as in Pericles' funeral oration, the halcyon days of Athenian grandeur were fleeting. The devastation of battle, especially a losing war, inevitably brought out the brutal underside of human existence. Where Aeschylus and Sophocles could still identify a divine plan in human affairs despite the horrendous evils woven into the web of fate that they retraced on the stage, for Euripides and the Sophists this world had become a play of contrary passions, and the cynical Thucydides interpreted the slogans of politics in terms of the raw grasping for power, as demagogue after demagogue led Athens to its ruin. In the destruction of the city and the subsequent juridical murder of Socrates, the most just of men, Plato could proclaim in his *Republic* that "for us good things are far fewer than evil" (ii, 379c), yet his profound belief in justice led him to postulate a purely spiritual world and eternal souls who somehow became involved in bodies. Aristotle turned his scientific attention to this-worldly nature with its consistent, necessary laws, and attributed freaks and chance to the accidental non-being of matter. He was not primarily interested in suffering for justice and he recognized when it was time to abandon Athens to the expanding Macedonian power.

24

With the breakdown of local political life and the growing sense of being unable to control one's destiny in the face of life's evils, many thinkers sought escape from the troubling upheavals of existence. Another disciple of Socrates, Aristipus, founded the Cyrenaic school which identified happiness with active pleasure. It flourished but briefly since its leading philosopher, Hegesias, considering the uncertainties of life and the impossibility of ever attaining pure pleasure, counselled suicide.[11] Just as radical, Pyrrhus of Elis identified the source of evil with thought, and, to attain a state free of disturbance, refused both to recognize any value in this world and to affirm or deny anything, leaving it to his few, unfaithful disciples to report his doctrine.

Stoics and Epicureans reacted less radically but in opposite ways.[12] The latter retreated into private gardens, to which only friends were admitted, in order that they might control what little bit of reality was to be found immediately before them and avoid as much as possible the shocks and disappointments of the outside world. The world was quite grey, and the individual hoped but to preserve a bit of green repose for himself and his friends. The Stoics tried to render themselves impervious to sufferings by the ascetical denial involved in not seeking excess pleasures as well as by taking the wider view, seeing how lesser evils contributed to the greater well-being of the whole universe, and then identifying themselves with the universe and submitting to its laws. For all its nobility Stoicism could not paint the universe in glowing colours nor arouse fierce enthusiasms in mortal breasts, and as the ideology of many intellectuals and conscientious officials in the middle Empire it could offer no lasting resistance to the fervid enthusiasm and vigorous charity of Christianity.[13]

The Old Testament [14]

The Jews knew and wrote of a different world. Certainly their histories tell of human passions and clever treacheries that wreaked woe upon men, and they knew of horrible sufferings. But behind and above the agony was the certitude that broke out ever again in songs of enthusiastic joy. The Psalmist raised his voice with the constant refrain, "Praise the Lord" or "I shall give thee thanks, O Lord." Two constant themes recurred as reasons for joy: Yahweh's creation of the wonders of the world and the mighty deeds that he accomplished in history for his people, especially the downtrodden and the poor (e.g., Ps 19; 35:10; 68; 108; 136; 146; 147; 148). [15] Psalm 8 serves an example of joy in creation:

> O Lord, our Lord, how majestic is thy name in all the
>   earth!
> When I look at thy heavens, the work of thy fingers,
>   the moon and the stars which thou hast established;
> What is man that thou art mindful of him,
>   and the son of man that thou dost care for him?
> Yet thou hast made him little less than God,
>   And dost crown him with glory and honour.
> thou hast given him dominion over the works of thy
>   hands;
>   thou hast put all things under his feet,...
> O Lord, our Lord, how majestic is thy name in all the
>   earth!

Nothing in Greek literature, not even Sophocles' famous choral ode beginning "Wonders are many on earth and the most wondrous of these is man" (*Antigone*, 332-383) can compare with Psalm 8 for pure joy and wonder. For, on the one hand, Sophocles' hymn reflected the ambiguity of human powers which can dominate everything and lead to evil and pride, as the consequent course of the play was to witness;

even the word translated "wonders" τὰ δεινά is somewhat ambiguous, meaning equally "fearful, dread, dire, terrible, marvellously strong." On the other hand, the Psalmist's vision was much broader, raising man's gaze to God, the giver of all gifts, and so opening his heart to joy and thanksgiving.

The ordering justice of the covenant

Among the Jews there was an exuberance unknown to the Greeks, for whom *nothing in excess*, what Horace termed *aurea mediocritas*, was the rule. The Greeks certainly did not always abide by the rule, and religious enthusiasms easily led to excesses, as Euripides' *Bacchae* recalls. The gods exceeded rational limits and frequently brought disaster on men.[16] But Israel's exuberant joy remained within the bounds of order. For Israel was always conscious of a benevolent providence ruling its history. Utterly foreign to Hebrew theology was the wanton arbitrariness of Greek divinities with their petty disputes into which men were embroiled willy-nilly to suffer the consequences. For the Jews God had really intervened in history to form a people uniquely his own. History as well as nature therefore provided reasons for joy and grounds for reflection. The biblical authors, especially those in the Wisdom tradition that began with fear of the Lord, returned often to such themes. Israel's gradual recognition that its God, Yahweh, was not just one national god among many, nor even the strongest of the gods, but the one God, supreme Lord of heaven and earth, was guided by its sense that Yahweh ruled Israel with justice (Deut 32:4; 2 Chr 12:6; Ex 9:15; Neh 9:32f; Ps 92; 15; 99:4; Is 5: 16; Jer 9:24; 12:1; Ezek 18:25).[17] For in an analogy, more or less exact, with standard models of international treaties God had entered a covenant of justice with Israel, swearing by himself to remain faithful to the stipulations of blessing and curse that requited Israel's pledged behaviour.

27

God ruled not with retributive justice alone. Included in the biblical notion of justice is the fundamental relationship of man with his fellow men, the world, and God. Even *Torah*, usually translated as "the law", expressed primarily the instruction about the wonders worked by God for his people as they are recorded in the Pentateuch and in the Bible as a whole, which includes, of course, a legal code in a strict sense.[18] For behind the covenant of justice were God's *hesed* and *rahamin*, his loving kindness and mercy, that led him to choose and maintain Israel as his own possession, as his own first-born.[19] So much love permeated God's justice that G. von Rad wrote, "The notion of a punishing justice (*sedakah*) cannot be verified; it would be a *contradictio in adjecto* [contradiction in the adjective]."[20] Though it is an obvious exaggeration in view of the punishments meted out by God, as we shall see below,[21] von Rad's statement serves to highlight the benevolence that motivates God's just dealings with men. In that perspective it is easy to understand Israel's great love for the law that appears so often in the Psalms (esp. 19:7-14; 111; 119).

On the basis of its own experience Israel could judge God's dealings with other peoples. For in the past, according to the priestly writer, God entered a covenant not only with the Hebrew patriarchs (Gen 15:18; 17:9-21) but also with Noah and all flesh after the deluge (Gen 9:8-17).[22] Indeed, some scholars saw in God's original dealings with mankind's first parents, as reported by the Yahwehist author, an implicit covenant with blessings or curses accruing to them and their descendants depending on their obedient faithfulness to God's initial command (Gen 2:16f).[23] Thus when they disobeyed, death followed for all. Yet God did not execute the sentence of death immediately; instead he clothed them with garments of skins – more comfortable and enduring than fig leaves – before expelling them from the Garden into the world, where Eve was to be mother of all the living, however tainted by mortality (Gen 3:20f). As

28

poignantly as Gilgamesh's laments and the *Iliad's* touching comparison of men's generations to the generations of the leaves (VI, 146-150; XXI, 462-467), the prophet knew of man's ephemeral transitoriness, passing like the grass and the flower of the field. But he did not protest against the injustice of uncaring gods, for "the word of our God endures for ever." (Is 40:6-8). And that word, the Jewish tradition had taught him, was just, rooted in Israel's covenant relation with God.

The notion of the covenant

The justice of Yahweh found its expression in the covenant, without doubt one of the dominant ideas and institutions of the Bible. G. Mendenhall had argued for an ancient, even Mosaic origin of the covenant on the basis of parallel structures in Hittite suzerainty treaties dating from the fourteenth and thirteenth centuries BC.[24] The debate about that dating has been brisk and recurrent. Other research has emphasized the lack of exact parallelism – certainly the relation established between God and his people could only be analogous to treaties regulating relations between human kings and their vassals – the unlikelihood of Hittite influence upon nomadic Semites in the Sinai desert, the existence of similar treaty-formulas at a later date and the strange failure of the prophets to harken back explicitly to the covenant.[25] Some recent scholarship has even assigned the origin of the covenant theology to the Deuteronomic writer or school (ca. 621 BC and therafter).[26]

Such late dating is most probably too radical. For, however, much influence the Deuteronomic writer exercised on the fixed formulation of the covenant tradition, making it into the centre of his theology, the notion could not have sprung full-formed from his head like Athena from Jove's headache. The reform of King Josiah claimed to effect only a restoration of the ancient covenant with Yahweh, even if it had been lost (2 Kings 22f). Moreover, the early prophets presupposed a special relation between Yahweh and his people, existing from the time of the exodus (e.g., Amos 3:1f; 9:7; Hos 2:14; 11:1; 13:4; Mic 6:4); that relation demanded faithfulness and threatened infidelity with punishment. At times the prophets constructed Yahweh's argument against Israel in the form of a legal complaint with covenant overtones (e.g., Mic 6:1-8; Is 1:2f, 10-20; Jer 2:4-13).[27] When Hosea referred to God's covenant (8:1) and accused Israel of "breaking the covenant" (*'bar berit*), he employed thereby the expression that, at least later, became the technical term to indicate the breach of the religious covenant as opposed to the violation of a secular treaty.[28] Furthermore, his recounting of God's promise to make a universal covenant guaranteeing Israel peace even with the animals (Hos 2:18f) would be easily comprehensible only against the background tradition of Yahweh's previous covenant with Israel.[29]

However late the actual formulation of Israel's covenant may have been set down in writing, its basic content had already been actively forming Israel's history. Indeed, given the fundamental notion of justice which the covenant incorporates, any earlier relation with God, necessarily implied in cult, most probably employed some schema of reward or punishment for proper or improper behaviour. In addition, there was no clearly defined realm of secular law opposed to religious law; profane and sacred everywhere intertwined in everyday life. The Deuteronomic school did not create the covenant *ex nihilo* but assembled various traditions of law, prophecy and wisdom.[30] Thus, even if the final legal articulation of the covenant came quite late, most of its constitutive elements were at hand from previous traditions, waiting to be organized and we can conclude that "the concept of a covenant between God and Israel is central to the Old Testament, even though the idea of a covenant may not always have been used with comparable frequency throughout all ages of Israelite-Jewish religion."[31]

The fundamental justice of the covenant

However basic was the *Torah* as the prime expression of Yahweh's love and mercy, reciprocal commitments, or promises, were involved.[32] Though the initiative for the covenant rested in Yahweh's freedom and Israel could never be imagined as his equal, their relations were formulated and organized in a series of promised requitals corresponding to Israel's conduct. No man might raise a legitimate claim in strict right against God. He shows gracious mercy to whom he will (Ex 33:19), and the phrase about God "merciful and gracious, slow to anger and abounding in steadfast love and faithfulness" became a recurring commonplace (e.g., Ps 86:5, 15; 145:8; Ex 34:6f; Num 14:18; Neh 9:17, 31; Joel 2:13). Yet God committed himself to be faithful to his own promises and his people had ratified the covenant by accepting a final series of curses and blessings. This concluding formula is found in two versions: Leviticus 26 and Deuteronomy 27-28. The promised rewards and punishments will attend the fulfilment or neglect of the obligations assumed.

Though the actual compilation of blessings and curses doubtless owes much to subsequent additions, especially in the longer version of Deuteronomy, which was probably completed in the post-exilic period (i.e., after the return from Babylon, beginning ca. 538 BC), what must strike the reader is the vast disproportion in length between the blessings (28:1-14; cf. Lev 26:3-13) and the curses (28:15-68; cf. Lev 26:14-39). Surely the list of material blessings, that were to accompany the possession of the land overflowing with milk and honey, alluringly attracted the Hebrews, who tenaciously retained their sense of this world's reality. Nonetheless, the horrifying catalogue of threats for disobedience would force most normal people to hesitate. Perhaps for that reason in his final discourse Moses, or the Deuteronomic writer, immediately reminded his people of the great wonders performed for them in Egypt and of God's fidelity to the promise made to their forefathers, a promise that would extend unto future generations (29:2-15). Then, after a brief warning against falling off into idolatry, Moses recalled the merciful forgiveness of the Lord who would receive back his people, if they repented of their wrong-doings and restore them to the fullness of blessings (30:1-10; cf. Lev 26:40-45). Finally, stressing that God's ordinances were eminently practical, Moses placed before the people the choice between life in the promised land and death. They chose life and fidelity, entering the offered covenant and on that basis they were to attempt to make sense of God's justice and human sufferings.[33]

God's justice and human suffering

The task of reconciling God's justice and human sufferings is not always easy in terms of the Old Testament. At times God is moved to compassionate intervention to relieve sufferings when the groans of his people or of individuals reach him (Gen 21:17; Ex 2:24; 3:7-10; 2 Kings 20:5; 22:19; Ps 22:24).[34] Yet, at other times, apparently to prevent anticipatorily any limitation of his power, he is recognized as the one who "makes weal and creates woe" (Is 45:7) and is responsible for evil (Lam 3:38; Amos 3:6; Eccles 7:14). Although these "evils" probably refer to his punishing of sinners (cf. Jer 18:11), some phrases in the Bible attribute less than benevolent intentions and effects to God: e.g., besides inflicting all types of material evils, he attempted to kill Moses (Ex 4:24), hardened Pharaoh's heart (Ex 4:21; 7:3; 10:20), sent evil spirits both to rouse conflict between Abimelech and the men of Shechem (Judg 9:23f) and to cause Saul's melancholy madness which ultimately almost killed David (1 Sam 16:14-23; 18:10f; 19:9f), let loose a lying spirit among the prophets (1 Kings 22:21-23) and, despite Jeremiah's protest (7:31; 19:4f; 32:35), was said by

Ezekiel to have made "bad statutes and ordinances", requiring human sacrifice, for Israel (20:25f).[35] However one interprets these texts, by appeal to God's permissive will, literary genres, dialectical statements or the wish to signify that everything exists under God's control, they obviously seem to contradict the norm of God's merciful dealings with men. Certainly insofar as the perfect revelation of God occurred in Jesus Christ and everything preparing for him in the Old Testament can accordingly be seen as provisional and less than perfect, Christians need not be bound to literalism in reading God's word.

The Old Testament recounts the story of love between God and Israel as God intervened in history, taking the Hebrews as they were in order to lead them to Christ. This stupendous election overwhelmed the Hebrew writers and they had to wrestle with the meaning of their history, including the mystery of iniquity. In struggling with their task they may have employed traditional ideas or borrowed mythological themes. However imperfect these expressions might be, the very fact that they are retained in Sacred Scripture prevents the believer from simply ignoring them. Even in their imperfection they compel the reader to ponder the truth intended, however partially, in them. For the sake of the present study, nonetheless, we need not now linger too long over them. Deeper than the mystery of iniquity is the mystery of election, which found its primary expression in the covenant. Only in its light can the problem of suffering be understood. Ultimately the full revelation of God in Jesus Christ alone allows an adequate understanding of such apparently difficult texts. Our study of the New Testament must return to them in order to interpret them properly. In the meantime the witness of the Old Testament about Israel's election should not be neglected but rather be penetrated as profoundly as possible in order to let it shed the maximum of preparatory light on the mystery of Christ.

The Old Testament explanations of suffering

The nine thematic headings chosen to guide our inquiry claim to be exhaustive neither in their choice of texts, which could have been multiplied almost endlessly, nor in enumerating possible subdivisions nor in following the evolution of Hebrew thought on the question of suffering. Truly it would be almost impossible to untangle the layers of tradition and interpretation in order to arrive at a pure explanation of suffering in any one epoch.[36] Even apart from the difficulty of dating texts, various interpretations of suffering can be found in the same period – they are more complementary than contradictory in dealing with a many-faceted mystery. Later generations prayed the prayers, sang the songs and repeated the stories of their predecessors; thus older views were repeated and remained alive. What we propose in the following pages, therefore, is not an historical analysis *per se* but a certain speculative consideration of the various themes found in the Old Testament. At times historical developments will be noted but they do not comprise our main concern. We shall indicate the insufficiencies of each answer, if taken in itself and then show the inherent need of discovering a more adequate reply. Only in their totality, therefore only in Christ, can these responses of the Old Testament persuade.

1. Good rewarded – Evil punished: This theme is grounded directly in the covenant, which clearly defined what God considered good and evil actions. Whether Israel remained faithful or slipped into infidelity determined its fate. A recent study claims to discover the basic theme of covenant retribution present and dominant in the early theologies of the Yahwehist and, possibly, Elohist writers and argues that the Deuteronomic writer found it already there and saw it as applicable, with a few modifications, to his own day.[37] Without doubt the simple notion of reward and punishment provided the consistent theme of Deuteronomic history, most clearly legible in *Judges*. There historical cycles repeated themselves: Israel fell away into infidelity, was punished until the people called out for mercy, then Yahweh was moved to intervene by raising up another judge to save his people. The theme was taken up and expanded in *1* and *2 Kings*, where the sins of Israel and Judah against the covenant were made responsible for the catastrophes of 721 and 587 BC, i.e., the fall of Israel, the northern kingdom and the destruction of Jerusalem.[38] The writer of *1* and *2 Chronicles* continued the same themes of sin and retribution but applied it more immediately to individuals in each generation.[39]

How God requites good and evil has been a subject of recent scholarly debate. K. Koch rightly questioned a legalist model of divine retribution apparently assumed without question by previous scholars.[40] He noted the Hebrews' recurrent tendency to see an inherent unity between an act and its consequences. Later he strengthened his case by noting the instances of unintentional sins for which the people suffered and offered sacrifices of expiation (Lev 4:2, 13, 27, 35; 5:15, 17f; Num 15:22-29; etc.).[41] Yet this "natural" law of retribution need not exclude God's meting out of justice. Koch himself noted that Yahweh was capable of upholding such a natural link, even expediting its completion, especially in the case of blessings, as well as of breaking the link or "forgetting" the sin.[42] In addition, insofar as Yahweh was the creator of the universe with its laws, his providence could be identified as working in and through them.[43] Wisdom literature certainly tended to see an intrinsic link between an act and its consequences (e.g., Prov 12:21; 13:21, 25). Yet the pious teachers of wisdom easily identified this with God's justice (Prov 3:33f; 10:29; 15:3-9, 25f, 29; 16:3-11); they even attributed long life and prosperity to "fear of the Lord" (Prov 1:29-33; 2:10-3:2, 9f; 10:27; 14:1f; 22:4; 28:25; Sir 33:1). The prophets in turn also saw God's hand behind the rewards and punishments of good and evil deeds. In this, wrote Koch, "Yahweh is preserving the covenant."[44] Certainly there is no contradiction between affirming a "natural law" uniting consequences to actions and preserving God's justice. Insofar as God acts consistently, one will perceive a constant relation, a law, between act and consequence; inversely, the experimental confirmation of a moral law of justice will lead the observer to conclude to an intelligent and moral power who guarantees the law. The non-personal cannot care for men. The biblical authors did not imagine a universe governed by impersonal, "scientific" laws of necessity, but one regulated by a benevolent God who concerned himself for human order and, insofar as it pertained to human beings, subhuman order.

Although the testimonies about early Israel tend to emphasize the corporate fate of God's people (cf. below "8. Vicarious suffering"), one should not conclude that only later times were concerned with the fate of individuals. In Israel's early history God was interested in the small successes or failures of apparently minor individuals (Gen 24:12; 27:20; 1 Sam 1:12-21; 17:37; Judg 14:8-20; Ruth 1:9) as well as in the fate of the patriarchs, Moses and great leaders. Names like Jonathan ("Yahweh has given") and Joiada ("Yahweh has regarded") expressed an awareness of God's answer to prayers. The "I" of the psalms, whose identity is so debated, whether private person, king, priest, prophet, chorus, or assembly, might have been applied by the individual to his situation of joy or anguish.[45] Often the Psalmist manifested his confidence in God's just requital of good and evil in his own case as well as in general. For example, Psalm 1, which emerged from the sapiential, or wisdom, tradition, seems to be the prayer of an individual. This psalm most probably borrowed its content from Jeremiah 17:5-8 and was then attached as a late preface to the whole book of the psalms.[46] In this psalm the author's simple trust in God as the rewarder of good and punisher of evil was stated in a straightforward manner:

Blessed is the man
who walks not in the counsel of the wicked, ...
but his delight is in the law of the Lord, ...
In all that he does, he prospers.
The wicked are not so,
but are like chaff which the wind drives away.

Such references can easily be multiplied: "My shield is with God, who saves the upright in heart. God is a righteous judge who daily requites the raging enemy" (Ps 7:10f). "The Lord is my shepherd, I shall not want; he makes me lie down in green pastures..." (Ps 23:1f).

Even *Proverbs*, representing the reflections of the wise and learned, could affirm simply, "The reward for humility and fear of the Lord is riches and honour and life" (22:4). However naive these and similar texts may at first appear, they were not and are not without justification. After all, not only did they find deep roots in the Hebrew experience of God's gracious mercy but also they apparently support the strongly ingrained sense of human justice and its fundamental norm, whether that be identified with the abstract notion *cuique suum* [to each his own], the modern adage "tit-for-tat," the ancient rule "life for life, eye for eye, tooth for tooth," (Ex 21:24; Lev 24:20; Deut 19:21) or the conviction that each deed is one with its consequences. "he who sows injustice will reap calamity and the rod of his fury will fail" (Prov 22:8). Indeed, in small, stable societies, whether on the land or in a ghetto, where each man knows his neighbours, such a rule of justice is eminently applicable. The just man wins the respect and appreciation of his neighbours; consequently, with their assistance to complement the internal discipline inculcated by justice, he prospers. Certainly within any good family the basic rule of justice holds: virtue is rewarded, the trespass deserves a spanking and shame before one's parents, one's neighbours and God serves as the final avenger of improper conduct.

37

Even after individualism rose in protest against the necessity of suffering for the sins of others, an apparent contravention of retributive justice in the cases of individuals, the prophets responded by affirming all the more vehemently God's justice in rewarding or punishing the individual, whether in the new covenant (Jer 31:23-34) or already at work in the present (Ezek 18). Later stories like *Tobit, 1 Maccabees* and the Daniel cycle told of God's miraculous interventions to vindicate the just, miracles almost as great as those recounted in the first books of the Bible when God was punishing sin (e.g., Deluge, Sodom and Gomorrah) or electing Abraham or liberating his people from Egypt. And the same late period of composition bore witness to both a greater demand of literal obedience to the law and a more pervasive sense of sin.[47] The subtle Sirach showed himself very cognizant of the essential complementary of opposites in created reality, which resulted in a certain ambiguity affixed even to God's actions on the good and on the evil (39:12-40:11); and, to gainsay the phenomenal prosperity of the wicked, he attributed psychological anxiety to them (31:1f; 40:1-11). This notion of psychological punishment had already been noted in the speech of Eliphaz (Job 15:20-24) and was developed later in greater detail in Wisdom 17.[48] Many were the devices which the human mind concocted or discovered to preserve the basic notion of justice that guaranteed the order of human society and the absolute uprightness of God.

Whether the defence of the simple norm of justice was due to an almost mystic love of the Law, as in Psalm 1, an embattled theodicy, or pious, utopian dreaming, many Jews trusted firmly in a just God who rewards good and punishes evil. So deep was the conviction that suffering was linked to sin that often people concluded from the pain in which a person found himself to the sinfulness of the sufferer. Job's consolers, for example, attempted to move him to renounce his innocence and confess his sin. Others turned against the sufferer or avoided him apparently lest they be contaminated by contact with his sin (Ps 31:11; 38:11; 41:4-12; 69:8, 26; 88:7f, 18; Jer 30:11-15; Is 53:2-4; Lam 4:11-16; Job 19:13-22; 30:9-20). Not surprisingly many of the texts in which such "prejudices" appear represent instances in which a different understanding of suffering was breaking through. Otherwise the connection between suffering and sin was so taken for granted that it needed not be averted to.[49] In view of these protests, however, it was clear that all the evidence does not support the conviction of simple justice in which the good are all rewarded and the evil all punished. Distinctions had to be drawn and new insights established.

2. Good rewarded – Evil punished in the future: Unfortunately wars disrupt society. Brigands grow rich through strikes against unsuspecting villagers whom they hardly know. Foreign kings oppress distant minorities. Analogously an expanding society, growing ever richer with international trade, large corporations and absentee landholders operating impersonally through middlemen, tends to ignore the plight of the poor in its concern with maximizing profits. Even in the best of times there generally was some interval between the sin and its consequences, as, for example, David's sin with Uriah's wife effected fratricidal strife as well as the child's death (2 Sam 12:7-12). Sometimes the swelling arrogance of sinners grew in order that their downfall might be more complete (Ps 37:1f; 34-38; 62:9f; Amos 6:1-8; Ezek 27:25-28:19). So the simple law of justice with immediate retribution no longer held. But, sure of God's fidelity, the pious Jew then projected the fulfilment of justice into the future.

The Wisdom tradition and many psalms testified to the firmness of Hebrew faith. Even in the most profound sense of abandonment the author of Psalm 22 retained his trust. In a most cleverly constructed prayer, between descriptions of his own misery he reminded God of his great fidelity in the past to Israel and to himself, thus identifying his own cause with God's and went on to describe how he would praise God's most assured, renewed saving deed toward himself in the great assembly, to the ends of the earth and to all posterity.

In many other psalms and in prayers scattered throughout the Old Testament there ruled the conviction that God will intervene to vindicate his justice, save his faithful ones and punish the ungodly: e.g., Ps 10; 13; 16; 26; 37; 1 Sam 2:9f; 12:19-25; 15:21f; 2 Sam 22; 1 Kings 3:6-9; 8:22-53; 17:20-22; 18:36-38; 2 Kings 19:15-19; Prov 22:22f; 23:10f; Eccles 11:9; 12:10f. Of course the time intervening between the crime and the punishment might extend itself longer than expected. The cry "How long, O Lord, how long?" was not infrequent upon Hebrew lips and in Hebrew hearts (e.g., Ps 13:1f; 35:17; 62:3; 74:10; 79:5; 80:4; 82:2; 89:46: 90:13; 94:3; 119:84; Jer 12:4; Hab 1:2). The ready assurance that the unjust man will not take his ill-gotten gains with him into the grave (Ps 37:1f; 10-21; 49; Job 20), however consoling for the moment, does not satisfy long. Neither does the just man enjoy his material rewards once he is dead. The difficulty concerning the present prosperity of the wicked remained. The fact of death only intensified the difficulty. Where was justice to be found in this world? Other reasons were sought out to explain the mysteries of sin, suffering and divine justice.

3. The experienced presence of God: This answer to the question of God's apparent silence before the wanton growth of iniquity in a sense transcends the problem. The one who feels God's greatness knows that he can never be placed in question and that just to remain in God's presence, even without material benefits, is reward and satisfaction enough. Psalm 73 well described the troubling confusion experienced by the believer at the prosperity of sinners. Yet his answer came upon entering God's sanctuary. "Truly thou dost set them in slippery places; thou dost make them fall to ruin. How they are destroyed in a moment, swept away utterly by terrors! They are like a dream when one awakes, on awaking you despise their phantoms" (18-20). Compared to the reality of God, sinners are as nothing and the believer has experienced God's reality:

> Nevertheless I am continually with thee;
>> thou dost hold my right hand. ...
> Whom have I in heaven but thee?
>> And there is nothing upon earth
>> that I desire besides thee.
> My flesh and my heart may fail,
>> but God is the strength of my heart
>> and my portion for ever (23-26).

The psalms often reflected this joy in God's presence, especially in his temple and compared with that all else became secondary (cf. Ps 16:5-11; 27:1, 4-10; 63; 84). Seeing in this psalm the height of Old Testament piety and the most adequate religious response to the problem of suffering in the acceptance of its unfathomable mystery along with the assurance of God's presence E. Balla wrote, "To have religion means to be blessed (*selig:* "blissful")."[50] Balla's presuppositions, apparently rooted in Schleiermacher's liberal theology, expired in the trenches of World War I. After Dachau such a simple answer sounds naive to modern man, who is prepared to reduce every religious experience to some type of psychological projection or wish-fulfilment.

Admittedly the universe of the Bible was generally a larger, happier, simpler one than our small world which tortures itself with intellectual contortions in terror lest it suffer the least suspicion of deception or illusion. The biblical intellectuals, therefore, could repeat, in however an attenuated form, the psalmist's insight. If the sage author of the Book of Proverbs did not rise to the heights of the inspired poet or mystic, he at least recognized the limits of his own wisdom and the contingency of earthly riches. "Better is a little with fear of the Lord than great treasure and trouble with it." "Better is a little with righteousness than great revenues with injustice. A man's mind plans his way, but the Lord directs his steps" (15:16; 16:8f; also 19:1; 30:8f). Wisdom points to the all-sufficiency of God and his justice beyond its own reasonings, when it cannot spell out all the Lord's ways. That negative theology might suffice for many a wise man.[51] Nonetheless, there were bound to be difficulties. For just as Old Testament believers did not remain on a mystical "high" forever nor could all Hebrews dwell always in God's temple, so the average man sought reasons less recondite to explain his experience of suffering. Hence other answers had to be excogitated by the Jews to explain more intelligibly their sufferings.

4. Medicinal suffering: The most obvious reason for suffering is sin. Yet for the Jews this punishment was not primarily conceived as the mere mechanical application of the rule enunciated in the covenant. For God's love stood behind the covenant and he had made provision for his people's conversion from sin by indicating that all the blessings would be showered upon them if they turned back to him. So behind the punishments the prophets saw the loving hand of God, constantly chastising Israel for its sins, constantly wooing Israel back to his love. Like a medicine that could be bitter and hard to swallow, these sufferings were for the good of the patient. The sufferings inflicted were to bring his people to reflection and to break sinful stubbornness. God wished to cure and reward Israel. So he constantly sent prophets to his people both to warn of impending doom and to interpret the castigations already administered.

The earliest of the canonical prophets, Amos, proclaimed God's vengeance not only against neighbouring peoples for ravaging Israel but, even more, over the luxuriously rich in Israel, who oppressed his poor. Chapter 4, initiating the complaint against Israel, interpreted Israel's woes, that had stretched from the planting to the harvest to the destruction of her children, with the repeated refrain, "'Yet you did not return to me,' says the Lord." There remained only the threat, "Prepare to meet your God, O Israel!" (4:12).

The day of the Lord would come not just at the end, but ever again in Israel's history (Amos 5:18-20; 8:9-14; Joel 1:15-2:11; Zeph 1:14-18; Is 13; Ezek 7; etc.). Yet God's mercy is long-suffering (Ex 34:6; Num 14:18; Neh 9:17, 31; Ps 86:15; Joel 2:13f). He takes no pleasure in the sinner's death (Ezek 18:23, 32; 33:11; Lam 3:31-33). If the virgin Israel had fallen with apparently no one to help her (Amos 5:2), the prophet Hosea showed in his own life as well as in his teachings how God seeks out the harlot Israel to marry her and despite her continuing infidelities he constantly brings her back, after inflicting her with sufferings, to his love (Hos 1-3). Yahweh wanted Israel to acknowledge his love, "Come let us return to the Lord; for he has torn, that he may heal us; he has stricken and he will bind us up" (6:1). Ultimately he is God himself who is involved in a relation of loving fidelity, who is himself touched and will not regret his choosing:

How can I give you up? O Ephraim!
    How can I hand you over, O Israel! ...
My heart recoils within me,
    my compassion grows warm and tender.
I will not execute my fierce anger,
    I will not again destroy Ephraim;
for I am God and not man,
    the Holy One in your midst,
    and I will not come to destroy (11:8f).

Long after Israel in the north was crushed by the Assyrian power, to Judah in the south the prophets would repeat again and again the same message of God's love in and through medicinal suffering (e.g., Is 30:12-33; Jer 3:21-4:2; 7:13; Ezek 16; Joel 2; Mic 7:9; Zech 10; Mal 3:6-12). Behind their chastisements was always the yearning of God's heart which beat in sympathy with his people (Jer 31:20; Is 63:9f, 15f).[52]

As for the nation, so for individuals. As individualism grew in Israel, especially after the exile, more reflection was dedicated to God's care for individuals. The psalms contain many confessions of God's goodness and mercy in chastising the sinner to turn him from his evil way.

> Before I was afflicted I went astray;
>> but now I keep thy word. ...
> It was good for me that I was afflicted,
>> that I might learn thy statutes. ...
> I know, O Lord, that thy judgments are right,
>> and that in faithfulness thou hast afflicted me.
>> (119:67-75; cf. also 32; 94:10f)

In the sapiential tradition which extended its roots back at least to the time of the Davidic monarchy, even if it was definitively formulated only after the exile, the same theme of God's constant love in inflicted sufferings was repeated. "My son, do not despise the Lord's discipline or be weary of his reproof, for the Lord reproves him whom he loves, as a father the son in whom he delights" (Prov 3:11f; cf. 13:24; 19:18; Wis 11:10; 12:2, 21). In such a context Wisdom easily acknowledged, "Faithful are the wounds of a friend" (Prov 27:6).

At the end of the sapiential tradition in a long reflection on God's patient mercy which chastises while granting abundant time to repent, the Book of Wisdom (11-19) also compared the punishments meted out to the Egyptians with the afflictions accorded the Israelites for similar sins. The author argued that however lenient God was to Israel's enemies, they were "scourged ten thousand times more" than Israel (11:12-22). Thus sufferings could continually reveal the kindness of the Lord always calling his people to fidelity, always desiring their good.

44

Although the answer of medicinal suffering must be satisfying to the vast majority of men who have to acknowledge themselves as backsliding sinners in need of a "boot in the backside", it obviously did not cover all possible cases. The old cynic Qoheleth knew that reward is not always proportioned to merit (5:8; 7:15; 9:1-3, 11-16; 10:5-7). At times the good undergo unexpected, apparently unmerited sufferings. To that problem Israel also turned its attention.

5. Testing: No Jew could have been oblivious of the opening verse of the twenty-second chapter of Genesis: "After these things God tested Abraham." "These things" included the miraculous birth of Isaac to the old Sarah in obvious fulfilment of the promise to bestow the land on Abraham's descendants as well as the expulsion of Ishmael, Abraham's son by the slave Hagar. Thus Isaac remained as the sole heir of God's promises to Abraham and God was demanding from Abraham the sacrifice of Isaac. The storyteller knew how to highlight the pathos of the tale. After an introductory address in which God demanded "your only son whom you love," the story repeated often the designations "father" and "son" and stressed the precocious questions of the child until God intervened to save the "lad" from his father's knife. The essential point of the story centred on Abraham's trust in God, even when it seemed that the sacrifice demanded of him would annul God's previous promises, the meaning and joy of his own present life and his entire future. As a result God went beyond the covenant promising the land between Egypt and the Euphrates to Abraham's descendants (Gen 15:18-21) and swore by himself to multiply beyond measure Abraham's progeny and to make them a blessing for all nations (22:16-18). For the Elohist writer, who began his history with Genesis 15 and basically ended with Genesis 22, Abraham was clearly intended as the paragon of obedience for all Jews to imitate. The Jews knew thereafter that they were chosen by God, not because of their own merits but because of the rock-like faithfulness of "father" Abraham while being tested (Deut 4:37; 7:6-8; 9:4-6; Neh 9:7f; Is 51:2f; Mic 7:20; Sir 44:19-22).[54] Henceforth the Lord would let himself be identified as the God of Abraham (Gen 26:24; 28:13f; 31:42, 53; 32:9; 48:15f; Ex 3:6, 15f, etc.).

Abraham's "testing" should not be considered as a huge practical joke by a God waiting to rush on the scene at the last possible moment like a *deus ex machina* to prevent a disaster that his own actions had previously prompted. Nor was it a matter of enlightening God about Abraham's future conduct. That intention is never predicated of God as it is of his creature, Wisdom, who originally torments the one seeking her "by her discipline until she trusts him and she will test him with her ordinances" (Sir 4:17). Despite this late anthropomorphic interpretation of the difficult initial stages of acquiring Wisdom's discipline, the "testing" by God, whose knowledge and power are unlimited, is probably best understood from the point of the human subject.[55] Indeed, as various scholars have pointed out, the opening verse about God "testing" was prefaced to a previous "family history" by the Elohist redactor.[56] Thus the emphasis was switched from the danger for Isaac to the obedience of Abraham; as is witnessed by Exodus 20:20 and Deuteronomy 33:8, which most probably were composed by the same author, God's intentions in "testing" were to do good to those tested.[57] There was no question of God murdering Isaac.

Just as overwhelming a child with gifts spoils him by denying him any sense of his proper worth (cf. Deut 8:5), so also Abraham and his posterity (cf. Jud 8:25-27) were to learn both the value of God's choice of them and what was demanded by it. As a life of ease enervates, so a challenge moulds the mettle of a man, an outcome for which one can be grateful. Suffering in itself need not be evil; lovers often wish to show their love by sacrificing for the beloved.[58] God often tested Israel's fidelity to him and his law (Ex 16:4; 20:20; Deut 8:2; Judg 2:22).[59]

In the wake of Abraham's testing the way was open for God to test Israel, especially during its wandering through the desert and in its struggle to possess the promised land (Deut 13:1-5; Judg 2:22; 3:1-4). Had not Israel often put God to the test and roused his anger by refusing to accept his signs? (Ex 17:2, 7; Num 14:22; Deut 6:16; etc.). Yet God's testing often preceded a saving intervention and, however fear-evoking, was intended to grant the Israelites a blessing for their obedience, "to do you good in the end." (Deut 8:16; Ex 16:4, 22-30; 15:25f; 20:20; Deut 4:32-40; 7:17-26; 8:2-10; 29:2-9; 33:8; Ps 81:7-16). A recent study by N. Lohfink even demonstrated how the "testing" at Marah (Ex 15:25) has to be understood in terms of the ordinance which was given as a blessing.[60] This German scholar even located the late texts, Deuteronomy 13:1-5 and Judges 2:22 and 3:1-4, within the whole tradition of testing in order to bless.[61] Thus even the lack of immediate references to the blessing intended does not allow a testing to be interpreted as an ambivalent event. The blessing was always presupposed as the purpose or "final cause" of the "test."

The Jews recognized that God tests the upright as well as the wicked to reward the former and scourge the latter (Ps 7:9-11; 11:4-7; Jer 11:20; 12:3; 17:10; 20:12; 2 Chron 32:31; 1 Macc 2:52). So they could pray for testing (Ps 17:1-3; 26:2; 139:23) and later glory in their tribulations victoriously endured. For God had tested them in order to save them for his praise:

Bless our God, O peoples,
    let the sound of his praise be heard,
who has kept us among the living,
    and has not let our feet slip.
For thou, O God, has tested us;
    thou hast tried us as silver is tried.
thou didst bring us into the net;
    thou didst lay affliction on our loins;

47

thou didst let men ride over our heads;
    we went through fire and through water;
yet thou hast brought us forth to a spacious place.
                                    (Ps 66:8-12; cf. also Deut 8:16)

Even when those tested failed to respond as God willed, his intention had always been to benefit them (Ps 81).

Despite all its excellences, testing inevitably contains the possibility that the one tested shall fail. The case of Adam and Eve springs immediately to mind. Yet in the third chapter of Genesis not only was the word "testing" avoided but also the serpent, later clearly interpreted as Satan (Wis 2:24), was the agent who put Adam and Eve to the test. They succumbed to temptation. In the other obvious "test" – without use of the word – which Satan conducted, the woes he worked upon Job served for the manifestation of Job's integrity and the justification of the Lord's trust and goodness in enriching him both before and then after his trial. Thus, despite the "evil" attributed to Yahweh (Is 45:7), there was a discernible tendency in later works to acquit the Lord of responsibility for moral evil, or sin. Yahweh's "incitation" that led to David's sin (2 Sam 24:1, 10) was later ascribed to Satan (1 Chron 21:1) and Sirach 15:11-20 refuted all attempts to blame God for leading men to sin. Even the earlier stories, as we saw, never implied that Yahweh wished to lead men to sin. On the contrary, his testing intended to induce fear of God so that his people would not sin (Ex 20:20).

The positive meaning of testing was brought out in later sapiential literature. Suffering serves to educate the individual and is appreciated as such by the wise. Although some texts stressed the lesson learned from sufferings previously undergone (Prov 3:11f; 15:5; Eccles 7:2-5; Sir 34:10) – a theme dear to Greek wisdom also – the main weight of Hebrew thought understood suffering as educative principally because it opened the sufferer to an existential recognition of Yahweh in a plea for help (cf. Ps 78:34; Ezek 6:7; 13:14; Job 33:19-

28; 36:15f).[62] Here the verb "to test" is employed for an existential turning to the Lord, even if no previous sin is mentioned. As gold is tested by fire, so the acceptable men are tried in the furnace of humiliation to move them to trust the Lord (Sir 2:1-6; Prov 17:3). God delivers and rewards those tested (Sir 33:1; Wis 3:5f; Jud 8:24-26). "The Lord scourges those who draw near to him, in order to admonish them" (Jud 8:27). If nothing else, God's paternal admonition served this positive purpose: "For when they were tried, though they were being disciplined in mercy, they learned how the ungodly were tormented when judged in wrath. For thou didst test them as a father does in warning" (Wis 11:9f). In the wide vision of the author of The Book of Wisdom, which extended to life beyond the grave (cf. below "9. *Life after death*"), that verse was more than just a means of exit from a difficult dilemma; it represented a successful admonition.

6. *Purificatory suffering:* Closely related to the notion of educatory testing is purification. Education means in its very root a "leading-out" from some situation, be it ignorance, laziness, prejudice or the like. Children have to be "led out" of childish whims and fits of passion. But these examples of selfishness do not cease with childhood. Often they become rooted in a person's life as habits. Education through sufferings will necessarily involve purification from sinful habits. The image of gold or silver submitted to the furnace served the prophets in explaining God's continual affliction of his people in their stubborn rejection of him (Jer 6:27-30; Ezek 22:17-22). Zechariah joined it to the traditional theme of the remnant of Israel that would remain faithful to the Lord through the tribulations of the final times:

In the whole land, says the Lord, two thirds shall be cut off and perish and one third shall be left alive. And I will put this third into the fire and refine them as one refines silver and test them as gold is tested. They will call on my name and I will answer them. I will say, "They are my people"; and they will say, "The Lord is my God" (13:8f).

As the basic quality of the metal emerges more purely after the furnace, so the goodness of Israel is refined to God's glory (Is 48:10f; 1:25; Mal 3:2f).

The text of Zechariah, insofar as it was describing the final purification of the just before the victory of God and his elect in the end time, recalls the recurrent theme of the "eschatological woes" in the late prophets. There will be a time of suffering and convulsion before final salvation arrives for the just and condemnation is awarded the wicked. Micah applied to the daughter of Zion, Jerusalem, the image of a woman in travail, suffering birth pangs before she brings forth the new shepherd king who shall gather his people and introduce the time of prosperity for the remnant of Jacob (4:8-5:15). Daniel 12:1 referred to "a time of trouble, such as never has been since there was a nation till that time" before the people will be delivered. Isaiah 65 noted the sins of the people for which they will be punished with the sword while his servants prosper in the creation of a new heavens and a new earth. Admittedly Isaiah inverted the image of Micah by saying that Jerusalem will give birth before she goes into labour (66:7-16). Since Jerusalem's parturition avoids pain for the faithful, whatever punishment is meted out in Isaiah's vision must apply to sinners. But aside from this prophecy of Isaiah all the other examples cited spoke of the sufferings of the just before the end of time; hence, the sufferings of their labour are to be considered purificatory.

Although the notion of purificatory suffering was usually tied to "testing," there were some psalms that exhibited an awareness that suffering cleanses. Psalm 38 recalls the plea and trusting confidence of a man who is following the good while being persecuted by enemies unjustly (19f). Yet he did not protest against God's justice. Instead he acknowledged these sufferings at God's hands as due to a past sin that he had confessed (1-4, 18). Through all his grievous pains he remained faithful to God and pleaded for his merciful assistance (cf. also Ps 39; 41; Mic 7:8-10). Clearly sin was not conceived as a punctual act that can be erased with a momentary conversion blotting out all past debts. As a mass-murderer who underwent a religious conversion in prison could not expect to be absolved from all punishment by a judge – in fact the murderer's sense of justice might even demand that he suffer the just castigation for his crimes – so also the psalmist recognized that the conversion to God involves a process that takes time until the proper dispositions are inculcated. One is inclined to see the same attitude in King David as he fled before Absalom and was cursed and stoned by Shimei in Bahurim. When Abishai wished to decapitate Shimei, David meekly responded: "Let him alone and let him curse; for the Lord has bidden him. It may be that the Lord will look upon my affliction and that the Lord will repay me with good for this cursing of me today" (2 Sam 16:11f). Similarly the conversions demanded by God were frequently conjoined to fasts and penances to make atonement, to turn aside God's anger and to manifest the sinner's determination to humble himself and follow fully God's will (Lev 16:29-34; 1 Kings 21:20-29; Jer 36:5-7; Joel 1:14; 2:12-17; Jon 3:5-10; Neh 9; Dan 9:3-19; Ps 69:10). This concretely involved the task of letting sinful habits, tied to desires for personal pleasures, be eradicated from his life (cf. Is 58:3-14; Sir 34:26; Zech 7:8-12).[63] "Blows that wound cleanse away evil" (Prov 20:30).

With "testing" and purificatory sufferings there has been a deepening of the biblical understanding of suffering, even though the basic lines of the covenant remain inviolate: evil is punished, good rewarded. But there are always cases in human existence where the suffering seems out of proportion to the evil to be atoned for and sometimes it seems that the innocent suffer outrageously. Such cases test human endurance and raise the greatest problem to theodicy[64] (cf. Ps 10:11; 73:11-16; 94:3-7; Job 21:14-16; Wis 2:1-20; Eccles 8:16-9:6; Mal 3:14f; 2:17). Does not God notice or has he ceased caring? The Hebrews, like all peoples, faced these problems and even more insistently than others because their notion of the one God, omnipotent, omniscient, just and loving, who "makes weal and creates woe" (Is 45:7; Amos 3:6; Lam 3:38; Jer 31:28), could not let them take refuge in polytheistic subterfuges. To their answers, the result of much pondering on the hidden ways of God, we must now turn.

7. *Job and the mystery of God:* That God can write straight in crooked lines must have been clear to every Jew reading the story of Joseph. Through all Joseph's innocent tribulations God's hand had been leading him in order to save his family. "For God sent me before you to preserve for you a remnant on earth and to keep alive for you many survivors" (Gen 45:4-8). There is a mystery to divine providence that only the subsequent outcome of a series of events can reveal as benevolent. Perhaps for that reason Jews continued to trust despite the appearances to the contrary. For the phenomenon of innocent suffering was not unknown in Israel. Many psalms (e.g., 7, 17, 26, 35, 44, 59, 86, 119) present the speaker, or singer, as an innocent victim, a true servant of God afflicted unjustly by others and therefore moved to call upon God for his vindication. Naturally the questions about the type of innocence intended, ritual purity or moral integrity, the speaker's identity and the occasion of the prayer are complex. But the psalmist appealed to his innocence precisely because he trusted in a God of justice, who, once averted to his need, should come to rescue him from his tribulations. A slight change of perspective, however, especially when divine intervention is long delayed, can result in the speaker's innocence being used no longer as a ground for confiding in God's help but as a reproach against his justice. Thence arose the problem of Job.

Although the book of Job is of unknown, undatable provenance – most scholars postulate, however, a Jewish author writing after the exile – its problem can be found at any time in any culture. In Mesopotamia several similar stories have been discovered, one of which goes back to the first half of the second millennium.[65] Yet what marks out the Bible's Job in world literature is not so much its magnificent poetry, replete with so many *hapaxlegomena*[66] and of such artistic complexity that it has resisted a secure translation, as its unceasing, dogged probing of the dilemma of undeserved suffering. As is universally recognized, the prose text of the introductory two chapters and the concluding verses (42:7-17) represent an older story which the inspired poet adapted as the frame for his own reflections. Actually more than one poet seems to have had a hand in the final product. Most commentators consider the speech of Elihu (32-37) a late addition and probably the hymn to wisdom (28) is to be reckoned a subsequent interpolation or an originally independent piece added by the "final redactor."[67]

The older story told how God let Satan have his way with Job, "a blameless and upright man, who fears God and turns away from evil" (1:8). For Satan had accused Job of mercenary service: if the good are always rewarded, who but a fool would not be good? To show Job's virtue, the superiority of goodness even in adversity and Job's steadfast fidelity, God let Satan deprive the just man, without cause, of all his possessions and children; finally Satan afflicted Job's entire flesh with loathsome sores so that "his suffering was very great" (2:13). In all of this Job did not sin and at the end God rewarded him by doubling his material prosperity and restoring seven sons and three daughters to make up for those lost (42:10-17).

Job might have continued to offer the simple solution of testing and reward, had not the second author intervened at the arrival of Job's friends, come to console him and explain his sufferings. Even in the original version their rationalizations were so seriously insufficient as to provoke God's wrath (42:7-12). Perhaps they failed to realize God's purpose in letting Job be put to the test, viz., that God's trust in Job be publicly vindicated. In the final version the rebuke held valid probably because their explanations tended to reduce God to a simple notion of retributive justice. In any case, one can hardly imagine any dialogue more moving than that composed by the second author. For him the central character was hardly the "patient Job" of later tradition (Jas 5:11). With a vehemence unmatched in the Old Testament, Job cursed the day of his birth and longed for death (3:3-26).[68] After each of his friends' "consolations" Job replied in "the bitterness of my soul" (7:11; 10:1), expressing disgust with human life and God's justice. He even turned the joy of Psalm 8 upside down:

What is man, that thou dost make so much of him,
    and that thou dost set thy mind upon him,
dost visit him every morning,
    and test him every moment? ...
Why dost thou make me thy mark?
Why have I become a burden to thee? (7:17-20)

Convinced of his innocence, even in his trials, Job recognized the impossibility of convincing God of injustice (9:15ff; 19:6f; 23:7-17; 31); yet he would call God to account (13:3; 23:2-7; 31:35-37). The wicked prosper and the innocent suffer (12:4-6; 21:7-26; 24:1-25). Nonetheless, throughout his plaint, Job recognized God's existence and the norm of justice. his comforters repeated the old saws about God's justice, but Job relentlessly rejected their rationalizations, knowing too well his own case. Were Job an historical person, his raging would seriously have put his innocent holiness into question, as his friend Eliphaz noted (15:2-16). Yet the author doubtless took for granted Job's innocence: the sins of his youth (13:26) are long past and hardly weigh in the balance of pain. Granted his innocence, the apparent excesses of Job's laments could serve a cathartic purpose for the reader. Job's plaints far surpassed in force of recrimination anything with which a pious reader would reproach God.[69] The very fierceness of Job let the reader identify his case with Job's, even if with some trepidation. For, though no one may rightly declare himself totally innocent of all fault (Job 4:17-20; 9:1; 14:4; 25:4; Ps 14:2f; 53:1-3; 143:2; 130:3), as Job did, his vehement sense of outraged innocence touches the bottom of our heart's protest, where we feel ourselves unjustly requited or handled. No one could be as violent as Job before God. Accordingly our identification with him can only be partial; but if God can answer him, certainly our complaints must likewise be dissipated. Hence the reader's festering bitterness will have been purged, and he will have been opened to the wonders of God's surpassing majesty. So the diatribe of Job against his comforters and against God continued almost to the end of the book.

Finally God answered Job out of the whirlwind, calling him to account, demanding how a man can put him into question. God's response pointed first to the wonders of creation and asked Job where he was on the day of creation. Facing God, aware of a mystery far greater than himself, Job replied: "Behold, I am of small account; what shall I answer thee? I lay my hand on my mouth. I have spoken once, and I will not answer; twice, but I will proceed no further" (40:4f).

Silent awe before the mystery of creation apparently did not satisfy Yahweh. The mystery lay deeper still. Job had no ground for a complaint against God unless he could "look on everyone that is proud and abase him ... and tread down the wicked where they stand." Only then, said God, "will I also acknowledge to you, that your own right hand can give you victory" (40:11-14). With that God had demonstrated how feeble and illusory would be man's sense of justice if man should wish to stand by himself. What is justice if no one can ensure punishment for the guilty and reward for the innocent?

55

With the foundations of Job's complaint destroyed, God then revealed that he is master over the primal monsters, symbols of chaos and evil, Behemoth and Leviathan, "a creature without fear. he beholds everything that is high; he is king over all the sons of pride." (41:33f). This revelation resulted in Job's total repentance and capitulation to God's mystery: "I had heard of thee by the hearing of the ear, but now my eye sees thee; therefore I despise myself, and repent in dust and ashes" (42:5f).

Here the answer given earlier, the presence of God, has been deepened immeasurably, as the abyss between man's limited knowledge and strength and the supreme majesty of God has been uncovered. Where previously the psalmist had been content with the experience of God's presence and needed no further explanation, now it is revealed that no explanation is possible. No longer did Job insist upon holding fast to his righteousness and the witness of his own heart (27:6). A greater norm of justice and reality had been revealed to him, even if he could not comprehend it. But does not that destroy the basis of man's sense of justice, which seemed to be enshrined in the covenant as God's justice?

That question is all the more relevant today, when, as a result of existentialist questioning, the relativity and even the absurdity of man's knowing and doing has been highlighted; yet self-conscious, wilful, modern man refuses to undergo the type of capitulation that would destroy man's humanity and lead him to "despise himself."[70] Apparently not all Jews were satisfied with the answer given to Job, despite the profundity of Job's questioning. Confronting the prosperity of the wicked and his own suffering, Jeremiah knew of the deeper mystery of divine providence surpassing human insight, but it brought him no peace (12:1-6). Inversely, looking upon the suffering, toil, and frustration of all, good and bad alike, Qoheleth saw the vanity of all earthly realities and rested his hope for wisdom not upon his own insight into the order of the universe but only upon God's pure gift to the one pleasing him (1:2f, 8, 13-18; 2:12-26; 3:16-22; 5:13-17; 6; 8:14-9:4, 11f). That wisdom ended in a confession of God's justice (12:13) despite all appearances. For Qoheleth as for Job the expected recompense for good and evil deeds had not been fulfilled. Like Job he finished with faith in a mystery, but where Job's universe was full of poetic wonder and amazing mystery, Qoheleth's world teemed with "weariness" (1:8). If the world does not reflect a just and benevolent order somehow perceptible to man, there is little to choose between Job and Qoheleth. What do wonders count if they pulverize man and justice is denied? Without intelligible meaning, wonder gives way to weariness and the void of absurdity yawns impolitely but inevitably. Neither Job nor Ecclesiastes could be or was the last word of the Old Testament. Other answers were attempted.

8. Vicarious suffering: Many parts of the Old Testament strike the modern era's exaggerated sense of individualism as strange and puzzling. For the Jews, as was the rule among ancient peoples, the so-called "rugged individual," if he lasted long, was someone more to be pitied than admired. The individual did not stand alone but belonged primarily to his family, his clan, his nation.[71] Outside their protection, outside the walls of the city, life was dangerous and insecure in a world without central police forces, social security, communal schools, easy communications, reserves of foodstuffs, and passports.

"Corporate personality" is a term coined by modern Scripture scholars to designate the Old Testament sense of reality whereby the individual is a representative as well as a constitutive member of the group to which he belongs.[72] In many and diverse ways this perception of personal relations found expression in the Bible. Three of its main characteristics have been identified. First, corporate personality implied an extension beyond the present into the past and future. So the covenant was sealed not only on the basis of promises made

to Israel's forefathers but also on behalf of "him who is not here with us this day," i.e., future generations (Deut 29:13-15). Indeed, the very names used repeatedly for the Jews in the Bible: Israel, Jacob, Judah, manifest how the descendants of the patriarchs identified themselves with the founders of the nation and tribe. The patriarch somehow lived on in his progeny. In Amos 3:1 God addressed the generation of Amos' day as if it were the generation he had led out of Egypt, and he addressed it in the singular.

Second, corporate personality intended not merely a personification, a metaphor or a juridical fiction but a reality upon which further relations, juridical and otherwise, were based. The so-called "levirate marriage" (Deut 25:5-10; Gen 38:8) provides a case in point: if a man died without leaving a son to carry on his name and inheritance, his brother, whether married or not, was obliged to beget a son by the dead brother's wife, and the child was to carry the name of the dead brother. Similarly Saul was bound by a treaty made centuries previously by Joshua, and his infringement of it brought a famine upon the land that only the hanging of seven of his descendants ended (2 Sam 21:1-14; Josh 9).

Third, there was a fluid transition in corporate personality from individual to group and back again. Num 20:14-21 offered a particularly interesting example of this transition and showed how "Edom" applied in turn to the king, the people, the land, and the ancestor. The closing of the covenant in Deuteronomy 28-30 marked also a transition from singular "you" (28) to plural "you" (29) back to singular again (30). Even more compactly, in Hosea 11:1f, God first designated Israel as "my son" before complaining in the next breath that "they" deserted him. Examples could be multiplied at length.

Against such a background the justice of the decalogue is unimpeachable: "For I the Lord your God am a jealous God, visiting the iniquity of the fathers upon the children to the third and the fourth generation of those who hate me, but showing steadfast love to thousands of those who love me and keep my commandments" (Ex 20:5; Ex 34:7; Num 14:18; Deut 5:9f).[73] So sinners and their families might be utterly extirpated (cf. Josh 7:24-26; 1 Kings 21:21). Nonetheless, such a rule of recompense reflected the supremacy of God's mercy over his justice.

Moreover, if solidarity existed in time, it also existed among members of the same generation. If one person broke the covenant, all would suffer for it (Deut 29:18f). The third chapter of Genesis clearly presupposed the solidarity of the whole race with Adam and Eve as the author explained the reason for human mortality as well as for the hard lot of men and women in tilling the land and bearing children (3:16-19).[74] So also for the fault of a king the whole land should suffer. David's sin resulted in a pestilence upon Israel, and it was turned aside only by David's prayer: "Lo, I have sinned, and I have done wickedly; but these sheep, what have they done? Let thy hand, I pray thee, be against me and against my father's house" (2 Sam 24:17). Notice that, even when asserting personal responsibility in order to protect his people, David could not separate himself from his family.

Individualism grew in Israel, especially in times of prosperity. Under Amaziah, who reigned at the beginning of the eighth century BC, those who had killed his father were put to death in turn, but Amaziah limited retribution to the immediate murderers, sparing their children (2 Kings 14:5f). That Scripture should note this limitation may indicate a novelty, yet the text cited to support such behaviour shows an antiquity of formulation. "The fathers shall not be put to death for the children, nor shall the children be put to death for the fathers; every man shall be put to death for this own sin" (Deut 24:16). Scholars disagree whether the familial retribution of Exodus 20:5 applied only to offences against God's prerogatives or also to civil matters; in the latter case Amaziah's conduct would represent an innovation.[75] But even in Amaziah's day the notion of collective retribution must have continued, at least in respect to the law touching God most directly. For approximately 200 years later a strong reaction against its apparent injustice to individuals found cynical expression in the bitter proverb, "The fathers have eaten sour grapes, and the children's teeth are set on edge" (Jer 31:29; Ezek 18:2). To refute such a charge of injustice God promised, through the mouths of the prophets Jeremiah and Ezekiel, to repay each sinner for his own sin and not requite his descendants (Jer 31:30; Ezek 18:3-20). Yet so strong was the sense of solidarity among the Jews that shortly after that apparent triumph of individualism in Jeremiah and Ezekiel its contradiction appeared. Jeremiah prayed apparently without hesitation the following verses:

Ah Lord God!... who showest steadfast love to thousands, but dost requite the guilt of fathers to their children after them, O great and mighty God whose name is the Lord of hosts, great in counsel and mighty in deed (32:17-19).

Ezekiel in his turn could announce God's judgment equally against the just and unjust on the basis of some sense of national solidarity:

Thus says the Lord: Behold I am against you, and will draw forth my sword out of its sheath, and will cut off from you both righteous and wicked. Because I will cut off from you both righteous and wicked, therefore my sword shall go out of its sheath against all flesh from south to north (Ezek 21:3f).

As a result of the destruction of Jerusalem and the exile, a rethinking of the covenant came about. On the one hand, the value of the individual, once discovered in his particular personal relation with God, could not be jettisoned. Indeed the pious Jew in exile concentrated on his interior life in fidelity to the Torah, as Tobit, the *Daniel* cycle, Wisdom, and 1 and 2 Maccabees witness.[76] For such a believer the validity of the basic norm of justice, good rewarded-evil punished, would be strongly reaffirmed, as we saw above. Yet Jerusalem's fall also introduced a very profound sense of sin and collective culpability. The Deuteronomic and priestly writers, who saw history in terms of Israel's recurrent collective rejection of Yahweh before punishment drove the people back to him, were composing their theological-historical works in the post-exilic period. Moreover, unique among the peoples of the ancient Orient, such was the collective consciousness of guilt from Jeremiah's day on that many confessions of sins employed the plural subject "we" or "we and our fathers" while admitting guilt and beseeching forgiveness (Jer 3:22-25; 14:7, 19-21; Lam 5:7, 16; Ezek 9:6-15; Dan 9:4-19; Neh 2:6f; 6:37; 9:2; Jud 7:28; Tob 3:2-5; Bar 1:15-3:8).[77]

As all can suffer for the sin of one, so all can profit from the accomplishment of one. As indicated above, all Jews reaped the reward of Abraham's fidelity under testing. Ten just men could have saved Sodom (Gen 18:22-33), and one could have saved Jerusalem (Jer 5:1).

As Jews and Philistines both united themselves with their champions, so at Goliath's fall and David's triumph the Philistines ran from the field, leaving victory and pursuit to the Jews (1 Sam 17:8f, 50-52). In a somewhat similar vein many leading Israelites, like Moses, Joshua, Phinehas and Samuel, acted for their people as mediators of God's will and sometimes petitioned God to forgive the people's sins (Ex 18:19f; 32:7-14, 31f; Num 14:11-24; 25:10-13; 1 Sam 12:23; 15:24-31; Sir 45ff). Kings, priests, and prophets functioned as mediators between God and his people.[78] They were intended to effect salvation in word and deed, but their failings could also be detrimental to their people. Kings functioned as mediators in the weakest sense, for they were responsible mainly for upholding the divinely established order, not initiating it, by securing peace and justice as well as by participating in the cult. In this way they were to bring blessings to the people. But neglect of their duties, especially if the people remained in solidarity with them, called down God's wrath on all. The priesthood taught Israel, brought expiatory sacrifices before the Lord, and prayed for Israel (Deut 33:10; Lev 10:8-26; 12:8; 14:10-32; 15:30; Ex 28:38; 1 Chron 15:16-27). But it is especially in the prophets that the link between their role and suffering is clearly highlighted.

From Moses onwards the prophets announced God's will to Israel. Their message often encountered rejection and entailed sufferings.[79] Against Moses' leadership the people repeatedly "murmured" and threatened to stone him (Ex 15:24; 16:2; 17:2f; Num 14:1-10; 21:4f). Difficulties drove him to request of the Lord a relief from his post (Num 11:10-14). Yet he "stood in the breach" (Ps 106:23) to staunch God's wrath against Israel's idolatry, a sin against which he had also raged (Ex 32); later, when the people, on the edge of the Promised Land, wished to choose a new leader and return to Egypt, Moses again overcame the divine anger (Num 14:13-20; cf. also 21:7-9). Elijah and Micaiah risked total abandonment, imprisonment, and death for their fidelity to the Lord's mission (1 Kings 19:4, 9f; 22:26f). Elisha wept for his people in carrying out God's will (2 Kings 8:11f), as did, later on, both Isaiah (22:4) and Micah (1:8f). Amos met rejection and banishment (7:10-13). Ezekiel was resisted by the people (2:5-7), and, in order to give a sign to Israel, he had to lose his wife, the delight of his eyes (24:15-27). Hosea had to live out his message in a painful marriage with a whore (1:2ff). Jeremiah's very sufferings were part and parcel of his mission. Besides the physical maltreatment (20:1f; 37:11-38:7) and hostile threats (25:7-11) he mourned for his people's sin (8:18-9:1) and for his own mission of woe (15:10, 17f). Under the weight of sufferings, his humanity broke down; he could not serve as the ultimate mediator.[80] For he not only wished, however temporarily, to reject God's commission (20:7-9, 14-18) but he also prayed for vengeance upon the people who refused to accept God's word after he had turned aside God's wrath (Jer 11:14-20; 15:11, 15; 17:18; 18:18-23; 20:12). Nonetheless, after his death Jeremiah was considered a prophet who continued to protect and pray for his people (2 Macc 15:13-16).

The most famous example of vicarious suffering is found in the Servant of Yahweh, the subject of the Servant Songs reported in Second Isaiah (42:1-4; 49:1-6; 50:4-10; 52:13-53:12). By the time of Second Isaiah the almost unreflective use of corporate personality in earlier times had been put into question by rampant individualism with its protest against God's justice. The simple assurance of divine justice for the individual (Ezek 18) did not correspond with empirical reality nor apparently did its projection into the future (Jer 31:27-34) resolve all questions. So the prophet harkened back to the deeper sense of solidarity that bound all Israelites together before the Lord in order to affirm the mystery of God's justice and to ground the hope of salvation in innocent suffering. Chosen by God from the beginning of his life to establish justice in Israel and the world, the Servant of Yahweh strove with meekness and persuasion, despite adversity, to fulfil the divine will. Yet in all his innocence he was unjustly rejected and put to death by those for whom he came. And this was willed by God. Then the contrast with Job and Jeremiah broke through most clearly. The Servant "opened not his mouth" in complaints and recriminations (53:7). Instead he accepted freely the sufferings so that he "might bear their iniquities... and make intercession for sinners" (53:12f).

The identity of this Servant remained somewhat unclear. At one point he was addressed as "Israel" (49:3); yet immediately thereafter his task was defined in terms of bringing Jacob back to God, "that Israel might be gathered to him" (49:5). Probably the flexible transition between people and representative individual characteristic of corporate personality can explain that oscillation of reference.

In the Servant's death, when "like a lamb led to slaughter... He makes himself an offering for sin" (53:7, 10), a juncture between corporate personality and the notion of sacrificial substitution for sin probably occurred. The sacrificial notion of substitution is found scattered throughout the Old Testament. The uncleanliness of leprosy was purified first by the killing of one bird and the release of another that had been bathed in the first bird's blood, then by the sin sacrifice of a lamb (Lev 14). Sin offerings involved the sacrifice of an animal in expiation for sin (Lev 4:1-7:10) and, of course, the scapegoat, carrying the people's sins, was driven into the wilderness on the Day of Atonement after another goat and a ram had been sacrificed for sin (Lev 16:1-22). A similar substitution, if not explicitly for sin, involved the redemption of first-born sons (Ex 13:12f; 34:19f). God seemed to will the substitution of a ram for Isaac (Gen 22:12-14). Finally, Jonathan was redeemed from death for an unwitting trespass, probably by some sacrifice (1 Sam 14:24-45).[81] Surpassing all these sacrifices was the Servant's expiation. Not only was he an innocent human being, but also he freely took upon himself the sins of others, standing in the greatest solidarity with them for their sake.

Though Zechariah 12:10-13:1 might well make another reference to the Servant "pierced" in order to cleanse others from sin and uncleanness, the Servant's role and identity did not provide a central focus for post-exilic theology.[82] Yet the notion of vicarious suffering would continue as the Maccabean martyrs saw themselves as propitiating God's wrath (2 Macc 7:32f, 37f), and a whole theology of vicarious, reconciling death arose in regard to martyrs, just men, the patriarchs and innocent children, who won merit applicable not only in this world but also in the next.[83]

However comforting for the rest of us the Servant's vicarious sufferings might at first appear, the question of God's justice cannot be long postponed. Why must the Servant be chosen to suffer so grievously, so disproportionately, for sinners? The reason for the subsequent Jewish lack of interest in the Servant, who suffered vicariously, may also be due to the increasingly legalistic emphasis of post-exilic Judaism. In a world increasingly dominated by the model of legal, retributive justice it would be ever harder to explain how one person could carry another's sin and actually take the place of a guilty person. Even today this apparent neglect of justice renders the Servant's model of redemption suspect.[84] In Dostoevsky's great novel, *The Brothers Karamazov*, Ivan Karamazov denied that any moral person could accept an edifice of universal human happiness, peace and tranquillity on the condition that he had to torture a single, innocent, human victim.[85] Thus the fate of the Servant introduces our study to its final theme.

9. Life after death: As a result of Adam's sin all men were doomed to death. However, already in Job 14:13f; 19:25-27 and in other Old Testament passages, viz., Is 26:19; Ps 73:24; 16:9-11; 49:15, there were occasional hints of something more.[86] The unrequited sufferings and death of the just person seemed to cry out for that "something more." In the figure of the Servant of Yahweh the new consciousness broke through clearly. After the Servant had been declared dead and buried, Isaiah 53:10f continued:

> When he makes himself an offering for sin,
> he shall see his offspring, he shall prolong his days;
> the will of the Lord shall prosper in his hand;
> he shall see the fruit of the travail of his soul and be satisfied;
> by his knowledge shall the righteous one, my servant,
> make many to be accounted righteous;
> and he shall bear their iniquities.
> Therefore I will divide him a portion with the great,
> and he shall divide the spoil with the strong.

Justice extends for the individual beyond the grave, and it was the sense of injustice in innocent suffering which demanded a recompense from the justice of God. The same theme was continued in the book of Wisdom 1-5. "Righteousness is immortal" (1:15). Contrasted with the ungodly, who considered this life everything and consequently lived riotously and unjustly, the godly man placed his hope in God and acted justly. Because his conduct was a rebuke to the ungodly, they killed him, testing to see if God was really his father, as he had claimed, and if God would deliver him. At his death their victory seemed complete. "But the souls of the righteous are in the hand of God, and no torment will ever touch them. In the eyes of the foolish they seemed to have died, ... but they are in peace" (3:1-3; also 5:15f). The just man was being tried previous to his acceptance by God and the evil would be punished hereafter (4:16-5:14).

As the typical Hellenistic contrast between appearance and reality indicated, Wisdom was written in the Greek-speaking world, probably in Alexandria. As a result, the Greek presupposition about immortal souls, so foreign to the previous Jewish culture with its emphasis on the reality and goodness of this world, had entered into the biblical tradition. There was apparently some hesitancy about its full acceptance in Wisdom, for the book also made reference to a later "visitation" when the just would rule over peoples and the ungodly would be stricken with remorse and punishments upon seeing the just man's exaltation (3:7-12; 5:1-23).

A more traditional interpretation, rooted in Jewish soil, appeared in apocalyptic literature, specifically Daniel. There, after great tribulations, at the end of time:

Many of those who sleep in the dust of the earth shall awake, some to everlasting life, and some to shame and everlasting contempt. And those who are wise shall shine like the brightness of the firmament; and those who turn many to righteousness, like the stars for ever and ever" (12:2f).

Some sort of corporeal resurrection, not immortal souls, seems to have been presupposed. How individual souls managed to survive the separation from their bodies offered room for rabbinic speculation about "soul chambers" and the like.[87] 2 *Maccabees* bears testimony to Jewish beliefs about the afterlife. Not only did the author assure his readers that God, even while chastising, does not abandon his people and intends to reward the sufferings of the just with eternal life (6:24-7:42) but he also took up speculation about the possibility of atoning for the sins of the dead in view of the resurrection. Offerings for the dead, he thought, could be efficacious in freeing them from their sin (12:39-45).

With the expansion of Israel's expectations to life beyond the grave, the significance of alienation from God, the source of life and justice, was deepened. Those pertinaciously resisting righteousness were damned to "shame and everlasting contempt" (Dan 12:2). The torments of the doomed represented the only type of suffering which did not yield a positive effect for those undergoing them (Wis 5:2-8). Judith preached woe to the nations in rebellion against the Lord, promising a bitter vengeance in the day of judgment: "fire and worms he will give to their flesh; they shall weep in pain for ever" (16:17). In this was echoed Isaiah's eternal condemnation of the rebellious when the new heavens and the new earth were to be formed (Is 66:22-24; cf. Sir 7:17). When the time of mercy has run out, the Lord "judges each man according to his works" (cf. Ps 62:13; Prov 24:12; Sir 35:19).

Thus by the end of the Old Testament fidelity to God's justice, a constant theme, as well as the new insight into the importance of the individual's destiny before God, had led to the affirmation of life after death.[88] That was quite a development, if not a reversal, of earlier themes which had looked for God's justice here on earth. This transposition of perspective, however necessary and correct, carried dangers with it. Wisdom recounted of the just man dead early:

There was one who pleased God and was loved by
    him,
and while living among sinners he was taken up.
he was caught up lest evil change his understanding
    or guile deceive his soul...
Being perfected in a short time, he fulfilled long years;
    for his soul was pleasing to the Lord,
therefore he took him quickly from the midst of
    wickedness (4:10-14).

An analogous view of a wicked world is glimpsed in Dan
12:10: "Many shall purify themselves, and make themselves
white, and be refined; but the wicked shall do wickedly; and
none of the wicked shall understand; but those who are wise
shall understand." This intimation was expanded in 2 Macc
6:12-17, where God was understood to show kindness in
punishing his people immediately while patiently letting
the Gentiles fill up, by sinning, the full measure of his
vengeance. Rabbinic theology, establishing an exact corre-
spondence of retribution for every deed, went further: God
allowed the wicked to prosper in order that they receive here
on earth the reward of their few good deeds so as to obtain
full punishment for all their bad deeds hereafter; conversely,
God punished the good here to requite their few evil deeds
and so assure their attainment hereafter of an unadulterated
reward.[89] In this way the belief in an afterlife has reversed
the original notion of inner-worldly justice: now the good
suffer while the evil are rewarded in order that the relation
may be reversed on the other side.[90] But is not this to abandon the present world to wickedness, to make it the place of
the devil, and to remove God from history, reducing him to
a celestial pastry vendor, offering "pie in the sky when you
die" or its apocalyptic, eschatological equivalent? The way
was thereby opened both to a profound pessimism, even
deeper than Qoheleth's, totally contradicting Judaism's faith

in a provident Creator, and to Gnosticism's rejection of this material world.[91]

Faced with such alternatives one more easily understands the fervid faith of the Jews in the basic principle of justice: good rewarded-evil punished. All the other answers proposed in the Old Testament, though they built upon that fundamental principle, never fully satisfied. In times of persecution and trial, such as the Jews underwent during and after the exile, it may have been best to hold on to the simple principles of morality and trust God to maintain them, even if appeal had to be made to miracles and apocalyptical interventions. God was faithful and just. That insight had to be preserved at all costs. So the Jews, having tried in so many ways to understand and explicate God's ways with men, still had to wait for light in face of dark conundrums. The miracle of Christ was to come as the fulfilment of their hopes in ways unsuspected. For, uniting in his own mystery all the strands of Old Testament reflection about the significance of suffering, Christ in his coming would save the meaning of this world and the next by bestowing an eschatological and supernatural profundity upon everyday joys and sufferings. Where man could go no further, even with the best will in the world, there God made space for his salvation.

NOTES

1. Cf. C.S. Lewis, *The Problem of Pain* (London: Bles, 1940), pp. 103f, on the "unimaginable sum of human misery"; cf. also the remarks of M.C. D'Arcy, S.J., *The Pain of this World and the Providence of God* (London: Longmans, Green, 1935), pp.125f.

2. In this study we wish to expand the conclusion of H. Schmidt, *Gott und das Leid im Alten Testament* (Gießen: Töpelmann, 1926), p.40, who saw nothing new about suffering in the New Testament except a heightening of joy. We also hope to show that Christian faith in the face of suffering and doubt is more than just an unwillingness to surrender God's mystery and the meaning

of one's life in whatever tradition one is brought up, as seems to be the conclusion, from their Old Testament studies, of J. Crenshaw, *A Whirlpool of Torment* (Philadelphia: Fortress, 1984), pp. 117-119, and R. Davidson, *The Courage to Doubt* (London: SCM, 1983), pp. 209-213. Christian faith has a structure, and it alone can respond adequately to the questions raised by suffering. Because it comes from God, faith drives out doubt and possesses the greatest certitude. Moreover, the theodicy of the Bible did not gnaw away at "the integrity and dignity of those who felt constrained to come to the defence of the creator" (J. Crenshaw, "Introduction: The Shift from Theodicy to Anthropodicy", in *Theodicy in the Old Testament*, ed. J. Crenshaw [Philadelphia: Fortress, 1983], 2, 6, 7). Although the Old Testament answers are only partial, they can rightly be seen as preparations for God's answer to man's wounded and tormented heart in the New Testament.

3. The following section represents a somewhat haphazard collection of views on life and suffering, gathered mainly from the author's reading in Greek and Latin literature. It is by no means complete. Other more positive views of suffering can be found in J. Coste, S.M., "Notion grecque et notion biblique de la 'souffrance éducatrice', *Recherches de Science Religieuse* 43 (1955), 483-497, and C. Moeller, *Sagesse grecque e paradoxe chrétien* (Tournai: Casterman, 1948), pp. 162-228. Moeller, however, finds the meaning of fragments only in view of Christian revelation. A. Sertillanges, O.P., *Le Problème du mal*, I (Paris: Aubier, 1948), pp. 73-98, is also helpful.

4. J. Pritchard (ed.), *Ancient Near Eastern Texts*, 2nd ed. (Princeton: Princeton U., 1955), pp. 44-52, 72-99.

5. Ibid., p. 91: X, ii, 12-15, repeated p. 92: X, iii, 28-31.

6. Ibid., p. 99: XII, 93-99.

7. C. Gordon, *The Common Background of Greek and Hebrew Civilizations* (New York: Norton, 1965), pp. 218-277, esp. 223f.

8. Anacreon, no. 66, in D.L. Page's edition, *Poetae Melici Graeci* (Oxford: Clarendon, 1963). Though it is difficult to judge from one fragment its proper meaning, the edition of *Anacreon* by G. Preisendanz (Lipsiae: Teubner, 1912) shows death as the power which Anacreon tries to exorcise or forget by his drinking. Cf. poems 36, 45, 48, 50, 52. Preisendanz's edition unfortunately is based upon many of his own reconstructions.

9. Herodotus, *Histories*, I, 29ff for the story of Croesus to whom this piece of wisdom was addressed. In Greek there was a play on the word ὄλβιος which signifies "rich", "happy", or some combination of both.

10. Theognis A 425-429. The new edition by D. Young (Lipsae: Teubner, 1961) lists other Greek authors who refer to this stanza. Sophocles' adaptation in *Oedipus at Colonus*, 1225ff, has been interpreted by some as reflecting the personal trials of his old age; cf. *Sophocle*, II, trans. P. Masqueray (Paris, 1924), p. 202, n. 2. Yet previously in *Oedipus Rex*, 1194f, he had echoed Solon's pessimistic wisdom about counting no mortal happy. See also Herodotus, I, 32, 86.

11. "Cyrenaici", *Harper's Dictionary of Classical Literature and Antiquities*, ed. H. Peck, 2nd ed. (1897; rpt. New York: Cooper Square, 1962), 459; Weinberger, "Hegesias von Kyrene", *Paulys Real-Encyclopädie der classischen Altertumswissenschaft*, ed. G. Wissowa u. W. Kroll, VIII (Stuttgart: Metzler, 1912), 2607.

12. For their doctrines cf. M. Pohlenz, *Die Stoa: Geschichte einer geistigen Bewegung*, I (Göttingen: Vandenhoeck & Ruprecht, 1947), pp. 1-158, esp. 111-158; J. Rist, *Stoic Philosophy* (Cambridge: Cambridge U., 1969); L. Edelstein, *The Meaning of Stoicism* (Cambridge: Harvard U., 1966); R. Hicks, *Stoic and Epicurean* (New York: Russell & Russell, 1962); G. Panichas, *Epicurus* (New York: Twayne, 1967), pp. 87-122; N. DeWitt, *Epicurus and his Philosophy* (Minneapolis: U. of Minnesota, 1964).

13. Cf. K. Prümm, S.J., *Christentum als Neuheitserlebnis* (Freiburg: Herder, 1939), pp. 332-347; K. Baus, "Inner Life of the Church Between Nicea and Chalcedon", *The Imperial Church from Constantine to the Early Middle Ages*, ed. H. Jedin and J. Dolan, trans. A. Biggs (New York: Seabury, 1980), 192, 197f, 202f, 213-217, 394-401, 406-411; W. Frend, *The Rise of Christianity* (London: Darton, Longman and Todd, 1984), pp. 292, 311-314, 421, 450f, 561.

14. Besides the books already mentioned we have relied on the following which treated the problem of suffering: G. von Rad, *Theologie des Alten Testaments*, 6th ed. (München: Kaiser, 1968-69), I, pp. 200-293, 366-473; II, pp. 108-270, 316-338, 413-436; W. Eichrodt, *Theology of the Old Testament*, trans. J. Baker (London: SCM, 1961-67), I, pp. 25-69, 206-288, 457-471; II, pp. 93-117, 151-529; A. Mattioli, *Dio e l' uomo nella Bibbia d'Israele* (Casale: Marietti, 1981), pp. 245-321; E. Balla, "Das Problem des Leides in der Geschichte der israelitisch-jüdischen Religion", in *EUXAPIΣTHPION* (Festschrift Gunkel) (Göttingen: Vanderhoeck & Ruprecht, 1923), 214-260; N. Peters, *Die Leidensfrage im alten Testament* (Münster, Aschendorf, 1923); J. Stamm, *Das Leiden des Unschuldigen in Babylon und Israel* (Zürich: Zwingli, 1946); E. Sutcliffe, S.J., *Providence and Suffering in the Old and New Testaments* (London: T. Nelson and Sons, 1955); J. Sanders, *Suffering as Divine Discipline in the Old Testament and Post-Biblical Judaism* (Rochester: Colgate Rochester Divinity School, 1955); J. Scharbert, *Der Schmerz im Alten Testament* (Bonn: Hanstein, 1955); A. Gelin, *The Key Concepts of the Old Testament*, trans. G. Lamb (New York: Paulist, 1963), pp. 63-94; A. Bertrangs, *Il Dolore nella Bibbia*, 2nd ed., trans. A. Sidoti (Bari: Paoline, 1967); G Fohrer, *Theologische Grundstrukturen des Alten Testaments* (Berlin: de Gruyter, 1972), pp. 133-184; J. Blenkinsopp, *Wisdom and Law in the Old Testament* (Oxford: Oxford U., 1983), pp. 41-158; J. L'Hour, "Pour une enquête morale dans le Pentateuque et dans l'Histoire Deutéronomiste", in M. Gilbert, J. L'Hour, J. Scharbert, *Morale et Ancien Testament* (Louvain: Université Catholique, 1976), 29-91. Our citations from the Bible, Old and New Testaments, are generally taken from the Revised Standard Version, *The New Oxford Annotated Bible with the Apochrypha*, ed. H. May and B. Metzger (New York: Oxford U., 1977).

Often we have made our own alterations on the basis of the original text to stress certain points.

15. For God's special love of the poor cf. R. McKenzie, S.J., *Faith and History in the Old Testament* (Minneapolis: U. of Minnesota, 1963), pp. 18-31; A. Gelin, *The Poor of Yahweh*, trans. K. Sullivan (Collegeville: Liturgical, 1964).

16. The classic study of E. Dodds, *The Greeks and the Irrational* (Berkeley: U. of California, 1951), is still useful for recalling the many aspects of Greek life and thought that recognized other norms besides that of rational clarity. Cf. pp. 28-134, 236-281, for sections especially concerning religion.

17. For the development, not always progressive, of Hebrew monotheism cf. J. Bright, *A History of Israel* (London: SCM, 1966), pp. 129-142; W. Albright, *From Stone Age to Christianity*, 2nd ed. (Garden City: Doubleday, 157), pp. 257-272; H. Rowley, *From Moses to Qumran* (London: Lutterworth, 1963), pp. 35-63; H. Renckens, S.J., *The Religion of Israel*, trans. N. Smith (New York: Sheed and Ward, 1966), pp. 25-40, 63-70, 97-139; 286-290; Mattioli, pp. 44-90.

18. R. Clements, *Old Testament Theology* (London: Marshall, Morgan and Scott, 1978), pp. 104-130.

19. Eichrodt, I, pp. 255f; MacKenzie, pp. 32-45; N. Lohfink, *Das Siegeslied am Schilfmeer* (Frankfurt: Knecht, 1965), pp. 151-173.

20. G. von Rad, I, p. 389.

21. Cf. also F. Nötscher, "Gerechtigkeit", in *Bibeltheologisches Wörterbuch*, I, 455.

22. Modern biblical scholarship has been very concerned to identify the sources of the early historical narratives in the Bible. Certain characteristic themes, literary styles and vocabulary keep reappearing in diverse contexts. By identifying them scholars have postulated the hypothesis of diverse authors or interpretative schools who introduced their own emphases or theologies in retelling and commenting upon earlier traditions. The priestly writer (school) shows a particular interest in cultic institutions. The creation account of Genesis 1, for example, concentrates on the seven days of creation leading to the Sabbath rest. The earlier creation account of Genesis 2:4bff is ascribed to the Yahwehist writer (school), so named because he habitually identifies God as Yahweh (Lord). The Elohist writer (school), on the contrary, habitually uses the name Elohim for God. The apparently oldest strand of narrative in the early histories is identified as those parts of the narrative which do not manifest the characteristics of the three other schools. Naturally in this hypothetical reconstruction there has been much debate about the exact contents of the various school, their theologies, the dates of composition and their relations to each other. More recent Old Testament criticism is turning its attention again to the final, overall message of the text. Nonetheless, the older categories are helpful in identifying recurrent theological themes. For a good introduction to the question cf. O. Eissfeldt, *The Old Testament: An Introduction*, trans. P. Ackroyd (Oxford: Blackwell, 1965), pp. 182-22. The

investigation of such sources does not put in question divine inspiration; rather it indicates the complexity of God's workings throughout history and stresses the open-ended aspect of the Old Testament that does not come to its definitive interpretation until Christ.

23. E.g., L. Alonso Schökel, S.J., "Motivos sapienciales y de alianza en Gn 2-3", *Biblica* 43 (1962), esp. 305-312; N. Lohfink, S.J., "Der theologische Hintergrund der Genesiserzählung von Sündenfall", in *Realität und Wirksamkeit des Bösen*, ed. K. Forster (Würzburg: Echter, 1965), 79-82; W. Roehrs, "Der alttestamentliche Bund und die Rechtfertigung durch den Glauben", in *Lutherische Rundblick* 12 (1964), 157.

24. G. Mendenhall, "Covenant", in *The Interpreter's Dictionary of the Bible*, ed. G. Butterick, I (New York: Abingdon, 1962), 714-723, esp. 714f, 718-720. These suzerainty treaties regulated the duties and obligations binding on overlord and vassal; in them the gods were summoned as witnesses to a series of blessings and curses dependent upon fulfilment or non-fulfilment of the treaty's stipulations.

25. D. McCarthy, S.J., *Treaty and Covenant* (Rome: P.B.I., 1963); E. Sellin-G. Fohrer, *Einleitung in das Alte Testament*, 10th ed. (Heidelberg: Quelle & Meyer, 1965), pp. 55-57, 77-80.

26. L. Perlitt, *Bundestheologie im Alten Testament* (Neukirchen-Vluyn: Neukirchner, 1969); E. Nicholson, *God and his People* (Oxford: Clarendon, 1986). The Deuteronomic writer (school) is one of the most influential in the final composition of the historical and legal books of the Old Testament. Most scholars link the school with the legal reform of Josiah in 621 BC Its views are clearly expressed in Deuteronomy and are found repeatedly in the historical books from Joshua to 2 Kings. Cf. Eissfeldt, pp. 171-176, 219-233, 241-301; G. von Rad, I, pp. 84-94, 232-244, 306-308, 316f, 319f, 343-359.

27. McCarthy, *Old Testament Covenant*, pp. 38-40, 78f.

28. Nicholson, pp. 179-188, despite his partiality to Perlitt's thesis, had to admit the very probable authenticity of this passage.

29. Though Nicholson, pp. 134-150, following Perlitt, rejected the Yahwehist authorship of the covenant in Exodus 34, he neglected R. Adamiak, *Justice and History in the Old Testament* (Cleveland: Zubal, 1982), pp. 10-31, who argued that a change took place in Yahweh's reaction to Israel's murmuring after the covenant was established and ratified. Before the covenant he had been most patient and lenient; after the covenant he showed his anger at Israel's infidelity. Even if the philological conjectures of Perlitt and Nicholson deny the present form of Exodus 34 to the Yahwehist writer, the pattern observed by Adamiak would be best explained by something like a covenant already known by the Yahwehist author. We would be left with an *Ur-Exodus* 34, i.e., a primordial version of Exodus 34 which existed before the Yahwehist revision. Adamiak's theory might also explain the existence of certain linguistic traces of the Yahwehist texts.

30. For the development of the law cf. J. Blenkinsopp, 41-129, 140-150; Sellin-Fohrer, pp. 112-209, esp. 144-156.

31. Clements, p.119.

32. This aspect of reciprocity, though mentioned by many, is especially accentuated by L. Köhler, *Theologie des Alten Testaments*, 3rd ed. (Tübingen: Mohr [Siebeck], 1953), pp. 48-55.

33. In his long treatment of covenant morality W. Eichrodt, II, pp. 316-379, tried to identify its essential element as the accomplishment of duty (Should) for God's sake alone. In this, as in some other aspects (cf. n. 88 below), he was probably too anxious to find Protestant theology, or his own particular understanding of it, in the Old Testament. Certainly even the prophets, who allegedly attained the peak of moral intuition, did not omit descriptions in materialistic terms of Israel's glorious future when, once the scourges for present sins would be past, Israel or the chosen remnant would enjoy again God's blessings (e.g., Is 11; 33:17-24; 35; 40; 55; 58; 66:10-14; Ezek 28:24-26; 36; Jer 30:10-31:14; Zeph 3:14-20; Zech 14). However perceptively the prophets recognized the primary obligation of fidelity owed to Yahweh for his own sake, they did not and, given their understanding of God's justice, probably could not imagine that God would be in return less than generous to his obedient people. Indeed, his past generosity was a reason for demanding present fidelity. The Deuteronomic and priestly writers, active after or contemporaneous with the great prophets, did not hesitate both to keep the more "primitive" notions of justice and even expanded them, as in Deut 29-30, emphasizing the material rewards and punishments of fidelity and infidelity. One must be careful, in a post-Kantian age, of separating man's service of God from God's generosity to man – there is an inherent link between them. Moreover, such a separation necessarily forced as insufficient and preparatory while judging later moral expressions, which re-employ earlier understandings, as a standard into scriptural morality and not letting God's revelation speak in its entirety.

34. More texts may be found in Scharbert, *Leid*, pp. 203-208.

35. For further instances cf. Peters, pp. 4-6; Stamm, pp. 33-36; Bella, 215-220; Eichrodt, II, pp. 178-180, 282-286.

36. E. Balla, "Problem", attempted to trace some development from an early notion of Yahweh as somewhat arbitrary in the distribution of blessings and punishments to a strict notion of retributive justice that would be surpassed in the Servant Songs, *Job,* and Psalm 73, the culmination of Old Testament spirituality, from which, however, later Judaism would regress into the schema of retributive justice. Besides the problem of dating texts, one must remember that later editors like the Deuteronomic school did not delete earlier passages that Bella considered had transcended. Further, most of the themes noted in our main texts seem to be recurrent throughout the Old Testament. Peters, p. 81, more wisely warned against any attempt to trace a development in the question of suffering – except concerning belief in a future life, the last of our thematic headings.

37. Adamiak, pp. 10-31, 56-77.

38. G. von Rad, I, pp. 340-359; Sellin-Fohrer, pp. 230f, 248-257, 255-257; cf. also pp. 181-194.

39. G. von Rad, I, pp. 359-365; Sellin-Fohrer, pp. 257-267.

40. K. Koch, "Is there a Doctrine of Retribution in the Old Testament", in *Theodicy*, 57-87; also G. von Rad, I, pp. 277-281, 395-399.

41. K. Koch "אטֶק hata' ", *Theologisches Wörterbuch zum Alten Testament*, ed. J. Botterweck u. H. Ringgren (Stuttgart: Kohlhammer, 1973-1986) [henceforth: *TWAT*], II, 860-862; cf. also G. Quell, "ἁμαρτάνω ", *Theologisches Würterbuch zum Neuen Testament*, ed. G. Kittel (Stuttgart: Kohlhammer, 1933-1973) [henceforth: *TWNT*], I, 274-276.

42. Koch, "Is there," 69-75.

43. Eichrodt, II, pp. 151-177.

44. Koch, ibid., 68. Mattioli's criticism of Koch, pp. 293f, has correctly stressed the hand of God behind all the punishments, but he exaggerated Koch's position somewhat unfairly to make his own points. Interestingly enough J. Scharbert, *Schmerz*, pp. 126, 171, earlier affirmed "the immanent sanction of the moral law", while allowing for God's place behind the "natural law", but in reaction to Koch's thesis he stressed Yahweh's personal intervention: "Das Verbum PQD in der Theologie des ATS", *Biblische Zeitschrift*, N.F. 4 (1960), 209-226, esp. 224f, and "SLM im Alten Testament", in *Um das Prinzip der Vergeltung in Religion und Recht des Alten Testaments*, ed. K. Koch (Darmstadt: Wissenschäftliche Buchgesellschaft, 1968), 300-324, esp. 321-323. Von Rad, I, p. 398, found the correct balance also. For a wider and more adequate discussion cf. the other articles in *Um das Prinzip*.

45. Eichrodt, II, pp. 175-177. Regarding the question of the psalmist's "I" cf. the recent complex thesis of S. Croft, *The Identity of the Individual in the Psalms* (Sheffield: JSUT, 1987).

46. Cf. Croft, pp. 20, 158, 160; H.-J. Kraus, *Psalmen*, 5th ed. (Neukirchen-Vluyn: Neukirchner, 1978), I, pp. 132-134, 141f; A. Anderson, *The Book of Psalms* (London: Oliphants, 1972), I, pp. 57f; P. Craigie, *Psalms 1-50* (Waco: Word, 1983), pp. 58-60.

47. J. Bright, *A History of Israel* (London: SCM, 1960), pp. 413-428.

48. The notion was not a sudden discovery. Mattioli, pp. 253-255, mentioned the frequent recurrence in Hebrew writings of polar expressions like good and evil, life and death, light and darkness, sweet and bitter, to express the totality of a reality. Mattioli, p. 268, also noted the use of psychological punishments in Job 15:20-24; 18:11; 20:27. These serve as corrections and expansions to J. Crenshaw, "The Problem of Theodicy in Sirach: On Human Bondage", in *Theodicy*, pp. 124-132.

49. Among the rabbis the same link was still widely affirmed; cf. H. Strack u. P. Billerbeck (ed.), *Kommentar zum Neuen Testament aus Talmud und Midrash*, 2nd ed. (1924-1928; rpt. München: Beck, 1956) [henceforth: Billerbeck], II, pp. 193-197, 529.

50. Bella, 255.

51. "Negative theology" is a technical term used to explain the possibility of speaking intelligibly about God. The philosopher, or natural theologian, argues to the existence of God from his created effects in the world. There must be some similarity between the cause and its effects. Otherwise no argument from effect to cause would be valid and all human reasoning would be put into question. That is the basis of every affirmative quality, or perfection, predicated of God by reason. This first step in speaking about God is termed the way of affirmation (*via affirmationis*). Nonetheless, the philosopher recognizes that every perfection possessed by a creature is enjoyed by God in an infinite way, in a way completely transcending our finite understanding and affirmation. There is an utter dissimilarity between our way of possessing and knowing a perfection and God's. This second step, recognizing the limitations of human language and thought about God, is generally designated the way of negation (*via negationis*) or negative theology. In a third step, the way of eminence (*via eminentiae*), the philosopher says, "Nonetheless, despite all limitations, there is an abiding analogy, or similarity, between God and our language about him." Various theologians emphasize various steps in man's manner of talking about God. Some see his hand immediately in creation, others recognize him in his transcendence of apparent absence, still others try to balance the presence and absence of God in the world. Of course, the same theologian may employ in turn the ways of affirmation, negation, or eminence, depending on his topic and audience.

52. Cf. T. Fretheim, *The Suffering of God* (Philadelphia: Fortress, 1984), for the collection of texts about God's sufferings because of, with, and for his people. Schmidt, p. 39, also pointed this out. Some speculative theologies have also built upon the sufferings of God: K. Kitamori, *The Theology of the Pain of God* (London: SCM, 1966); J. Moltmann, *The Crucified God*, trans. R. Wilson & J. Bowden (New York: Harper & Row, 1970); E. Jüngel, *Gott als Geheimnis der Welt*, 3rd ed. (Tübingen: Mohr [Siebeck], 1978). For a more traditional interpretation of God's "sufferings" cf. Scharbert, *Schmerz*, pp. 216-225.

53. H. Reventlow, *Opfere deinen Sohn* (Neukirchen-Vluyn, Neukirchner, 1968), pp. 70f. (pp. 72-75: Abraham was also such a model for the final redactor of the story); R. Kilian, *Die vorpriesterlichen Abrahams überlieferungen* (Bonn: Hanstein, 1966), pp. 274, 276, 310f.

54. The role of Abraham was very highly esteemed by late Judaism: J. Jeremias, " 'Αβρααμ", *TWNT*, I, 7f. For Abraham's position among the rabbis cf. Billerbeck, I, pp. 117-121.

55. Crenshaw, *Whirlpool*, p. 2, speaks of "the divine act of self-limitation" that resulted from the creation of human freedom and led to the necessity of testing; on p. 14 he has God beseeching Abraham as if he were aware of the monstrosity of the test to which he was subjecting the patriarch. (Cf. also Crenshaw, "Introduction," 10.) More fundamentally, Fretheim, pp. 34-78, saw the Old Testament God as limited by the world in space, time, knowledge

and power. Admittedly it is difficult to decide to what extent anthropomorphic metaphors are intended as such in speaking to God. Not only is a response to such a question dependent on the stage of evolution of monotheistic belief, the dating of the texts, the conception of divine transcendence, the author's intentions and the presuppositions about personal relations between God and man but also a great deal of modern philosophy is implied in such questions and answers. Surely the ancient author was not bothered by such complexity of hermeneutical questions and probably had not elaborated all his presuppositions. Given the rather early entrance of monotheism into the Israelite tradition and the tendency to attribute the complete control of Israel's history to God, it seems best not to limit God's power and knowledge, even before Second Isaiah. (Cf. Peters, p. 48.) For a philosophical groundwork that would allow God's infinity, omnipotence and omniscience to coexist with a certain "waiting on" man's freedom cf. J. McDermott, S.J., "A New Approach to God's Existence", *The Thomist* 44 (1980), 219-250. Our identification of the central conundrum of metaphysics in terms of the one-many problematic is better reformulated in terms of the infinite-finite problem that bedevils modern philosophy and of which the one-many problematic is but one aspect. A very brief résumé of the argument is found in "Proofs for the Existence of God", *The New Dictionary of Theology*, ed. J. Komonchak, M. Collins, D. Lane (Wilmington: Glazier, 1988), 804-808.

56. "Redactor" is a technical term of exegesis to indicate the editor-writer of a scriptural text. he takes over previous traditions, orders them according to his understanding of their significance, and even adds to or interprets them by his comments. The notion of "redactor" emphasizes the elements of compiling, ordering and editing traditional texts or stories more than the element of free composition.

57. L. Ruppert, "Das Motiv der Versuchung durch Gott in vordeuteronomischer Tradition", *Vetus Testamentum* 22 (1972), 55-63; cf. also Reventlow, pp. 67-70; Kilian, *Isaaks*, pp. 50f, 72-74.

58. Crenshaw, "Introduction", 8, objected to such an answer, confusing suffering with evil. But limitation necessarily involves the possibility of suffering, which in turn seems to be the condition of possibility for growth, adventure, and self-sacrificial love. Cf. J. McDermott, S.J., "The Loving Father and the tormented Child: Professor Flew and St Irenaeus", in *Thought* 53 (1978), 70-82. Even the Abraham story shows the implication of love of God, the readiness to prefer him to all else and the mercy of the Creator who gives himself and the world in return. As for Crenshaw's objection, 8, 11, against God's pact with Satan in *Job*, the original author may well have been trying to "excuse" God by attributing the initiative for Job's woes to Satan. The second author saw deeper and recognized God's mastery even over evil. That suffering occurs for the innocent is undeniable, the ultimate reason for it was hidden in God until he revealed the mystery of his love in Christ.

59. Cf. F. Helfmeyer, "נִסָּה, nissah", *TWAT*, V, 473-487; also S. Wagner, "יָגָה, jagah", *TWAT*, III, 406-412; R. Moses, "bak, k'b", *TWAT*, IV, 8-13.

60. N. Lohfink, "'Ich bin Jahwe, dein Artz' (Ex 15, 26)", in *"Ich will euer Gott werden"*, ed. H. Merklein u. E. Zenger (Stuttgart: Kath. Bibelwerk, 1981), 15-29 (41).

61. Ibid., 63-66.

62. For more on educative suffering cf. Coste, 497-508. The texts he cited do not specifically speak of "testing" but of "learning" or "coming to know".

63. J. Gamberoni, "Fasten", *Bibeltheologisches Wörterbuch*, I, 335-337.

64. "Theodicy" refers to philosophical or theological discipline attempting to vindicate God's justice in permitting evil's existence.

65. For an interesting comparison of these stories with the Old Testament cf. Stamm, esp. pp. 76-83. Cf. also Blenkinsopp, pp. 61-63.

66. A "hapax legomenon" (pl. "hapax legomena") is a technical term of classical philology and biblical exegesis to designate a word that occurs but once either in the author, the larger work (e.g., the Bible), or in the whole literature of a language. Clearly the meanings of words that occur but once, especially in poetic contexts, are extremely difficult to decipher. "Hapax legomenon" comes from two Greek words meaning "said once."

67. An "interpolation" refers to an addition made to an already completed text. The "final redactor" designates the one ultimately responsible for the text as it now stands. Presumably he saw the meaning in the various parts placed together. Exegesis usually tries to discover the mind of the final redactor. Exegesis can become very complicated once it is recognized that the final redactor might not have properly appreciated the significance of the texts which he joined in his final interpretation. Exegetes may debate such matters, but the final sense of Scripture becomes clear only in Christ. *Novum in vetere latet, Vetus in novo patet* [The New Testament is hidden in the Old, the Old Testament becomes clear in the New: a frequent phrase of the Church Fathers from Irenaeus on].

68. Jeremiah 20:14-18 also expresses a curse upon the prophet's day of birth. Ecclessiastes 4:2f. recalls the wisdom of Solon about the dead being more fortunate than the living and the never born most fortunate of all. These texts go contrary to the strong, main current of Jewish piety, but neither matches the prolonged vehemence and existential passion of Job. For a very stimulating and reflective analysis of *Job* cf. D. Cox, O.F.M., *Man's Anger and God's Silence: The Book of Job* (Slough: St Paul Publications, 1990). Though at times excessively emphasizing an existentialist interpretation, Cox's book raises the essential questions and finds a surprising unity.

69. Even granting the frankness with which some Jews, like Moses and Jeremiah, spoke to God, Job's case is unique. Doubtless the vast majority of Jews never considered themselves such close companions of God as Moses or Jeremiah.

70. Crenshaw, "Introduction", 6; A. Camus, *The Plague*, trans. G. Stuart (New York: Vintage, 1972), pp. 203f, 207-213, 216. Much of this critique doubtless

derives from L. Feuerbach, *The Essence of Christianity*, trans. G. Eliot (New York: Harper, 1957), who opposed God and man so that the magnification of the one led to the diminution of the other: cf, e.g., pp. 25f.

71. J. Scharbert, *Solidarität in Segen und Flucht im Alten Testament und in seiner Umwelt* (Bonn: Hanstein, 1958), pp. 72-112, shows how this sense of solidarity still persists among the Bedouin of Arabia, and the rest of the book shows the deep sense of solidarity in ancient Israel. Cf. also J. Scharbert, *Prolegomena eines Alttestamentlers zur Erbsündelehre* (Freiburg: Herder, 1968), esp. pp. 31-44, 108-117. In Greek literature the individual in formal introductions would present himself by identifying first his nation or people, then his father, and only then his own personal name: e.g., Homer, *The Iliad*, V, 227; VI, 145ff; XV, 254-256; XXI, 154-160; XXIV, 396-400; Aeschlylus, *Libation Bearers,* 674; Sophocles, *Oedipus at Colonus*, 214-223. Euripides' age of individualism brought a breakdown of this structure of presentation. A similar structure is found in the ancient English epic *Beowulf*, 260-269, 408.

72. H.W. Robinson, "The Hebrew Conception of Corporate Personality," *Zeitschrift für alttestamentliche Wissenschaft:* Beihefte 66 (1936), 49-62; J. de Fraine, S.J., *Adam and the Family of Man*, for the different meanings of the slight changes in the formulation.

74. Scharbert, *Prolegomena*, esp. pp. 60-77, 103-107, finds in Genesis 3 a strong witness to what, in accord with St Paul, the later Church would call "original sin."

75. Most of the older German literature considers the law a later interpolation: A. Sanda, *Das Zweite Buch der Könige* (Münster: Aschendorff, 1912), p. 163; R. Kittel, *Die Bücher der Könige* (Göttingen: Vandenhoeck & Ruprecht, 1900), p. 260; I. Benzinger, *Die Bücher der Könige* (Freiburg: Mohr [Siebeck], 1899), p. 164; A. Bertholet, *Deuteronomium* (Freiburg: Mohr [Siebeck], 1899), p. 76; H. Junker, *Das Buch Deuteronomium* (Bonn: Hanstein, 1933), p. 102; G. Hentschel, *2 Könige* (Würzburg: Echter, 1985), p. 64. Yet G. von Rad, *Das Fünfte Buch Mose*, 3rd ed. (Göttingen: Vandenhoeck & Ruprecht, 1978), p. 109, was very cautious about judging the law's provenance. A. Mayes, *Deuteronomy* (London: Oliphants, 1979), p. 326, argued on the basis of form and context that the law is older than the usual forms of Deuteronomic legislation, and he was followed by G. Jones, *1 and 2 Kings* (Grand Rapids: Eerdmans, 1984), II, p. 508.

76. Though *1* and *2 Maccabees* recount the bravery of faithful Jews under persecution in Palestine, the fact that the books were written in Greek, in the Diaspora, indicates that the authors shared the values of the Jews who died for obedience to the Torah and whom they praised so highly. *Daniel*, though written in Palestine, nonetheless tells of fidelity to the law in the Diaspora. Obviously there was a communality of culture faithful to the *Torah* in Palestine and in the Diaspora that continued even after the return of the exiles, who carried that culture with them.

77. Scharbert, *Solidarität*, pp. 247f, 270-274.

78. Cf. C. Spicq, "Mittlerschaft", in *Bibeltheologisches Wörterbuch*, II, 869-873; Peters, pp. 60-62; Eichrodt, *Theologie*, II, pp. 448-453, 462f; de Fraine, pp. 152-202; Scharbert, *Heilsmittler im AltenTestament und in seiner Umwelt* (Freiburg: Herder, 1964), pp. 237-320.

79. Cf. Stamm, pp. 59-68.

80. G. von Rad, "The Confessions of Jeremiah", in *Theodicy*, 88-99.

81. Stamm, pp. 68-70, even suggested a human volunteer who offered himself for death, but the text does not state that clearly, and speculation about what "really might have happened" not only remains very hypothetical but also does not immediately concern God's word.

82. Bright, p. 442; E. Lohse, *Märtyrer und Gottesknecht* (Göttingen: Vandenhoeck & Ruprecht, 1955), pp. 104-109.

83. Peters, pp. 67ff; Lohse, pp. 64-110; K. Kuhn, "Rm 6:7 ὁ γὰρ ἀποθανὼν δεδικαίωται ἀπὸ τη~ ἁμαρτία'", *Zeitschrift für die Neutestamentliche Wissenschaft und die Künde der älteren Kirche* 29 (1930), 305-310. A Leaney, "The Eschatological Significance of Human Suffering in the Old Testament and the Dead Sea Scrolls", in *The Scottish Journal of Theology* 16 (1963), 290-296, tries to link two psalms from Qumran with 2 Maccabees 6:27ff, in order to show that suffering is with the people for the birth of the Messiah; yet the notion of satisfaction for others is not clear, even if the psalmist desires the suffering.

84. Crenshaw, "Introduction", pp. 9f; I. Kant, *Die Religion innerhalb der Grenzen der bloßen Vernunft*, 2nd ed. (1974; rpt. Stuttgart: Reclam, 1974), pp. 90f, 172f. Actually this "modern" complaint, revealing a very legalistic mentality, can be found already in Socinus: cf. C. Gonzalez, S.J., "Fausto Socino: La salvación del hombre en las fuentes del racionalismo", *Gregorianum* 66 (1985), 475f.

85. F. Dostoevsky, *The Brothers Karamazov*, trans. A MacAndrew (Toronto: Bantam, 1981), p. 296.

86. For a background on Hebrew belief in life after death cf. H. Rowley, *The Faith of Israel* (London: SCM, 1956), pp. 153-176. Cf. also Peters, pp. 81-94; though he over-interprets some texts, Peters well outlines the steps preparing for belief in personal immortality. On the "dialectical" relationship between the negation of life after death by Qoheleth and its affirmation in *Wisdom* cf. Lohfink, *Siegeslied*, esp. p. 238f.

87. Cf. P. Hofmann, *Die Toten in Christus* (Münster: Aschendorf, 1966), pp. 94-174, for an interesting study of Jewish conceptions of the after life in the centuries surrounding Christ's birth. Faced with the problem of imagining how a human being could continue existing after death when his body had turned to dust, some Jews postulated the existence of "chambers" or rooms somewhere in the universe where the individual souls might be deposited as

they awaited the resurrection of their bodies. It was hard for Jews to imagine a bodiless existence as a real human life.

88. In his consideration of immortality Eichrodt, *Theology*, II, pp. 510-526, apparently careful to prevent any argument from the human experience of justice from impinging upon God's utterly transcendent liberty, held that the Bible's discovery of resurrection was due to its hope of the revelation of God's glory (Is 26:19; 53; Ps 22; Dan 12) and individuals' "realization that in direct contact with God life acquires an indestructible content" (Job; Ps 73; 16). This view reflected too obviously Eichrodt's Protestant presuppositions (cf. also above n. 33). There need be no opposition between God's glory and man's sense of justice, especially if the latter is rooted in God's justice, that admittedly transcends retributive justice and expresses his free, loving mercy. God's kindness always surpasses what men desire of themselves, and only through its continual experience of God's love, which did not and cannot abandon the just man, did Israel receive the revelation of a destiny far surpassing this earth. The Old Testament is replete with requests for God's intervention in restoring justice for his name's sake, to defend his fidelity (e.g., Ps 35; 44; 109:1-5, 20-27). This was more than just a clever rhetorical device to involve God's honour with the fate of Israel or the individual Hebrew. For insofar as Israel is God's people, God's honour is really involved (cf. Ex 32:11-14; Num 14:13-16; Is 48:9-11; Ezek 36:22f). Moreover, Koch's argument showing the inherent, internal connection between deed and consequence (cf. above n. 40), though under God's ultimate providence, can easily be applied to a "justice" beyond the grave: God gives "more" than man can expect on his own. Finally, the texts alleged by Eichrodt not only often fail to provide an unambiguous witness to life after death but also are found, for the most part, in contexts recalling God's justice (Is 26:7-10, 21; 53:6-9, 11; Dan 12:3, 10; Ps 73:1-14; Job throughout).

89. Peters, pp. 62f; W. Wichmann, *Die Leidenstheologie: Eine Form der Leidensdeutung im Spätjudentum* (Stuttgart: Kohlhammer, 1930), pp. 51-80.

90. Bertrangs, p. 35, had noted this inversion but considered it a "step forward" in his understanding of Psalms 16, 49 and 73; these psalms, in his interpretation, recognized an after-life. Not only is his interpretation of the psalms debatable but also the reversal of values, once the next life is acknowledged, is hard to resist. That denigration of this world can hardly be called a "step forward".

91. Although the problem of Gnosticism's origin is still wrapped in the obfuscating shadows of conjecture and scholarly debate congenial to such a doctrine of extra-worldly salvation, its similarities with late Judaism have been well noted. Cf. K. Rudolph, *Gnosis*, trans. R. Wilson (San Francisco: Harper & Row, 1987), pp. 275-282. Gnosticism designates a spiritual movement at the beginning of the Christian era. Though some of its forms evolved into Christian heresies, others developed on their own. The main tenets of Gnosticism, building upon a dualistic anthrosophy and cosmology, stressed

81

the opposition between matter and spirit, the need of salvation through knowledge (not love, as in Christianity), and a return to the spiritual *pleroma* from which, through a series of crises, souls had fallen and become entrapped in matter. The best introduction remains H. Jonas, *The Gnostic Religions*, 2nd ed. (Boston: Beacon, 1963).

Part II

The New Testament's response
to suffering

The Old Testament's doctrine on sin and suffering is taken up, purified and deepened in the New Testament.[1] The same themes recur but their emphasis and their overall structure have been altered in view of Christ and his cross. The new covenant is now in Christ's blood (1 Cor 11:25; Lk 22:20; Mk 14:24; Mt 26:28; Heb 9:11-22; 12:24; 13:20). Obviously it cannot be reduced to a legal contract which God in his mercy initiated and in which he remains a partner to whom certain obligations are due with respect to the responsibility of balancing the legal books in and beyond history. Such was not even the case in the Old Testament when the mighty Lord of mercy retained his supreme freedom to bestow favour on whom he wished. Now all is done with, through, and in Christ (e.g., Rom 6:4-11; 8:32, 39; 11:36; 1 Cor 8:6; etc.). "Without me you can do nothing" (Jn 15:5). God is most intimately involved in the covenant's process of salvation. "Work out your salvation in fear and trembling. For God is working in you both the willing and the working according to his good pleasure" (Phil 2:13). Justice is no longer imaginable as a neutral standard by which man or, in Job's case, God can be called to account. Justification, or justice, is achieved through Christ and given as a free gift to men (Rom 3:21-30; 4:24f; 5:15-21; 10:4; etc.). In fact, Christ has become our justification (1 Cor 1:30). The New Testament's whole perspective manifests a fundamental Christocentricity. "No one comes to the Father if not through me" (Jn 14:6). Yet Christ also refers all to the Father greater than himself (Jn 14:28). "No one can come to me unless the Father, who sent me, draws him" (Jn 6:44, 65). In that oscillation of love between Jesus, the unique mediator, who recapitulates in himself the universe, and the Father, to whom all is ultimately referred, the Christian lives (1 Tim 2:3-6; Col 1:15-23; Eph 1:3-23; 1 Cor 3:22f; 8:6; 15:20-28). Keeping that tension vital and fruitful is the Holy Spirit, the bond of love uniting believers with the triune God (2 Cor 13:13; Jn 15:26; 16:13-15; 20:22f). For the Spirit of Christ has been poured into the hearts of believers (Rom 5:5), and only in that Spirit can they call out as sons, "Abba, Father" (Rom 8:15: Gal 4:5). Within the context of the new covenant, therefore, the Old Testament explanations of suffering must be read again.

Good rewarded – Evil punished now and in the future

Most assuredly God remains the uncorrupted judge without partiality who shall repay each according to his deeds (Acts 10:34f; 1 Pet 1:17; Rom 2:5-11; Gal 2:6; Eph 6:9; cf. Col 3:25). As had the Jews previously under the old alliance, the Christians now enjoy a special place in God's providence since they are identified with Jesus (Acts 9:5). So in the final judgment "God deems it just to repay with affliction those who afflict you, and to grant rest with us to you who are afflicted" (2 Thess 1:6f; Mt 25:31-46). Similarly as in the Old Testament an inherent connection was affirmed between a man's deeds and its consequences: "Do not be deceived; God is not mocked, for whatever a man sows, that he will also reap. For he who sows to this own flesh will from the flesh reap corruption; but he who sows to the Spirit will from the Spirit reap eternal life" (Gal 6:7f). Indeed, in many cases the punishment of God consisted in this, that God gave impure men over to their own unnatural impurities and passions so that they dishonoured themselves (Rom 1:24-32). Clearly God need not reserve all his judgments for the hereafter. he could also intervene directly before the end. his judgments occur already in this world, as the Old Testament witnesses, for "the Lord knows how to rescue the godly from trial, and to keep the unrighteous under punishment until the day of judgment" (2 Pet 2:9). The cases of Ananias and Sapphira, Herod Agrippa, and Elymas illustrated how God's justice can be strict and immediate (Acts 5:1-10; 12:1-5, 20-23; 13:7-12). Yet the immediate application in this world of the simple rule of justice, good rewarded-evil punished, has been radically put into question by the cross of Christ, the innocent one who suffered and died. Wisdom's story of the just man assailed unjustly in this life and rewarded in the next was fulfilled on the cross (Mt 27:41-43), forcing Christians to look for a justice transcending this world. Jesus himself refused to apply a direct tit-for-tat measure to sufferings for sin (Mt 5:45; Jn 9:1-3), while affirming nonetheless a real connection between sin and physical punishment (Jn 5:14; possibly Mk 2:5-12). Thus in referring to the Galileans massacred by Pilate and the victims killed by a falling tower Jesus denied that they were worse sinners than all the others, yet he used these catastrophes as occasions to call his audience to repentance lest they all likewise perish (Lk 13:1-5). The parable of the rich man and Lazarus recounts the piety and reward of a poor man while the rich man is condemned to respiteless torment (Lk 16:19-31). God's reward and retribution are most often referred to the future (Gal 6:7-10; 1 Pet 4:3-5; etc.), especially to the last judgment when Christ will return to judge the world, separating the wheat from the weeds, the sheep from the goats, the godly from the ungodly (Mt 13:37-43; 25:31-46; Jude 14-23, etc.).

Eschatological deepening

The eschatological judgment dominates the New Testament. The Apocalypse calls up before our eyes the universal backdrop against which the acts of our individual destinies are played out. The cosmic struggle between Christ and Satan began with the latter's fall from heaven and the battle conducted by Michael against him and his minions (Apoc 12). The fallen angel opposes the Church in the present age (2:9f, 13, 24; 3:9). Many acts, in which the faithful undergo persecutions, have to pass by before Christ, the faithful and true one, who judges with justice, emerges on a white war horse to overcome the false seducer. Then "that ancient serpent" is confined in the bottomless pit for a thousand years until he will be loosed for his final battle, decisive defeat and everlasting torment (19:11-20:15).

The Apocalypse only painted in bright colours what was more than implicit in the Gospels and the Epistles. Paul called upon the Christians to take up the armour of God in the war not just against flesh and blood but also against "principalities and powers, the world rulers of this darkness, and the spiritual hosts of wickedness in the heavenly places" (Eph 6:10-20; 2:2f; Gal 4:3, 8f; Col 1:13; 2:8, 20).[2] But with his resurrection and ascension Christ has already vanquished such powers (Col 2:15), and it only remains for their definitive conquest at the end when through Christ "God will be all in all" (1 Cor 15:20-28). St Peter likewise called upon Christians to stand fast in faith against the devil, the raging lion, so that after suffering a little while, that which is required of the brotherhood throughout the world, they might be restored, established, and strengthened by "the God of all grace who has called you to his eternal glory in Christ" (1 Pet 5:8-10). St John employed the cosmic imagery of light against darkness (1:4-13; 3:19-21; 8:12; 12:35f, 46). He knew that the Christian battle was directed against the "ruler of this world" (12:31; 14:30; 16:11), who was a liar and a murderer from the beginning (8:44); for when Satan entered Judas and led him to abandon Christ, "it was night" (13:27-30). Luke had earlier reported Jesus' words as he was taken prisoner through Judas' betrayal, "This is your hour and the power of darkness" (22:53). Similarly symbolic, the evangelists had noted that at Jesus' crucifixion and death "there was darkness over the whole land" (Mk 15:33; Mt 27:45; Lk 23:44).

In the synoptic Gospels the same universal struggle was announced from the beginning of Jesus' public life as he was driven out into the desert to be tempted by Satan (Mk 1:12ff). After gathering the first disciples, Jesus performed his first miracle, an exorcism (Mk 1:21-27). Given the connection still vividly felt by Jesus' contemporaries between sin and material evil, Jesus' subsequent miraculous healings marked not only a further attack on Satan's empire (Lk 16:16) but also the irruption into the present of the kingdom of God, which the prophets had predicted with images of physical well-being and material prosperity. Hence, in response to John the Baptist's question whether he was "the one who is to come," Jesus merely pointed to his healings and exorcisms:

Go and tell John what you have seen and heard: the blind receive their sight, the lame walk, lepers are cleansed, and the deaf hear, the dead are raised up, and the poor have the good news preached to them. And blessed is he who takes no offence at me" (Lk 7:22f; Mt 11:4-6).

Consequently, when Jesus' disciples returned from their first mission to report their success in subjecting even the demons to his name, he responded, "I saw Satan fall like lightning from heaven" (Lk 10:18).

Not that Satan yielded the field gracefully. Peter's rejection of Christ's words about the necessity of the Son of Man's sufferings merited the strong rebuke: "Get behind me, Satan. You think the thoughts not of God, but of men" (Mk 8:33; Mt 16:23). Though Luke omitted those words, he noted, after Satan had already entered into Judas, that Satan sought to sift Peter like wheat (22:31), and during the reign of "the power of darkness", Jesus' passion, Peter was thoroughly shaken. The sufferings of Christ certainly overflowed onto all those who had put their faith in him as the earthly Messiah. They should have known better, for the Old Testament prophets had foreseen the "eschatological woes", a period of severe trials before the introduction of God's reign, and Jesus' eschatological discourse (Mk 13 par.) had accentuated the fierceness of suffering that believers would have to undergo before the Son of Man ultimately appeared in the heavens with his angels to summon all to the final judgment.

Realized eschatology: the necessity of present choice [3]

This apocalyptic scenario that both identified as Satan the mendacious serpent who had seduced Eve in the garden at the beginning of human history and promised the victory of Christ at the end, revealed the imperative need for a decision about loyalties. Life's fundamental option can in no way be imagined as a choice between hard-necked, obstinate independence and obedience to an external law; after Christ the person hearing God's message is forced to choose between Christ, on the one hand, and the world, the flesh and the devil, on the other (Jas 1:27; 4:4; 1 Jn 2:15-19; Rom 8:6-8; 13:14; Eph 2:1-3; Gal 5:16-24; 1 Pet 2:11). For Christ partook of our nature "in order that through death he might destroy him who had the power of death, the devil, and deliver all those who through fear of death were subject to lifelong bondage" (Heb 2:14f; 1 Jn 3:8). Christ had to conquer Satan before subduing "the last enemy, death," and leading his followers to a blissful union with God far surpassing the earthly paradise (1 Cor 15:20-28, 51-56; Apoc 20:7-22:5).

Besides highlighting the ultimate personal dimensions of the conflict, the apocalyptic imagery brought home the imperative necessity of declaring one's loyalty immediately. For, unlike the accounts in Jewish apocalyptic writings, the eschatological judgment and the arrival of God's kingdom are not relegated just to the "beyond" or to the "hereafter". Both are presently effective. Christians know that they already live in the "last hour" (1 Jn 2:18; cf. Rom 13:11f) and that they are already children of the light (Eph 5:8; Col 1:12f; 1

Thess 5:5; cf. 1 Pet 2:9f). As St Paul wrote with regard to Christ's incarnation, "the fullness of time had come" (Gal 4:4). That fullness empowered the Apostle to turn the demand for effective conversion upon his audience: "Behold, now is the acceptable time; behold, now is the day of conversion" (2 Cor 6:2). So overwhelming is that plenitude that those who accept God's call are in a sense already liberated, saved, reconciled, justified, and glorified (Rom 5:9f; 8:2, 24, 30; 10:10). Developing the image of God's saving mercy, Ephesians 2:5f referred to God who not only "saved us" but also "raised us up" with Christ and "made us sit with him in the heavenly places." Yet such effective, present salvation did not destroy the need of free, human co-operation. Otherwise there would have been no need for the imperative of conversion to complement the indicative, or the fact, of salvation accomplished in Christ. Salvation is still a future event (Rom 5:9; 10:9, 13; 1 Cor 5:5; 10:33). Christ's Spirit has been given only as the pledge of what is to come (1 Cor 1:22; 5:5; Eph 1:13f), as the "first fruits" of redemption dependent upon Christ's resurrection (Rom 8:23; 1 Cor 15:20, 23). So Paul was continually addressing the imperative of the Gospel not just to those outside the Church but also to Christians in the process of "being saved" (1 Cor 1:18; 15:2; 2 Cor 2:15; 3:18).

This vital tension between present and future, in which the imperative of conversion finds its place, is rooted in Jesus' own preaching and action. Though he urged his disciples to pray for the coming of God's kingdom (Mt 6:10) and saw it as a future reality (Mk 4:25; 10:15, 23; Mt 8:11; 22:2-14; etc.), in responding to the charge that collusion with Beelzebul explained his exorcisms, Jesus emphasized the kingdom's presence in his miracles: "But if I with the finger of God cast out demons, then the kingdom of God has come upon you" (Lk 11:20). The very beginning of his preaching announced the equivalent message: "The time has been fulfilled and the kingdom of God has drawn near. Repent and believe in the gospel" (Mk 1:15 par.). The miracles and preaching functioned not as artificial signs pointing to a reality different from them; but they expressed in a form comprehensible to men the reality of the one effecting them. The point of conversion and loyalty was neither a verbal ideology nor an impersonal empire waiting to be staffed by bureaucrats. Rather, men were called to accept Jesus with total dedication. he is "more" than Jonah, whose preaching converted Nineveh, and "more" than Solomon, whose wisdom attracted the queen of the South "from the ends of the earth" (Lk 11:31f). Consequently, by rejecting the call to conversion issued by Jesus, who had performed such mighty works, Corazin, Bethsaida and Capernaum are doomed in the final judgment (Lk 10:13-15). More than his words in themselves, Jesus' person had become the ultimate measure of salvation and damnation: "Whoever confesses me before men, the Son of Man will confess before the angels of God; whoever denies me before men will be denied before the angels of God" (Lk 12:8f par.).

In John's "realized eschatology", even though it did not deny a future for free choices, the sending of the Holy Spirit, and the final resurrection, the emphasis nonetheless rested on the fullness already attained in Christ. In such a way John reveals what was implicit in Jesus' claim, reported by the synoptic evangelists, for total fidelity to him. Only God could demand such fealty as Jesus demanded. Consequently in the Johannine vision Jesus' presence and word made the eschatological judgment already present; for as acceptance of him enlightens and vivifies, so rejection already blinds, causes sin, and brings judgment (3:18-21; 5:24-29; 9:39-41; 11:25f; 15:22-25; 16:8-11). Thus, as witnessed by all the Gospels, the absoluteness of God's claim for human faith and love is found historically present and effective in the person of Jesus of Nazareth. In Origen's words, he is himself the kingdom ($\alpha\dot{\upsilon}\tau o\beta\alpha\sigma\iota\lambda\epsilon\acute{\iota}\alpha$).[4] On such a basis of the life shared with the disciples who followed him before being sent out to continue his work of preaching repentance and exorcising demons (Mk 1:17, 20; 3:13f; 6:7-13 par.; Mt 10:1-15), Jesus might say, "To you has been entrusted the mystery of the kingdom of God" (Mk 4:11).

Christ might raise such an absolute claim to fidelity in his own person because in him "the fullness of divinity dwells bodily" (Col 2:9; 1:19). Equivalently, in St John's words, the Word who was God became flesh; thus we might hear, see and touch the Father's Son who was from the beginning (Jn 1:1-14; 1 Jn 1:1-3). Insofar as the fullness is already present in time, the indicative of God's love has been definitively grounded; yet insofar as the response of freedom to that love still has to take place, the future retains the indeterminacy necessary for freedom. In the Johannine vision of "realized eschatology" Jesus could announce in his lifetime, "The ruler of this world is already judged" and "Have courage, I have overcome the world," even if tribulations remained in store for his disciples (Jn 16:11, 33; 12:31). The indicative of Christ's triumph grounds the imperative that supports and encourages believers.

Jesus' sufferings

If the Christian experiences in the Holy Spirit the tension between present and future as well as the oscillation of love between Father and Son, Jesus had previously lived those relations most profoundly. The whole purpose of his life, that for which he had been sent, was to bring a sword of division, to call sinners, to save the lost and ultimately to give his life as a ransom for many (Mt 10:34f; Mk 2:17; Lk 19:10; Mk 10:45). He himself was to experience the sufferings of human life due to sin. Besides hunger, thirst, and fatigue (Mt 4:2; 8:24; Jn 4:6-8; 19:28), he felt compassion for the widow of Nain who had lost her only son (Lk 7:15) as well as for the crowds that hungered for food and wandered without

93

spiritual direction (Mk 8:2f; 6:34). From that source of pity welled up his miracles and teaching. It was not a condescending, superficial pity, but it rose from the depths of his heart. he wept for the death of his friend Lazarus (Jn 11:35) and over the destruction of Jerusalem on which he would have bestowed peace if only its inhabitants had turned to him (Lk 19:41-44). Seeing the effects of sin in the fate of others, he did not refuse to share their fate so that they might share his glory. The Letter to the Hebrews described Christ's life as follows:

> In the days of his flesh Jesus offered up prayers and supplications, with loud cries and tears to him who was able to save him from death, and he was heard for his piety. Although he was the Son he learned obedience from what he suffered; made perfect, he became for all obeying him the cause of eternal salvation, since he had been called by God high priest according to the order of Melchizedek (5:7-10; cf. 2:9-15).

His obedience was put to the test not only during the temptations in the desert (Mt 4:1-11) but especially during the passion, that crucible of agony which culminated all his past sufferings and showed most clearly the meaning of his life and the person that he is. In the Garden Jesus was racked by the resistance of his own human will to the cup of pain, rejection and death that awaited him. Only his obedient love for the Father let him accept the Father's will as his own (Mk 14:32-42 par.). So in the mystery of his freedom he chose to go the way that the Son of Man was destined to go (Mk 8:31 par.; Lk 17:25; 24:7, 26). In the one moment of apparent hesitation recounted in John's gospel Jesus prayed: "Now is my soul troubled. And what shall I say? 'Father, save me from this hour'? Yet for this I have come to this hour. Father, glorify your name" (12:27). Despite inner resistance Jesus was determined to complete the Father's will and go to the cross.

The cross

The cross stands at the centre of Christian belief, and from it the significance of suffering must be illuminated. For St Paul, though he did not describe in any detail the events of the passion, the cross, "a scandal to Jews and a folly to Greeks", represented the weakness of God that is stronger than men and the foolishness of God that is wiser than men. Even "the rulers of this age" failed to comprehend the hidden wisdom of God; otherwise "they would not have crucified the Lord of glory" and destroyed thereby their own dominion. Hence none may boast except in the Lord, and Jews and Gentiles, who have accepted the necessary conversion of life and perspective, can be united in the Spirit to the mind of Christ, "our wisdom, righteousness, sanctification, and redemption" (1 Cor 1:17-2:16). The ancient hymn Paul quoted in Philippians 2:6-11 stressed the paradox of Jesus Christ, who, though "in the form of God", "emptied" and "humbled" himself even to an obedient death on the cross so that God might indeed raise him in praise above all creation. Paul employed the hymn to exhort Christians to humility in order that they might be united in love and care for each other (2:1-5). Certainly in Christ's death and resurrection was illustrated most convincingly the truth of Jesus' words, "Whoever exalts himself will be humbled and whoever humbles himself will be exalted" (Mt 23:12 par.). For Paul, however, Christ was much more than an example confirming a general rule. As God's word does not merely report a fact but creates what it announces (Gen 1; Is 55:10f; Ps 33:6-9; Heb 11:3; 2 Pet 3:5-7), so Christ's cross and resurrection provided the norm for Christian existence by creating that new existence. Christ's passion touches all most intimately. "he was handed over on account of our trespasses and rose for our justification" (Rom 4:25; cf. 1 Cor 15:17). Before studying the effects of Christ's life-giving death, however, it seems best to investigate how the cross was interpreted by the evangelists.

a. Mark

The same notion of the paradoxical revelation *sub contrario* reappears in Mark's gospel.[5] There the cross stands at the culmination of Jesus' whole life and revelation. The initial verse of the gospel served as its title and table of contents, "The beginning of the gospel of Jesus Christ, the Son of God."[6] The gospel moves with insistence to the confession of Jesus' two main titles: Christ and Son of God, paralleling Jesus' own movement, with inevitable consistency, through life to the death which was his full revelation. The first half of Jesus' life, a time of conquest and challenge, full of exorcisms, miraculous healings, authoritative preaching, and confrontations with the Jewish leaders, resulted in the confession of Peter, "You are the Christ" (8:29). Immediately thereafter the confessed Messiah, instead of beginning a public campaign for recognition, paradoxically began to withdraw from the crowds to prepare his disciples for the further revelation of his fate and person. he announced repeatedly the necessity of the Son of Man's suffering and death, but, eyes blinded by the transfigured glory of the one just confessed to be the Messiah and by their own conceptions of Messianic glory, the disciples refused to comprehend his meaning (8:31-38; 9:9f, 30-34; 10:32-45).[7] As a consequence of their misunderstanding, during his passion they fell away, and Judas betrayed him (14:43-50). Thus, rejected by his people, betrayed by a friend, forsaken by all, calumniated, maltreated, he died alone on the cross, apparently abandoned by God himself "My God, my God, why have you forsaken me?" (15:34). Yet in his death, God's revelation, the gospel, reached its goal, as the centurion exclaimed, "Truly this man was God's son." For the first time in Mark's gospel Jesus was acknowledged by a human being for who he was.

Jesus had lived what he preached. he had called men to conversion, to "follow him," leaving behind all possessions, family, honour, even their own wills in order to carry the cross, to serve and give their lives, trusting in God alone like a child. For he was God's Son and wished others to become his relatives by obedience to God's will (1:15-20; 2:13; 3:33-4:20; 8:34-38; 10:13-31; 12:41-44; 13:9-13). For some the challenge to leave all to follow Jesus and enter the kingdom, to love God and one's fellow beings, was too difficult (compare 12:28-34 with 10:17-21); hence from the beginning Jesus had aroused the opposition of the powers that be and they plotted his death (2:1-3:6; 7:1-23; 10:2). Unable to refute him in argument, they had recourse to violence (11:15-12:38). So the revelation of God in historical humility marked the point of decision, the cross for those called to abandon their own attempts at self-justification and self-preservation in order to follow Christ.

b. Luke

The same tensions between divine weakness and omnipotence, humility and judgment, are found in the accounts of the first and third evangelists, but with different emphases. The gentle Luke had constantly stressed the meek and merciful condescension of God in Christ come to heal sickness and forgive sins, in short, to announce peace. He saw then in the cross no rupture but the ultimate confirmation of Jesus' love for men and for his Father. In the midst of his own sufferings Jesus showed constant concern for others, not rebuking harshly the disciples on the Mount of Olives who "for sorrow" fell asleep (and only once, not three times as in Mark and Matthew) (22:45f), avoiding violence and healing the ear of the high priest's servant (22:51), moving

Peter to tears of contrition by a look (22:61f), consoling the women of Jerusalem in the face of approaching judgment (23:28-31), praying for his executioners' pardon (23:34), and promising paradise to the good thief (23:43). So merciful and reconciling was his death that, ironically, he served as the occasion of joining in friendship Herod and Pilate, previously enemies (23:12). Pilate and Herod had repeatedly, but inefficaciously, found him innocent (23:4, 14f, 22). In view of his death the centurion was moved to praise God in confessing Jesus' innocence. Even the onlooking crowd returned to the city beating their breasts (23:47f). For at the end, just as he had enjoyed the continual union of prayer with the Father during his life, Jesus – without any indication of abandonment – had trustingly committed his spirit into his Father's hands (23:46).

The resurrection simply continued and confirmed the life and death of the "prophet mighty in deed and word before God and men" (24:19). For Christ commissioned his disciples to "preach repentence and forgiveness in his name to all nations, beginning from Jerusalem" (24:47). In that way he left the world with a blessing in order that his disciples might continually bless God (24:50-53).

c. Matthew

For Matthew the cross of Christ marks the historical point of judgment dividing the old from the new Israel. The unique Son of God had gone his way to the cross with full awareness and authority, yet in complete agreement with the Father's will, to fulfil Scripture (26:39, 42, 54, 56). As God's Son he had predicted his future rejection in a parable (21:33-44) and forced the Pharisees to see that the Christ must be more than David's son (22:41-45). Such was his majesty that the Jewish rejection of him resulted in their self-willed rejection by God (21:41-44). To make clear what was at stake, the titles "King of the Jews" and "Christ" recurred frequently throughout the passion (26:63, 68; 27:11, 17, 22, 29, 37, 42), and the Jews called down Jesus' innocent blood, shed for the forgiveness of sins, upon their own and their children's heads; they acknowledged no king but Caesar (23:35f; 26:28; 27:4, 19, 24f). Judas' betrayal and his horrendous fate were both clearly predicted (26:21-25; 27:3-10). Jesus was handed over to "sinners" (26:45) while freely forgoing the assistance of angelic legions and chiding his enemies (26:53-56). Aside from the answer to the solemn adjuration of the High Priest, asking if he were "the Christ, the Son of God" (26:63f) – a confession that only highlighted the import of his rejection by the Jews – Jesus kept a majestic silence throughout his trial and passion until the last cry of Psalm 22 passed his lips on the cross.

At Jesus' death the temple veil split in two, an earthquake occurred and from open tombs the dead arose, clear anticipations of the general resurrection as well as signs of Jerusalem's rejection by God (27:51-54). For the cross is not the final catastrophe but only a necessary way-station willed by God in Jesus' authoritative progress through time. Once the Jews had rejected their chance, the way was open to the new people of God (21:41-43; 8:11f). With Jesus as the corner stone the Church could be constructed on the rock of Peter to whom authority was entrusted by Jesus (16:17-19; 21:42). For in authoritatively sending his disciples out into the whole world to preach and baptize, Jesus promised to remain with them "until the end of the age" (28:18-20). Then the Son of Man, clearly identified with Jesus (16:13-16), would return as eschatological judge to reward or punish those who accepted or rejected him and his brethren, the members of his Church (10:32f; 24:29-31; 25:31-46; cf. 18:15-17).

d. John

John's theology of the cross is very complex, precisely because his gospel is such a tightly constructed unity with so many themes overlapping. Without doubt the hatred of the Jews was responsible for Jesus' death, for they handed him over to Pilate, desiring his death so much that they renounced every king but Caesar (18:29; 19:12-16). Their hatred for Jesus had a double root: his healings on the Sabbath (5:10-18; 9:14) and his alleged blasphemy in calling God his Father (5:18; 10:30-39; 19:7). Behind the opposition to his unity of love with the Father and his deeds of love for men Jesus espied the devil (8:42-47). Nonetheless it was with the greatest freedom and determination that Jesus affronted his death. Not only did he predict Judas' betrayal (13:21, 26) but he also ordered him to do it quickly (13:27) before going to the customary garden that Judas knew (18:2). With the approach of the soldiers and the Pharisees' servants Jesus took the initiative in addressing them. After they fell to the ground at his revelation, "I am", he had to offer himself again to them while simultaneously restraining his disciples from resistance and assuring their safety (18:3-11).

So dominating was Jesus that he acted during his passion to fulfil his own word (18:9, 32). Yet behind his self-assurance stood the Father who handed him the chalice of suffering (18:11). The unity of love and obedience (3:34; 5:18f; 6:38; 8:28f, 38; 14:10; 17:4-8), which is also an ontological unity (10:30, 38; 14:9; 17:11, 21f), involved Jesus' self-giving:

> The Father loves me because I give my life in order that I may take it again. No one takes it from me, but I give it of myself I have power to give it, and I have power to take it away. This command I have from my Father.
>
> (10:17f)

As the grain dies in order to bear fruit (12:24), so the crucifixion marked the hour of Christ's glorification (12:27f).

The "lifting up" or "elevation" of the Son of Man was a favourite description of the crucifixion since it telescoped into one movement crucifixion, resurrection, ascension, and enthronization. Then the Son, in glorifying the Father (14:13; 15:8; 17:1-4, 24), received the glory that he had with the Father before the world's creation (1:14; 17:5). For in his being lifted up he is recognized and draws all men to himself in order to heal (3:14; 8:28; 12:32-34). After Jesus had entrusted his mother to the beloved disciple and fulfilled the Scripture with the statement, "I thirst", from the cross Jesus exclaimed, "It is consummated" (19:25-30). Then he handed over the Spirit and from his pierced side blood and water, most probably symbolizing the Eucharist and baptism, flowed forth (19:30, 34). In this way the Church was founded. In this way was fulfilled the mission entrusted to the Son by the Father, the revelation and the communication of divine life to men (1:43; 3:15f, 36; 4:14; 5:40; 6:40, 47-68; 10:10, 28; 11:25f; 17:2f; 20:31). Therefore in the great movement of going forth from and returning to the Father that characterizes the essential structure of revelation (8:14, 21-23, 42; 13:3; 14:12; 16:27-30; 17:8, 11), Jesus takes believers with him. While they remain in the world, they are not of it, but only continue the Son's mission (17:14-18). They share his life and they receive his Spirit (14:16f, 26; 15:26; 16:7, 13-15; 20:22f) in order that they may be one in him with the Father and with each other (14:16-21; 15:1-11; 17:11, 20-26). Thus the same love of God that motivated the sending of the Son even to the cross, that event which manifested the greatness of his love (3:16f; 13:1ff; 15:13), continues in the believers who have become God's children by faith in Christ (1:12f; 13:34f; 15:12, 17; 16:27; 17:26). In loving one another Jesus' disciples are to maintain unity among themselves, with Jesus, and in Jesus with the Father; for their unity is grounded in the Son's unity with the Father (3:35; 8:56; 14:10, 20f; 15:1-11; 17:11, 20-26).

The supreme manifestation of love also functions as

judgment. Even as Jesus went willingly to the cross, hatred and sin drove him to it. Consequently, through Jesus' acceptance of the ignominy of the cross, the ruler of this world and all his followers were condemned for preferring darkness to light (3:18f; 9:39; 12:31; 16:8-11).

The understanding of the cross of Christ, presented in these major, fundamental witnesses to the mystery of Christ, contains an implicit theology of suffering which has only to be explicated. Doubtless the evangelists' accounts of the fundamental facts of historical revelation, committed to final form many years after Christ's death, would have been influenced by speculative reflection about the significance of Jesus' death – the much earlier Pauline epistles manifest an abundance of such reflection. More than that, the facts themselves, stark in their challenge for the comprehension of victory in defeat and elevation in humiliation, forced the sacred authors to meditate ever more profoundly the underlying intention of Jesus throughout his passion. For, given Jesus' unity of volition with the Father, his intention revealed the whole, divine plan of salvation. Thus Paul, the evangelists and all the New Testament writers had a common, unifying object of their contemplation and reflection in Christ's death and resurrection. Of itself that object evoked a further penetration of human insight into the divine intention. This divine intention, in turn, revealed the ultimate nature of the intending, saving God: pure, selfless, triune Love. Hence it should hardly be surprising to find an underlying unity of theological affirmation and vision in the diverse perspectives and accentuations of the various authors of the New Testament.

If the ultimate reason for the cross was the salvific love of God, the four perspectives of the evangelists centred on that mystery of divine love. The Markan abandonment of Jesus indicated the length of suffering to which the love of God's Son was willing to go. The Lukan theme of reconciliation marked the final intention of God's redeeming love. Matthew's stress on Jesus' authority not only revealed the dignity of the person and the majestic freedom of his sacrifice but also clarified the demand upon men for a decision implicit in the historical manifestation of self-sacrificial love. John's complex, meditative vision revealed how Christians are already taken up into the event of redemption, God's eternal love for the world, which the cross signifies even in its moment of judgment.

Insofar as the cross constitutes God's supreme, earthly self-revelation, it sheds light also on the meaning of human suffering. Jesus Christ is more than a model for men. he is the saviour of the world (Jn 4:42; 1 Jn 4:14). What Jesus suffered redeemed man. When Christians are introduced into the mystery of Christ, their sufferings then find their meaningful place. This defines the further progression of our investigation. First we shall attempt to uncover the full meaning of Christ's sufferings. For only in him, the crucified one, is there salvation (Acts 4:10-12). Then we shall study how Christ's sufferings illuminate and give value to human sufferings. All the while we shall be discovering how the Old Testament answers to the problem of suffering are reforged in the burning furnace of God's infinite love, to which the New Testament bears unsurpassable witness.

Insofar as the cross marks God's supreme earthly self-realization, from it light must be shed on the meaning of all suffering.

Christ's vicarious, redemptive suffering

a. The Suffering Servant and sacrifice

The unusual harmony of wills among Father, Son, and the Son's executioners, the silent innocence of the abandoned Christ offering himself for the sins of others and his victory beyond death – all these cannot but recall the Servant of Yahweh described by Isaiah. Assuredly the early Church in searching the Scriptures did not overlook the parallelism between Christ and the Servant of Yahweh. St Paul was quoting an early credal formula when he wrote, "Christ died for the sake of our sins according to the Scriptures" (1 Cor 15:3). The reference must be to Isaiah 53. Probably the Apostle of the Gentiles was reflecting the same tradition of interpretation when he formulated his own brief synopsis of the redemptive mystery: "he was handed over on account of our trespasses and he rose on account of our justification" (Rom 4:25; cf. Gal 1:4). But, without doubt, other direct citations from the Servant Songs show the early Church's identification of Jesus with the figure described by Isaiah (Mt 8:17; Lk 22:37; Jn 12:38; Acts 8:32f; Heb 9:28; 1 Pet 2:18-25). In addition, John 19:37 applied the dependent text of Zechariah 12:10 about the pierced one to the crucified Jesus. Though this remains a point strongly debated among scholars,[8] it seems most probable that Jesus understood himself in the light of the Servant Songs. For he came "to serve and give his life as a ransom for many" (Mk 10:45), an intention symbolized anticipatorily by his institution of the Eucharist in which he announced his "blood poured out for many" (Mk 14:24 par.). In accordance with his usual practice Jesus did not simply identify himself with any Old Testament title or figure lest he be limited to it. Rather he borrowed themes and made references to the Old Testament in ways that allowed it to interpret his person and actions without limiting him to narrow categories. he retained his freedom of going beyond it even while fulfilling it. his was the wine that could not be trapped in old wineskins (Mk 2:22), and his good measure, himself, was superabundant, "pressed down, shaken together, running over" (Lk 6:38; cf. Mk 4:24f; Mt 13:12; 25:29). This superabundance in turn allowed room to employ imagination in interpreting Christ in his uniqueness and novelty.

The notion of vicarious, redemptive suffering and the sacrificial imagery found further development in the early Church's theology. St John may have borrowed from Isaiah

53:7 the designation of Christ as the Lamb of God carrying the sins of the world (1:29, 36), a theme of sacrificial offering illustrated in his account of the crucifixion which not only had Jesus dying at the hour of the paschal lamb's sacrifice but also cited the verse about not breaking any of the paschal lamb's bones (19:33-36). 1 John 2:1f portrayed the "just Jesus Christ" as the propitiation for our sins and those of all the world (cf. also 4:10, 14). The Lamb dominates the action and imagery of the Apocalypse, for, though slain, he stands in the centre of heaven's liturgical adoration (5:6-8:1; 14:1-15; 19:1-8; 21:9-22:5). In both the Apocalypse (5:9; 7:14) and 1 Peter 1:18-21 the blood of the spotless Lamb redeems men from sin and futility. Long before St Paul had proclaimed, "Christ, our paschal Lamb, has been sacrificed," as he urged men to live in the newness of sincerity and truth (1 Cor 5:7).

A parallel development of Isaiah's sacrificial imagery that went beyond the Eucharist's institution may be found in the Letter to the Hebrews. There Christ was recognized as the eternal high priest who offers himself freely to expiate sins, to redeem sinners, and to mediate the new covenant by his blood (2:17; 4:14-5:10; 6:19-10:22; 13:1-16, 20f). The notions of liberating sacrifice and redemption from sin likewise underwent further expansion beyond Mark 10:45 in various New Testament writings (Acts 20:28; Rom 3:24f; 8:23; Gal 1:4; 2:20; Eph 1:7, 14; 5:2f, 26f; 1 Tim 2:6; Tit 2:14; Apoc 14:4f; cf. also 1 Cor 6:20; 7:23; 2 Pet 2:1).

These images of sacrifice and redemption should not be pressed too hard. They are only analogies. Other images are also applied by Scripture to Christ's work of salvation. Moreover, it is difficult to reconcile in the imagination the priest who is simultaneously victim. The offering priest better symbolizes the free voluntariness of Christ's self-donation while the victim image shows how Christ underwent suffering because of others' sins. This paradoxical juncture of activity and passivity is reflected in turn through the apocalyptic Lamb that, though slain, conquers. Similarly, unlike later systematizers who tended to take the image for the full reality, Jesus and the New Testament authors never specified to whom the ransom was paid. As is obvious, difficulties arise inexorably once that question must be answered: God cannot be subject to the devil or mankind, and it must be a cruel or limited God who wishes to or must demand the death of his innocent Son in order to pay off a debt of justice. Analogies always limp. They cannot be extrapolated simply from their usage in the secular world or the sphere of natural religion to apply exactly to the mystery of God's supernatural revelation. Even the Old Testament's preparatory analogies are only shadows compared to the brilliant glory of Christ's full revelation (Heb 10:1; 8:5; Col 2:17). Without doubt salvation as a "ransoming" or carrying another's sin is not to be conceived as a magic rite, nor as a legal transferral of guilt, nor as a sacrificial substitution. The message of Christ demanded personal conversion, and his person constituted the concrete point of decision and adherence where ultimate loyalty was to be manifested. Salvation must involve a personal relation with Christ, and all attempts to explain it in terms of a juridical or mechanical substitution cannot grasp the full import of God's saving deed.

b. Corporate personality in the unity of love

Besides the imagery of sacrifice, the Suffering Servant of Isaiah exhibited the traits of corporate personality, and upon the basis of that notion vicarious suffering may be best understood. No man is an island. All human beings after Adam and Eve had parents and relatives from whom they inherited life, love and many cultural advantages as well as many inconveniences, the results of sins and erroneous judgments. Clearly the world is suffused with the results of sin, sometimes obscuring our vision to such an extent that

God's love might be doubted or denied. It took the cross of Christ to enlighten humanity as to God's true nature. St Paul wrote:

> While we were still weak, at the proper time Christ died for the ungodly. Scarcely does anyone die for a just man – for a good man perhaps one might even dare to die. But God made known his love for us in that while we were still sinners Christ died for our sake.
>
> (Rom 5:6-8; cf. 8:32-39)

John expressed the same insight into the basis of our salvation, "For God so loved the world that he gave his only Son in order that everyone believing in him might not perish but have everlasting life" (3:16). When one considers the hostile connotation of the "world" in John's gospel as the evil power opposed to the Son's revelation (e.g., 1:10; 3:19; 7:7; 8:23; 9:39; 12:31; 14:17; 15:18f; 16:8-11, 20; 17:9, 13-16; 18:36f), such love can only indicate the justification of the sinner, of which St Paul had written at such length (Rom 5:1-11; 3:21-26; 4:1-25; etc.). In view of Christ's cross, therefore, John could draw the staggering conclusions about God and the nature of Christian life:

> Beloved, let us love one another; for love is of God, and he who loves is born of God and knows God. he who does not love does not know God; for God is love. In this the love of God was made manifest among us, that God sent his only Son into the world, so that we might live through him. In this is love, not that we loved God but that he loved us and sent his Son to be the expiation for our sins. Beloved, if God so loved us, we also ought to love one another. No man has ever seen God; if we love one another, God abides in us and his love is perfected in us (1 Jn 4:7-12).

Reflecting on that statement, one may argue that, if God is love and man is made in his image (Gen 1:26f; Mk 12:13-17),[9] man was created in love for love, and is intended to enjoy the love of God forever (cf. 1 Jn 3:1f; 1 Cor 13:8-13; 2 Cor 3:18). Sin, by contrast, breaks the unity of love between God and man as well as among men, as the author of Genesis 3:11-14 recognized in his portrayal of the results of the original sin: after the fall Adam and Eve, who were made of and for unity (2:21-24), not only denied their freedom by casting the responsibility for sin upon another (ultimately God, in Adam's case) but also separated themselves in guilt from each other. Sin broke the primordial unity of the race, and every subsequent refusal to bear responsibility for one's brother (cf. Gen 4:9) only manifests and deepens the rents of sin in the fabric of human society. Corporate personality therefore reflects what remained of love, of the image of God, in man after the fall (Gen 9:6). But once the original unity of mankind was shattered, man was doomed to live apart from God, who is Love, and in enmity with others (Rom 5:15-21). Indeed, insofar as each man is constituted in himself and by his relations with others, the disruption of relations with others is bound to introduce division and enmity into himself (Rom 7:13-25). Such enmity, confusion and forsakenness characterize man's state apart from Christ.

c. The restoration of love's unity

When Christ entered the world and raised the absolute claim to fidelity in his own person – a claim that no mere creature can raise on his own behalf – he established himself as the new Adam, the new head of redeemed humanity (Rom 5:15-21; 1 Cor 15:20-24, 45-50). His "incarnation", his prevenient love of us, which achieved its clearest expression in the unrestricted self-giving of the cross, provides the indicative, the fact, in which the imperative of responsible love is grounded.[10] Love moves love, and the total, self-offering love of God, revealed in its profundity on the cross and in its victory at the resurrection, demands an absolute response of love from us. Love means personal union, for the lover joins himself to the beloved at that point where he is most himself, in his freedom. On that basis Paul could write:

> Now no longer I live, but Christ lives in me. What I now live in the flesh, I live in the faith in the Son of God who loved me and gave himself up for me. I do not reject the grace of God (Gal 2:20f).

That same grace of God, which is attributable to Christ's grace (Rom 5:15; 2 Cor 8:9; Gal 1:6; 6:18; Eph 1:6f), penetrated all Paul's accomplishments as well as his being:

> By the grace of God I am what I am, and his grace in me has not been void. On the contrary, I have laboured much more than all of them [the other apostles], not I, but the grace of God which is with me (1 Cor 15:10).

The experience of being loved grants the beloved the greatest sense of his own dignity, existence and power while paradoxically rendering him most humble, even "the least of the apostles" and an unworthy one at that (1 Cor 15:8). In love the last become first and those humbling themselves are exalted (Mt 19:30 par.; 20:16, 27 par.; 23:12; Jas 4:10; 1 Pet 5:6). Because the beloved knows that he cannot demand or rationally justify being loved, the bestowal of the gift of love must awaken gratitude even while drawing him out of himself in joy. Then he experiences the paradox of love, that while he concentrates most upon his beloved, he also knows that he is living as he has never lived before. "To me, to live is Christ" (Phil 1:21). The more his attention is concentrated on the beloved, the more he lives in joy and finds his own "I" confirmed. "I can do all things in him who strengthens me" (Phil 4:13; cf. 2 Cor 12:10; 2 Tim 4:17). In all this Paul was only witnessing to the paradoxical truth of Jesus' words, "Whoever loses his life for my sake will save it" (Mk 8:35 par.; Jn 12:24f). That experience of love is common to all men; in faith it is in principle open to all believers, and if St Paul experienced it so profoundly – this joy of living outside oneself could be deepened into true mysticism (2 Cor 12:1-7; 1 Cor 15:8; Gal 1:15f) – it is only because by God's grace he appreciated more than most the overwhelming, limitless love of God made manifest in the cross and resurrection of Jesus. The divine omnipotence manifested in the love poured into human hearts (Rom 5:5) does not obliterate human freedom, but calls it to be most itself.[11]

d. The conflict between love and sin

Obviously this union of love with Christ is not always bathed in pure bliss. The original unity of mankind had been shattered and Christ's coming as the historical manifestation of divine love occurred in a world of sin, the object of God's wrath (Rom 1:18-3:20). Hence Christ's demand for total fidelity in love for himself through his humanity (Lk 12:8f) must involve a break with the past, revealing, as it does, the chasm between Love and sin. As a consequence, Satan and sinners, trying to justify themselves, would resist violently the submission of love. One easily understands their hatred of Christ and their desire to remove his challenge to themselves, even by violence, thus employing death, the result of sin (Gen 2:17; 3:19; Rom 5:12-21; Jas 1:15), against love. Christ's death on the cross out of love led to the manifested victory of the resurrection. But those responding to his love must let his love conquer the hardness of their hearts and their fear to entrust themselves to what seems at first a foreign dominion, even to him. This involves a dying to self and Paul could speak of being baptized into Christ's death, of a dying with Christ in baptism, that sacrament in which the believer confesses his faith in Christ, in order to rise to life in God (Rom 6:1-11). Analogously, John called this Christian faith a rebirth and a passage from death to life (3:3-8; 5:24; 1 Jn 3:14). Even more succinctly Paul wrote, "With Christ I have been crucified" (Gal 2:19). That union with Christ provided the basis of his joy and hope:

But far be it from me to glory except in the cross of our Lord Jesus Christ by which the world has been crucified to me and I to the world. For neither circumcision counts for anything, nor uncircumcision, but a new creation (Gal 6:14f).

e. Corporate personality as the Church of the redeemed

The new, supernatural union with Christ in love, which is salvation, does not just involve individuals. Christ died for the "many," (Mk 10:45; 14:24; etc.) an expression that most probably derived from the Aramaic and stands for "all".[12] Not only is love expansive in itself but also those sharing Christ's love are united by the same love to Christ and to each other. This provides the basis for the expressions "in Christ," "with Christ," "through Christ," that recur frequently in the Pauline and Johannine writings as well as for the "σuν" prefix ("with") that is added to so many verbs in the Pauline corpus. This lived experience of corporate personality found other images even better adapted to show the full extent of the vivifying union with Christ: the vine and the branches (Jn 15:1ff; cp. 1 Cor 3:6-9), the body of Christ (1 Cor 10:16f; 12:12-31; Rom 12:4-8; Eph 2:14-18; 4:1-16; Col 1:18), the bride of Christ or of the Lamb who is also one body with him (Eph 5:21-33; Apoc 19:7-9; 22:17; cp. Mk 2:19), and the living temple constructed on Christ (1

Cor 3:10-17; 14:12; 2 Cor 6:16; Eph 2:19-22; 1 Pet 2:4-8; cp. Jn 2:19-21). Insofar as Christ demands total fidelity to himself, no aspect of human life is excluded from his control (cf. Phil 4:8f; 1 Cor 10:31-33; 1 Thess 5:16-22; Col 3:17). The union with him cannot remain purely spiritual insofar as man is also essentially corporeal. On the basis of corporeal union with Christ, Paul argued against corporeal union with prostitutes (1 Cor 6:12-20). Furthermore, in the Eucharist Christ's body and blood remained present in the Church as the creative symbol of unity and the touchstone of faith (Lk 22:14-20 par.; 1 Cor 10:16f; 11:23-34; Jn 6:50-69); on the basis of its celebration and reception concrete rules for the Church were drawn up and laid down (1 Cor 10:14-22; 11:27-34). Consequently there had to be structure and order in the Christian Church, according to the various ranks and duties in love, for the common good (1 Cor 12-14). Such is the Christian *koinonia*. *Koinonia*, as used by St Paul, signifies in turn community, Eucharistic communion, receptive participation, active sharing, and monetary collection. Since Paul employed this same multifaceted word, at times twisting it into grammatical novelties and fresh meanings, to express his thought, he obviously saw a profound connection among all its significations. In a synthetic view, then, *koinonia* designates the spiritual and visible community of grace and material goods, to which all are called in faith in order that, participating fully in the life of the Father, Son and Spirit, they might both respond in love to God's gift of himself, which is most clearly manifested in Eucharistic communion, and assist each other spiritually and materially, thereby contributing to the upbuilding of the Church.[13] By that sharing in the divine life through faith in Jesus, Jesus' relation to the Father whom he addressed so intimately as *Abba* (Daddy) could be extended to believers; in Jesus' Spirit they enjoy adoption as children and in turn call out in prayer *Abba* (Rom 5:5; 8:14-17; Gal 3:26-4:7). On the basis of that dynamic communion of love preachers were sent out into the whole world to announce Christ's saving deeds and words and in that way to bring all to faith, baptism and salvation (Mt 28:18-20; Mk 16:15-18; Lk 24:45-49; Acts 1:8; 2:1ff; 1 Tim 2:4-7; Rom 10:13-18). For through Christ's death, in his blood, the true reconciliation of God and humanity has occurred, and all are called to be reconciled; this reconciliation is the new creation, the justification and peace achieved in Christ (Rom 5:9-11; 2 Cor 5:17-21; Gal 6:15; Col 1:19f; Eph 2:11-18).

Human suffering, especially Christian suffering

a. Eternal life as reward of suffering sustained faithfully

It is with reference to that fundamental saving community of Christ and his Church that the full significance of suffering is revealed. For one thing, the union with Christ, the sharing of his life of divine love, relativizes all suffering. Just as the resurrection overcame the cross, so the eternal life presupposed and promised to the faithful everywhere in the New Testament leads them to discount the temporal tribulations of this world:

Amen, Amen, I say to you, you will weep and lament, but the world will rejoice; you will be sorrowful, but your sorrow will be turned to joy. When a woman is in labour she has sorrow because her hour has come; but when she has given birth to the child, she does not remember the travail any longer on account of the joy that a human being has been born into the world. And you therefore have sorrow now, but I shall see you again, and your heart will rejoice, and no one will take your joy from you (Jn 16:20-22).

The second coming of the Lord was a great comfort and served as a motive for the exhortation to stand fast in good works and in tribulation (Mt 24:32-35, 45-51; 25; Rom 13:11-14; 1 Thess 5:1-11; Jas 5:7-11; 1 Pet 4:7-11; Heb 10:23-25; Apoc 22:10-13).

Sufferings were relativized in their intensity as well as in their duration by comparison with what was to come. In a type of *praeteritio*[14] Paul wrote, "I consider that the sufferings of this present time are not worth comparing with the glory that is to be revealed to us" (Rom 8:18). Even more strikingly was that final glory magnified over present sufferings when the Apostle denied all comparison between the eternal realities and the things of this world:

So we do not lose heart. Though our outer nature is wasting away, our inner nature is being renewed every day. For this slight momentary affliction is preparing for us an eternal weight of glory beyond all comparison, because we look not to things that are seen but to the things that are unseen; for the things that are seen are transient, but the things that are unseen are eternal (2 Cor 4:16-18).

With that statement St Paul seemed to be close to a Platonic or late Jewish downgrading of this world in favour of a future life. With a reference to the shortness of time and the argument, "The form of this world is passing away" (1 Cor 7:31), he advised a distancing of self from all the goods and sorrows of this world (1 Cor 7:29-31). Similarly John urged Christians to refrain from love of the world. "The world passes away and the desire of it, but the one doing God's will remains forever" (1 Jn 2:17). Surely life with and in Christ is of a value beyond compare – all else without it is "refuse" (Phil 3:9) – and that life flowers in eternity. Yet Paul's unceasing activity in this world amply demonstrated that he did not reject it and its values. For the eternal life promised to the Christian is not just a future reality. In Christ the time has been fulfilled (Mk 1:15; Gal 4:4), the kingdom of God is already present (Lk 11:20; 17:21; Mt 5:3, 10; etc.), and

Christians have already died and risen to life with Christ (1 Thess 5:10; 2 Cor 5:15; Rom 6:3-13; 14:7f; Eph 2:1-7). John's "realized eschatology" understood that the life of our resurrection was already present in the Son, who is the resurrection and the life, and he gives life to believers (5:25-27; 11:25-27; 14:6; 20:31). "And this is eternal life, that they may know you, the only true God, and Jesus Christ, whom you have sent" (17:3). With this new life suffering acquires a new meaning already in this world as a result of Christ's cross. We must now consider in the light of Christ the significance of the tribulations invariably attendant upon all human life, and especially upon Christian life.

b. Medicinal suffering

Suffering as such is certainly a punishment of God for sin in the New as well as in the Old Testament. But it is not just that. For it inexorably reveals to man his inability to save himself; much less can he control the world. Hence it can liberate him to abandon all self-justification and to seek a salvation outside himself The sick and the lame, the lepers and the blind in their affliction all sought mercy and help from Jesus. Such petitions implied a faith in Jesus. Indeed, he often demanded, praised or rewarded faith in the sick person healed (Mk 5:34; 10:52; Mt 9:29) or in their friends or relations (Mk 2:5; 9:23f; Mt 8:10:25-28; Jn 4:50), thereby acknowledging human solidarity for weal as well as for woe. Moreover, his miracles were often intended to create faith (Jn 2:11, 22f; 4:53; Mt 11:4-6). At times no miracles were performed due to a lack of faith. Mark even wrote of Jesus' visit to his own country and the people's rejection of him: "And he could do no mighty work there, except that he laid his hands upon a few sick people and healed them. And he marvelled because of their unbelief" (6:5f).

Obviously Jesus did not destroy human freedom in offering

healing. Within such a context, therefore, the deeper reason for sicknesses can be revealed. "It was not that this man sinned, or his parents, but that the works of God might be made manifest in him" (Jn 9:3). So the cure of the blind man led to his full faith in Jesus (9:35-38; cf. 6:29). Similarly the death of Lazarus, painful as it was to Jesus as well as to Lazarus' sisters and friends, served to build up the faith of the disciples and others (Jn 11:15, 45).

If suffering can bring to faith those who did not believe, it can also recall to themselves those who believe but do not act accordingly. The Apocalypse's letter to the angel of the Church of Thyatira warned against the "prophetess Jezebel" and her followers:

I gave them time to repent, but she refuses to repent of her immorality. Behold, I will throw her on a sickbed, and those who commit adultery with her I will throw into great tribulation unless they repent of her doings; and I will strike her children dead. And all the churches shall know that I am he who searches mind and heart, and I will give to each of you as your works deserve (2:21-23).

Analogously, the Corinthians misusing the Eucharist were stricken with sickness and death so that, "judged by the Lord" and "chastened", they "might not be condemned along with the world" (1 Cor 11:23-33).

If God so worked on small scales, he also used the impending destruction of cities, like Jerusalem, as admonitions for conversion (Mt 26:24; 27:35; Mk 13; Lk 13:1-5). While grief of the world brings death, grief "according to God" brings conversion (2 Cor 7:8-12; cp. 1 Cor 11:25-32). All these punishments recall the divine chastising that God paternally employs for his children in order that like the Prodigal Son they may "come to themselves" and return to him (Lk 15:11-24). "Those whom I love I reprove and chasten; so be zealous and repent" (Apoc 3:19). And Hebrews 12:5-

11 cited Proverbs 3:11f to remind believers that God was treating them like sons in his chastisements "for our good".

c. Suffering as a test

Behind all the suffering in this world stands God's infinite, merciful love (Rom 2:4; 9:22-24; Jas 5:11; 2 Pet 3:9, 15). He grants sinners time to turn back to him, and in the worst of their tribulations and temptations his grace is always sufficient to support them (Rom 5:3-5; 1 Cor 10:13; 2 Cor 12:9; Phil 4:12f; 2 Tim 4:16f). The believer who stands firm in temptation for the love of God is called "blessed" insofar as he will receive the crown of life (Jas 1:12; Mk 13:13; 2 Tim 4:6-8). The element of love is so paramount that the theme of "testing by God" frequently referred to in the Old Testament is almost completely abandoned. Though Hebrew 11:17 spoke in passing of Abraham "being tempted" as he conquered by faith, the notion of testing seems incompatible with the Father of Jesus Christ to whom Christians pray daily, "Lead us not into temptation" (Mt 6:13; cf. also 26:41).

Without doubt a change of meaning in the term πειράζειν had occurred in the intertestamental period. The Septuagint translation of the Old Testament[15] had employed that word with the primary signification: "to make trial of," even "to have an experience of" Yet the New Testament, following in the wake of other intertestamental writings, understood the word primarily as "to tempt (to sin)".[16] Hence, St James angrily rejected the excuse of Christians who claimed that God had tempted them and attributed the temptations instead to their own base desires (1:12-15). "The tempter" was the name bestowed on the devil (Mt 4:3; 1 Thess 3:5). Jesus himself had been tempted repeatedly, not by his Father but by the devil and his enemies (Mk 1:13; 8:11; 10:2; 12:15). In his agony he was torn between his will and his Father's so as to learn the full meaning of obedience and save others

(Lk 22:42 par.; Heb 2:18; 5:7-10). Jesus' disciples apparently shared his fate (Lk 22:28), yet at the time of his agony he repeatedly urged his disciples to pray that they may not enter into temptation (Lk 22:40, 46).

The Old Testament image of "testing by fire" was retained, but not directly attributed to God in the present. Rather the day of the Lord would test with fire to see if Christians have built securely on the foundation of Jesus Christ (1 Cor 3:10-15), and they were assured in the midst of their sufferings that their faith was more valuable to the God who guards them than gold "tested by fire" (1 Pet 1:3-8). It should also be noted that in these passages the verb "to test" δοκιμάζειν differed from the verb "to tempt" πειράζειν. Moreover, the only passage speaking of God "testing our hearts" actually assured Christians that they had already been approved: "just as we have been approved by God to be entrusted with the gospel, so we speak, not to please men, but to please God who tests our hearts" (1 Thess 2:4). In that verse the same verb δοκιμάζειν was used twice with its double possibility of translation: "to approve" and "to test." Clearly God "tested" in order to "approve". Nowhere was there the slightest hint of a comparison of God to an examination proctor coolly sitting back like a proctor to observe how his charges had learnt their lessons; much less was he imagined as tempting others to sin.

Such a revised understanding of "testing" was doubtless rooted in the life and practice of Jesus. For he demanded conversion in order to follow him. That in turn involved sacrifices. He had come, he said, to bring not peace but a sword that would cleave the unity of the family and turn one member against another: "He who loves father or mother more than me is not worthy of me, and he who loves son or daughter more than me is not worthy of me" (Mt 10:34-38; Lk 12:51-53; Mk 13:12f par.; Lk 9:59-62 par.). The abandonment of the goods of this world in favour of Jesus was a real challenge that not all could accept but only those moved by God's grace (cf. Mk 10:17-27). Yet to those who responded positively Jesus promised an abundant recompense, "Everyone who has left houses or brothers or sisters or father or mother or children or lands, for my name's sake, will receive a hundredfold and inherit eternal life" (Mt 19:29). Here the sacrifice of Abraham was repeated in true followers of Jesus. The hundredfold reward, promised already in this life (Mk 10:29f), probably referred to the new community which Jesus was founding: for whoever did God's will was to Jesus "brother and sister and mother" (Mk 3:34f). In this new relationship surpassing all natural ties, love was destined to rule and goods would be shared (Acts 2:44f; 4:32-36; Rom 15:25-28; 1 Cor 16:1-4; 2 Cor 9; 1 Tim 6:17-19; Jas 1:27-2:8, 14-17; etc.). In this was verified the often repeated, simple law of love, "Whoever wishes to save his life, will lose it; but whoever loses his life for my sake will find it" (Mt 16:25; 10:39; Mk 8:35; Lk 9:24; 17:33; Jn 12:25). Clearly this testing of men's hearts which Jesus worked was meant to bring an immense reward.

d. Suffering as purification

If trials come, they are allowed by God for purification. Not only are all men sinners (Rom 3:10, 23; 5:12, 19), but they are also afflicted by concupiscence, or evil desires (Rom 7:5, 13-25; 1 Pet 1:14f). Of bad desires resulting from original sin and their own personal sins Christians must be purified. Although the word purification was usually restricted to the overall forgiveness of sins effected by Christ's blood, especially in faith, baptism and the confession of sins (1 Jn 1:7f; Heb 9:14; Eph 5:26; Acts 15:9), conversion's ongoing process in the Christian life was assured. Believers bearing fruit would be pruned, or purified, in order that they produce even more fruit to the Father's glory (Jn 15:2, 8). They were urged to purify themselves from every defilement to attain perfect holiness (2 Cor 7:1), a perfection ultimately modelled, in Jesus' words, after the perfection of their heavenly Father (Mt 5:48). Even though, for John, Christians believed in Jesus and possessed eternal life already, they were still to be sanctified in truth and perfected (17:17-23).

Paul based his imperative to overcome the desires of the flesh squarely upon the indicative of the salvific grace of divine love poured into every Christian's heart (Gal 5:16-25; Rom 5:5; 8:4-14) and he laboured in order that that Christ be formed in believers (Gal 4:19). For Christians still groan, awaiting with patience their full redemption (Rom 8:22-25). They undergo suffering to be made worthy of the kingdom of God (2 Thess 1:5). Paul did not lament having to carry about in his own body Christ's wounds (Gal 6:17). He bore in his body the dying of Jesus so that through his weakness the power of grace and the resurrection might be the better manifested (2 Cor 4:7-15). Although baptism bestowed as a gift the crucifixion of the old man in his body of sin (Rom 6:6), Paul also continually urged Christians to crucify themselves in the ongoing struggle against the flesh, "Those who belong to Christ Jesus have crucified the flesh with its passions and desires" (Gal 5:24). Perhaps for this reason of purification, to prevent excessive elation, Paul received his "thorn in the flesh" and learned humility and greater trust in Christ (2 Cor 12:7-10). Certainly the Apostle practised self-control and chastised his body lest, despite his preaching, he himself be lost (1 Cor 9:25-27). And, in view of Jesus' example and teaching, fasting was practised in the early Church, often with the accompaniment of prayers and vigils (Mt 4:2; 6:16-18; 9:15; Acts 13:2f; 14:23; 2 Cor 6:5; 11:27). Sexual abstinence was likewise recommended in order to obtain the freedom to pray (1 Cor 7:5); virginity, celibacy and poverty for the sake of the kingdom of heaven and following Jesus were highly praised (Mk 10:43f; Mt 19:11f, 16-30; 22:30; Lk 6:20f, 24f; 7:22; 16:20-22, 25; Acts 2:44; 4:32-35; 1 Cor 7:1, 7-9, 25-40; 2 Cor 6:10; 8:1-

5; Apoc 14:3-5). Baptism obviously was not the goal but the beginning of life in and with Christ.

Since the daily struggle is not easy but directed against principalities and powers, the Christian is urged to arm himself for war by developing supernatural habits (Rom 13:12-14; 2 Cor 10:3-5; Eph 6:10-20). Thus the evil habits inculcated by sin will be eradicated and replaced by Christ's life, planting itself ever more deeply in the believer's whole being. If a believer proves recalcitrant in obeying the commands of Christ he may be excommunicated or "handed over to Satan", but even this desperate measure is intended to bring the person to his senses and effect his further purification after baptism (1 Cor 5:5; 1 Tim 1:20; Mt 18:15-17). Probably in prevision of sins committed after baptism, the disciples received from the risen Jesus the power of forgiving as well as of retaining sins (Jn 20:22f; cf. Mt 18:15-18; 16:18f).

e. The vicarious, redemptive suffering of Christians

The sufferings just discussed seemed to come from without, intended to convert or purify. But anyone reading the New Testament cannot understand Christian suffering just in terms of impositions from without. So often do sufferings appear in the New Testament that they seem to flow from the Christian vocation itself In Ananias' vision St Paul's vocation and mission were described by the Lord thus: "he is a chosen instrument of mine to carry my name before the Gentiles and the sons of Israel; for I will show him how much he must suffer for the sake of my name" (Acts 9:15f). In Acts Paul willingly and knowingly took sufferings upon himself for the sake of Christ and the Gospel (20:23f; 21:10-14). Paul's epistles also presupposed a necessary connection between the Christian vocation and suffering. "Share in sufferings," he wrote, "as a good soldier of Jesus Christ. No soldier on service gets entangled in civilian pursuits, since his aim is to satisfy the one who enlisted him" (2 Tim 2:3f). St Peter, in turn, found nothing "strange" or "foreign" ξένον in suffering:

> Beloved, do not be surprised at the fiery ordeal which comes upon you, as though something strange were happening to you. But as you participate in the sufferings of Christ, rejoice, in order that you may also rejoice exultingly in the revelation of his glory. If you are reviled because of the name of Christ, you are blessed, because the Spirit of glory and of God rests upon you. If one suffers as a Christian, let him not be ashamed, but under that name let him glorify God" (1 Pet 4:12-16).

After all, did not Jesus also consider blessed those who were reviled and persecuted for his sake? (Mt 5:10f). And did he not call upon all who wished to follow him to deny themselves and take up their cross daily? (Lk 9:23; 14:27). As Christ, so the Christian; for the disciple is never above the Master (Mt 10:24f; Jn 13:16). Even more pointedly Jesus warned of the world's hatred for the disciples because they belonged to him. "If they persecuted me, they will also persecute you" (Jn 15:18-21). Following Christ, i.e., discipleship, involves confessing him before men and standing fast in persecution (Lk 12:8f; Jn 15:18-27; Mk 13:9-13; Mt 10:17-22). The only way to glory is based on divine adoption, and that involves suffering, as St Paul reminded the Romans: "If [we are] children, then [we are] heirs, heirs of God and fellow heirs with Christ, provided that we suffer with him in order that we may also be glorified with him" (Rom 8:17). It seemed almost a commonplace to say that "we must enter the kingdom of God through many tribulations" (Acts 14:22). The early Christian hymn stated as the simple truth: "If we have died with him, we shall also live with him; if we endure, we shall also reign with him" (2 Tim 2:11f). Consequently the Apostle could sum up and apply the New Testament doctrine, "All who desire to live piously in Christ Jesus will be persecuted" (2 Tim 3:12).

Just as following and confessing Christ consists much less in a mere external imitation and preaching than in a real sharing of his life, so the sufferings attendant upon discipleship are not simply attributable to fortuitous, external events. The Father is the one who prunes the vine's branches (Jn 15:2). Moreover, the suffering believers, as members of the Christian *koinonia* communicating in Christ's body and blood, actually share in Christ's sufferings (Phil 3:10; 1 Pet 4:13). The sufferings of Christ are even pictured as "superabounding," flowing over onto the disciples (2 Cor 1:5). Paul sees his own sufferings as borne "for the sake of" his fellow Christians who share in his sufferings, which are their glory (2 Cor 1:6f; 4:8-12; Eph 3:13). This probably is not to be interpreted in terms of a merely external service that entails suffering, like preaching the Gospel or caring for the needy. Some scholars, noting the sufferings in superabundance that attended Paul's ministry and the alacrity with which he bore them for others, attempted to identify Paul's understanding of his person and mission with that of the Suffering Servant.[17] Although the texts cited by them do not unequivocally support that interpretation, those scholars may be close to the truth. Paul commended all to put on the mind of Christ, who humbled himself as a servant in obedience unto the cross (Phil 2:5-11) and he urged them to be imitators of him as he was of Christ (1 Cor 11:1; 4:15-17; 1 Thess 1:6; 2:14f; 2 Thess 3:7-9).

As the union with Christ is interior and exterior, so the mission and efficacy of Christ continues in his members, the Church on earth. What each member of Christ's Body accomplishes and suffers affects all other members (1 Cor 12:26). For the Christian *koinonia* is a community of sharing, passively accepting and actively contributing, in the goods of others, spiritual as well as material. Insofar as this community of love is centred on and grounded in Jesus, the Lord, just as his sufferings are salvific, so are the Christian's. Indeed, Paul wrote, "Now I rejoice in the suffering for your sake and I fill up in my flesh what is lacking to the sufferings of Christ for the sake of his Body, which is the Church" (Col 1:24). This is not as if Christ's passion were insufficient for our salvation; the Greek word "what is lacking" ὑστερήματα generally stands in opposition to "what is superabundant" περίσσευμα (1 Thess 3:10; 1 Cor 8:8; 12:24; 2 Cor 8:14; 9:12; Phil 4:11f).[18] Just as God's Being superabounds in letting us be, finite "alongside" the Infinite, and God's omnipotence does not obliterate but rather creates our freedom, so also the plenitude of Christ's redemptive sufferings does not suppress the need for the sufferings of Christians, but gives them a new value. The expansiveness of love that marks the divine generosity does not cease when it enters the human heart but expands that heart so that it may bear fruit and, going beyond itself, bring benefits to all others. So Paul wrote, "I can do all things in him who empowers me" (Phil 4:13; Gal 2:19f).

The mystery of God's presence: Job transcended

The very possibility of vicarious suffering is not deduced from abstract reasoning. For the Christian it is given actuality by its relation with Jesus Christ, that historical and eternal person who died and rose for all. In Christ the love of God has been revealed unsurpassably. In his humanity he is the unique mediator between God and us (1 Tim 2:4-7; 1 Cor 8:6; Acts 4:12; Jn 14:6) and ultimately the final revelation of God's nature: Love. Even in the weakest analogy drawn from human experience love remains a mystery, for it depends on human freedom which cannot be forced by any type of rational, hence abstract, persuasion to dedicate itself concretely. All the greater is the mystery when sacrifice is involved and greater still when one gives one's life for one's enemies, as Christ gave his for sinners, the very ones responsible for his death. Yet love cannot remain a theory, mere words. It plunges on to concrete dedication (1 Jn 3:18). God did not rest content in sending messengers, the prophets, to turn Israel from sin. Mistreated as they were, he also knew their incapacity to hold out under the strain of bearing God's word of love to sinful men. For a word of divine love, if it is to be completely credible, has to be lived entirely by the speaker or messenger. So at the proper time he sent his only Son (Mk 12:1-6; Heb 1:1f). Words do not suffice; hence the eternal Word, God himself, "became flesh and dwelt among us" (Jn 1:1-14). That is the true presence of God, *Emmanuel*, in history. Surpassing the Old Testament in which the pious recognized God's presence in some inner experience, Christ's presence is public, accessible to all who have ears to hear and eyes to see the mystery of God breaking through the crucified humanity of Christ.

Job experienced God as the mysterious, creative power dominating good and evil. Yet the extent of God's mastery remained undreamt of by Job. In taking flesh Christ apparently hid the effulgence of the Father's glory that he is (Heb 1:3; cf. Mk 9:2-8). He "emptied himself" of the form of God in assuming the form of a slave (Phil 2:6f). For he first took upon himself not glorious but mortal flesh, indeed, sinful flesh (Rom 8:3). St Paul went to the limit in the force of his language when he wrote of God's appeal to us for reconciliation made through Christ, "For our sake [God] made him sin who knew no sin in order that we might become the justice of God in him" (2 Cor 5:21). In coming to be hanged upon a tree Jesus "became a curse for our sake" in order to redeem us from the law and give the blessing of Abraham to the nations (Gal 3:13f). In a related image Paul said that the legal bond of sins that told against us was nailed to the cross, cancelled, and set aside in order to let us enjoy life with Christ (Col 2:13f). The total abandonment of the cross described by Mark (15:33-37) shows God's horror of sin which Jesus carried. he who was utterly sinless and spent his whole life doing good in full obedience to the Father's will (Heb 4:15; Acts 2:22; 10:38), experienced in his innocence an abandonment more rending than Job's and scarcely imagined even by the inspired author of the Servant Songs. In a startling paradox, out of solidarity with sinful humanity, Jesus took upon himself the utmost consequences of sin, total alienation and abandonment, in order that by his unjust condemnation to death others might receive the justice of God, his very life, the life of the one who is justice (1 Cor 1:30), and so become "partakers of the divine nature" (Rom 3:22; 5:17f; 8:10; 2 Cor 4:10-12; Jn 3:15f, 36; 6:47, 54; 10:10; 20:31; 2 Pet 1:4). At the same time that Christ reconciled the world to God, he brought peace and reconciliation to us by destroying the walls of division that the sin of Adam and Eve had originally erected (Eph 2:11-22; Gal 3:28; 2 Cor 5:18; Col 1:20). Sin has been thoroughly overcome in Christ.

By joining the extremes, God and world, Infinite and finite, and, even more, the pure holiness of divine love and sinful man, Jesus eviscerated the power of death and sin, revealing the hollow nothingness of their ferocious threats to one who lets himself be ruled by divine love. For to Christians, unlike the Jews, the veil has been lifted; on the cross they recognized the glory of triumphant love, the likeness of God in the face of Christ, and in a love responding to love they themselves grew in the Spirit ever more into the glorious likeness of God (Gal 3:18-4:6). Thus God has mastered death and evil not by pure play of power, destroying the enemy from without, but, emptying himself and taking on the servile likeness of man even unto death (Phil 2:7f), he overcame sin and death from within. Fittingly in his resurrected glory Christ bears the wounds of his hard won victory (Jn 20:20, 25-29). In his own way God not only showed the depth of his love, the extreme to which he would go, but also he established the cross as the axis on which the revolution in mankind's view of the world was to be accomplished.

The fundamental change in man's perspective could occur

only before the revelation of God's mystery. By "mystery" St Paul intended God's entire plan of salvation decreed before all ages and manifested in Christ. For by the blood shed on the cross sinners have been redeemed in the fullness of time. This redemption is not to be imagined as a merely mercantile or juridical transaction taking place behind the closed curtains of God's counsel chamber. For believers have become, in the Holy Spirit, sons of God through Jesus Christ; therefore in Christ they have become truly holy and blameless before the Father. God's mystery, Paul told the Colossians, "is Christ in you, the hope of glory," as he urged them to grow in the knowledge and understanding of that mystery through love (Col 1:11-2:3; Eph 1:3-14). Ultimately the divine mystery consists in love's overflowing plenitude revealed on the cross to touch the hearts of all in order that, when "Christ dwells in your hearts through faith, you, being rooted and grounded in love, may be strong enough to comprehend with the saints the breadth and the length and the height and the depth and to know the love of Christ which exceeds all knowledge, that you may be filled unto all the plenitude of God" (Eph 3:17-21). It is not a mystery of unlimited force that conquered sin and death and before which the Christian is to be humbled and silenced. Job has been left far behind, and Qoheleth's sceptical distance has been overcome. Rather the mystery of self-giving love that reveals the open heart of God forces man to surrender the posture of sapiential observer and judge (1 Cor 1:18-2:16). Man can no longer remain in a hard-hearted neutrality. By loving Christ the believer has entered the very heart of love and there in silent wonder before the mystery of mysteries he understands its dimensions as those of infinite Love – for God is Love – and his silence melts into grateful praise and joyful adoration of the God too vast for the human head and heart, who nevertheless became man. God's wisdom has been revealed to be his love, and his ways are confessed to be truly inscrutable (1 Cor 3:18-23; Rom 11:33-36).

The ultimate meaning of Christian suffering

Through Christ's cross the very meaning of suffering has been transmuted. It is not simply attributed to human finitude as something to be overcome by insight or asceticism that destroys or absolutizes individuality, as the Hindu and Buddhist wisdoms teach.[19] Neither is it any longer just the result of sin, which leads to death, the manifestation of God's wrath against those who seek to avoid accepting his salvation in favour of justifying themselves (Rom 1:18-2:12; 5:1-30). Now for believers, through the folly of the cross that is wiser than human wisdom, suffering becomes an invitation to share in Christ's redemptive love, the very life of God himself, and, by offering themselves in sacrifice for God and their fellow Christians, to grow in love and contribute to the growth of the whole body of Christ. Not without reason sacred authors applied sacrificial imagery to the Christian life (Rom 12:1; 15:16; Phil 2:17; 4:18; Heb 12:28; 13:15; 1 Pet 2:5); for in the following of Christ they were summoned to give all, to be united to him in his self-sacrifice. Luke wisely added the word "daily" to Christ's injunction to take up one's cross (9:23), probably indicating thereby the ordinary character of the Christian life, where every day Christians are challenged to prove themselves faithful disciples. In and through love's daily sacrifice they are called to grow into the fullness of Christ, the head, "from whom the whole body, joined and knit together by every joint with which it is supplied, when each part is working properly, makes bodily growth and upbuilds itself in love" (Eph 4:16; 2:22f; Col 2:19).

Only such an understanding of suffering in union with Christ can explain the authentic Christian reaction to suffering. Not only do Christians find comfort from Christ in their affliction (2 Cor 1:3-7) and rejoice after punishment for having been found worthy to suffer dishonour for the name of Christ (Acts 5:41) but they also actually desire to share Christ's sufferings, considering it a grace to suffer for Christ

(Phil 1:29; 3:8-10; 1 Pet 2:19-22). In the midst of and because of their tribulations they seem to be constantly rejoicing (Rom 5:3; 2 Cor 6:8-10; 7:4; 8:2; 12:9f; Col 1:24; Phil 2:17f; Heb 10:34; 1 Pet 1:6-8; Jas 1:2-4). In the eyes of unbelievers this must appear incredible madness, but truly here the programme of the beatitudes has been realized as all await the final day when the sorrowful shall be comforted, the hungry sated and the persecuted rewarded (Mt 5:3-12). At the end all tears shall be wiped away as the faithful are introduced into apocalyptic joy (Apoc 7:16f; 21:4). In the meantime, in the joy of suffering Christians, a valid testimony to the eschatological character of Christ's message is given and the kingdom of God is realized anticipatorily upon earth. Thereby sufferings, both Christ's and the Christian's, have become the means of "manifesting God's works" and "glorifying" the Son and the Father (Jn 9:3; 11:4; 12:27f).

The New Testament thus teaches that suffering reflects God's punishment only as long as we remain under his wrath by rejecting his proffered mercy in Christ (cf. Rom 1:18-2:11; 5:9f; 11:22f; 1 Thess 5:9f; Eph 1:1-10; 2:16; 5:3-6; Col 3:5-17). His mercy is admittedly fierce, for it is the burning of a love that forces us to abandon self-justification, to confess our sins and to accept salvation as a pure gift, letting him become all in us as we receive all in him. The sufferings which he sends or allows are revealed thereby as invitations to love. God's wrath results not from any pleasure of his in punishing but from our refusal to accept his love. Yet even against the background of infinite Love there is a terribly hard message that remains forever ineradicable from the "good news": the existence of hell.

Hell, fire, damnation and election

a. Hell

The eschatological background and apocalyptical imagery of the New Testament message serve, as we saw, to place men before a radical decision. "No one can serve two masters; for either he will hate the one and love the other, or he will be devoted to the one and despise the other. You cannot serve God and mammon" (Mt 6:24). Paul asked, "What accord has Christ with Belial?" (2 Cor 6:15). Similarly James wrote, "Do you not know that friendship with the world is enmity with God? Therefore whoever wishes to be a friend of the world makes himself an enemy of God" (4:4). That stark contrast also reflects the Johannine antitheses between God and the world (14:17-19; 15:18f; 16:8-11; 17:13-26; 18:36f) as well as between light and darkness (1:4f; 3:19-21; 8:12), life and death (1:4; 5:21-27; 8:51; 11:24f), truth and lie (8:31-55; 1:14-17; 14:6, 17; 16:13; 17:17-19; 18:37f). Paul preferred to contrast faith and God's justification with sin, death and man's self-justification (Rom 1:16-5:1; 14:23; Gal 2:15-3:29) or, more simply, the life-giving spirit with the flesh (Rom 8:1-17; Gal 3:1-3; 4:28-31; 5:16-26). All these dualisms but continue Jesus' initial summons to convert and believe the Gospel before the inrushing kingdom of God and to confess him boldly before men even at the risk of one's life (Mk 1:15f; 8:34-38).

The choice forced upon men by Christ does not meet an impartial, innocent observer. There is none righteous, all are sinners (Rom 3:10-12; 5:12). Even before Christ's coming Paul found men "without excuse" since they had rejected God's witness to himself given in creation (Rom 1:18-2:1). For his part John considered Jesus' presence and words to deprive men of any excuse for their guilt (3:36; 12:48; 9:39-41; 15:22-25). Even the gentle Luke who attempted to excuse the Jews' rejection of Israel on account of their ignorance

(23:34; Acts 3:17), insisted upon the absolute need of repentance for sin after Easter (Acts 3:19-26). "There is salvation in no one else, for there is no other name under heaven given among men by which we must be saved" (Acts 4:12).

If for Paul "to live is Christ" (Phil 1:21), one immediately understands his judgment about life without Christ. If Christ did not rise from the dead, faith is vain and Christians, remaining in their sins, are the most pitiable of men (1 Cor 15:17-19). Not Christians alone but the whole universe has been subjected to vanity, or futility, in expectation of liberation (Rom 8:20). Indeed, if Christ had never come, the pessimism of Qohelet – whose Greek translation employed the same word for "vanity," or "futility" ματαιότης as Paul later used – would be far outdone by Paul. For all the reckonings of the wise are futile (1 Cor 3:20). Paul, of course, did not win through to that insight all on his own. Only through the cross of Christ did he both acknowledge the paradoxical foolishness of God that is so much wiser than men and confess that the wisdom of this world has become folly. No human being may boast before God (1 Cor 1:18-2:14; 3:18-21). Thus all the reasons which Paul had for boasting in the flesh, after knowing Christ Jesus, he counted loss and refuse (Phil 3:3-11). These affirmations must be attributed to something more than an excessively enthusiastic, subjective experience of conversion. For Paul's attention was centred not on himself but on Christ, and if Christ, as he believed, is really the unique Son of God, who raised an absolute claim to fidelity in his own person, nothing else really mattered (cf. Acts 20:24; 21:13f).

If Christ shares his resurrected life with the baptized who believe in him (Rom 6:1-11), how horrendous must be exclusion from Christ! There are probably no more chilling words found in all of Scripture than those spoken by Christ about his betrayer, "It would be better for that man not to have been born" (Mt 26:24). Judas's fate must be referred to the equivalent of "eternal damnation," the exclusion from the Lord's presence (2 Thess 1:9) or "the second death", the lake of punishing fire (Apoc 20:6, 14f; 21:18). That is Gehenna, or the hell of eternal, inextinguishable flame and the ever-gnawing worm (Mk 9:42-48; Lk 16:24-26, 28; Mt 5:22, 29f; 13:41f; 18:8f; 25:41, 46). It is the outer darkness whose inhabitants weep and gnash their teeth and remain unknown to the Lord (Mt 25:12, 30; 7:23; 24:51; 22:13; 8:12). The fullness of revelation has but increased the punishment for those who refuse Christ. After discussing Jesus' sacrifice for sins and the necessity for remaining faithful, the author of the Letter to the Hebrews concluded:

> For if we sin deliberately after receiving the knowledge of the truth, there no longer remains a sacrifice for sins, but a fearful prospect of judgment, and a fury of fire which will consume the adversaries. A man who has violated the law of Moses dies without mercy at the testimony of two or three witnesses. How much worse punishment do you think will be deserved by the man who has spurned the Son of God, and profaned the blood of the covenant by which he was sanctified and outraged the Spirit of grace?... It is a fearful thing to fall into the hands of the living God (10:26-31).

How are these terrible torments to be reconciled with the Lord of infinite love and mercy? It is too flimsy an answer to say that people choose their own destiny, for such a response would impinge upon the majesty of God, as if men were primarily responsible for their fate.[20] Scripture invariably attributes the expulsions into hell as either God's work, signified by the "divine passive" habitually used by Jews to avoid naming the divine name, or in the explicit judgment of the Son of Man. One must look deeper to find an adequate answer.

b. Fire

Linked most closely with the image of hell is the symbol of fire, eternal and quenchless. This symbol actually is found frequently in the Scriptures, yet in a much wider context, extending far beyond hell. Early on God appeared to Moses as a flame of fire in the bush that burned without being consumed (Ex 3:2-4), and for the bestowing of the Law he descended in fire upon Sinai (Ex 19:18). From the midst of the fire, as Horeb was ablaze, God spoke and roused the terror of death among the people (Deut 4:12; 5:4f, 22-27; 18:16). So God revealed himself a jealous God, a "devouring fire" whose wrath should not be lightly kindled (Deut 4:24; 6:15: 32:21f). He led his people through the desert by a column of fire at night (Ex 13:21f; 40:38; t. 1:33). Certainly fire often served as a sign of Yahweh's holiness and presence (Ex 3:5f; Ps. 50:3; Ezek 1:4-28). Elijah called down fire from heaven upon his sodden sacrifice in the contest with the priests of Baal. "The God who answers by fire, he is God" (1 Kings 18:24, 38). Similarly, other sacrifices were consumed by heavenly fire to indicate God's approval (Lev 9:24-10:3; 1 Chr 21:26; 2 Chr 7:1-3; Judg 6:21; 2 Macc 1:18-36; 2:10). If God is holy, he could purify Isaiah's lips with a burning coal to remove guilt and make him a fit instrument for his word (Is 6:1-9). Jeremiah in his turn found the word of God a fire so scorching in his heart that he could not contain it but had to speak it out (20:9; 23:29). Consequently it was not surprising that the prophets and their words themselves could burn (Jer 6:27-30; Sir 48:1), for fire also represented the anger of God that punishes sin (Amos 1:3-2:5; Is 9:18f; 30:27, 33; Jer 15:14; 17:4, 27). Similarly, besides punishing Egypt as the seventh plague, fire was sent from heaven to destroy Sodom and Gomorrah, the rebels against Moses, disobedient priests, and the soldiers come to arrest Elijah (Ex 9:23f; Gen 19:24f; Num 16:35; Lev 10:1f; 2 Kings 1:10, 12). But it was especially in the prophetic predictions of the day of the Lord that the element of divine fire breaks forth most clearly. The Lord is to come in the fire of his wrath and execute judgment by fire (Is 66:15f; Dan 7:10; Zeph 1:18). That same fire would apparently purify and protect the chosen (Is 4:5f; Zech 2:9; 12:6; 13:9; Mal 3:2f) even as it consumes the wicked (Mal 4:1), burning rebels' bodies for ever (Is 66:24).

In the vast majority of texts the New Testament links the symbol of fire to the final day when Christ will return to judge the world in fire, destroying the ungodly and searing each man's work to see if it stands the test (1 Pet 4:12, 17; 2 Pet 3:7, 12; 2 Thess 1:8; 1 Cor 3:10-15; Jude 18-23). Sodom and Gomorrah stood as exemplary warnings to convert before the final and eternal fire (Lk 17:29; Jude 5-7). Fruitless branches and trees, chaff and weeds will all be thrown into the fire (Mt 3:10, 12; 13:40-42; Jn 15:6). John the Baptist clearly intended that fire when he contrasted his baptism in water with the coming one's baptism in the Holy Spirit and fire (Mt 3:11; Lk 3:16). When the eschatological fire did not burst out to consume the wicked, the imprisoned John sent his disciples to inquire whether Jesus was "the coming one" (Mt 11:3; Lk 7:19). Jesus responded, as we noted earlier, by pointing to his miracles and preaching, signs of the kingdom already present.

Jesus' eschatology involved a fulfilment which leaves time for human responses. So he restrained his disciples from calling down fire from heaven (Lk 9:54f). He had a fire to ignite and a baptism to undergo: "I came to cast fire upon the earth; and would that it were enkindled! I have a baptism to be baptized with; and how I am constrained until it is accomplished!" (Lk 12:49f). Just as Jesus, in John's gospel, could not pour out the Spirit until he had been "glorified", i.e., crucified and risen (7:39f), so only after Easter, at Pentecost, did the Apostles receive their "baptism with the Holy Spirit", when tongues of fire descended upon them, and, filled with the Holy Spirit, they spoke "in other tongues as the Spirit gave them utterance" (Acts 1:5; 2:3). Thus was fulfilled Joel's prophecy about the end time when the Spirit was to be poured out for prophecy amidst signs of fire (Acts 2:17-21). Anticipating that Spirit, Jesus' words explaining Scripture's fulfilment had already inflamed the hearts of the two disciples on the way to Emmaus (Lk 24:32). If the Spirit is the Spirit of love, poured into human hearts (Rom 5:5), it may not be too fanciful to see in Paul's use of Scripture, which recommends heaping coals upon an enemy's head through good works, an indication of love's conquest of evil (Rom 12:17-20). If the inspired author of the Letter to the Hebrews wrote, "Our God is a consuming fire" (12:29). that fire can easily be identified with the Love that is God (1 Jn 4:8, 16).

c. Damnation and election

The same fire that enlightens, guides, purifies and warms, also terrorizes and torments. Does not love do the same? Anyone who knows the guilt of sin recognizes the fear of confessing sin, an agony that can grow greater proportionately as the one injured is more innocent and shows himself ever more loving. Does not the tenacious craving to maintain oneself in the right involve a terrible hardening of the heart, a tendency to self-justification that becomes ever more habitually ingrained, so deep that it can escape our superficial consciousness unless an "accident" of grace bring it again to full awareness? The very goodness of God can harden our hearts. he effects that by being himself, self-giving Love. The texts in Scripture about God's hardening of Pharaoh's heart are balanced by other texts speaking of Pharaoh's hardening of his own heart (Ex 8:32; 9:34; cf. 10:16). With this we touch the central mystery of philosophy, the relation between God's omnipotence and human freedom; both poles of the unequal relation must be retained

135

in vital tension and neither must be reduced to a mere appendage of the other nor can both be resolved into some higher, rational synthesis.[21] If God is love, then he is responsible for man's punishment insofar as God's goodness has forced man to harden his heart and so driven man away from God's love. If such truths are valid apart from Christ, the overwhelming love of the crucified one must prove even more irresistible or ultimately drive the sinner, like Judas, to the utter despair of hell.

The initiative is always God's, for he is creator and redeemer. "he has mercy upon whomever he wills, and he hardens the heart of whomever he wills" (Rom 9:18). Conversion and salvation are always considered pure gifts of God beyond man's meriting (Rom 3:24; 5:15; 11:6; Apoc 21:6; 22:17) – love can never be earned. Yet Love demands a response of love from human freedom. So the indicative of God's salvific activity grounded the imperative addressed to the Christian and each was assured of being judged according to his works (Mt 16:27; 25:34-46; Rom 2:6-10; 1 Cor 3:10-15; 2 Cor 5:10; Apoc 14:13; 22:12). Here is the nub of the mystery: neither the infinite God nor the working of human freedom allows a reduction to a rational, much less, mechanical, scheme of explanation. As we saw before, the lover is drawn by the objective goodness and beauty of the beloved and attributes the "necessity" of his free response to the "irresistible" attraction of the beloved. Here human freedom corresponds with the omnipotence of God who calls men to himself through chosen signs in this finite world: the humanity of Christ, miracles, the Church, the Bible, sacraments, etc. But human freedom can resist that "irresistible", "necessary" appeal and attraction and prefer itself to God. That choice of evil as such cannot be attributed to God, for God is summoning the person to respond differently. When speaking of "predestination", the Apostle referred it only to the works of salvation, divine sonship through Christ and eternal glory (Rom 8:29f; 1 Cor 2:7; Eph 1:5, 11f). Luke, doubtless recalling the "necessity" of the passion, which he mentioned much more frequently than any other evangelist (9:22; 13:33; 17:25; 22:22, 37; 24:7, 26, 44-46), spoke also of the preordained accomplishment of God's plan of salvation in Christ's passion (Acts 4:28; 2:23).[22] Yet this "necessity", again, must not be conceived as a mechanical necessity. Rather the verb employed to denote "necessity" δεῖ is otherwise used in the gospel with an appeal to human freedom and, hence, is best understood as a "moral necessity" or a "should".[23] All in all, there is no mention of any "predestination" to hell or evil.

Moral evil cannot be attributed directly to God. If responsibility was apportioned to anyone besides man, the devil was often recognized as blinding, seducing, and possessing men (1 Thess 3:5; 1 Cor 7:5; 2 Cor 4:4; 11:14; Eph 2:2; 1 Tim 3:7; Jn 8:43-47; 1 Jn 3:7f; Mt 13:19; Mk 5:6-9; Lk 11:14-26; etc.). At most God only hardens men in their evil. So the angel of the Apocalypse apparently ordered persistence in sin, "Let the evildoer still do evil, and the filthy still be filthy, and the righteous still do right, and the holy still be holy" (22:11). St Paul, pondering the mystery of the Israelites who failed to obtain election, explained their failure by citing a combination of Isaiah 29:10 and Deuteronomy 29:4, "God gave them a spirit of stupor, eyes in order not to see, ears in order not to hear, until this very day" (Rom 11:8). This passage in its turn recalls other from Isaiah, verses, 6:9f, cited by our Lord when the disciples inquired about the meaning of the parables:

To you has been given the mystery of the kingdom of God. But to those outside everything is in parables in order that seeing they may see and not perceive, and hearing they may hear and not understand lest they convert and be forgiven (Mk 4:11f).

It would be strange indeed if Jesus preached in parables in order that his audience may not understand him. Rather

137

this passage can serve as the key of interpretation for the other passages. For recent studies have indicated that the parables were meant as challenging addresses, summoning the hearers to let themselves be taken up into the address, trust themselves to the narrator and understand the parable from within.[24] The disciples had eyes and ears to perceive and understand the signs of love which Jesus worked and preached because they had entrusted themselves to him, sharing his life in following him; but the outsiders who held back were prevented from understanding due to their lack of love. Only a lover rightly knows love. Every finite action, even the giving of one's life, can be wrongly motivated as well as wrongly interpreted (cf. 1 Cor 13:1-3; Jn 11:49-53). Those who reject Jesus' claim and harden their hearts against the testimony of his pierced heart must consider his sacrifice madness, but for those who accept him the cross is the wisdom and the power of God. That God should love them so much! The Jews unfortunately had closed their hearts to Jesus' signs of love, his life given for them, and the spirit of stupor was sent upon them, a stupor in which they persisted.

This interpretation of God's hardening of human hearts, which does not deny human freedom, finds confirmation in John 12:36-43, a passage about the unbelief of the Jews and Jesus' self-concealment from them. After citing Isaiah 53:1 from the final Servant Song, John appealed to Isaiah 6:10 about God "blinding their eyes and hardening their hearts" lest they see, understand and turn to be healed. The evangelist then attributed Isaiah's word to the fact that he had seen and spoken of God's glory, an apparent reference to the great, initial vision that commissioned the prophet's preaching (Is 6:1-9). Jesus had revealed the eternal glory received from his Father as God's only-begotten Son, full of grace and truth, in order to call men to faith (1:14; 2:11; 5:44; 11:4, 40; 17:5, 22, 24). But before him the Jews drew back. For John, the evangelist of divine love, the reason was indisputable: despite their "belief" in Jesus, many, even among the rulers, feared to confess it publicly, for "they preferred the glory of men much more than the glory of God." Without doubt human freedom is responsible for its rejection of Christ and its concomitant hardening of heart. The same glory of God that empowered Isaiah's prophetic word and rouses Christian faith causes hardening of heart. God's omnipotence does not obliterate human freedom nor does human freedom limit the power of God's love, which thoroughly penetrates men for their salvation or damnation. That central mystery pervades the New Testament.

God has bestowed the ultimate sign of his love in Jesus' death and resurrection, and on the basis of that love Paul, in the face of the Jews' hardhearted rejection of his Lord, could still hope in God's mercy for their salvation (Rom 11:25-32). Indeed, once the fullness of the Gentiles had entered upon salvation, Paul was sure, in view of God's unrepentant election and his love for their forefathers, "All Israel will be saved" (Rom 11:26). That was a great hope, but it was grounded in a greater mystery of love and mercy. So, in the peroration,[25] citing a text from the Book of Job, he could entrust himself totally to divine providence:[26]

> O the depths of the riches and wisdom and knowledge of God! How unsearchable are his judgments and how inscrutable his ways! "For who has known the mind of the Lord, or who has been his counsellor?" "Or who has given a gift to him that he might be repaid?" For from him and through him and to him are all things. To him be glory for ever. Amen.
> (Rom 11:33-36; cf. 1 Cor 2:16; Eph 3:14-21)

Where Job was reduced to silence, Paul, even while humbling himself, could rise to a joyful doxology. For he was sure, in ways unimaginable to Job, that behind all of history, sated with its horrid sin and gruesome death, there ruled the boundless love of God. Even sinners, despite

139

themselves, are compelled to acknowledge God's infinite love and so render him glory.

In acknowledging the divine mystery of love, Paul certainly humbled himself before God. But he was not forced to "despise himself". God raises the lowly even while abasing the proud and mighty of this world (Lk 1:51f), and Paul knew in his humility the elevation to the third heaven and Paradise (2 Cor 12:1-10). For he knew God's love in Christ, the new Adam and the new creation. Before Ivan Karamazov protested against the construction of a blissful world order on the sufferings of any innocent creature, Paul recognized in joy that for the new creation it was not a creature who was forced to undergo torments but God who took the crucifixion upon himself freely, out of love for sinful men. Confronting the fact of the superabundant immensity of God's love no creature is justified in insisting upon his own meager notion of retributive justice, a mere tit-for-tat measure elaborated by his rational, three-dimensional mind.[27] As philosophers recognize today, the human mind can construct no closed and consistent explanation of reality. And if reality always exceeds the mind's grasp, it is mental suicide to insist on remaining within the limited bounds of finite reason.

We had previously seen in our study of corporate personality that to demand justice only for oneself in isolation from everyone else, apart from the sins of one's forefathers, involved a rejection of solidarity and of love that could only augment the evil of the world. It is the fate of a finite creature that he cannot and should not sunder himself from humanity. he can never reason himself out of the conditions of finitude and the heart of anyone really trying to do so would inevitably shrivel up. Yet if the bitterness of injustice still festered in human hearts for having to suffer the penalties of Adam and Eve's sin, the love of God revealed and mediated to men by their fellows, starting with "the man Christ Jesus" (1 Tim 2:4), the first-born from the dead of many brethren (Rom 8:29; Col 1:18; Apoc 1:5; Acts 26:23), leaves no place for the petty reckoning of mean accounts. God certainly "closed all under disobedience", or "sin", as St Paul wrote, but only "in order that he might have mercy on all" (Rom 11:32; Gal 3:22). God's predestination intends all men's salvation and it will be accomplished if only men let go of themselves, their self-justifying claims, and their limited perspectives to fall trustingly into the hands of the Father of our Lord Jesus Christ.

Only from the perspective of God's all-surpassing love revealed in Christ can man finally acknowledge that love is the meaning of reality (cf. Jn 3:16; Rom 5:6-11). Only there the Christian receives the power to recognize that he too is bound in the solidarity of love with Adam intended by God from the creation of the world. Previously, recognition of solidarity with Adam involved him in damnation, and against that judgment his whole being rebelled. He preferred his self-justifying individuality to any binding relations with others, even if that meant refusing love, which is the essence of sin. Thus he had been caught in a trap: acknowledge solidarity with Adam and share his damnation or reject that solidarity and, by so refusing love and repeating Adam's sin, merit damnation (Rom 5:12-21; 3:23). For hopeless man – "damned, if he did, and damned, if he didn't – Christ's love was liberating and vivifying (cf. 1 Cor 15:20-22; Phil 3:8-11). "It is not the man who commends himself who is accepted but the man whom the Lord commends" (2 Cor 10:18). The immensity of Christ's love justified the sinner. In that love, all fear of hell, the eternal privation of God, was definitively extinguished. God stood revealed not as a baneful judge applying a merciless rule of inflexible justice, but as a merciful Father willing to share his infinite life of love with sinful men through the pierced heart of his Son (cf. 1 Thess 5:9f; Gal 4:4-8; Rom 8:14-17, 28-39; Eph 1:3-14; 2:4-10). It is only in accepting the demands of love, in acknowledging solidarity in sin with Adam, that the fullness of the divine mystery of love is bestowed upon man's sinful heart, and only the sinner so justified knows and praises the fullness of God's love (cf. Rom 11:30-36). All men are therefore called to confess their guilt in the sin of the human race, a sin that finally crucified God's only Son; only by confessing that sin of deicide can men receive the divine life which Christ poured out for them on the cross. For, if men's sin nailed Christ to the cross, he also went freely to that death to show his love even for his enemies, all those who were murdering him (cf. Rom 5:6-8; 4:25). The confession of such a horrendous sin involves the pains of hell, the being crucified with Christ, and the confession of God crucified out of love for man entails boundless joy (cf. 2 Cor 5:13-15, 20f). Both are possible only because God in grace shared his life with men (cf. Col 2:13f).

Difficult Old Testament texts revisited

Before concluding this section, it is now possible to turn back to those Old Testament texts attributing evil to God and to attempt from the perspective of divine love, with a bit of speculative imagination, to understand their intent. Most of the "evils" were physical or at least referred to sufferings for sins. Yet sometimes the sending of evil spirits or an incitation to evil was also predicated of God. These latter texts caused the real difficulty. Insofar as sin destroyed the original unity of men among themselves and with God, the world could not longer function simply as a symbol revealing God. Touched by evil, the world became at best an ambiguous place, and the possibilities of suffering, which any finite world of sentient as well as free creatures necessarily entails, became felt threats to man's self-subsistence and comfort instead of vivifying challenges and invitations to help others.[28] Death, which otherwise might have been conceived as a painless transition to a greater proximity to God, was warped into a special menace, and on account of their selfishness men were ever more tempted to close in upon themselves. Insofar as they yielded to that egocentric movement, God's hardening of hearts was "effective". Since this closing further skewed men's perspective, any threat to their self-sufficiency was to be absolutely resisted; and these threats would multiply in proportion to men's lack of self-assurance. Insofar as God's very goodness produced the hardening of heart that led to such malformed interpretations of reality, these baneful results of human bias may be indirectly attributed to God. "Bad statutes and ordinances" resulted from Israel's turning from God to the worship of idols and from their consequent blindness about the significance of the love of the God who was to be worshipped. "Evil spirits" found entry into men's hearts and minds because of their jealousies and desires for power – and this need not have been willed explicitly by men in each case, for original sin affects all men and concupiscence's power can grow in the individual in proportion to a society's decay. The same may be said about "inciting" David to hold a census. Even the strange story of God seeking to kill Moses (Ex 4:24-26) depends upon a fear of death seen as a threat.

Be that as it may, these stories serve as forerunners to the effecting of God's plan of salvation through the unjust death of his only Son. God willed that death on the cross even though in itself it entailed objectively a supreme injustice committed by men (cf. Acts 4:24-28). In Luke's writings it is admittedly attributed to ignorance, which would mitigate the gravity of the fault (Acts 3:17; Lk 23:34). But John left no doubt that sin was involved (19:11). Here again God, recognizing the hardness of men's hearts, gave them over to themselves (cf. Ps 81:12); indeed, the very revelation of his meekness in Christ may have excited their rage and increased their blindness. The greatness of the goodness revealed makes clearer the horror and depth of the sin pertinaciously resisting it. If God were to conquer sin in its entirety, it would have to swell up against him in its arrogant usurpation of power, and that arrogance would bring its downfall as it overstepped itself in trying to destroy God. So Love "humbled" and "emptied" himself in servitude. The powers of this world could not understand according to their measures how victory could be won through such apparent helplessness. There is a real "necessity" in sin's rejection of God, and if sin is ultimately incorporated in a person, Satan, the battle with all the means at his command was inevitable. God called it forth by his supreme gesture of love in sending his Son. Yet only in the Son's rejection was the full grandeur and goodness of God's love revealed to men. Therefore man, impeded by ignorance of the ultimate implications of the cosmic battle between God and Satan, contributed to Christ's crucifixion but only in order that, in God's plan, once Christ was risen, man might convert, confessing his sin, and receive God's everlasting life of love. God then can be said to have "done evil", to have "willed the death of his Son at men's hands", but only indirectly as a result of his revealed goodness and only in order that men's co-operation with Satan might be broken through seeing the horrendous consequences of their sin in the death of the God-man and the boundless love of the God who let himself be harried to death out of love for sinful man. he did not wish men's sin as such, only their redemption.

Résumé

The cross of Christ bears witness to a double truth: the sinfulness of all men, whose sins nailed the innocent Son of God onto the cross of death, and the self-sacrificial love of God, who gave all, his very life, freely for sinners. If sin justly arouses God's wrath, God also took the just effects of wrath upon himself in sending his only Son to the utter abandonment of the cross. Because God had to go so far, the distance between Father and Son could only be bridged by an infinite love in the Spirit.[29] Therefore there is always hope for every sinner; no matter how high his sins are heaped, he can always find a place for himself in his Saviour's heart, opened to men out of love on the cross. Thus, as long as death has not intervened and God has not yet rung down the curtain to close our historical play, the Christian, knowing God's will to save all men through the man Christ Jesus, can always hope and work for the conversion of all, himself included. How man's ultimate destiny is achieved remains a mystery hidden in the depths of God. When no one can be sure of his own fate (cf. 1 Cor 4:1-4), it is best to entrust oneself and all others to God's infinite love. Then looking on the cross, the eschatological sign of human sin and divine love, Christians can only heed the command of the Apostle: "Work out your salvation in fear and trembling, for it is God who is working in you both the willing and the working for the sake of his good pleasure" (Phil 2:12f).

NOTES

1. As mentioned in our introduction there is apparently very little written explicitly about the problem of suffering *per se* in the New Testament. Some of the books mentioned in the previous chapter, however, have sections dealing with the New Testament: E. Sutcliffe, S.J., *Providence and Suffering in the Old and New Testaments* (London: T. Nelson and Sons, 1955), pp. 127-150; J. Schmidt, "Leiden: Neues Testament", in *Bibeltheologisches Wörterbuch*, ed. J. Bauer, 2nd ed. (Graz: Styria, 1962), I, 760-765; J. Scharbert, "Leid", *Handbuch theologischer Grundbegriffe*, ed. H. Fries, II (München: Kösel, 1963), 41-44; F. Petit, *Il Problema del Male*, trans. P. Graziani (Catania: Paoline, 1959), pp. 52-68; A. Bertrangs, *Il Dolore nella Bibbia*, 2nd ed., trans. A. Sidoti (Bari: Paoline, 1967), pp. 59-87.

2. Cf H. Schlier, *Mächte und Gewalten im Neuen Testament* (Freiburg: Herder, 1958), esp. pp. 50-63.

3. For a more complete development of the presuppositions and argument of the following section cf. J. McDermott, S.J., "Jesus and the Kingdom of God in the Synoptics, Paul, and John", in *Eglise et Théologie* 19 (1988), 69-91, which in turn summarizes various other articles of the author.

4. Origen, *Matthäuserkläung*, xiv, 7, in *Origenes Werke*, X, ed. E. Klostermann (Leipzig: Heinrich, 1935), p. 289, on Matthew 18:23.

5. The expression "*sub contrario*" [under a contrary aspect] was frequently used by Luther to indicate that God revealed himself in a way that contradicted sinful man's expectation of God. Where man expected God to be omnipotent, on the cross he was weak; where glorious, despised; where victorious, defeated; etc. In this Luther was correct. he went too far, however, in opposing God's word to human reason and denying the ability of the latter to know God apart from Christian revelation. Actually love joins opposites, the highest with the lowest, and it would have been possible for man to know God as love before sin entered the world. The same structure of reason, its same capacity to know love and the God of love, remains after the fall; otherwise man could not recognize the revelation of God for who he is, when God reveals himself (This does not, however, say that in the concrete order of sin man has a sure knowledge of God apart from revelation. Love can only be recognized by love, and love is God's gift.)

6. K. Stock, S.J., "'Gesù è il Cristo, il Figlio di Dio', nel vangelo di Marco", *Rassegna di Teologia* 17 (1976), 242-253.

7. Even the glory of the transfiguration should not have misled the disciples, for the scene culminated in the voice from heaven which commanded, "Hear him" (9:7). Since Jesus had said nothing to the disciples during the event the command clearly referred to the preceding words of Jesus about the necessity of carrying one's cross, denying oneself and confessing him (8:34-38); even the first words of Jesus after the transfiguration refer to the rejection as well as the resurrection of the Son of Man (9:9-12). The transfiguration clearly cannot be isolated from the cross.

8. Cf J. McDermott, S.J., "Jesus and the Son of God Title", in *Gregorianum* 62 (1981), 311-315, for a discussion of the debate and a solution.

9. Cf the article by C.H. Giblin, S.J., "'The Things of God' in the Question Concerning Tribute to Caesar (Lk 20:25; Mk 12:17; Mt 22:21)", in *Catholic Biblical Quarterly* 33 (1971), 510-527.

10. The term "prevenient" is used especially in treatises on grace to indicate that God's grace precedes any meritorious action on our part. All the initiative in the realm of grace is God's; we human beings just respond to the offer of his grace. Therefore we cannot boast of our good works nor make any demands upon God. In our text the term is used analogously to indicate that our response as Christians is possible only because of Christ's incarnation. Unless he had come, we could not believe in him and love him. The divine initiative began in the incarnation, Jesus' conception in the Virgin Mary, and manifested itself ever more convincingly through Jesus' life, death and resurrection. The fact, or indicative, of Jesus' love then moves our hearts, as we are called imperatively to respond to that fact of supreme love.

11. For the metaphysics underlying many of these interpretations of St Paul cf. J. McDermott, S.J., "A New Approach to God's Existence," *The Thomist* 44 (1980), 219-250.

146

12. J. Jeremias, "πολλοί", in *Theologisches Wörterbuch zum Neuen Testament*, ed. G. Kittel, VI (Stuttgart: Kohlhammer, 1959), 536, 540-545.

13. For the basis of this understanding of *koinonia* cf. J. McDermott, S.J., "The Biblical Doctrine of KOINONIA", in *Biblische Zeitschrift* 19 (1975), 64-77, 219-233. The whole notion of a supra-individual unity of free persons can sometimes present imaginative difficulties for modern individualists. As helps to overcome these difficulties cf. E. Mersch, S.J., *The Theology of the Mystical Body*, trans. C. Vollert (St Louis: Herder, 1951), esp. pp. 96-128, 271-322; H.U. von Balthasar, *Theodramatik: III. Die Handlung* (Einsiedeln: Johannes, 1980), pp. 379-395.

14. *Praeteritio* is a classical rhetorical device whereby the orator allegedly passes over a point or issue even while mentioning it. A crass example: "I do not wish to offend the fine sensibilities of the jury by mentioning the cruel torments to which the accused submitted his victims. It is already too well known how he sadistically plucked out their fingernails, etc."

15. The Septuagint (Greek: seventy) refers to the translation of the Hebrew Bible into Greek which, according to legend, was accomplished by seventy or seventy-two rabbinical scholars in the third century BC, at the request of Ptolemy II Philadelphus, at Alexandria in Egypt. More probably the Septuagint translation was assembled over centuries, from the third BC until the second century AD. It also includes Greek texts not found in the Hebrew Bible. These texts are recognized by the Church as canonical (what the Protestants call "Apocrypha"). Although New Testament authors often cite it as Scripture and many Church Fathers considered it inspired, many modern exegetes deny the Septuagint's inspiration: Protestant exegetes deny the entire translation, Catholics only those writings found also in the hebrew original. Although the Church has declared to be inspired, some books found only in the Greek Septuagint (DS 1334f, 1501-1504, 30067, 3029), the magisterium has never pronounced authoritatively upon the question whether the Hebrew or Greek version of the others is to be considered the authentically inspired writing. Even if the Septuagint should not be inspired, it serves as an early, excellent, interpretative commentary upon the meaning of the Hebrew original.

16. The shift in meaning can be seen clearly in the texts cited in the debate between S. Lyonnet, S.J., "Le sens de πειράζειν en Sap 2, 24 et la doctrine du péché originel", in *Biblica* 39 (1958), 27-36, and A. Dubarle, O.P., "La Tentation diabolique dans le Livre de la Sagesse (2, 24)", in *Mélanges Eugène Tisserant*, I (1964), 187-195.

17. Bertrangs, pp. 71-84; D. Stanley, S.J., "The Theme of the Servant of Yahweh in Primitive Christian Soteriology and its Transposition by St Paul", *Catholic Biblical Quarterly* 16 (1954), 385-425.

18. McDermott, "Biblical Doctrine," 75-77, 221f. In an unpublished doctoral thesis approved at the Gregorian University, Rome in 1974, L. Ramaroson, S.J., *La Théologie de l'église en Ep 1, 15/20*, wrote on p. 113: "It is proper to recall here that the ancients, whether of the East or of the West, did not possess exactly the same notion of plenitude as modern man. For them

'plenitude' frequently meant 'overflowing'. For the people of the Bible, flowers are full when they overflow (Jos 3:15; 1 Chron 12:15 or 16; Sir 24:25f), and the same applies to the vat (Joel 3:13b: [LXX]); the fingers of the beloved are full of myrrh when they drip with it (Song 5:5); the clouds are filled with water when they pour it upon the earth (Eccles 11:3); the measure of wheat is full only when it falls in small, peaked avalanches from the upper rims of the vessel (Lk 6:38). For Homer and Hesiod the filled river is the one which leaves its bed and carries away everything along its passage (*The Iliad* XI, 492; *The Odyssey* XIX, 207; *Aspis* 477f; cf. 314)." In a footnote to this passage he commented: "Cf also Herodianus (2nd century AD): 8, 7, 1. The examples which we have offered contain πληρόω - πλήρη, except for Homer and Hesiod who use πλήθω. The 'full measure' of Luke 6:38 can still be found today in some 'bazaars' of Asia and Africa: it is the buyer who himself often measures the grain which he is buying."

Insofar as in Christ, the head of the body, the "plentitude" of the divinity dwells bodily (Col 1:19; 2:9) and all have come to fullness of life in him by being buried with him (2:12), his fullness does not deny their fullness even through a type of death. As his death, which brought life, overflowed on Christians in baptism, so his sufferings can overflow on them also for the upbuilding of the Church. For the body really grows in fullness precisely because it is joined to the head, who is the fullness (2:19). If the members of the body can grow to a fullness of knowledge of God's will and of Christ (1:9; 2:2), there seems to be no reason why his fullness, or sufficiency, of suffering, as his fullness of knowledge, cannot overflow onto believers. Cf also von Balthasar, esp. pp. 381-386. The Infinite and the finite cannot be played off against each other.

19. There are admittedly many different interpretations of Hinduism and Buddhism. Some Hindu teachings, as in the worship of Siva or in the *bhakti* cult, allow for a union of love with a personal god. The earlier interpretations certainly put much more stress on Yoga and meditation as means either of achieving a union of *Brahman* and *Atman* (the all and the soul, or self) that resulted in the loss of personal consciousness or its expansion to the infinite or in isolating the individual so as to obtain perfect self-control and avoid disturbances from without. Cf R. Zaehner, *Hinduism* (London: Oxford University, 1966), esp. pp. 48-56, 67-79. Buddha and Hinayana Buddhism stress asceticism and contemplation to overcome desire, the source of pain. Basic is the doctrine of the *anatta*, the denial of a permanent soul-self, and *nirvana* accordingly is interpreted as an abolition of consciousness or is merely defined negatively. Cf K. Ch'en, *Buddhism: the Light of Asia* (New York: Barron, 1968), pp. 33-60. The more popular Mahayana Buddhism considers Buddha an eternal being. Even though the cult of Buddha Amitabha allows for a blissful paradise for the devout, *nirvana* consists in the insight into the undifferentiated emptiness of the sole absolute truth, in which all things are the same; so the individual eradicates from his mind the concept of his own individuality, merges with the substanceless absolute and becomes the eternal buddha-nature. Cf Ch'en, pp. 61-80.

20. This seems to be the tendency among some recent Catholic authors who see death as the final, decisive opportunity of choice for men when they are most in possession of themselves and aware of their relation to the centre of reality. In this direction go such works as L. Boros, *Mysterium Mortis*, 4th ed. (Olten: Walter, 1964), throughout, but cf. esp. pp. 122-138, where death itself frees man from original sin – this seems to reverse the biblical teaching about death as the consequence of original sin. Cf also P. Schoonenberg, S.J., *Man and Sin*, trans. J. Donceel (Notre Dame: U. of Notre Dame, 1965), pp. 30-40, in which the author saw no definitive sin before death when man "chooses eternity itself for better or for worse" (32), "chooses his eternal attitude, thus definitively and irrevocably deciding his action" (34), and so "reaches a decision about God" (35). Then the author denied that "God punishes sin" in favour of his view that "sin punishes itself". For a criticism of these views cf. B. Schüller, S.J., "Todsünde – Sünde zum Tod? Bedenken zur Theorie der Endentscheidung", in *Theologie und Philosophie* 42 (1967), 321-340; J. McDermott, S.J., "Metaphysical Conundrums at the Root of Moral Disagreement", in *Gregorianum* 71 (1990), 718-734.

21. In our "A New Approach" we do not consider this "mystery" as a nebulous area alongside the area of clear, philosophical precision; rather all the philosophical conundrums are resolved into this central mystery of divine omnipotence and human freedom in the sense that philosophy, human thought, becomes meaningless unless these two fundamental poles of created reality are affirmed.

22. Acts 4:28 does not imply that God made Pilate, Herod, Israel, and the Gentiles do an evil thing, but that he accomplished his plan through their "empty things" (4:25). What the Jews did, they did in ignorance (3:17; Lk 23:34), and thereby even the "good" of Herod's and Pilate's reconciliation was accomplished (Lk 23:12). The verb ὁρίζειν, usually meaning "to divide as boundary, bound, mark out, limit, appoint, determine, or define," seems sometimes to bear the notion of "predestination" (Lk 22:22; Acts 2:23; 10:42; 17:26, 31; Rom 1:4), but always in reference to Christ and his role.

23. Luke 21:9 uses δεῖ of the events preceding the end of the world. It is the sole exception to the usage noted. Modern physics has rejected the notion of absolute, mechanical necessity, seeing in past systems just models more or less successful in approximating and controlling reality. As we indicated in our article, "A New Approach", the most valid understanding of necessity does not exclude, but necessarily incorporates human freedom.

24. Cf McDermott, "Jesus and the Kingdom of God", 80-82; E. Jüngel, Paulus und Jesus (Tübingen: Mohr [Siebeck], 1962), pp. 139-174; E. Schweizer, "Jesus Christus", in *Theologische Realenzyklopädie*, ed. G. Müller, XVI (Berlin: de Gruyter, 1987), 715f.

25. The "peroration" of a speech is its final part, usually summing up an argument and applying it to the conclusion desired. Though Paul's letter continues, this "peroration" concludes a major section of the epistle.

26. It was this confidence in God's mercy that could let Paul feel and speak of his desire to be anathema from God if only his fellow Israelites might be saved (Rom 9:1-3). But just as Christ's sense of abandonment on the cross was undergirded by the invincible surety of his Father's love, Paul also knew that he, like Christ, could feel the pains of abandoned love for those who persisted in their rejection of love without, however, being rejected by the Father. So Romans 9:1-3, the beginning of Paul's consideration of the mystery of Israel's rejection, has to be read together with the very end of that same reflection, a pure paean of praise to God's love that shall save Israel. Paul's true Christian vision of God's revelation *sub contrario*, of the paradox of love that is highest when it most lowers itself, rules in service and conquers sin by apparently losing, supported the apparently "exaggerated" expressions of his love for his fellow Jews. For that divine love penetrated him.

27. Such were the conditions laid down by Ivan Karamazov in F. Dostoevsky, *The Brothers Karamazov*, trans. A. MacAndrew (Toronto: Bantam, 1980), pp. 282f, 294f his brother Alyosha already anticipated the answer of God who "gave his innocent blood for everyone's sins" (p. 296; 284). The whole novel, Dostoevsky's masterpiece, is an answer to the complaints of rationalistic atheists like Ivan.

  Regarding the relation of God's justice to human justice, the former clearly surpasses the latter without destroying it. For the norm of human justice is an approximation of the reality of God's justice, which is one with his love. Cf McDermott, "New Approach", 238-242. A strict adherence to human justice *alone* must fail. At its best it results in self-justifying Pharisaism; at its worst it can release torrents of blood in never-ending cycles of retribution. Aeschylus' *Oresteia* trenchantly indicted the "necessary" chain of the human vindications of justice that repeatedly propelled men to crime and madness. Only a divine intervention in establishing the Court of the Areopagus was able to sever the chain of vengeance and bring peace to human hearts. In his own way the great Athenian dramatist, who acknowledged both fate and freedom, prepared the way for Christ's salvation.

28. For a further speculative grounding and development of these themes cf. our articles referred to in n. 55 of the first chapter.

29. Cf H.U. von Balthasar, "Mysterium Paschale", in *Mysterium Salutis*, ed. J. Feiner u. M. Löhrer, III/2 (Einsiedeln: Benziger, 1969), 133-319, esp. 182-18, 193-202, 216-230, 237-249, 267-278.

Conclusion

In Jesus Christ all the explanations of suffering offered in the Old Testament are recapitulated. As well as being preserved, God's justice is given as a gift to man in Jesus' self-sacrifice. Though the ultimate reward for the faithful comes in the future, the *eschaton* is already breaking into the present to chastise, admonish and purify. For Christians share already now in Christ's eternal life by grace. This sharing, or *koinonia*, though first received in accord with God's sovereign initiative, does not remain a passive given; rather it actualizes human freedom so that the believer in return contributes to the spiritual and material well-being of Christ's Body, the Church. Even his sufferings, joined to Christ's, work for the salvation of others in "corporate personality". Thus he is challenged to bear out of love the sins of others and offer his sufferings with Christ for the increase of love in the world. For the Christian has met God, directly present in Christ, and that encounter of love has opened to him the unfathomable mystery of divine providence. God has taken evil upon himself for men's good, suffering the extreme of alienation on the cross, in order that henceforth all men might live no longer for themselves but for Christ, who died and rose for them (2 Cor. 5:15). That is the ultimate mystery of love, God's self-humiliation in the flesh, before which all, like Job, must repent in humility, surrendering all attempts at self-justification. For it reveals the innocent heart of God in his weakness for men such that this weakness may be paradoxically manifested as God's strength conquering sin and death.

The Christian mystery of self-sacrificial love transmutes,

like the fabled elixir of the alchemists, the very meaning of suffering, from dross metal into precious gold tested by fire. What had been perceived as the most negative and oppressive element of human existence, something that was to be fled or overcome by prayer, ascetical practices or philosophical wisdom, now can be accepted with patience and even joy. Though the figure of this world is not ultimate in its passing away, its meaning is preserved, for here love is sown and the lover must die to self in order to rise to eternal life. Here love is lived and witnessed as Christians strive to help their fellows in building up the Body of Christ, and on such a foundation of love true justice is established in mutual service. Justification is primarily God's gift, but, once accepted, it inaugurates new relations among men. It has to go beyond retributive justice; the measure "eye for eye, tooth for tooth" no longer suffices. Love of enemies is demanded and, with trust in God's justice, vengeance is forsworn, forgiveness is demanded without measure in response to God's limitless willingness to forgive, and even persecutors are blessed so that evil may be conquered by good (Mt 5:38-48; Rom 12:14-21; Lk 17:3f; Mt 18:21-35). Following Christ's example Christians, like Stephen, should beseech pardon for their murderers (Acts 7:60); who knows but that another Saul of Tarsus might be among them?

Men have to experience love in this world in order to affirm a meaning transcending this world – such is the analogy of love. The Son of God came to give us the example of pure love and establish the community which henceforth was to function as the sacrament of his love. Before the testimony of this sacrament the rebellious, atheistic heart of man is faced with a choice. On the one hand, he can choose to keep his gaze fixed upon himself, complaining of injustice, incapable of finding a rational answer to the sufferings of the individual. For the individual as such, as the Scholastics said so well, is ineffable, rationally unintelligible. Suffering only compounds the conundrum. If suffering is only an evil, and if an evil is what should not be, no cause for suffering can be discovered. For a cause implies a necessity: the effect proceeds necessarily from the cause; otherwise the alleged "cause" would be only an occasion or a condition for an event's occurrence. There must be an inherent connection between effect and cause such that the cause can be recognized in its effect and the cause necessarily produces its effect. Now, if suffering, precisely as an evil, is "caused", it must somehow be necessary. But in such a case the universe would be inherently immoral; for evil must then be attributed to God, the first cause, or, if such a God does not exist, to a universe running according to mechanistic laws, which annul human freedom. Hence the distinction between "is" and "should" has become unintelligible, and all thought ends in frustration.

On the other hand, he can choose to lift up his eyes to the hills, from which the psalmist awaited help (Ps 121:1). There on the most prominent of hills, against a darkening sky, the heart of God is revealed in the pierced heart of Christ. The hard-hearted "Why me?" in the complaint of suffering is transformed into the cry of wonder "Why me?" as the individual recognizes that he is loved with an unsurpassable, inexplicable love. The innocent Son of God has gone his way into alienation in order that we may no longer be isolated and abandoned but joined to him and to others in his love. The testing of Abraham has here been turned topsy-turvy for the testing of the Christian. The Church Fathers rightly saw in Isaac's sacrifice the prefiguration of Christ's sacrifice. At the beginning of the typological exegesis Origen wrote, "Observe God struggling with men in magnificent generosity: to God Abraham offered a mortal son who was not to die; for the sake of men God handed over to death an immortal Son."[1] Ultimately the loving obedience demanded of Abraham, who was called to sacrifice his all, his only son, is grounded in the limitless love of the eternal Father who is ready to sacrifice his all, his only Son, in order that all men may be blessed with Abraham in the Son, becoming sons and heirs of the promise (Gal 3:6-18, 25-4:7; Rom 4:16-25). The final test of man then consists in his willingness to believe in a love so divine and so humble that God sacrificed himself for his sinful creatures. What appears at first an imposition, a foreign domination, because it must penetrate the inured callousness of our selfish hearts from without, reveals itself, once accepted, as God's vivifying, healing and elevating love. What we can offer to him, ourselves, is given back to us as a gift, and with ourselves the whole world; even more, God gives us himself. Such is God's measure of generosity. The overwhelming beauty of that love must rend the sinful, self-justifying human heart, opening it up to the revelation of God's heart. For those believers loving Jesus Christ's heart innocent suffering then ceases to be the basis of the complaint against God's justice and becomes instead the surest proof of God's justifying love:

If God is for us, who is against us? he who did not spare his own Son but gave him up for us all, will he not also give us all things with him? Who shall bring any charge against God's elect? It is God who justifies; who is to condemn? Is it Christ Jesus, who died, yes, who was raised from the dead, who is at the right hand of God, who indeed intercedes for us? Who shall separate us from the love of Christ? Shall tribulation, or distress, or persecution, or famine, or nakedness, or peril, or sword? As it is written, "For thy sake we are being killed all the day long; we are regarded as sheep to be slaughtered." No, in all these things we are more than conquerors through him who loved us. For I am sure that neither death, nor life, nor angels, nor principalities, nor things present, nor things to come, nor powers, nor height, nor depth, nor anything else in all creation, will be able to separate us from the love of God in Christ Jesus our Lord (Rom 8:31-39).

NOTE

1. Origen, *In Genesim Homilia*, viii, 8, in *Origenes Werke*, VI, ed. W. Baehrens (Leipzig: Hinrichs, 1920), p. 84. In his critique of the typological exegesis for destroying revelation's historicity and remaining on a superficial level G. Reventlow, *Opfere deinen Sohn* (Neukirchen-Vluyn: Neukirchner, 1968), p. 82, unfortunately missed the deeper comparison of the divine love that called for Abraham's sacrifice. The prevenient grace moving Abraham to sacrificial love was finally revealed in its fullness on the cross, in the eternal Father's love for man. Cf D. Lerch, *Isaaks Opferung Christlich gedeutet* (Tübingen: Vandenhoeck & Ruprecht, 1950), pp. 27-115, for the patristic tradition on Genesis 22. Though Reventlow cited Lerch's work, he did not share Lerch's appreciation of the "richness" (115) of the typological interpretation of Genesis 22. Be it remarked in passing that St Paul's exegesis of the Old Testament was much closer to the method of the Fathers than to that of modern scholarship – and St Paul was inspired. Moreover, many modern interpretations of Scripture, especially in the wake of Bultmann, apparently eviscerate God's word of its historical accuracy and meaning. The exegesis of the Fathers has much to recommend it.

THE DANCE OF THE MERRYMAKERS

A way to explore the Scriptures
with confidence

by Joseph O'Hanlon

Like the poor, the Scriptures are always with us.
Indeed, to judge by the number of new translations
that appeared recently, they are with us much more
than they used to be. Yet there is unease about. How
can we listen to so many words, understand them,
make them live in the turmoil of our lives? We declare,
"This is the word of the Lord." But is it? Most people
find the Bible strange, even boring.

The Dance of the Merrymakers seeks to provide a
way through the Bible which makes sense. It is not a
book about the Scriptures. Rather, the reader is taken
on a journey through the text, is provided with
necessary information along the way and invited to
turn study into prayer. What is on offer is a method
which enables the reader to tackle most, if not all, of
the books which make up the library of Scripture. This
is the ideal book for Bible Study groups that are unsure
of themselves and need to find confidence to explore
boldly the word of the Lord. It will be welcomed by all
who care passionately that good scholarship should
find its way from the desk to the pew.

272 pages   ISBN 085439 331 5   £7.50

LIKE THE DEER THAT YEARNS

Salvatore Panimolle (ed.)

This book is about *lectio divina*. It is not easy to give a literal translation of the term which has its roots in the Benedictine monastic tradition and spirituality. Literally it means the reading of the Sacred Scriptures; the particularity of which is in the attitudes, goals of the reader and the manner in which it is done – prayerful and listening attitudes. The purpose is not to engage in scholarly pursuits.

The *lectio divina* has a vital and existential purpose – it seeks to nourish faith, to aid the deepening of a personal relationship with God. The inner disposition with which one engages in the *lectio divina* is the heart's thirst to drink from the living water of the Word, to satisfy the vital need for happiness and salvation. Thus the term *lectio divina* means a religious of dutiful listening to Scripture that leads to personal reflection, prayer and contemplation.

In *Like the deer that yearns* a team of well-known masters of spirituality initiate and guide to the listening to Scriptures through this age-old method those who do not live in monasteries and yet would like to "be graced" by intimate contact with the Word of God.

128 pages   ISBN 085439 319 6   £5.95

SWISS RAILWAYS

LOCOMOTIVES, MULTIPLE UNITS & TRAMS

FOURTH EDITION

The complete guide to all Locomotives, Multiple Units and Trams of the railways of Switzerland

David Haydock

Published by Platform 5 Publishing Ltd.,
52 Broadfield Road, Sheffield, S8 0XJ, England.

Printed in England by The Lavenham Press, Lavenham, Suffolk.

ISBN 978 1 909431 23 2

Above: Sursee–Triengen 0-6-0T no. 5 (SBB 8479) heads a special on the Sursee–Triengen line on 22 July 2012. **Andrew Thompson**

Front cover: MGB Deh 4/4 24 "TÄSCH" passes Oberalppass whilst working train 835 12.14 Disentis–Andermatt on 2 February 2016. **Laurence Sly**

Back cover, top: SBB Re 460 039 rounds the curve through the closed station of Céligny on 5 July 2013 with an IR service from Brig to Geneve. **Gordon Wiseman**

Back cover, bottom: CEG electric railcar Be 4/4 116, built in 1922 and preserved by GFM, operates a special train from Broc Fabrique to Bulle on 23 June 2012. **Jan Lundstrøm**

CONTENTS

INTRODUCTION TO THE FOURTH EDITION

Welcome to the fourth edition of Swiss Railways, which contains details of all locomotives and multiple units of Swiss Federal Railways (SBB), and around 50 independent railways, varying from 381 km down to 294 metres, which are mainly owned by the Swiss cantons, open access freight operators and track maintenance contractors.

Since the third edition of this book was published, Swiss railways have continued to modernise their fleets, and there have been many changes. The European Vehicle Number system is now applied to all trains operating on the "main line" and operators other than SBB and BLS on the national network are now very common. For this reason we have completely revised the way we show data in this book. Instead of SBB, BLS and the biggest narrow gauge operators being followed by a section on the smaller operators, we have first set out all standard gauge stock in numerical order, no matter what the operator. Thus SBB Class 514 is followed by BLS Class 515. We believe that this new format will make it easier to look up a train seen in Switzerland, as the operator's name may not be immediately obvious. The section on "Other Railways" gives details of all operators other than SBB, with narrow gauge stock of various gauges listed under each operator and standard gauge stock listed in numerical order within section one.

ACKNOWLEDGMENTS

We would like to thank all who have helped with the preparation of this book, especially Christian Ammann, Martin Baumann, Stéphan Frei, Sylvain Meillasson, Mathias Rellstab, Bruce Smetham, Mario Stefani, various officials and staff of the numerous railways and all who submitted photographs.

A BRIEF HISTORY OF SWITZERLAND

Switzerland is a very beautiful mountainous country which makes up for being landlocked with its many lakes. The spectacular scenery, ease of travel, welcoming people and well-run towns attract around 10 million tourists a year.

The position of Switzerland on the major trade routes, particularly north–south between today's Germany and Italy, led to early settlement. Among the early settlers were a Celtic people known as the Helvetes – today's country is known as the Helvetic Confederation which reversed explains the CH letters used for the country. The area was fought over by German people from the north, Burgundians from the area now in France and the Lombards from the south, now Italy. This explains Switzerland's multilingual status. It was early as 1 August 1291 that the first part of the federation was formed by the cantons of Schwyz, Uri and Unterwald. The name Switzerland, plus Schweiz, Suisse and Svizzera in German, French and Italian all come from founder member Schwyz. Between 1332 and 1353, five cantons joined and by 1513 the total reached 13, all German-speaking. In 1815, the treaty of Wien took the total to 22 and the modern federal state was created in 1848. Other changes have taken the total to 26 cantons today.

Switzerland has a long history of neutrality – the country has not been at war since 1815 – and therefore has attracted many humanitarian agencies. The Red Cross was created by Henry Dunant here. The country also has a long history of direct democracy through referenda.

Switzerland is not part of the EU but its crucial position between Member States and the need for free trade has led Switzerland to adopt certain EU rules – including those on open access to neighbouring rail networks. Switzerland joined the Schengen area in 2005.

LANGUAGES

Switzerland has four official languages. The most widely spoken is German, with a large French-speaking area in the west of the country and Italian spoken in the areas south of the Gotthard and Bernina passes. The fourth language, Romantsch, is spoken in parts of Graubünden canton in the south-east. The national timetable uses all languages as appropriate to each table; this system has been adopted in this publication for place names. It should be noted that some towns are bilingual, Biel/Bienne (German/French) being the best-known example.

THE RAILWAYS OF SWITZERLAND

The first train in Switzerland arrived in 1845 – at Basel from France. It was not until 1847 that the first railway opened within Switzerland from Zürich to Baden (30 km). Known as the Spanisch-Brötli Bahn, as it carried fresh rolls from Baden to Zürich. A plan for a national network from Britain's Stephenson family was rejected in favour of the cantons granting concessions to private railways. Development was quite slow but by 1870 the first rack railway had started to allow access for tourists to the mountains and in 1882 the monumental 15 km Gotthard tunnel opened. Many private lines were a limited success and power over planning the railways was transferred to the Confederation in 1872. A plan to create a national network was accepted by referendum in 1898 and in 1902 Swiss Federal Railways was born from the merger of eight railways of which the Schweizerische Nordostbahn and Schweizerische Centralbahn were the biggest. In the following years the whole of the Swiss standard gauge network was electrified at 15 kV AC 16.66 Hz (now 16.7 Hz), the same system as in Germany and Austria.

Despite the creation of a national network, Switzerland has retained many local railways, mainly owned by the cantons. The biggest is BLS which owns one of the main north–south lines through the Alps, although this is managed as part of the national network. BLS also owns many of the suburban lines serving Bern. Other local standard gauge lines are also electrified at 15 kV AC and through working onto the SBB network often occurs.

Despite closures over the years there are also many narrow gauge lines in Switzerland, metre gauge being the most common, with a variety of electrification systems.

RACK OPERATION

Many Swiss mountain lines are fitted with rack equipment to allow trains to climb very steep gradients, and brake the train on its way back down. These are known as cog-wheel railways in the USA as rack systems work by pinions (cogs) fixed on the train's axles engaging in teeth on a rail between the running rails. Four different systems were devised by Swiss engineers Abt, Locher, Riggenbach and Strub and all are still in use today. As a general rule all coaches of multiple units used on rack lines are fitted with rack equipment but if a rack locomotive or power car is used, the coaches are not equipped. Generally the locomotive is positioned at the lower end of the train so that it is pushing up a mountain and braking from underneath on the way down to prevent unpowered coaches from running away if they become uncoupled. In a small number of cases in this book, a power unit is used at the front of a train on the way up a mountain section. This is the case with Class HGe 4/4 locos on the Glacier Express from Visp to Zermatt. In these cases, the hauled coaching stock is also fitted with rack equipment for braking purposes. In the technical details of rack/adhesion trains in this book, two speeds are given – for rack and adhesion operation. However, space is not availabe to include all speed limits for rolling stock. In general, the limit uphill on a rack railway is higher than that on the way downhill and even these limits may vary according to the gradient.

TICKETS & PASSES

Despite the Swiss railway network being operated by many different companies, the national rail timetable is planned so that all trains connect as far as possible and almost all tickets are valid on all companies.

Apart from the ordinary single and return tickets (the cost of a return being less than twice the single fare for journeys of about 40 km), numerous concessions are available, usually through the purchase of "passes" or "cards".

The **Swiss Travel Pass** (the name Swiss Pass is now used for smart cards for commuters) gives unlimited travel on almost all railways, boats, the transport systems of 24 cities and many post buses together with a reduction on many privately-owned funiculars and mountain railways. This pass is available for three, four, eight or 15 consecutive days' travel.

The **Swiss Travel Pass Flex** covers the same undertakings as the Swiss Travel Pass but gives three, four, eight or 15 days free travel in one month.

The **Swiss Transfer Ticket** provides a transfer from the point of entry into Switzerland to the holder's destination and back. It is valid for one month. In fact, the first and last days are effectively rover tickets, giving opportunities limited only by the timetable, ingenuity and stamina!

The **Swiss Half Fare Card** gives a 50% reduction on almost all transport, including urban transport in cities, for a month.

Regional Passes can be obtained covering many different areas. The length of validity (two to five days out of seven to 15) and class of travel available varies according to the area. Day, family and half-fare cards are also available and the latter two can be used to obtain a reduction on the cost of regional passes.

Full details of all these tickets and other facilities are available from Switzerland Travel Centre, 30 Bedford Street, London, WC2E 9ED, England. URL: www.swisstravelsystem.com

HOW TO GET THERE

By Rail
Lyria TGVs run direct from Paris to Basel, Zürich, Lausanne, Bern and Genève. DB ICEs from Germany run to Basel, Zürich, Bern and Interlaken. SBB and Trenitalia trains from Milano, Italy run to Montreux, Lausanne, Genève, Bern, Basel and Zürich. Zürich can be reached with ÖBB from Austria. A Brussels–Lille–Basel TGV service is to be introduced in 2016.

By Air
There are flights from all over Europe to Genève and Zürich which have very good onward rail services. In addition, Basel-Mulhouse airport is situated in France but has a bus shuttle to Basel.

LAYOUT OF INFORMATION

For each class of vehicles technical and historical information is given followed by a list of individual vehicles arranged as follows:

(1) Number.
(2) Previous number in parentheses (if any).
(3) Livery code (if applicable) – in bold condensed type.
(4) Sector (operating division) code (if applicable).
(5) Minor difference notes (if applicable).
(6) Code for depot allocation.
(7) Names and detailed notes (if any).

Where a company hires a locomotive, which is increasingly common, this will be shown under "Company" with the owning leasing company code first, followed after a slash (/) by the company using the loco. For example AT/BLS – the loco is owned by Alpha Trains used by BLS. A list of Train Leasing Companies can be found at the start of section 1.2.

ABBREVIATIONS

Standard abbreviations used in this book are:

de	Diesel-electric
dh	Diesel-hydraulic
dm	Diesel-mechanical
e	Electric
E	Equipped with ETCS signalling system.
ecs	Empty coaching stock
ETCS	European Train Control System
GSM-R	Global System for Mobile Communications - Railways
HSL	High Speed Line
km/h	Kilometres per hour
kN	Kilonewtons
kW	Kilowatts
m	Metres
mm	Millimetres
mw	Multiple working possible
TSI	Technical Standards for Interoperability
ZUB	Zugsicherung Integra-Signum (signalling)

CLASSIFICATION OF SWISS MOTIVE POWER

All Swiss railways use a standard classification system for their motive power. Separate systems are used for locos and railcars, so it is possible for a loco and a railcar to have the same classification.

PREFIX LETTERS (Locomotives)

R   Maximum speed more than 110 km/h
A   Maximum speed 85 to 110 km/h
B   Maximum speed 70 to 80 km/h
C   Maximum speed 60 to 65 km/h
D   Maximum speed 45 to 55 km/h
E   Shunting locomotive
G   Narrow gauge locomotive

H   Rack fitted locomotive (combined with above if rack & adhesion)
O   Open wagon body
T   Tractor
X   Departmental vehicle (some of these are ex-railcars)

PREFIX LETTERS (Railcars/Multiple Units)

Note: Further prefixed by R if maximum speed is more than 110 km/h.

A   First class accommodation
B   Second class accommodation
D   Baggage compartment

S   Saloon vehicle
Z   Postal compartment

SUFFIX LETTERS (All Motive Power)

a   Battery powered.
e   Electric powered.
em   Electric & diesel powered (i.e. an electro-diesel).
h   Rack fitted (only used with railcars & tractors); if this precedes the a, e or m then the unit is pure rack; if it follows, the unit is rack & adhesion.
m   Diesel or petrol powered.
r   Restaurant vehicle.
rot   Rotary snowplough.
t   (only used with X in the form of Xt) Self propelled departmental vehicle, but not a loco (e.g. a self propelled crane or snowplough).

NUMBERS

These indicate the number of powered and total number of axles, e.g.
4/4 = all four axles powered (e.g. Bo-Bo)
3/6 = six axles of which three are powered (e.g. 2-Co-1)

SUB-CLASS INDICES

To differentiate between classes with otherwise similar classifications, superscript Roman numerals are used, e.g. Re 4/4^{I}, Re 4/4^{II} etc.

All the above are combined as required to give full classifications, e.g.

Ae 6/6   Co-Co electric loco, maximum speed 85–110 km/h
Be 4/6   1B-B1 electric loco, maximum speed 70–80 km/h
ABDe 4/4   Bo-Bo electric railcar, first, second & baggage accommodation

The above system is now being replaced by new computer numbers. The classification letters are retained, but the "fraction" numbers are replaced by a three digit class number. The system originally only included SBB but has since been expanded to incorporate most of the standard gauge private railways. This has caused some new computer numbers to be changed! See the section on SBB numbering system for further details.

SIX-DIGIT SWISS NUMBERING SYSTEM

In 1989, a new numbering system, with six digits, was introduced for new classes. This was only applied to new classes and existing classes where renumbering has been carried out (for example the rebuilt Ee 3/3^{IV} 16555 became 934 555, even though all trains were allotted new class numbers. The system was then extended to include the standard gauge private railways, and worked as follows.

First Digit:	0	Steam locomotive or historic railcar
	1	Metre gauge locomotive (Brünig Line)
	2	Tractor
	3	Electric locomotive (three powered axles)
	4	Electric locomotive (four powered axles)
	5	Electric railcar
	6	Electric locomotive (six powered axles)
	7	Departmental stock (self-propelled, but not a loco e.g. crane or tamper)
	8	Diesel locomotive
	9	Electric shunting locomotive
Second Digit:	0	Express stock (railcars only)
	1–6	Sub class index (bogie electric locomotives)
		Type of electric railcar
		No. of powered axles (diesel locomotives)
	7–8	Not used
	9	Used in lieu of / on rigid frame electric locomotives (but in practice, not used)

Third Digit: Used to differentiate between classes with identical first and second digits. However, in some cases indicates the following:

	2–4	two, three, or four voltage loco or railcar
	5–8	stock owned by private railways.

Fourth to Sixth Digits: Generally the last three digits of the old number, but with many exceptions.

Check digit: After the running number there is a computer check digit. This does not form part of the serial number but is a calculated value used by data systems to check the preceding combination of digits gives a valid result. It is arrived at by multiplying the class and running number digits alternately by 1 and 2. The resulting digits are added together and the sum deducted from the next whole ten gives the check number.

Example 460 033-4

$$
\begin{array}{cccccc}
4 & 6 & 0 & 0 & 3 & 3 \\
\times \quad 1 & 2 & 1 & 2 & 1 & 2 \\
\hline
\end{array}
$$
$= 4+1+2+0+0+3+6 = 16.$
$20-16 = 4.$

EUROPEAN VEHICLE NUMBER & VEHICLE KEEPER MARKING

The UIC system of 12 digit numbers (used for loose coaches and wagons in Switzerland, but not for locos or multiple units) has now been superseded by an Europe-wide system managed by the European Railway Agency. Under this, every vehicle on EU main lines must have a European Vehicle Number (EVN). This consists, like the UIC system, of a 12-digit number, including a check digit, plus a Vehicle Keeper Marking (VKM) which consists of a country code plus letters showing the "keeper" (which is usually the owner) of the item of stock. A National Vehicle Register (NVR) exists in each country and in early 2016 it was announced that these had been merged by the European Railway Agency.

Taking electric loco 460 033 as an example again, its full EVN is 91 85 4460 033-4 CH-SBB which breaks down as follows:

Type of traction
The first digit is a code for a traction unit with the second digit giving the type of traction. In Switzerland the main types are:

91 Electric Locomotive, faster than 99 km/h
92 Diesel locomotive, faster than 99 km/h
93 High speed EMU
94 Other EMU
97 Electric shunting locomotives or electric locomotives with maximum speed under 100 km/h
98 Diesel shunting locomotives or diesel locomotive with maximum speed under 100 km/h

Country code
The old UIC system gave each railway company a number – the third and fourth digits. These now indicate the country. 85 is the country code for Switzerland.

Stock "running number"
The next seven digits show the "running number" (the six figure number composed of class number plus serial number) of each item of stock. This is 460 033 in our example, "460" being the "class". There is also a "4" added to the front. At present, this "4" is not significant, unlike in Austria where class numbers are four digits, such as Class 1116 electric locos. In Germany, the move is also towards four-figure class numbers. The running number is followed by the check digit, then the country code and the VKM.

The full EVN is shown on the sides of locomotives and vehicles and can be very small. For this reason numbers on the front of locomotives and units only show the basic number, with or without a check digit. Check digits have not been shown in the main lists.

Initially, when EVNs started to be created for Swiss motive power, the existing six-digit Swiss numbers were extended to 12-digits. However, it is clear that someone must have noticed that some of this numbering was illogical and started to put some order in the system. This has meant that some rolling stock has been renumbered during the production of this book, while others were receiving EVNs for the first time. Many shunters have been renumbered more logically – for example, 236 341 has become 230 436, reflecting the fact that it used to be SBB 436. Members of this class which are preserved, but work on the national network have also been given 230 xxx numbers. In some cases, a private loco of the same design as an SBB type has been given a follow-on number.

So this book comes somewhere in the middle of renumbering and may be a little confusing at times. It will all work out in the end!

LIVERIES

Until 1984, most SBB main line electric locomotives and railcars were painted dark green, while diesels and shunters were reddish-brown. In 1984, a red livery was adopted for locomotives (except for Class 450), while new railcars are blue and cream. Recent EMUs are white with black window band plus red front end, doors and roof. ICN sets do not have red doors. Class 514 has dark blue below sole bar level. A few tractors used as works pilots are yellow. A number of non-standard liveries also exist, but several of these will disappear in the near future. The various liveries are shown in the lists using the following letter codes:

A Overall advertising livery.
B Brown. The original electric loco livery, a few "museum" locos have been restored to this livery.
C SBB Cargo livery. Red front ends, blue sides with Cargo in large letters on side.
G Dark green. The standard livery for most electric locomotives and railcars prior to 1984.
K BLS dark blue.
N NPZ (*Neue Pendel Zug*). Blue and grey with red ends. The 1990s livery for SBB local trains.
O Orange/Grey ('Swiss Express') livery, applied to Mark III coaching stock and some Re4/4^{II} locos during the 1970s).
P Reddish-brown. The standard livery for SBB shunters and tractors until 1984.
R Red. The current standard SBB Passenger and Infra locomotive livery. Many Cargo locos are still in this livery.
S S-Bahn. Dark blue with white band and red ends, applied only to SBB Class 450.

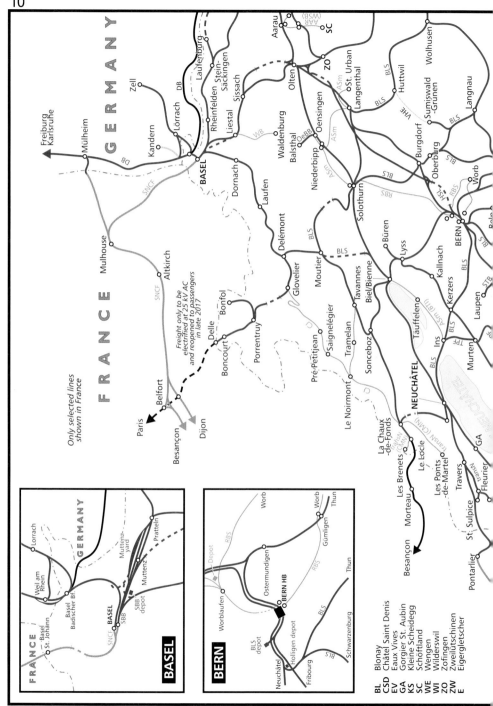

Only selected lines shown in France

Freight only to be electrified at 25 kV AC and reopened to passengers in late 2017

BASEL

BERN

BL Blonay
CSD Châtel Saint Denis
EV Eaux Vives
GA Gorgier St. Aubin
KS Kleine Scheidegg
SC Schöftland
WE Wengen
WI Wilderswil
ZO Zofingen
ZW Zweilütschinen
E Eigergletscher

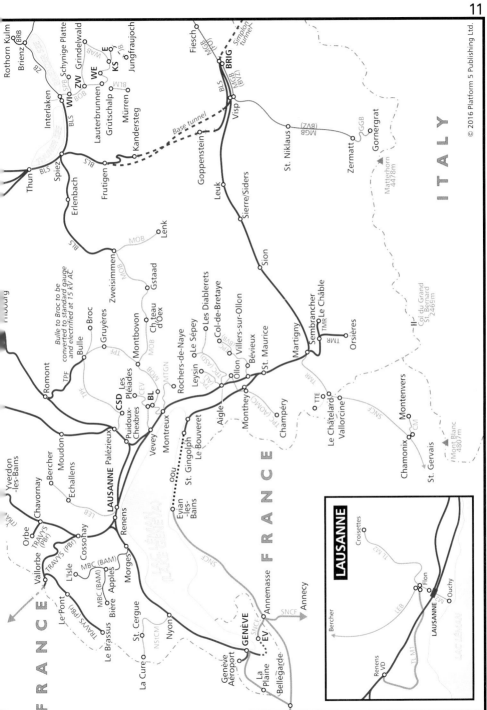

12

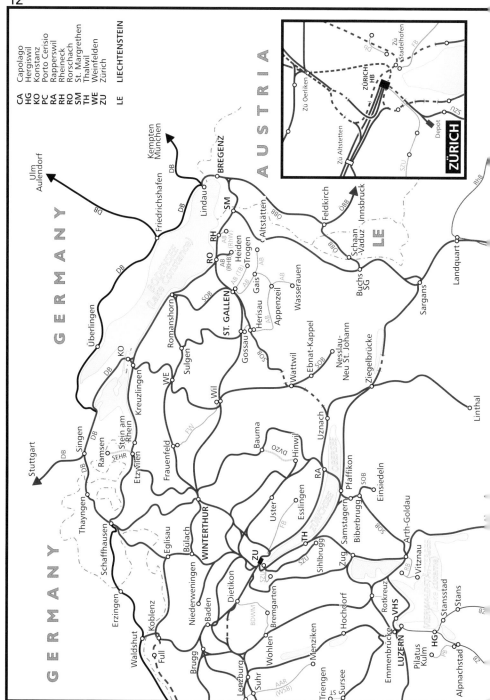

CA Capolago
HG Hergiswil
KO Konstanz
PC Porto Cerisio
RA Rapperswil
RH Rheineck
RO Rorschach
SM St. Margrethen
TH Thalwil
WE Weinfelden
ZU Zürich

LE LIECHTENSTEIN

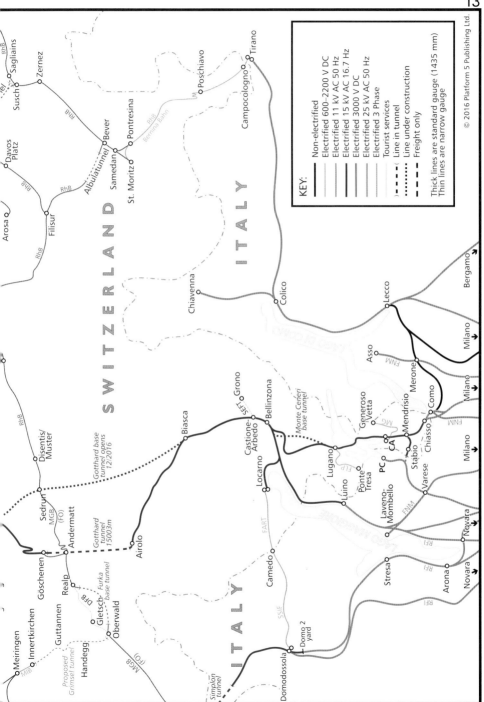

KEY:

Non-electrified
Electrified 600–2200 V DC
Electrified 11 kV AC 50 Hz
Electrified 15 kV AC 16.7 Hz
Electrified 3000 V DC
Electrified 25 kV AC 50 Hz
Electrified 3 Phase
Tourist services
Line in tunnel
Line under construction
Freight only

Thick lines are standard gauge (1435 mm)
Thin lines are narrow gauge

PLATFORM 5 MAIL ORDER

EISENBAHNATLAS SCHWEIZ
2ND EDITION
Schweers & Wall

Fully revised and updated atlas of Switzerland's railways in 1:150 000 scale. Shows all lines with identification of double track, single track, narrow gauge lines, freight only lines, closed lines, rack railways and lines under construction. Different colours are used to show different electrification voltages and Swiss timetable numbers

are shown for all passenger carrying lines. Also shows all stations, junctions, yards, freight depots, preservation centres, heritage lines, tramways and funiculars, as well as general geographical features including rivers, motorways and lakes. Includes enlargements of key railway locations and a full index of station names. Key is in German, English, French and Italian. Published 2012. Large format hardback. 112 pages. **£32.95** *TR Subscriber Price £29.95*

Also available in the same series:
TR subs price

Eisenbahnatlas Deutschland.................................. £44.95...... £39.95
Eisenbahnatlas Österreich..................................... £28.95...... £25.95
Eisenbahnatlas Frankreich Band 1: Nord .... £30.95...... £27.95

To place an order, please follow the instructions on page 224 of this book.

1. STANDARD GAUGE ROLLING STOCK

SWISS FEDERAL RAILWAYS   SBB

The official use of three languages in the areas where Swiss Federal Railways operates requires it to display an official name in each of the three languages:

German: Schweizerische Bundesbahnen   SBB
French: Chemins de Fer Fédéraux   CFF
Italian: Ferrovie Federali Svizzere   FFS

The Romantsch name – Viafers Federalas Svizras (VFF) – appears only in the national timetable, which also has an introduction in English.

Swiss Federal Railways locomotives and coaches are either lettered "SBB CFF FFS" on both sides or "SBB CFF" on one side and "SBB FFS" on the other. Their controls are labelled in German, French and Italian. In this publication, the initials "SBB" are used throughout.

The SBB was formed in 1902 when most of the major private companies were nationalised, and a few other railways have been absorbed since.

The SBB network is electrified at 15 kV AC 16.7 Hz overhead, the only exceptions being a few lines in border areas where the systems of neighbouring countries are used. SBB electric stock can only operate on the above system unless stated otherwise. The SBB network is standard gauge (1435 mm). SBB's former metre gauge Brünig line, is now part of Zentralbahn.

ORGANISATION

SBB is now divided into Passenger, Cargo and Infrastructure divisions, each with its own dedicated fleet. Depots and works are now generally allocated by activity.

In response to market liberalisation in the EU (of which Switzerland is not a member) it was decided to allow open access to the Swiss rail network in exchange for allowing Swiss operators into the rest of the EU. SBB Cargo decided on a strategy of operating its own trains over the whole of the north–south corridor from Germany via Switzerland to Italy then founded a subsidiary in Germany (SBB Cargo Deutschland) and another in Italy (SBB Cargo Italia) – both now part of SBB Cargo International. The companies operate extensively in these two countries; SBB Cargo Deutschland is now the second largest freight operator in Germany, behind incumbent DB Schenker.

One of the unfortunate consequences of the division of the SBB fleet is a policy of not giving specific depot allocations to many traction units.

Switzerland once had a diverse train building industry, but the historic works of SLM and Schindler closed or were broken up, then ADtranz also closed the former BBC works. Only Bombardier retains a small plant at Villeneuve. However, Stadler has gone from a tiny family business to one of Europe's leading multiple unit builders in the space of two decades!

PASSENGER SERVICES

International passenger services serving Switzerland are now mainly tributaries of high speed services in neighbouring countries. Lyria, jointly owned by SBB and SNCF, operates TGVs from Zürich, Basel, Bern, Lausanne and Genève to Paris and Genève to the south of France. DB operates ICEs from Basel to Berlin via Frankfurt and to Köln, with some trains starting back from Zürich or Interlaken plus from Zürich to Stuttgart. SBB and Trenitalia separately operate services using tilting train sets from Genève, Basel and Zürich to Milano. Less frequent EuroCity services run from Zürich to München and Austria.

Within Switzerland, a very frequent network of regular interval passenger trains operate from long distance IC services down to suburban level. SBB's IC and IR services are operated by a limited number of loco and stock types – mainly double-deck IC2000 stock or single-deck IC IV stock in push-pull or conventional mode, mainly with Class 460 electric locos. A small number of routes are operated by Class 500 ICN tilting EMUs. IR services are often formed of more lowly stock with Class 460 or older Re 4/4ʲ electrics. Suburban trains are increasingly operated by Class 521–524 FLIRT EMUs or double-deck EMUs. All of the conurbations are developing networks known as S-Bahn in German-speaking areas and RER where French is spoken.

FREIGHT SERVICES

Traffic in Switzerland is dominated by north–south international flows over the Gotthard and Lötschberg routes although there is still a great deal of traffic elsewhere. Intermodal traffic, be it containers or complete lorries on trains, is heavy on the north–south routes. Switzerland retains, however, an extensive wagonload network based on yards at Muttenz (Basel), Denges (Lausanne) and Limmattal (Zürich). There is also still a busy network of postal trains.

SBB NUMBERING SYSTEM

Steam locomotives were numbered below 10000, and consequently when main line electric locomotives first appeared, they were numbered 10001 upwards. However, when railcars, shunting tractors and later diesel locomotives were purchased, they each had their own separate numbering systems, railcars being initially numbered in the carriage series. This resulted in many duplicated numbers; to eliminate these much renumbering occurred during the 1950s and 1960s. Although this eliminated duplicated numbers, the result was a non-too-logical system, particularly in the case of the 8xxx and 9xxx series tractors which were numbered in these blocks when vacant numbers in the earlier series were exhausted. The traditional SBB number series were as follows:

1–250	Electric tractors (traffic stock)
251–399	Electro-diesel tractors (traffic stock)
401–599	Diesel tractors (traffic stock)
601–950	Diesel tractors (departmental stock)
951–963	Electric tractors (departmental stock; all now withdrawn)
964–979	Battery tractors (all are departmental)
1001–1899	Electric railcars
2001–2999	Electric railcars
8001–8399	Electric tractors (traffic stock)
8401–8999	Diesel tractors (traffic stock)
9401–9999	Diesel tractors (departmental stock)
10001–11999	Electric locomotives, max speed more than 80 km/h
12001–13999	Electric locomotives, max speed 70 to 80 km/h
14001–14999	Electric locomotives, max speed 60 to 65 km/h
15001–15999	Electric locomotives, max speed 45 to 55 km/h (all now withdrawn)
16001–16999	Electric shunting locomotives
17001–17999	Electro-diesel locomotives (being converted to diesels)
18001–18999	Diesel locomotives

SECTOR ALLOCATIONS

SBB locomotives are now all allocated to one of three activities, each with subdivisions, which we give a code in this book:

C	Cargo
C-I*	Cargo Instandhaltung (maintenance).
C-O*	Cargo Ost (east) division.
C-S*	Cargo Süd (south) division.
C-W*	Cargo West division.
I	Infrastructure
I-B*	Infrastructure Betriebsführung, Lösch- und Rettungszüge: fire-fighting and rescue trains.
I-R*	Infrastructure Rangierbahnhöfe (marshalling yards – Switzerland opens up its yards to all, so shunting is carried out by Infra.)
I-S* (I-U*)	Infrastructure Strategischer Einkauf-Fahrzeugmanagement (rolling stock management)
P	Passenger
P-O	Passenger Operations

*   Where a loco is not given a specific depot allocation, the second letter above is shown in the "depot" column to denote the sub-sector allocation.

SBB DEPOTS

In the past decade SBB has been reorganised by activity and maintenance has also been changed so that traction is less attached to a specific geographic location. Data on "allocations" is now difficult to obtain and much of the data here comes from "inside knowledge".

Code	Depot	Main activity
BE	Bellinzona	Cargo
BI	Biel/Bienne	Passenger
BN	Bern	rented to BLS
BR	Brig	Cargo
BS	Basel Wolf	Passenger
CH	Chiasso	Cargo
ER	Erstfeld	Cargo (to close in 2016)
GE	Genève	Passenger
LS	Lausanne	Passenger
LZ	Luzern	Passenger
OL	Olten	Historic
OW	Oberwinterthur	Passenger
ZU	Zürich	Passenger

In addition to the above, many stations and other locations have small sheds housing one or more shunting tractors; often these belong to the permanent way or other engineer's departments.

The following codes for stabling points are also used:

AI	Airolo
BU	Buchs
DE	Delémont
GI	Giubiasco
GO	Goldau
LI	Limmattal yard (also known as RBL)
LO	Locarno
LT	Lausanne Triage (Denges yard)
NE	Neuchâtel
RO	Romanshorn
RW	Rapperswil
SA	Sargans
SG	St. Gallen

(S)	stored serviceable
(U)	stored unserviceable

SBB WORKSHOPS

Four workshops are responsible for the repair and overhaul of SBB motive power. These have now been dedicated by activity. Meiringen is now part of Zentralbahn and Zürich has closed.

Code	Works	Activity
BW	Biel/Bienne	Diesel locomotives.
NW	Bellinzona	Cargo locomotives and wagons; passenger locomotives Re 4/4^{II}.
OW	Olten	Passenger coaches.
YW	Yverdon	Passenger locomotives, except Re 4/4^{II}, and EMUs.
ZW	Zürich Altstetten	Zürich S-Bahn

1.1. SHUNTING TRACTORS

SBB has a much reduced fleet of tractors for light shunting duties following the division of activities between Passenger, Cargo and Infra, plus the rationalisation of wagonload freight. Those numbered between 1 and 599 and in the 8000 series traditionally belonged to the traffic department and were mainly used in station goods yards where they are driven by station staff. Those numbered between 601 and 999 and in the 9000 series were in departmental use, now known as SBB Infra, the greatest number being allocated to the permanent way department, with others being used by the overhead line and signals departments and as depot and works pilots.

In the past decade, most older shunters have either been withdrawn or rebuilt and renumbered with a six-figure number or a full 12-digit EVN, the traditional six-figure number being incorporated as part of this. It is no longer possible to give full data on depot allocation and the location of each tractor as this information is not readily available and most tractors move around far more than in the past.

The shunters owned by other companies are often the same or similar designs to those with SBB. BLS has a large fleet but other companies have only a few. All standard gauge shunters are now shown in this section. In the case of small classes, or single locos, technical details are not given and the locos are listed with details of builder, works number and build date.

Electric shunters have been allocated EVNs in the series 97 85 1xxx xxx-c. Diesel shunters have been allocated EVNs in the series 98 85 5xxx xxx-c. These are not always carried!

CLASS Te^{III} (CLASS 212)   Bo

Small electric shunters; the last few with SBB are used by the Passenger department. 157 and 176 are both normally at Locarno. MBC (BAM) has two for shunting wagons between metre and standard gauge at Morges. Note that locomotives in this class will have their serial number reduced by 100 if renumbered, so 144 will become 212 044 etc. 212 080 is ex SOB 216 035, ex BT 35.

Built: 1965/66.
Builder–Mechanical Parts: SLM.
Builder–Electrical Parts: MFO.
Traction Motors: 2 single-phase axle-suspended.
One Hour Rating: 245 kW.   **Maximum Tractive Effort:** 67 kN.
Wheel Diameter: 950 mm.   **Weight:** 28 tonnes.
Length over Buffers: 6.64 m.   **Maximum Speed:** 60 km/h.

Number	Company	Sector	Depot		Number	Company	Sector	Depot
144	SBB	P	GE		157	SBB	P	LO
147	MBC		Morges		176	SBB	P	LO
155	MBC		Morges		212 080	SOB		

CLASS Tem^{I} (CLASS 220.2)   B

This class, and the following Tem^{II} and Tem^{III} classes, are electric tractors fitted with a diesel engine to enable them to shunt in non-electrified sidings. This class ran from 251 to 275.

Built: 1950–57.
Builder–Mechanical Parts: Tuchschmid.
Builder–Electrical Parts: BBC/MFO.
Engine: Saurer C615D of 65 kW.
Maximum Tractive Effort: 36 kN (electric), 31 kN (diesel).
Traction Motors: 1 single-phase axle-suspended with side rod drive.
One Hour Rating: 90 kW (electric), 50 kW (diesel).
Wheel Diameter: 950 mm.   **Weight:** 15 tonnes.
Length over Buffers: 5.87 m.   **Maximum Speed:** 60 km/h.

Number	Company	Sector	Depot		Number	Company	Sector	Depot
251	SBB	C	LS		268	SBB	I	OW
262	SBB	C	LS					

CLASS Tem^{II} (CLASS 221)   B

A dual-mode tractor; the last one with SBB is used by Passenger. The class ran from 276 to 298. Two locos are in industrial use.

Built: 1967.
Builder–Mechanical Parts: SLM/Tuchschmid.
Builder–Electrical Parts: MFO.
Engine: Saurer C615D of 85 kW.
Traction Motors: 1 single-phase axle-suspended with side rod drive.
One Hour Rating: 120 kW (electric), 60 kW (diesel).   **Maximum Tractive Effort:** 33 kN.
Wheel Diameter: 950 mm.   **Weight:** 26 tonnes.
Length over Buffers: 6.70 m.   **Maximum Speed:** 60 km/h.

Number	Company	Sector	Depot		Number	Company	Sector	Depot
276	Sika, Düdingen				221 284	SBB	P	LS

CLASS Tem^{II} (CLASS 220.3)   Bo

Another dual-mode tractor, now used only by SBB Cargo. The class ran from 321 to 365. One loco has been acquired by Travys. A large number are preserved.

Built: 1954–62.
Builder–Mechanical Parts: SLM.
Builder–Electrical Parts: BBC/SAAS.
Engine: SLM 12BD11 of 145 kW.
Maximum Tractive Effort: 59 kN (electric), 64 kN (diesel).
Traction Motors: 2 single-phase axle-suspended.
One Hour Rating: 260 kW (electric), 95 kW (diesel).
Wheel Diameter: 1040 mm.   **Weight:** 32 tonnes.
Length over Buffers: 7.29 m (†7.35 m)   **Maximum Speed:** 60 km/h.

Number	Company	Sector	Depot	Notes
325	SBB	C	CH	
220 329	Travys (PBr)			Ex SBB 329
~~333~~	Chocolat Fret, Buchs			Ex SBB 333
347	† SBB	C	W	
348	† SBB	C	W	
365	† SBB	C	W	

CLASS Tm^I (CLASS 230.4)   B

A small diesel tractor with many variations. Originally all fitted with SLM engines, many have been rebuilt with Deutz or VM engines since 1971. The series once ran from 401 to 513. The last SBB machine was withdrawn in December 2015.

Built: 1957–65.
Builder: RACO Type 85 LA 7.
Engine: SLM 6VD11 of 66 kW.   a. SLM 4VDIII of 44 kW.
                               b. Deutz of 87 kW.
                               c. Deutz F6L413 of 90 kW.
                               d. VM of 90 kW.

Transmission: Mechanical.   **Maximum Tractive Effort:**
Driving Wheel Diameter: 600 mm.   **Weight:** 10 tonnes.
Length over Buffers: 5.19 m.   **Maximum Speed:** 45 km/h.

Number	Company	Sector	Depot	Notes
402	Hügler, Dübendorf			
403	Pre Beton, Avenches			
409	Stahlrohr, Rothrist			
411	Tiger Käse, Langnau			
230 414	Scherer & Bühler, Meggen			
415	MEKA, Kallnach			
427	Vaparoid, Turtmann			

▲ Travys Tem 220 329 (showing both new and old numbers) is seen at Sentier-Orient on 9 October 2014. **David Haydock**

▼ Travys loco 238 305 (not a number on the national system) is former SBB Tm 458. Formerly on the Pont Brassus line, it is seen at Orbe where it is depot shunter on 9 October 2014. **David Haydock**

429		Brenntag, Avenches	
432		Prodo, Domdidier	
230 436		Kentaur, Lintzelflüh-Goldbach	Ex 236 341
442	b	Bahnhof Kuhlhaus, Basel	
446	b	Bahnhof Kuhlhaus, Basel	
447	b	Coop, Vernier	
448		Zwicky, Müllheim-Wigoltingen	
449	c	Filipini & Filio, Airolo	
450	c	Rhenus, Romanshorn	
451		Thommen-Furler, Rüti bei Büren	
452	b	Robert Wild, Muri AG	
457	b	Terrazzo & Jurasitwerk, Bärschwil	
238 305		Travys (OC)	Ex SBB 458
461	d	Thommen-Furler, Rüti bei Büren	
470	c	Spinnerei, Linthal	
471	c	Wander, Neveregg	
472	b	Trottet, Collombey-Muraz	
230 477	c	STAG, Maienfeld	
479		Silo Olten, Olten	
230 496	d	Rhenus, Romanshorn	
498	d	Thommen-Furler, Ruti bei Büren	
499	c	Cartiere Cham-Tenero, Tenero	
502		Papier Metso, Delémont	
504		Cablofer, Bex	
505	c	Stihl, Wil	
506		Ferro AG, Birr	
507	b	LANDI, Les Hauts-Geneveys	

CLASS Tm^{II} (CLASS 230.6)   B

A small track trolley with a cabin for four personnel and a platform for carrying tools and materials. Capable of hauling a few wagons for permanent way work. Once ran from 601 to 853. Only three left with SBB but many in industrial use.

Built: 1950–68.
Builder: RACO.
Engine: Saurer C615D of 70 kW.
Transmission: Mechanical.   **Maximum Tractive Effort:**
Wheel Diameter: 600 mm.   **Weight:** 10 tonnes.
Length over Buffers: 5.24 m.   **Maximum Speed:** 45 km/h.

*   Fitted for snowplough use.

Number		Company	Sector	Depot	Notes
601		Nexans, Cossonay			
605		Stauffer			
622		Thevenaz-Leduc, Eclubens			
624		Chiesa Altmetal, Pratteln			
230 635	*	SBB	I	LI	
637	*	Chiresa, Turgi			
230 643		SOREC, Gossau			
644		Lagerhaus, Buchmatt			
230 647		SBB	I	O	
649		EFSA, Châtillens			
237 910		Chemie Uetikon, Uetikon am See			Ex SBB 652
656		Galvachrom, Rivera			
675		KFOR, Effingen			
680		EFSA, Châtillens			
236 342		LSB			Ex SBB 700
237 931		Stauffer			Ex SBB 726
735		Tiger Käse, Langnau			
236 317^{II}		Blaser Swisslube, Hasle			Ex SBB 739
230 751		Stauffer/Stadler, Sargans			Ex SBB 751
756		Ries Mühle, Brunnen			
760		Stauffer			

789	Thommen, Kaisersaugst			
806	Tensol Rail, Piotta			
809	Chemie Uetikon, Uetikon am See			
810	Leim & Düngerfabrik, Märstetten			
230 816	SBB	P	BW	
818	AMAG, Birrfeld			
230 834	BOAG, Trimbach			
839	EFSA, Châtillens			
844	Stauffer			
847	Lagerhaus, Buchmatt			
230 849	Stauffer			Ex SBB 849
230 863	SOB			Ex 236 001, ex BT 1
230 864	SOB			Ex 236 002, ex BT 2

"CLASS Ta" B

This assortment of battery tractors of widely differing designs are used as works pilots. Not in capital stock – owned by the works themselves. Ta 966, 969 and 971 are preserved.

Number	Builder	Built	Rating	Weight	Length	Max. Speed	Owner/Location
968	Stadler	1977	4 kW	7 tonnes	2.85 m	10 km/h	Yverdon works
974	SBB Zürich	1965	4 kW	6.5 tonnes	3.32 m	10 km/h	Zürich works
975	Stadler	1971	35 kW	6.5 tonnes	2.85 m	25 km/h	Zürich works
976	Stadler	1971	35 kW	6.5 tonnes	2.85 m	25 km/h	Bellinzona works
978	AEG	1913	145 kW	24 tonnes	8.40 m	25 km/h	Bellinzona works (S)

"CLASS Ta 205" Bo

This classification covers a variety of BLS battery shunters.

Number	Company	Builder	Built	Notes
205 001	BLS	BLS Böningen	1941	
205 002	BLS	BLS Spiez	1975	
205 003	Olten Works	BLS Böningen	1943	ex SBB Ta 967
205 031	BBC	BLS Böningen	1915	ex WM Ta 31

CLASS Te 210 (CLASS Te^{II}) Bo

A small former SBB electric shunter. The only one still in use is with Travys (Orbe–Chavornay).

Built: 1968.
Builder–Mechanical Parts: SLM/Tuchschmid.
Builder–Electrical Parts: MFO.
Traction Motors: 1 single-phase axle-suspended with side rod drive.
One Hour Rating: 120 kW.   **Maximum Tractive Effort:** 33 kN.
Wheel Diameter: 950 mm.   **Weight:** 22 tonnes.
Length over Buffers: 6.70 m.   **Maximum Speed:** 60 km/h.

Number	Company	Notes
210 086	Travys (PBr)	Ex SBB Te^{II} 86; ex 218 306

"CLASS Te 216 (CLASS Te^{III})" Bo

This classification covers a variety of electric shunters, mainly with SOB.

Number	Company	Builder	Works No	Built	Notes
216 036	SOB	SLM/SAAS	3810	1945	ex SOB 2/2 51, ex 31
216 038	SOB	SLM/MFO	3753	1947	ex SOB Te 2/2 53, ex SBB 953
216 039	SOB	Tuchschmid/MFO		1956	ex SOB Te 2/2 54, ex SBB 52
216 302	SOB	SLM/SAAS	3907	1945	ex SBB 137, ex VHB 163
216 303	BLS	SLM	4075	1952	Te^{III}
216 924	OFEFT, Bure (army depot)	SLM/MFO	4583	1965	

CLASS Ee 217 (CLASS Ee 2/2)   Bo

A single electric shunter now with TPF. Formerly GFM Ee 2/2 91. The all-electric version of the Em 2/2 - see Class Em 238.5. There are two similar locos with Travys (OC) nos. 1 and 2.

Number	Company	Builder	Works No	Built
217 091	TPF	SIG/BBC	6127	1960

CLASS Tem 225   B

BLS "Turmwagen" – electric shunters with an overhead inspection platform – originally Tm 55 to 58. Makies has equipped its loco as a driving trailer for trains of ballast! CJ has numbered its loco 183 to fit into its own system.

Number	Company	Builder	Built	Notes
225 055	Makies	MFO/SAAS	1966	ex BLS Tm 55
225 056	BLS	MFO/SAAS	1967	ex Tm 56
225 057 (U)	BLS	MFO/SAAS	1967	ex Tm 57
225 183	CJ	MFO/SAAS	1967	ex BLS Tm 58

CLASS Tm 230.5

A small shunting locomotive for which few technical details are available.

Number	Company	Builder	Works No	Built	Name	Notes
230 514	Sersa	RACO Type 100 DA3H	1826	1975	ROLF	Ex EBT Tm 14

CLASS Tm 230.9   B

A unique design of low-slung tractor for shunting the traverser at Biel/Bienne works, previously numbered Tm 900.

Built: 1963.
Builder: SBB Biel/Bienne.
Engine: VW of 22 kW.
Transmission: Mechanical.   **Maximum Tractive Effort:**
Wheel Diameter: 600 mm.   **Weight:** 2.3 tonnes.
Length over Buffers: 2.00 m.   **Maximum Speed:** 20 km/h.

Number	Company	Sector	Depot
230 900	SBB	C	BN

CLASS Tm 231.0 (CLASS Tm^{III})   B

Diesel-electric tractors for use as shed and works pilots, originally numbered 901 to 924. About half are still working with SBB. Several others have gone to dealer Stauffer. 231 025 and 231 180 are former industrial locomotives built to the same design.

Built: 1958–66.
Builder–Mechanical Parts: SLM.
Builder–Electrical Parts: BBC.
Engine: SLM 12BD11 of 145 kW.
Transmission: Electric.   **Maximum Tractive Effort:** 92 kN.
Wheel Diameter: 950 mm.   **Weight:** 28 tonnes.
Length over Buffers: 6.54 m.   **Maximum Speed:** 30 km/h.

Number	Company	Sector	Depot	Notes
902	Stauffer			Ex SBB Tm 902
231 003	Stauffer			Ex SBB Tm 903
231 004	SBB	I	CH	Ex Tm 904
905	SBB	P	BW	For spares
231 006	SBB	I	YW	Ex Tm 906
231 007	Stauffer			Ex SBB Tm 907; ex 237 934

231 008	SBB	I	ZU	Ex Tm 908
231 009	SBB	I	ZU	Ex Tm 909
231 010	SBB	I	ZU	Ex Tm 910
231 011	Stauffer			Ex SBB Tm 911
912	SBB	I	BS	
231 013	Stauffer			Ex SBB Tm 913
915	SBB	I	ER	
231 017	Stauffer			Ex SBB Tm 917
918	SBB	P	BW	For spares
231 019	SBB	P	ZU	Ex Tm 919
231 020	SBB	I	GE	Ex Tm 920
231 021	SBB	I	GE	Ex Tm 921
237 906	Stauffer			Ex SBB Tm 922; "Andrin"
231 023	SBB	C	LT	Ex Tm 923
231 024	SBB	I	BI	Ex Tm 924

Number	Company	Works No	Built	Notes
231 025	Stauffer	4586	1966	ex Dreispitz Tm 12 (ex 237 866)
231 180	CJ	4438	1962	ex Dreispitz Tm 10 (ex 237 480)

▲ Tm 232 005 heads a works train through Genève Cornavin station on 28 May 2013.

David Haydock

CLASS Tm 231.9   B

This is the former Sensetalbahn Tm 2/2 number 11 (238 111).

Built: 1969.
Builder: Stadler/BBC.
Engine: Originally Saurer of 185 kW. Re-engined.
Transmission: Electric.
Weight: 23.5 tonnes.   **Maximum Speed**: 55 km/h.

Number	Company	Works No.	Notes
231 900	Imbach Logistik (IMLOG), Schachen	130	Ex SBB

CLASS Tm 232.0 (CLASS Tm^{III})   B

When built, these were similar to Tm^{III} tractors 9451–9463 (now Class 232.4), but fitted with a 3-tonne hydraulic crane and an open platform for use on permanent way work. Originally numbered 9501–43, 9551–9597, 52 of the class were modernised by Windhoff and Stadler Winterthur (formerly Winpro) from August 2003 to February 2006. The rebuild involved the installation of a more powerful engine which satisfies Euro III emissions standards, with particle filters, an increase of 80% in tractive effort and an increase to 80 km/h maximum speed. The tractors now have Signum signalling system for main line running, radio control and a new crane. The other 9501–9597 shunters were all withdrawn from SBB service. 9511 and 9515 are now in Denmark as 99 86 9281 511 and 515. A few others still carry their original numbers.

Built: 1976–88; rebuilt 2003–06.
Builder: RACO; rebuilt by Winpro, Windhoff.
Engine: Iveco of 260 kW.
Transmission: Hydraulic.   **Maximum Tractive Effort**:
Wheel Diameter: 950 mm.   **Weight**: 25 tonnes.
Length over Buffers: 8.74 m.   **Maximum Speed**: 80 km/h.

Number		Company	Sector		Number		Company	Sector
232 001	(9566)	SBB	I		232 027	(9524)	SBB	I
232 002	(9516)	SBB	I		232 028	(9591)	SBB	I
232 003	(9510)	SBB	I		232 029	(9552)	SBB	I
232 004	(9512)	SBB	I		232 030	(9577)	SBB	I
232 005	(9584)	SBB	I		232 031	(9507)	SBB	I
232 006	(9588)	SBB	I		232 032	(9520)	SBB	I
232 007	(9525)	SBB	I		232 033	(9538)	SBB	I
232 008	(9528)	SBB	I		232 034	(9541)	SBB	I
232 009	(9518)	SBB	I		232 035	(9531)	SBB	I
232 010	(9586)	SBB	I		232 036	(9504)	SBB	I
232 011	(9522)	SBB	I		232 037	(9542)	SBB	I
232 012	(9508)	SBB	I		232 038	(9536)	SBB	I
232 013	(9555)	SBB	I		232 039	(9543)	SBB	I
232 014	(9559)	SBB	I		232 040	(9537)	SBB	I
232 015	(9579)	SBB	I		232 041	(9534)	SBB	I
232 016	(9523)	SBB	I		232 042	(9575)	SBB	I
232 017	(9558)	SBB	I		232 043	(9519)	SBB	I
232 018	(9589)	SBB	I		232 044	(9539)	SBB	I
232 019	(9553)	SBB	I		232 045	(9563)	SBB	I
232 020	(9567)	SBB	I		232 046	(9540)	SBB	I
232 021	(9561)	SBB	I		232 047	(9556)	SBB	I
232 022	(9582)	SBB	I		232 048	(9532)	SBB	I
232 023	(9533)	SBB	I		232 049	(9557)	SBB	I
232 024	(9585)	SBB	I		232 050	(9535)	SBB	I
232 025	(9562)	SBB	I		232 051	(9506)	SBB	I
232 026	(9521)	SBB	I		232 052	(9554)	SBB	I

CLASS Tm 232.1, 232.2 & 232.3 (CLASS Tm^{IV})   B

Small shunters 8751–8781 were delivered as 551–581. Between batches, SLM delivered identical 9651–9685, 9651–9658 being delivered as 861–868. 8761 was re-engined and modernised by Biel/Bienne works in 2007 for SBB Cargo then renumbered 232 111 and was followed by 27 others from the 8751–8796 batch as Class 232.1 and 18 from the 9651–9684 batch as Class 232.2. More locos were modernised as 232 301 to 315 for Infra in 2013, this time from both batches. Few of these shunters now remain with SBB in their original state. A few have been sold to other operators. Other companies have examples of the design such as CJ 232 181 and SOB 232 288/290. In addition to the hydraulic transmission, these tractors have a two-ratio gearbox giving a maximum shunting speed of 30 km/h.

Built: 8751–8797 1968–78; 9651–9685 1974–77.
Builder: SLM.
Engine: Original MAN R8V 16/18 of 280 kW; 232.1 & 2 Caterpillar 13C Acert of 280 kW; 232.3 MTU of 280 kW.

Transmission: Hydraulic.	**Maximum Tractive Effort:** 90 kN.
Wheel Diameter: 950 mm.	**Weight:** 30 tonnes.
Length over Buffers: 7.67 m.	**Maximum Speed:** 30/60 km/h.

EVN: 96 85 5232 101-c and so on.

*   Purchased 1994 from Sulzer, Winterthur.
§   Purchased 1987 from SLM (was their works pilot).
z   Fitted with ZUB signalling system for main line running.

Number			Company	Sector	Depot	Name
232 101	(8751)	z	SBB	C		
232 102	(8752)		SBB	C		
232 103	(8753)		SBB	C		
232 104	(8754)		LSB			
232 105	(8755)		LSB			

▲ SBB Cargo Tm 232 103 stands in front of the goods shed at Sion on 16 April 2014. 232 201 to 235 are very similar.   **David Haydock**

8756			LSB			
232 107	(8757)		LSB			
232 108	(8758)		SBB	C	O	
232 109	(8759)		LSB			
232 110	(8760)		SBB	C	O	
232 111	(8761)		Serfahr			
232 112	(8762)	z	SBB	C		
232 113	(8763)		SBB	I		
232 115	(8765)		SBB	I		
232 116	(8766)	z	SBB	C		
232 117	(8767)		SBB	C		
232 118	(8768)		Serfahr			
232 119	(8769)	z	SBB	C		
232 121	(8771)	z	SBB	C	O	
232 122	(8772)		SBB	C		
8773			Thommen, Kaisersaugst			
232 124	(8774)	z	SBB	C		
232 126	(8776)	z	SBB	C		
232 127	(8777)	z	SBB	C		
232 128	(8778)	z	SBB	C		
232 129	(8779)		SBB	C		
232 131	(8781)		SBB	C	O	
232 132	(8782)	z	SBB	C	O	
232 134	(8784)		LSB, Jura Cement, Wildegg			
232 135	(8785)		SBB	P	RO	
232 136	(8786)	z	SBB	C		
232 137	(8787)		LSB			
232 139	(8789)		SBB	C	O	
232 140	(8790)	z	SBB	C		
232 141	(8791)	z	SBB	C		
232 143	(8792)	z	SBB	C	W	
232 144	(8794)		SBB	I		
232 146	(8796)	z	SBB	C		
232 147	(8797)	*z	SBB	C		
232 164	(8764)		Stauffer			
232 175	(8775)		Stauffer			
232 181	(ex Tm 181, ex EBT)		CJ			
232 182	(9595)		CJ			
232 183	(8783)		SRT			
232 192	(8792)		Marti			Albert
232 201	(9651)		SBB	C	W	
232 202	(9652)		SBB	C	O	
232 203	(9653)		SBB	C	O	
232 207	(9657)		SBB	C		
232 208	(9658)	z	SBB	C		
232 209	(9659)		SBB	C	W	
232 210	(9660)		SBB	P		
232 211	(9661)	z	Sersa			
232 212	(9662)	z	SBB	C		
232 216	(9666)	z	SBB	C		
232 218	(9668)		Sersa			
232 223	(9673)		SBB	C	O	
232 224	(9674)		SBB	C	O	
232 225	(9675)		SBB	C	O	
232 226	(9676)		SBB	C	O	
232 227	(9677)		SBB	P		
232 229	(9679)	z	SBB	C	O	
232 230	(9680)		SBB	C	W	
232 233	(9683)		SBB	C		
232 235	(9685)	§	SBB	P	OW	
232 254	(9654)		SBB	C	U	

Number		Company	Builder	Works No	Built	Notes
232 256	(9656)	Schöni, Niederbipp				
232 286	(8701)	WRS			1976	ex ST "2"
232 287		Ciments Vigier, Reuchenette-Péry	SLM	4951	1973	"4" "Carole"
232 288		EDG	SLM	4952	1973	Ex SOB 236 006; "Max"
232 289		TAU, Muttenz Auhafen	SLM	4983	1973	Ex 237 814
232 290		SOB	SLM	4984	1973	Ex SOB 236 007

Number		Company	Sector	Notes
232 301	(9664)	SBB	I	
232 302	(9665)	SBB	I	
232 303	(9684)	SBB	I	
232 304	(9667)	SBB	I	
232 305	(9671)	SBB	I	
232 306	(8795)	SBB	I	
232 307	(8780)	SBB	I	
232 308	(8788)	SBB	I	
232 309	(9655)	SBB	I	
232 310	(9672)	SBB	I	
232 311	(9681)	SBB	I	
232 312	(9682)	SBB	I	
232 313	(9663)	SBB	I	
232 314	(9678)	SBB	I	
232 315	(9670)	SBB	I	

CLASS Tm 232.4 (CLASS Tm^{III})   B

These tractors are fitted with a hydraulic platform for overhead line maintenance work.

Built: 1981–86.
Builder: RACO.
Engine: Saurer D2K of 165 kW.
Transmission: Hydraulic.
Wheel Diameter: 950 mm.
Length over Buffers: 8.74 m.

Maximum Tractive Effort:
Weight: 28 tonnes.
Maximum Speed: 60 km/h.

Number		Company	Sector	Names
232 451	(9451)	Stauffer		
232 453	(9453)	Müller		
232 454	(9454)	Kummler+Matter		
232 456	(9456)	Stauffer		
9457		SBB	I	
232 460	(9460)	Müller		
232 461	(9461)	Müller		"Nonno"
232 463	(9463)	Stauffer		

CLASS Tm 232.5 (CLASS Tm^{III})   B

Similar to Class 232.4, but fitted with a three-tonne hydraulic crane and an open platform for use on permanent way work. Most of this class were rebuilt as Class 232.0.

Built: 1976–88.
Builder: RACO.
Engine: Saurer D2K of 165 kW.
Transmission: Hydraulic.
Wheel Diameter: 950 mm.
Length over Buffers: 8.74 m.

Maximum Tractive Effort:
Weight: 24 tonnes.
Maximum Speed: 60 km/h.

Number		Company		Number		Company
232 501	(9501)	SRT		9565		EFSA, Châtillens
232 517	(9517)	WRS		9587		Reismühle, Brunnen
232 526	(9526)	EDG		9593		Tensol Oil, Giornico
232 530	(9530)	WRS		9594		Tensol Oil, Giornico
9551		Carrière du Lessus, St Triphon		232 596	(9596)	SOB

CLASS Tm 233.9   B

Various Stadler tractors.

Number	Company	Works No.	Built	Notes
233 900	Sersa	235	1994	Ex SBB 233 900, ex STB 238 114
233 909	SOB	158	1983	Ex Tm 33, ex 236 009; "Wilen"
233 910	DSM, Sisseln	531	1999	Ex MThB 236 643; "Richard"
233 911	SZU	532	1999	Ex MThB 236 644, ex RM
233 914	CMS, Basel	325	1998	Ex 237 860
233 915	CMS, Basel	838	2003	Ex 237 869
233 916		522	1999	Ex PTT P16, ex 237 916
233 917		523	1999	Ex PTT P17, ex 237 917

CLASS Tm 234   "AMEISE"   B

The first batch of 50 (orders of 13 plus 37) of these track maintenance machines (*Ameise* means ant) was ordered by SBB in 1997 and this was followed by a further 50 in 2000 and 25 in 2005. The vehicle consists of an engine compartment and cab at one end and a platform with crane at the other. The 234 200–224 batch have a number of differences including a crane with basket, particle filters, GSM-R radio and redesigned roof. 234 000–012 are equipped with radio for the Zürich S-Bahn area, plus Winterthur and St. Gallen districts. 234 087 and 090 are respectively former MThB 236 648 and 649.

Built: 2000 (234 000–012); 2000/01 (234 050–086); 2002/03 (234 100–149); 2006–08 (234 200–224).
Builder: SLM Stadler, except 234 200–224 Stadler Winterthur.
Engine: MTU 12V 183 TD13 of 550 kW.

Transmission: Hydraulic.	**Maximum Tractive Effort:** 81 kN.
Wheel Diameter: 800 mm.	**Weight:** 30 tonnes (234 200–224, 37 tonnes).
Length over Buffers: 11.36 m.	**Maximum Speed:** 80 km/h.

All operated by SBB, except 234 087.

E   Equipped with ETCS Level 2.

Number	Sector		Number	Sector		Number	Sector
234 000	I		234 067	I		234 107	E I
234 001	I		234 068	I		234 108	I
234 002	I		234 069	I		234 109	E I
234 003	I		234 070	I		234 110	I
234 004	I		234 071	I		234 111	E I
234 005	I		234 072	I		234 112	I
234 006	I		234 073	I		234 113	I
234 007	I		234 074	I		234 114	E I
234 008	I		234 075	I		234 115	I
234 009	I		234 076	I		234 116	I
234 010	I		234 077	E I		234 117	E I
234 011	I		234 078	E I		234 118	I
234 012	I		234 079	I		234 119	I
234 051	I		234 080	I		234 120	E I
234 052	I		234 081	I		234 121	E I
234 053	I		234 082	I		234 122	E I
234 054	I		234 083	I		234 123	I
234 055	I		234 084	I		234 124	E I
234 056	I		234 085	I		234 125	E I
234 057	I		234 086	I		234 126	E I
234 058	E I		234 087	TPF		234 127	E I
234 059	I		234 090	I		234 128	E I
234 060	I		234 100	I		234 129	I
234 061	I		234 101	E I		234 130	E I
234 062	I		234 102	E I		234 131	E I
234 063	I		234 103	E I		234 132	E I
234 064	I		234 104	E I		234 133	E I
234 065	I		234 105	E I		234 134	E I
234 066	I		234 106	E I		234 135	E I

234 136	E	I	234 149	E	I	234 212	E	I
234 137	E	I	234 200		I	234 213		I
234 138	E	I	234 201	E	I	234 214		I
234 139	E	I	234 202		I	234 215	E	I
234 140	E	I	234 203	E	I	234 217		I
234 141	E	I	234 204		I	234 218		I
234 142	E	I	234 205	E	I	234 219		I
234 143	E	I	234 206	E	I	234 220		I
234 144	E	I	234 207		I	234 221		I
234 145	E	I	234 208		I	234 222		I
234 146	E	I	234 209		I	234 223		I
234 147	E	I	234 210		I	234 224		I
234 148	E	I	234 211	E	I			

CLASS 234.4

In 2015 SBB ordered 35 trolleys for infrastructure work from Windhoff. They will have a cab at one end and a platform with crane, and will have two diesel engines. Delivery will be from spring 2017 – five will initially be delivered for tests, then deliveries will go on to 2021.

Built:
Builder: Windhoff.
Engine:
Transmission: **Maximum Tractive Effort:**
Wheel Diameter: **Weight:** 40 tonnes loaded.
Length over Buffers: **Maximum Speed:** 100 km/h.

Number	Sector				
234 401	I	234 413	I	234 425	I
234 402	I	234 414	I	234 426	I
234 403	I	234 415	I	234 427	I
234 404	I	234 416	I	234 428	I
234 405	I	234 417	I	234 429	I
234 406	I	234 418	I	234 430	I
234 407	I	234 419	I	234 431	I
234 408	I	234 420	I	234 432	I
234 409	I	234 421	I	234 433	I
234 410	I	234 422	I	234 434	I
234 411	I	234 423	I	234 435	I
234 412	I	234 424	I		

CLASS 234.5 B

New trolleys for SOB with a cab at one end and a platform with crane at the other.

Built: 2015.
Builder: Robel.
Engine: Deutz TCD 2015 V8 4V of 500 kW.
Transmission: Hydraulic. Voith T212 bre + HA. **Maximum Tractive Effort:**
Wheel Diameter: 920 mm. **Weight:** 41 tonnes.
Length over Buffers: 15.10 m. **Maximum Speed:** 80 km/h.

Number	Company		
234 501	SOB	234 503	SOB
234 502	SOB		

▲ SBB 234 143 is seen at Fribourg with a short works train on 17 April 2014. BLS 236 380–384 are very similar. **David Haydock**

▼ BLS shunter 235 091 is seen at Stalden on 18 March 2015. Sersa loco 237 862, looks very similar. **Mario Stefani**

CLASS Tm 235.071–089 (CLASS Tm 2/2)　　　　　　　　　　　　　　　B

18 of these track trolleys, with cranes or diggers, were built by RACO, mainly for BLS, and are known as Types 240 DT4H and 270 DT4H. Others were built for metre gauge operators as Type CR4H. 235 085 was sold to Vanoli as 237 959 and is now preserved. 235 086 and 087 were sold to Italy. 235 082 and 088 were withdrawn.

Built: 1977–93.
Builder: RACO.
Engine: Deutz of 176 kW (§ 204 kW).
Length: 9.96 m; (235 076, 9.24 m).

Transmission: Hydraulic.
Weight: 19 tonnes.

Maximum Speed: 75 km/h (* 45 km/h).

Number		Company	Notes
235 071	*	Müller Gleisbau	Ex VHB Tm 56
235 072	*	Müller Gleisbau	Ex SMB Tm 72
235 073		transN	Ex RVT 12
235 074		Travys (PBr)	Ex PBr 238 303
235 075	*§	Müller Gleisbau	Ex BT 5, 236 005
235 076	*§	Müller Gleisbau	Ex BT 4, 236 004
235 079		BLS	Ex Tm 79
235 080	*	Extrazug	Ex BLS Tm 80
235 081		BLS	Ex Tm 81
235 083		BLS	Ex Tm 83
235 084		BLS	Ex Tm 84
235 089		EDG	Ex BLS Tm 89

CLASS 235.091–094　　　　　　　　　　　　　　　　　　　　　　B

Centre-cab shunters received by BLS Netz from Stadler.

Built: 1980/81.
Builder: Stadler: works numbers 151–154.
Engine: 2 x Mercedes of 350 kW each.
Transmission: Hydraulic.
Length: 10.30 m.

Weight: 40 tonnes.
Maximum Speed: 80 km/h.

Number	Company	Notes
235 091	BLS	Ex Tm 91
235 092	BLS	Ex Tm 92
235 093	BLS	Ex Tm 93
235 094	BLS	Ex Tm 94

CLASS 235.095–098　　　　　　　　　　　　　　　　　　　　　　B

End-cab shunters received by BLS Netz from Stadler.

Built: 1984.
Builder: Stadler: works numbers 163, 165, 164 & 166.
Engine: 1 x Mercedes of 350 kW.
Transmission: Hydraulic.
Length: 7.95 m.

Weight: 29 tonnes.
Maximum Speed: 80 km/h.

Number	Company	Notes
235 095	BLS	Ex Tm 95
235 096	BLS	Ex Tm 96
235 097	BLS	Ex Tm 97
235 098	Müller Gleisbau	Ex BLS Tm 98; "Bruno"

CLASS 235.100　　　　　　　　　　　　　　　　　　　　　　　　B

End-cab shunter received by BLS Netz from Stadler. 235 099 (works no. 282) was scrapped after an accident at Thun in 2006.

Built: 1996.
Builder: Stadler: works number 283.
Engine: 1 of 550 kW.
Transmission: Hydraulic.
Length: 8.90 m.

Weight: 38 tonnes.
Maximum Speed: 75 km/h.

Number	Company
235 100	BLS

CLASS 235.2 B

These are track maintenance trolleys owned by BLS Netz. All have cranes, but are of different designs. 201, 202 and 208–210 also have test pantographs. Similar to Robel vehicles recently delivered to CFL. 235 201, 202, 213 and 214 are equipped with ETCS so should be found near the Lötschberg base tunnel.

Built: 235 201–210 2006/07; 235 211–214 2011.
Builder: Robel.
Engine: 2 x Deutz 6-TCD20154V of 330 kW each.
Transmission: Hydraulic.   **Weight:** 32 tonnes.
Length: 14.396 m.   **Maximum Speed:** 100 km/h.

Number	Company		Number	Company
235 201	BLS		235 208	BLS
235 202	BLS		235 209	BLS
235 203	BLS		235 210	BLS
235 204	BLS		235 211	BLS
235 205	BLS		235 212	BLS
235 206	BLS		235 213	BLS
235 207	BLS		235 214	BLS

"CLASS Tm 236"

Tractors of a variety of designs. 236 001/2 became 230 863/864, 236 004/5 became 235 076/77, 236 006/7 became 232 288/290, 236 009 became 233 909, 236 341 became 230 436, 236 371/72 became 235 071/72.

Number	Company	Builder/Type	Works No	Built	Notes
236 008	SOB	Stadler/CAT	158	1983	Ex SOB Tm 2/2 33
236 067	Petroplus, Niederhasli	SLM/DZ		1965	Ex BLS Tm 67
236 310	CT-X Rail Service, Attisholz	Diema/DZ	4220	1978	Ex EBT Tm 10, ex BLS 236 310
236 317^{II}	See Class Tm^{II} (Class 230.6)				
236 340	BLS	Henschel DH250B	29968	1959	Ex RM, ex Preussen Elektra
236 342	See Class Tm^{II} (Class 230.6)				

CLASS 236.380–384 B

Track machines with BLS Netz, almost identical to SBB Class 234, and formerly numbered 234 380–384. All have cranes, but 236 384 has a "cherry picker" with basket. Details as SBB Class Tm 234 except:

Built: 2003/04.   **Builder:** Winpro.
Length: 11.36 m.   **Maximum Speed:** 80 km/h.

Number		Company		Number		Company
236 380	(234 380)	BLS		236 383	(234 383)	BLS
236 381	(234 381)	BLS		236 384	(234 384)	BLS
236 382	(234 382)	BLS				

"CLASS Tm 236" (others)

Number	Company	Builder/Type	Works No	Built	Notes
236 508	SZU	Robel Tm 3/3		1994	Ex Tm 508, ex 337 508
236 647	Stadler, Winterthur	RACO Tm^{II}	1537	1959	Ex MThB Tm 62
236 903	LBA, Brenzikon	Kronenberg DT120	146	1963	
236 910	LBA, Claro	Stadler	117	1965	

"CLASSES Tm 237 & 238"

A wide variety of smaller shunters (larger ones are in the 837 series), most with industrial users.

Number	Company	Builder/Type	Works No	Built	Notes
237 087	TPF	Stadler	532	2000	Ex MThB Tm 2/2 649
237 554	RA	RACO Tm 234	2026	1995	"Barry"
237 701	LBA, Thun	Stadler	141	1973	Ex K+W, Thun
237 708	SOB	Jung	13180		Ex SOB 34, ex DB 323 812; "s'MANDARINLI"
237 803	Sygenta, Monthey	Henschel DHG300B	32474	1985	"493A"
237 804	Elektrozinn, Oberrüti	Gmeinder 190PS	5246	1961	Ex Südzucker
237 806	Railcare, Härkingen	Schöma CFL350DCLR	4942	1987	
237 808	Jura Cement, Wildegg	Henschel DHG200B	30877	1965	Ex 837 808
237 810	Alcosuisse	O&K MB125N	26696	1970	
237 818	Landor Fenaco Genossenschaft	Jung	13272	1960	"Marco"
237 819	Chemie Uetikon	Jung	13154	1960	Ex DB 323 786
237 822	Delicia, Birsfeld Hafen	O&K MHB101	26799	1975	"1"
237 824	Delicia, Birsfeld Hafen	Henschel	30868	1964	"2"
237 825	Migros, Oberbuchstein	O&K MB280N	26791	1974	
237 852	Vanoli	Henschel DH500C	30258	1960	
237 856	Timcal, Bodio	O&K MB280N	26781	1973	
237 857	Ultra-Brag, Muttenz Auhafen	O&K	26971	1981	"1"
237 859	Saurefabrik, Schweizerhalle	KM ML225B	18701	1960	
237 861	Sersa	Stadler	235	1994	Ex SBB 233 900, ex STB 14
237 862	Sersa	Stadler	162	1984	Ex WM Em 2/2 103
237 864	Ultra Brag, Basel Port	Jung RK15B	13399	1961	"5"
237 865	Meyerhans Hotz, Frauenfeld	SLM	4587	1965	
237 867	TAU, Muttenz Auhafen	Gmeinder D35B	5468	1970	"Ronny"
237 868	TAU, Muttenz Auhafen	Henschel DHG275	31098	1967	
237 871	Altola, Olten	O&K MV3	26596	1966	
237 873	Sappi Schweiz, Biberist	Henschel DH240B	30585	1963	
237 874	KEBAG, Zuchwil	Schöma CFL200DCLR	5362	1994	
237 875	Stauffer	Deutz KG230B	57938	1965	
237 880	UFA	O&K MB200N		1975	
237 881	Contargo	Deutz A12L614R	56282	1956	
237 900	EDG, Railogistics, Zollikon	Schöma CFL 150DBR	2292	1960	
237 902	Jurachimie, Cornaux	MaK	500052	1970	Ex 837 902
237 904	ZAF, Frauenfeld	Gmeinder DS20B	5678	1989	
237 905	Chemie Uetikon, Uetikon am See	Gmeinder Köf II	4686	1952	Ex DB 324 013
237 906	see Class Tm 231.0				
237 907	Sersa	SIG/BBC/SAU		1967	Ex DSM. "FRIDOLIN"
237 908	Sersa	Cockerill	4143	1964	Ex Migros, Suhr
237 909	Ferro AG, Birr	RACO 95MA3RS	1798	1971	Ex 236 312
237 910	see Class Tm^{II} (Class 230.6)				
237 911	Eurovapor	Deutz KS230B	57069	1960	Ex ÖBB Em 2/2 9
237 915	Bühler, Uzwil	Henschel DHG300B	31988	1978	
237 923	Weiacher Kies, Weiach	Moyse BN40E260D	1264	1977	
237 924	Jura Cement, Wildegg	O&K MB220N	26721	1972	
237 925	LSB	O&K MB9			
237 926	Weiacher Kies, Weiach	Schöma CHL 350GR	5712	2002	
237 927	Migros, Gossau	O&K	26679		
237 929	Stadler, Altenrhein	Jung RK11B	14038	1968	
237 931	see Class Tm^{II} (Class 230.6)				

▲ 237 906, owned by Stauffer, is former SBB Tm^{III} 922. It is seen at Gwatt on 25 October 2013.
Charles-André Fluckiger

▼ 237 960 is an O&K MB5N and shunts for Railcare at Roggwil-Weynau, where it is seen on 15 April 2013. **Mario Stefani**

237 932	Ems-Chemie	CKD T239-S		1994	
237 933	Stauffer	Stadler	119	1966	Ex MThB 51; "Seppi"
237 935	Ziegler Papier, Grellingen	Henschel DHG160B	30874	1964	
237 937	Holcim, Niederstetten	Schöma	2151	1958	"Alex"
237 942	LBA, Claro	Stadler	117	1965	Ex BABHE 236 910
237 944	LBA, Claro	RACO	2023	1975	
237 948	Kibag Kies Seewen	Moyse BN32E150B	1067	1954	
237 950	Sersa	Robel Barnow AG54	2353	1994	"CHRISTIAN"
237 952	Sersa	Henschel DH240B	30336	1962	Ex BBC Oerlikon, Ex Ems Chemie; "ERWIN"
237 954	LSB	KM M250B	19279	1965	
237 956	Febex, Bex	Deutz A6M617R	55754	1955	Ex DB 323 085
237 957	Kummler + Matter	Robel			
237 960	Railcare, Roggwil-Wynau	O&K MB5N	26586	1965	
237 963	LSB, Railcare, Härkingen	Henschel DHG240B	31092	1965	
237 966	Greuter, Bülach	Henschel DH240B	30594	1964	Previously numbered 237 906 (Duplicate number!)
237 969	Migros Ostschweiz	Henschel DHG300B	32473	1982	
237 970	Sersa	Robel 54.22		2005	"MAX"
237 971	Sersa	Robel 54.22		2005	"PETER"
237 972	VDM	Deutz A8L614R	56900	1956	

CLASS Em 238.5 (CLASS Em 2/2)   Bo

Formerly known as Type Em 2/2, and mainly built for industry, these locos were once numbered in various series but are now almost all in the series 238 501 to 509. There was also an all-electric version: GFM has 217 091 and Travys (OC) has Ee 2/2 1 and 2. 238 503 was scrapped.

Built: 1959–67.   **Builder:** SIG/BBC.
Engine: Saurer SD of 240 kW.   **Transmission:** Electric.
Length: 7.50 m.   **Weight:** 39 tonnes.

Number	Company	Works No	Built	Notes
238 501	Sersa	6088	1959	Ex 237 953; ex BBC, "FRITZ"
238 502	Kaufmann Thörishaus	6089	1960	Ex 237 928; ex BBC
238 504	Sersa	7701	1967	Ex 237 907; "FRIDOLIN"
238 505	Bombardier Zürich	6405	1964	Ex 237 905, ex BBC, "WALTER"
238 506	ST	6406	1965	aka Em 2/2 1
238 507	SZU	6149	1961	Ex 236 507; ex Stadt Bern
238 508	Sersa	7639	1961	Ex 237 914, ex WM 101; "ERICH"
238 509	Sersa	7640	1966	Ex 237 897, ex WM 102; "Madeleine"

CLASS Tea 245   B

Electric/battery shunters built for BLS – very similar in appearance to BLS diesel locos 235 095–097.

Built: 1993/94.   **Builder:** Stadler: works numbers 197, 198, 199 & 234.
Length: 7.95 m.   **Weight:** 34 tonnes.
Maximum Speed: 80 km/h.

Number	Company		Number	Company
245 021	BLS		245 023	BLS
245 022	BLS		245 024	BLS

▲ 237 932 was built by ČKD (Type T239) in the Czech Republic and shunts for Ems Chemie near Chur. It is seen on 12 July 2007. **Mario Stefani**

▼ 237 966 is one of many Henschel shunters operating in Switzerland and is seen at Gummenen, working for Greuter AG. **Charles-André Fluckiger**

CLASS Ta 251   Bo

SBB battery tractors, not in capital stock, owned by the works themselves for use as pilots. 251 001 and 251 003 are now preserved.

Built: 1990.
Builder–Mechanical Parts: Stadler.   **Traction Motors:**
Builder–Electrical Parts: Bosch.   **Power Rating:** 4 kW.
Transmission: Electric.   **Maximum Tractive Effort:**
Wheel Diameter: **Weight:** 7 tonnes.
Length over Buffers: 3.36 m.   **Maximum Speed:** 10 km/h.

Number	Location		Number	Location
251 002	Olten works		251 005	Olten works
251 004	Olten works			

CLASS Tm 283   Bo

A second hand tractor purchased by SBB from Scheuchzer in 1989 then sold to Rhenus. Yellow livery. Used in the port of Basel-Kleinhüningen.

Built: 1972.
Builder: Gmeinder Type DE-SF-3. Works number 5490.
Engine: MAN 650 kW.
Transmission: Electric.   **Weight:** 23 tonnes.
Length over Buffers: 7.63 m.   **Maximum Speed:** 60 km/h.

Number	Company
283 000	Rhenus, Kleinhüningen

1.2. MAIN LINE ELECTRIC LOCOMOTIVES

Swiss electric locomotive classes have traditionally been numbered from 401 for Bo-Bo types and from 601 for Co-Cos. However, cross-border operations have led to increasing numbers of locos being leased – and numbered in the German class system from 100 upwards. BLS Cargo has said its new Vectron locos will be Class 193 – as in Germany.

Electric locomotives registered in Switzerland carry EVNs 91 85 4xxx xxx-c. It should be noted that some of the locomotives listed here, particularly modern multi-voltage locomotives, are registered outside Switzerland and carry EVNs respective to their country of registration.

Many locomotives are now being leased including by SBB itself. Leasing company codes are:

AK	Akiem	MER	Macquarie European Rail
AT	Alpha Trains	MRCE	Mitsui Rail Capital Europe
BRL	Beacon Rail Leasing	RPOOL	Railpool
HML	Hannover Mobilien Leasing		

CLASS Ae 1042   Bo-Bo

Nine of these former ÖBB locos were imported from Austria; three were approved for use by WRS in late 2014 and started operation in mid 2015. Others may be prepared for traffic but some will serve as spares banks.

Built: 1963–68.
Builder–Mechanical Parts: SGP.
Builder–Electrical Parts: Elin/Siemens/BBC.
One Hour Rating: 3560 kW.
Wheel Diameter: 1250 mm.
Length over Buffers: 16.22 m.
EVN: 91 85 1042 007-c and so o

Maximum Tractive Effort: 255 kN.
Weight: 84 tonnes.
Maximum Speed: 130 km/h.

Number	Company	Number	Company	Number	Company
1042 007	WRS	1042 020	WRS(S)	1042 034	WRS(S)
1042 013	WRS(S)	1042 032	WRS	1042 036	WRS(S)
1042 018	WRS(S)	1042 033	WRS(S)	1042 041	WRS

CLASSES 185.1 & 185.2   TRAXX AC   Bo-Bo

The Bombardier TRAXX electric locomotive has been a major success in Switzerland and exists in several versions, although both versions 1 and 2 look the same. TRAXX AC locos (15/25 kV AC) are known as Class 185 (DB and leasing companies) Class 482 (SBB) and 485 (BLS). TRAXX MS (multi-system), in various version are Classes 186 (DB and leasing companies), 484 (SBB) and 486 (BLS). All can work in multiple with each other. These locomotives (version D-A-CH for Germany, Austria and Switzerland) are used by DB Schenker, which has 185 095–149 (Type 185.1 – see German Railways Part 1) for use in Switzerland, mainly on the Gotthard route. They generally work singly from Germany to Basel, then add a second loco there or at Erstfeld, from where a banker can also be provided. 185 101–110 are equipped with ETCS Level 2 and the others are now also being equipped in preparation for the opening of the Gotthard base tunnel in December 2016. BLS also hires locos numbered in the 185.5 series (Type 185.1) from Alpha Trains when required. Crossrail hires locos in the 185.5 series (Type 185.2) both long-term, which are in Crossrail livery, and to cope with traffic peaks. Captrain Deutschland also hires Class 185 for transit traffic.

Built: 2000–10.
Builder: Bombardier Transportation (Kassel).
Electric Brake: Regenerative.
Continuous Rating: 5600 kW.
Wheel Diameter: 1250 mm.
Length over Buffers: 18.90 m.

Systems: 15 kV AC 16.7 Hz, 25 kV AC 50 Hz.
Maximum Tractive Effort: 300 kN.
Weight: 84 tonnes.
Maximum Speed: 140 km/h.

Number	Company	Names	Number	Company
185 525	AT/XRAIL		185 536	AT/XRAIL
185 527	AT/Lokomotion		185 541	HML/Captrain DE
185 535	AT/XRAIL	Christine	185 549	MRCE/Captrain DE

▲ WRS 1042 041 is seen on a test run at Grenchen Süd on 8 April 2014.   **Mario Stefani**

▼ Crossrail 185 596 and three more of the company's electric locos head a southbound container train at Silenen on 14 August 2014.   **Laurence Sly**

185 550	MRCE/BLS Cargo		185 593	BRL/XRAIL		
185 571	MRCE/SBB CI		185 594	BRL/XRAIL		
185 576	AT/XRAIL		185 595	BRL/XRAIL	Ruth	
185 577	AT/IGE		185 596	BRL/XRAIL	Suzy	
185 578	MER/Captrain DE	Christine	185 597	BRL/XRAIL		
185 579	MER/Captrain DE	Adriana	185 599	BRL/XRAIL		
185 580	MER/Captrain DE	Jana	185 600	BRL/XRAIL		
185 581	MER/XRAIL	Celine Alia	185 601	BRL/XRAIL		
185 590	BRL/XRAIL		185 602	BRL/XRAIL		
185 591	BRL/XRAIL		185 607	AT/XRAIL		
185 592	BRL/XRAIL		185 613	AT/XRAIL		

CLASS 186   TRAXX MS   Bo-Bo

Class 186 is the multi-system version (TRAXX MS) of the TRAXX and can be configured for almost any European country or corridor. These are version D-A-CH-I – 15/25 kV AC plus 1500/3000 V DC for Germany, Austria, Switzerland and Italy. BLS has hired several to operate container trains throughout from Germany to Melzo in Italy. BLS and Crossrail also use Class 186s into Italy. BLS Cargo took some Class 186s in exchange for leasing Class 465s to Railcare.

Built: 2006–08.
Builder: Bombardier Transportation (Kassel).
Electric Brake: Regenerative.   **Systems:** 15 kV AC 16.7 Hz, 25 kV AC 50 Hz, 1500/3000 V DC.
Maximum Tractive Effort: 300 kN.   **Continuous Rating:** 5600 kW (4000 kW under 3000 V DC).
Wheel Diameter: 1250 mm.   **Weight:** 84 tonnes.
Length over Buffers: 18.90 m.   **Maximum Speed:** 140 km/h.

*   Subhired from Lokomotion

Number	Company		Number	Company		Number	Company
186 101	RPOOL/BLS		186 109	RPOOL/BLS		186 904	MER/XRAIL
186 102 *	RPOOL/BLS		186 110	RPOOL/RTB Cargo		186 905	MER/XRAIL
186 103	RPOOL/BLS					186 906	MER/XRAIL
186 104	RPOOL/BLS		186 251 *	RPOOL/BLS		186 907	MER/XRAIL
186 105	RPOOL/BLS					186 908	MER/XRAIL
186 106 *	RPOOL/BLS		186 901	MER/XRAIL		186 909	MER/XRAIL
186 107	RPOOL/BLS		186 902	MER/XRAIL		186 910	MER/XRAIL
186 108	RPOOL/BLS		186 903	MER/XRAIL			

CLASS 187   TRAXX AC3 LM   Bo-Bo

Class 187 is the first version of the third generation of TRAXX loco; these feature a new front end design and body sides which are designed to take advertising. The locos are the AC version (15/25 kV AC) with the addition of a small diesel engine for "last mile" operations in non-electrified sidings. BLS was an "early adopter" of the loco, allowing Bombardier to test the loco, hiring three from Railpool – which ones may change over time. The design was approved in Switzerland and is now used regularly. SRT has bought identical 487 001. All Class 187 have ETCS Level 2. 187 001 to 003 are test locos. Railpool has now ordered 18 more locomotives, of which 13 will be equipped for NL-BE-D-A-CH-I. SNCF leasing subsidiary Akiem has four Class 187 equipped for D-A-CH-I. 187 010 was sold to Westfälische Landes-Eisenbahn.

Built: 2013–   **Systems:** 15 kV AC 16.7 Hz, 25 kV AC 50 Hz.
Builder: Bombardier, Kassel.   **Maximum Tractive Effort:** 300 kN.
Diesel Engine: Deutz 2013 BR-4V of 230 kW.   **Weight:** 84 tonnes.
Continuous Rating: 5600 kW.   **Wheel Diameter:** 1250 mm. **Length** over
Buffers: 18.90 m.   **Maximum Speed:** 160 km/h.

Number	Company	Names		Number	Company
187 001				187 008	RPOOL/BLS
187 002				187 009	RPOOL/LOCON
187 003		Hans Werner		187 011	AK/Captrain DE
187 004	RPOOL/BLS			187 012	AK/Captrain DE
187 005	RPOOL/BLS			187 013	AK/Captrain DE
187 006	RPOOL/BLS			187 014	AK
187 007	RPOOL/BLS				

▲ 187 008 and 186 103, both on hire from Railpool to BLS Cargo, head a train of containers south from Erstfeld on 24 June 2015. **Mario Stefani**

▼ SBB Historic's preserved loco 10001 (410 001) carries out a test run with electric railcar 1001 at Boudry on 17 June 2015. **Mario Stefani**

CLASS 189   TYPE ES64F4   Bo-Bo

Class 189 is a multi-voltage locomotive used across Europe. Only locos likely to operate across Switzerland (others work from Germany to Basel Muttenz) are included here.

189 101–115 are version VL (delivered as Version VE) for the Netherlands, Germany, Austria, Switzerland, Italy, Belgium, Slovenia, Hungary and Romania. 982–999 are version VE for the Netherlands, Germany, Austria, Switzerland, Italy, Slovenia and Croatia. SBB Cargo International has hired a dozen of them from MRCE and uses them from Germany to Switzerland. SBB CI may hire other Class 189s for use outside Switzerland – they are not included here.

Built: 2003–09.
Builder: Siemens, München Allach.
Systems: 15 kV AC 16.7 Hz, 25 kV AC 50 Hz, 1500/3000 V DC.
Continuous Rating: 6400 kW.   **Maximum Tractive Effort:** 300 kN.
Wheel Diameter: 1250 mm.   **Weight:** 86 tonnes.
Length over Buffers: 19.58 m.   **Maximum Speed:** 140 km/h.

Number	Company
189 101	MRCE/WLC
189 102	MRCE/SBB Cargo International
189 103	MRCE/CFI
189 104	MRCE/Captrain DE
189 105	MRCE/LTE NL
189 106	MRCE/SBB Cargo International
189 107	MRCE/SBB Cargo International
189 108	MRCE/Trenitalia Cargo
189 109	MRCE/SBB Cargo International
189 110	MRCE/ISC
189 111	MRCE/Captrain DE
189 112	MRCE/SBB Cargo International
189 113	MRCE/LTE NL
189 114	MRCE/Captrain NL
189 115	MRCE/TXL
189 982	MRCE/SBB Cargo International
189 983	MRCE/SBB Cargo International
189 984	MRCE/SBB Cargo International
189 985	MRCE/InRail
189 986	MRCE/TXL
189 987	MRCE/SBB Cargo International
189 988	MRCE/off lease (accident)
189 989	MRCE/TXL
189 990	MRCE/SBB Cargo International
189 991	MRCE/SBB Cargo International
189 992	MRCE/TXL
189 993	MRCE/InRail
189 994	MRCE/Captrain DE
189 995	MRCE/TXL
189 996	MRCE/SBB Cargo International
189 997	MRCE/TXL
189 998	MRCE/TXL
189 999	MRCE/DB Schenker IT

CLASSES Re 410 & 416   Bo-Bo

These are former SBB Class Re 4/4^{I} locos, which were originally numbered 10001 upwards, and are now used by private operators. 10008 and 10019 are preserved in Germany by Centralbahn but are not equipped to operate in Switzerland. Centralbahn also bought 10006 for parts; we believe it has been scrapped. Four locos were numbered 416 626 to 629, and may still carry those numbers, but EVNs are in the 410 series.

416 011/013/014/015/102/171 are preserved Class Be 4/4.

Built: 1946–51.
Builder–Mechanical Parts: SLM.
Builder–Electrical Parts: BBC/MFO/SAAS.
Traction Motors: 4 single-phase commutator type, fully suspended with BBC spring drive.
One Hour Rating: 1854 kW.   **Maximum Tractive Effort:** 137 kN.
Wheel Diameter: 1040 mm.   **Weight:** 57 tonnes.
Length: 14.90 m.   **Maximum Speed:** 125 km/h.

Number		Company	Notes
10001		SBB H	
416 625	(10002)	Classic Rail	No. 2012
410 009	(10009)	Trans Rail	Ex 416 626
410 016	(10016)	VEhE Ae 6/6	Ex 416 627
410 032	(10032)	TEE AG	
410 034	(10034)	TEE Classics	"Sissach"
416 628	(10039)	SRT (S)	
10044		SBB H	
10046		THURBO	

CLASSES Re 420 & 430 (ex Re 4/4ᴵᴵ & Re 4/4ᴵᴵᴵ) Bo-Bo

This was the standard SBB electric locomotive for some 20 years and is still to be found throughout the system. The first six appeared in 1964 with series production beginning in 1967. The different lengths arise from variations in the body below the cabs. Those which have carried "Swiss Express" livery were fitted with automatic couplers, but have now reverted to standard. 11172, 11282, 11312, 11323 and 11365 were withdrawn following accidents. The current 11172 was originally MThB Re 4/4ᴵᴵ 21.

The first of the class, 11101, was withdrawn in mid 2014. 11102 to 11107, 11110, 11117, 11119, 11123, 11137 and 11142 were sold to BLS as part of a deal when work was divided between BLS and SBB. They were renumbered 420 501 to 512 in random order and carry only the 5xx number on the front end; 420 507 to 512 were later withdrawn. The remaining locos are used on push-pull passenger services from Bern to Neuchâtel with ex-SBB Mark III stock. 420 503 was sold to Travys (red/grey livery) and 420 506 to MBC (green/grey livery) in 2013, both to allow these small companies to operate on the main line.

In late 2014 SBB Cargo started to modernise its locos, the first being 11275, renumbered 420 275.

Class Re 4/4ᴵᴵᴵ (11350–11370) is a variation with a lower gear ratio for use on mountain lines. 11351–11353 were sold to the Südostbahn but returned to SBB together with an identical locomotive built new for the SOB in exchange for the Re 4/4ᴵⱽ class.

11201–11230 are being overhauled and equipped to top-and-tail sets of double-deck coaches on Zürich area peak workings. These trains are known as *Hauptverkehrszeit-Doppelstock-Pendelzug* (HVZ) and are part of the "LION" project. Modified locos are renumbered and turned out in a red livery with large symbols on the side.

11371–11397 have been equipped for use in Germany, turned out in Cargo livery and renumbered 421 371–397 (see below). 421 382 has since been withdrawn.

Crossrail 430 (formerly 436) 111–113 are ex-EBT Re 4/4 111–113, 430 114 is ex-VHB 141 and 430 115 is ex-SMB 181. All are equipped with ETCS Level 2 and are used mainly on freight from Basel to Domodossola. Details are the same as SBB Class 420.

Built: 1964–85; Crossrail 430 111, 112 1969; 430 113 to 115 1983.
Builder–Mechanical Parts: SLM.
Builder–Electrical. Parts: BBC/MFO/SAAS.
Traction Motors: 4 single-phase commutator type, fully suspended with BBC spring drive.
One Hour Rating: 4700 (4650*) kW.   **Maximum Tractive Effort:** 255 (280*) kN.
Wheel Diameter: 1260 mm.   **Weight:** 80 tonnes.
Length over Buffers: 14.80–15.52 m.   **Maximum Speed:** 140 (125*) km/h.

Pantographs:

11101–11155: One, double arm Swiss (s single arm).
11195–11198: Two, single arm, one Swiss and one DB/ÖBB-type for through working to Lindau.

There are many variations in length.

11101–11106 (Prototypes)	14.80 m
11107–11155 (First production series)	14.90 m (15.52 m §)
11156–11219, 11236–11238 (Second production series)	15.41 m (15.465 m†, 15.52 m §)
11220–11235, 11239–11254 (Second production series, mod.)	15.51 m
11255–11349, 11350–11397 (Final production series)	15.52 m

E   ETCS Level 2 fitted.
L   LION project (HVZ).
r   Equipped with radio for e.c.s. working.
u   Equipped with UIC 18 pole cable.

Notes:
All are push-pull and mw fitted and can multiple with Classes Re 4/4ᴵᴵᴵ, Re 4/4ᴵⱽ, Re 6/6 and RBe 4/4. 11350–11353 were formerly SOB 41/4/2/3 respectively. 11172 was formerly MThB Re 4/4ᴵᴵ 21.

SBB locomotives. Depot allocations are not shown, as locos of this class are common user.

Number	Livery	Sector			Number	Livery	Sector	
11108	0	P	§		11112	R	P	§
11109	0	P	§		11114	R	P	u
11111	R	P			11115	R	P	u

11116	R	P	u		11156	R	P	Eu
11118	R	P	u		11157	R	P	†u
11120	R	P	r		11158	R	P	u
11121	R	P			11159	R	P	u
11122	R	P	u		420 160	C	C	
11124	R	P	u		11161	G	P	Eu
11125	R	P			11162	R	I	
11126	R	P	u		11163	R	I	
11127	R	P			11164	R	P	u
11128	R	P			420 165	C	I	
11129	R	P	u		11166	R	C	§
11130	R	P			11167	R	C	
11131	R	P			11168	R	C	
11132	R	P	u		420 169	C	C	§
11133	R	P			420 170	C	C	
11134	R	P	u		11171	R	C	
11135	R	P	u		11172	R	P	Eu*
11136	R	P	u		11173	R	C	
11138	R	P	u		11174	R	C	
11139	R	P	u		11175	R	C	
11140	R	P			11176	R	C	
11141	R	P	§u		11177	R	C	
11143	R	P	u		420 178	C	C	
11144	R	P			11179	R	C	
11145	R	P	u		11180	R	C	
11146	R	P			11181	R	P	Eu
11147	R	P	u		11182	R	C	
11148	R	P	u		11183	R	C	
11149	R	P	u		11185	R	C	
11150	R	P	u		420 186	C	C	
11151	R	P			11187	R	C	
11152	R	P	u		11188	R	C	
11153	R	P			11189	R	C	
11154	R	P	u		11190	R	C	
11155	R	P	u		11191	R	P	Eu

▲ Class Re 420 11320, which was previously hired to Interregio Cargo, pairs with Re 6/6 11664 with an intermodal service through Airolo on 1 February 2015. **Laurence Sly**

11192	**R**	P	Eu		11256	**R**	C	E
11193	**R**	P	Eu		11257	**R**	P	Eu
11194	**R**	P	Eu		11258	**R**	P	Eu
11195	**R**	P	Eu		11259	**R**	C	E
11196	**R**	P	Eu		11260	**R**	C	E
11197	**R**	P	Eu		11261	**R**	C	E
11198	**R**	P	Eu		11262	**R**	C	E
11199	**R**	P	Eu		11263	**R**	C	E
11200	**R**	P	Eu		11264	**R**	C	E
420 201	**R**	P	L		420 265	**R**	C	E
420 202	**R**	P	L		11266	**R**	C	E
420 203	**R**	P	L		11267	**R**	C	E
420 204	**R**	P	L		420 268	**A**	C	E
420 205	**R**	P	L		11269	**R**	C	E
420 206	**R**	P	L		11270	**R**	C	E
420 207	**R**	P	L		11271	**R**	C	E
420 208	**R**	P	L		11272	**R**	C	E
420 209	**R**	P	L		11273	**R**	C	E
420 210	**R**	P	L		420 275	**R**	C	E
420 211	**R**	P	L		420 276	**C**	C	E
11212	**R**	P			11277	**R**	C	E
420 213	**R**	P	L		11278	**R**	C	E
420 214	**R**	P	L		11279	**R**	C	E
420 215	**R**	P	L		11280	**R**	I	E
420 216	**R**	P	L		11281	**R**	C	E
420 217	**R**	P	L		11283	**R**	C	E
420 218	**R**	P	L		11284	**R**	C	E
420 219	**R**	P	L		11285	**R**	C	E
420 220	**R**	P	L		11286	**R**	C	E
420 221	**R**	P	L		11287	**R**	C	E
420 222	**R**	P	L		11288	**R**	C	E
420 223	**R**	P	L		11289	**R**	C	E
420 224	**R**	P	L		11290	**R**	C	E
420 225	**R**	P	L		11291	**R**	C	E
420 226	**R**	P	L		11292	**R**	C	E
420 227	**R**	P	L		11293	**R**	C	E
420 228	**R**	P	L		11294	**R**	C	E
420 229	**R**	P	L		11295	**R**	C	E
420 230	**R**	P	L		11296	**R**	C	E
11231	**R**	C			11297	**R**	C	E
11232	**R**	C			11298	**R**	C	E
11233	**R**	C			11299	**R**	P	
11234	**R**	C			11300	**R**	P	
11235	**R**	C			11301	**R**	P	
11236	**R**	C			11302	**R**	P	
11237	**R**	C			11303	**R**	P	
11238	**R**	C			11304	**R**	P	
11239	**R**	C			11305	**R**	C	
420 240	**C**	C	E		11306	**R**	C	
420 241	**R**	C			420 307	**C**	C	
11242	**R**	C			11308	**R**	C	
11243	**R**	P	Eu		11309	**G**	C	
11244	**R**	C			420 310	**C**	C	
11245	**R**	C			11311	**R**	C	
11246	**R**	C			11313	**R**	C	
11247	**R**	P	Eu		11314	**R**	C	
11248	**R**	P	E u		11315	**R**	C	
11249	**R**	P	Eu		11316	**R**	C	
11250	**R**	P	Eu		11317	**R**	C	
11251	**R**	P	Eu		11318	**R**	C	
11252	**R**	C			11319	**R**	C	
11253	**R**	C			11320	**A**	C	E
11254	**R**	C	E		11321	**R**	C	E
11255	**R**	P	Eu		11322	**R**	I	E

11324	R	C	E		11348	R	I	E	
11325	R	C	E		11349	R	I	E	
11326	R	I	E						
11327	R	C	E		430 350	R	C	*	
11328	R	C	E		430 351	R	C	*	
11329	R	I	E		11352	R	C	*	
11330	G	I	E		430 353	R	C	*	
11331	R	I	E		430 354	R	C	*	
11332	R	I	E		11355	R	C	*	
11333	R	I	E		430 356	C	C	*	
11334	R	I	E		430 357	R	C	*	
11335	R	I	E		~~11358~~	R	C	*	*430 358*
11336	R	I	E		430 359	R	C	*	
11337	R	I	E		11360	R	C	*	
11338	R	I	E		11361	R	C	*	
11339	R	I	E		11362	R	C	*	
11340	R	I	E		11363	R	C	*	
11341	R	I	E		430 364	G	C	*	
11342	R	I	E		11366	R	C	*	
11343	R	I	E		11367	R	C	*	
420 344	C	I	E		430 368	R	C	*	
11345	R	I	E		~~11369~~	R	C	*	*430 369*
420 346	C	I	E		11370	R	C	*	
420 347	C	I	E						

Name:

11239 PORRENTRUY (name taken from Ae 6/6 11483 in 1979).

Other companies' locomotives.

Number		Company	Names				
420 501	(11110)	BLS			430 111	XRAIL	Sara
420 502	(11117)	BLS			430 112	XRAIL	Zita
420 503	(11119)	Travys (PBr)			430 113 (U)	XRAIL	Marianne
420 504	(11123)	BLS			430 114	XRAIL	Natalie
420 505	(11137)	BLS			430 115	XRAIL	Ivon
420 506	(11142)	MBC					

CLASS Re 421   Bo-Bo

These are Class 420 (Re 4/4ᴵᴵ) locomotives modified for operation into Germany and allocated to SBB Cargo. Also used on Zürich–Lindau passenger trains. Modifications include changes to fit within the loading gauge, a new Schunk Type WBL 85 pantograph, and German radio and signalling equipment. Former numbers 11371–11397. 11382 was destroyed in a fire. About half are hired and reach the far north of Germany.

Details as Class Re 420 except:

Maximum Speed: 140 km/h (120 km/h in Germany).

All locomotives are with SBB.

Number	Livery	Sector		Depot/Hired to	Number	Livery	Sector		Depot/Hired to
421 371	C	P	u	BS	421 385	C	I		BS
421 372	C	C		HSL	421 386	C	I		TXL
421 373	C	C		TXL	421 387	C	I		BS
421 374	C	C		BS	421 388	C	I		Staudenbahn
421 375	C	C		TXL	421 389	C	C		HSL
421 376	C	C		TXL	421 390	C	C		BS
421 377	C	C		TXL	421 391	C	C		TXL
421 378	C	C		BS	421 392	C	P	u	BS
421 379	C	P	u	BS	421 393	C	C		BS
421 380	C	C		BS	421 394	C	P	u	BS
421 381	C	C		HSL	421 395	C	C		HSL
421 383	C	P	u	BS	421 396	C	C		HSL
421 384	C	C		TXL	421 397	C	C		HSL

▲ The 30 "LION" Class 420 locomotives are normally used on peak extras to/from Zürich but 420 202 turned up on an InterRegio service at Luzern on 1 June 2015. **Mario Stefani**

▼ All four of the serviceable Crossrail Class Re 436 locos (now renumbered as Re 430) are seen running light through Pratteln on 23 April 2015 led by 436 115. **Mario Stefani**

CLASS Re 425 (ex Re 4/4) Bo-Bo

This was originally the standard BLS electric locomotive. They are found mainly on the Basel–Lötschberg route, now only on freight. 161–165 were Ae 4/4 ^{II} 261–265 until 1969. All are now with BLS Cargo. They still all carry the original brown livery and the original three-digit number.

Built: 1964/65 161/162; 1967 163–165; 1970 166–173; 1972 174–189; 1982/83 190–195.
Builder–Mechanical Parts: SLM.
Builder–Electrical Parts: BBC.
Traction Motors: Four DC type, fully suspended with BBC spring drive.
One Hour Rating: 4980 kW. **Maximum Tractive Effort:** 314 kN.
Wheel Diameter: 1250 mm. **Weight:** 80 tonnes.
Length over Buffers: 15.47 (15.10 m *). **Maximum Speed:** 140 km/h.

All locos multiple-working fitted.

E Equipped with ETCS Level 2 for Lötschberg base tunnel.
p Push-pull and door control equipped. No longer used.

All locomotives are with BLS.

Number	Livery		Names		Number	Livery		Names
425 164	B	*	LENGNAU		425 180	B	E	VILLE DE NEUCHÂTEL
425 165	B	*	MOUTIER		425 181	B	E	INTERLAKEN
425 167	B	*	AUSSERBERG		425 182	B	E	KANDERGRUND
425 168	B	*	BALTSCHIEDER		425 183	B	E	KANDERSTEG
425 169	B	*	BÖNIGEN		425 184	B	E	KRATTIGEN
425 170	B	*E	BRIG-GLIS		425 185	B	E	LALDEN
425 171	B	*E	DÄRLIGEN		425 186	B	E	LEISSIGEN
425 172	B	*E	EGGERBERG		425 188	B	E	NATERS
425 173	B	*E	LÖTSCHENTAL		425 189	B	E	NIEDERGESTELN
425 174	B	E	FRUTIGEN		425 190	B	E	RARON
425 175	B	E	GAMPEL		425 191	B	p	REICHENBACH
425 176	B	E	HOHTENN		425 192	B	p	SPIEZ
425 177	B	E	ZWEISIMMEN		425 193	B	p	STEG
425 178	B	E	SCHWARZENBURG		425 194	B	p	THUN
425 179	B	E	BERN		425 195	B	p	UNTERSEEN

Locomotives numbered in the 430 xxx series can be found under Classes Re 420 & 430.

CLASS Re 446 (ex Re 4/4^{IV}) Bo-Bo

These locos were built as prototypes 10101 to 10104 for SBB but were not followed by a production run. They were initially numbered Re 446 445 to 448 by SOB. Now used to power the Voralpern Express passenger service from St Gallen to Luzern.

Built: 1982 (as SBB Re 4/4 ^{IV} 10101 to 10104).
Builder: SLM/BBC.
One Hour Rating: 4960 kW. **Maximum Tractive Effort:** 210 kN.
Wheel Diameter: 1260 mm. **Weight:** 80 tonnes.
Length over Buffers: 15.80 m. **Maximum Speed:** 160 km/h.

All locomotives are with SOB.

446 015	446 017
446 016	446 018

▲ Class Re 421 work deep into Germany, mainly on hire to other companies. 421 388 is seen here heading south through Boppard (Germany) with a container train on 22 March 2012. **Robin Ralston**

▼ Two BLS Class Re 425 locos headed by 188 climb out of Erstfeld on the Gotthard with a train of clay for the Italian ceramics industry on 2 July 2015. **Brian Denton**

CLASS Re 450 — Bo-Bo

These are single-ended locos to work push-pull trains on the Zürich S-Bahn, which commenced operation in May 1990. They have three-phase traction motors, SLM "shifting axle drive", which allows radial adjustment of the axles within the bogies, and regenerative braking. The locos operate in fixed formation sets with two intermediate trailers and a driving trailer. SBB has replaced one coach in each set with a new low-floor trailer to conform with modern standards of access. The trailers replaced have been formed into hauled sets for use in the peak under the "LION" project with locos 420 201 to 230. Locos/sets 450 067 and 070 were transferred to SZU in 2008. They are in an all red livery. Class 450 are currently receiving a mid-life overhaul. The overhauled power cars can be distinguished by the new logo on the front end.

Built: 1989–97.
Builder–Mechanical Parts: SLM.
Builder–Electrical. Parts: ABB.
Traction Motors: Four 3-phase axle-hung, nose-suspended.
One Hour Rating: 3200 kW.　　　　**Maximum Tractive Effort:** 240 kN.
Wheel Diameter: 1100 mm.　　　　**Weight:** 74 tonnes.
Length over Buffers: 18.40 m.　　　**Maximum Speed:** 130 km/h.

All locomotives except 450 067 and 070 are with SBB.

Number	Livery	Depot	Names/Notes	Number	Livery	Depot	Names/Notes
450 000	S	ZU	Seebach	450 042	S	ZU	Hettlingen
450 001	S	ZU	Schwerzenbach	450 043	S	ZU	Rorbas
450 002	S	ZU	Oberwinterthur	450 044	S	ZU	Henggart
450 003	S	ZU	Zollikon	450 045	S	ZU	Feldbach
450 004	S	ZU	Stettbach	450 046	S	ZU	Zürich Affoltern
450 005	S	ZU	Kilchberg	450 047	S	ZU	Seegräben
450 006	S	ZU	Rafz	450 048	S	ZU	Elgg ZH
450 007	S	ZU	Fehraltorf	450 049	S	ZU	Nänikon
450 008	S	ZU	Riesbach	450 050	S	ZU	Wien
450 009	S	ZU	Hedingen	450 051	A	ZU	Kleinandelfingen
450 010	S	ZU	Steinmaur	450 052	S	ZU	Lottstetten
450 011	S	ZU	Oberrieden	450 053	A	ZU	Witikon
450 012	S	ZU	Schwamendingen	450 054	S	ZU	Oberglatt
450 013	S	ZU	Niederglatt	450 055	S	ZU	Küsnacht ZH
450 014	S	ZU	Männedorf	450 056	S	ZU	Otelfingen
450 015	S	ZU	Erlenbach	450 057	S	ZU	Dielsdorf
450 016	A	ZU	Altstetten	450 058	S	ZU	Niederhasli
450 017	S	ZU	Bubikon	450 059	S	ZU	Knonau
450 018	S	ZU	Hirslanden/Hottingen	450 060	S	ZU	Glattfelden
450 019	S	ZU	Stäfa	450 061	S	ZU	Mönchaltorf
450 020	S	ZU	Pfäffikon	450 062	S	ZU	Gossau ZH
450 021	S	ZU	Seuzach	450 063	S	ZU	Hombrechtikon
450 022	S	ZU	Richterswil	450 064	S	ZU	City of Osaka
450 023	S	ZU	Greifensee	450 065	S	ZU	Bonstetten
450 024	S	ZU	Pfungen	450 066	S	ZU	Neerach
450 025	S	ZU	Winterthur Seen	450 067		SZU	(Re 551)
450 026	S	ZU	Birmensdorf	450 068	S	ZU	Waltalingen
450 027	A	ZU	Zürich Enge	450 069	S	ZU	Wiesendangen
450 028	A	ZU	Urikon	450 070		SZU	(Re 552)
450 029	S	ZU	Altikon	450 071	S	ZU	Altenburg
450 030	S	ZU	Rümlang	450 072	S	ZU	Rheinau
450 031	S	ZU	Wald	450 073	S	ZU	Wettswil
450 032	S	ZU	Mettmenstetten	450 074	S	ZU	Stadel
450 033	S	ZU	Thalheim	450 075	S	ZU	Ossingen
450 034	S	ZU	Oberweningen	450 076	S	ZU	Unterstammheim
450 035	S	ZU	Schöfflisdorf	450 077	S	ZU	Oberstammheim
450 036	A	ZU	Dietlikon	450 078	S	ZU	Au ZH
450 037	S	ZU	Niederweningen	450 079	S	ZU	Jestetten
450 038	S	ZU	Wollishofen	450 080	S	ZU	Rüschlikon
450 039	S	ZU	Embrach	450 081	S	ZU	Weiningen
450 040	S	ZU	Hinwil	450 082	S	ZU	Feuerthalen
450 041	A	ZU	Buchs/Dällikon	450 083	S	ZU	Trüllikon

▲ SOB 446 015 arrives at Pfäffikon SZ with a Voralpern Express service to St Gallen on 13 June 2014. On the left is Sersa shunter 237 862, formerly WM Tm 2/2 103. **David Haydock**

▼ 450 099 arrives at Zürich Stadelhofen on 12 June 2014 with an S6 service to Uetikon while a Class 511 EMU departs in the opposite direction. **David Haydock**

450 084	S	ZU	Neftenbach	450 100	S	ZU	Rudolfingen
450 085	S	ZU	Rickenbach ZH	450 101	S	ZU	Obfelden
450 086	S	ZU	Benken ZH	450 102	S	ZU	Wangen-Brüttisellen
450 087	S	ZU	Zell ZH	450 103	S	ZU	Marthalen
450 088	S	ZU	Wangen SZ	450 104	S	ZU	Zürich Hard/
450 089	S	ZU	Bäretswil				Zürich Aussersihl
450 090	S	ZU	Turbenthal	450 105	S	ZU	Herrliberg
450 091	S	ZU	Dürnten	450 106	S	ZU	Winterthur Töss
450 092	S	ZU	Wila	450 107	S	ZU	Maschwanden
450 093	S	ZU	Wil ZH	450 108	S	ZU	Uetikon
450 094	S	ZU	Hüntwangen	450 109	S	ZU	Kappel a./A.
450 095	S	ZU	Wasterkingen	450 110	S	ZU	Hittnau
450 096	S	ZU	Winterthur Veltheim	450 111	A	ZU	Neuenhof
450 097	S	ZU	Maur	450 112	S	ZU	Flurlingen
450 098	S	ZU	Grüningen	450 113	S	ZU	Humlikon/Adlikon
450 099	S	ZU	Volketswil	450 114	S	ZU	Dänikon

CLASS Re 456 — Bo-Bo

456 091–096 are former BT locos 91–96 (the short version of the number is still shown on the front), now SOB, and are used to top-and-tail the Voralpen Express service between St Gallen and Luzern.

SZU 456 101 to 106 (formerly 546, 547, 542 to 545) power push-pull trains of mixed double- and single-deck coaches on the Zürich HB–Sihlwald suburban line.

456 142 and 143 are owned by the BLS, having been inherited from Regionalverkehr Mittelland (originally VHB 142 and 143), and are hired to other companies as required. Their EVNs make them 456 111 and 112!

Built: 1987/88 (091–096, 101/102), 1992/93 (103–106, 142/143).
Builder: SLM/SGP/BBC.
Power Rating: 3000 kW (101–106 3200 kW). **Continuous Tractive Effort:** 140 kN.
Wheel Diameter: 1100 mm. **Weight:** 68 tonnes.
Length over Buffers: 16.60 m. **Maximum Speed:** 130 km/h.

Number	Company		Number	Company
456 091	SOB		456 103	SZU
456 092	SOB		456 104	SZU
456 093	SOB		456 105	SZU
456 094	SOB		456 106	SZU
456 095	SOB			
456 096	SOB		456 142	BLS/Müller Gleisbau
			456 143	BLS/SRT
456 101	SZU			
456 102	SZU			

CLASS Re 460 — Bo-Bo

High speed locomotives built for the "Bahn 2000" project. Originally used on mixed traffic, they are now all passenger locos, very often used in push-pull mode with IC2000 double-deck or Mark IV single-deck stock. Locos temporarily in advertising livery often do not carry their names – which are thus shown in italics. All are equipped with ETCS Level 2.

In 2014 460 084 received an extensive mid-life refurbishment, under which the GTOs are replaced by IGBTs, plus a slightly revised livery. The rest are following. Refurbished locos have the cross symbol in the middle of the nose and the number on the right. The "2000" is removed.

Built: 1991–96.
Builder–Mechanical Parts: SLM/Krauss Maffei.
Builder–Electrical. Parts: ABB.
Traction Motors: Four three-phase fully suspended.
One Hour Rating: 6100 kW. **Maximum Tractive Effort:** 275 kN.
Wheel Diameter: 1100 mm. **Weight:** 84 tonnes.
Length over Buffers: 18.50 m. **Maximum Speed:** 230 km/h.

All locomotives are with SBB.

▲ SOB 456 095 stands at Arth-Goldau with a Luzern–St Gallen "Voralpern Express" on 15 April 2014. **David Haydock**

▼ SBB 460 111 climbs out of Lausanne at La Bossière with a Genève Aéroport–St Gallen IC service on 25 January 2016. **Charles-André Fluckiger**

Number	Livery	Names
460 000	R	Grauholz
460 001	R	Lötschberg
460 002	R	Seeland
460 003	A	*Milieu de Monde*
460 004	R	Uetliberg
460 005	R	Val d'Anniviers
460 006	R	Lavaux
460 007	R	Junior
460 008	R	La Gruyère
460 009	R	Le Jet d'Eau
460 010	R	Löwenberg
460 011	R	Léman
460 012	R	Erguël
460 013	R	Nord Vaudois
460 014	R	Val-du-Trient
460 015	R	uf u dervo
460 016	R	Rohrdorferberg Reusstal
460 017	R	Les Diablerets
460 018	R	
460 019	R	Terre Sainte
460 020	R	
460 021	R	
460 022	R	Sihl
460 023	A	*Wankdorf*
460 024	R	Rheintal
460 025	R	Striegel
460 026	R	Fricktal
460 027	R	Joggeli
460 028	A	*Seetal*
460 029	A	*Eulach*
460 030	R	Säntis
460 031	A	*Chaumont*
460 032	R	
460 033	R	
460 034	R	Aare
460 035	A	
460 036	R	Franches-Montagnes
460 037	R	Sempacher See
460 038	R	Hauenstein
460 039	R	Rochers-de-Naye
460 040	R	Napf
460 041	A	*Mendrisiotto*
460 042	R	Albis
460 043	R	Dreispitz
460 044	R	Zugerland
460 045	R	Rigi
460 046	R	Polmengo
460 047	R	Maderanertal
460 048	A	*Züri Wyland*
460 049	R	Pfannenstiel
460 050	A	*Züspa*
460 051	R	Staffelegg
460 052	R	Eigenamt
460 053	R	Suhrental
460 054	R	Dreiländereck
460 055	R	Lillehammer
460 056	R	
460 057	R	Val-de-Ruz
460 058	R	La Côte
460 059	R	La Béroche
460 060	R	Val-de-Travers
460 061	R	Wiggertal
460 062	R	Ergolz
460 063	A	*Brunegg*
460 064	R	Mythen
460 065	R	Rotsee
460 066	R	Finse
460 067	R	Hohle Gasse
460 068	R	Gütsch
460 069	R	Verkehrshaus
460 070	R	
460 071	R	Mittelland
460 072	R	Reuss
460 073	R	Monte Ceneri
460 074	R	
460 075	R	Schafmatt
460 076	R	Leventina
460 077	R	Chunnel
460 078	R	Monte Generoso
460 079	R	Weissenstein
460 080	A	*Tre Valli*
460 081	R	Pfänder
460 082	R	Ceresio
460 083	A	
460 084	R	Helvetia
460 085	A	*Pilatus*
460 086	R	Ägerisee
460 087	A	*Säuliamt*
460 088	R	Limmat
460 089	R	Freiamt
460 090	R	Goffersberg
460 091	R	Werdenberg
460 092	R	Fridolin
460 093	R	Rhein
460 094	R	Rätia
460 095	R	Bachtel
460 096	R	Furttal
460 097	R	Studenland
460 098	A	*Biasca (Balsberg)*
460 099	R	Bodensee
460 100	R	Tösstal
460 101	R	Bözberg
460 102	A	*Lägern*
460 103	R	Heitersberg
460 104	R	Toggenburg
460 105	A	*Fürstenland*
460 106	R	Munot
460 107	A	*Glärnisch*
460 108	R	Engadin
460 109	R	Alpstein
460 110	R	Mariaberg
460 111	R	Kempt
460 112	R	Thurtal
460 113	R	Irchel
460 114	R	Circus Knie
460 115	R	Heidiland
460 116	R	Ostschweiz
460 117	R	Zürichsee
460 118	R	Gotthard/Gottardo

CLASS Re 465   Bo-Bo

General purpose BLS locomotives in dark blue livery and based on SBB Class 460. They are now used on passenger services from Bern to Neuchâtel and La Chaux de Fonds and on Basel–Domodossola freights, especially RoLa services carrying complete lorries. In 2015 four were on hire to RailCare in exchange for Class 186 locos.

Built: 1994–97.
Builder–Mechanical Parts: SLM.
Builder–Electrical Parts: ABB 465 001–008; ADtranz 465 009–018.
Traction Motors: Four 3-phase fully suspended.
One Hour Rating: 7000 kW.   **Maximum Tractive Effort:** 320 kN.
Wheel Diameter: 1100 mm.   **Weight:** 82 tonnes.
Length over Buffers: 18.50 m.   **Maximum Speed:** 230 km/h.

All locos are push-pull & multiple working fitted (can work with BLS Re 425, plus SBB Re 420, 430, 460, and 620). All are equipped with ETCS Level 2. All locomotives are with BLS (465 015–018 on hire to RailCare in 2016).

Number	Livery	Names
465 001	A	Simplon / Sempione
465 002	K	Gornergrat
465 003	K	3454 m JUNGFRAUJOCH TOP OF EUROPE
465 004	A	Trubschachen
465 005	K	Niesen
465 006	K	Lauchernalp-Lötschental
465 007	K	Schilthorn/Piz Gloria
465 008	A	Niederhorn/Beatenberg
465 009	K	Napf
465 010	K	Mont Vully
465 011	K	Wisenberg
465 012	K	Eurotunnel
465 013	K	Stockhorn
465 014	K	Spalenberg
465 015	A	Cat's Eye
465 016	A	Black Pearl
465 017	A	Pink Panther
465 018	A	Flash Fire

▲ BLS 465 014 and another of the class pass Ostermundigen near Bern on their way to the Lötschberg tunnel and Italy with a heavy freight train on 8 May 2015. **Mario Stefani**

CLASS Re 474   ES64F4   Bo-Bo

These locos are the same Siemens ES64F4 (Class 189, see above) design but are configured only for 15 kV AC in Switzerland and 3000 V DC in Italy. They work mainly southwards from Bellinzona and Chiasso. Siemens won the contract by claiming to be able to deliver the locos faster than Class Re 484 from Bombardier. This turned out not to be the case and SBB penalised the builder by refusing to accept six of the locos. The first versions of 474 007 and 008 were damaged during delivery then rebuilt and became MRCE Dispolok 189 919 and 920. 474 001 and 010 plus the second versions of 474 007 and 008 went to Italian operator Del Fungo Giera which went bankrupt, as E.474.101 to 104. E.474.101 to 103 then went to Rail One in Italy as E.474 101 to 103 and E.474.104 to NordCargo in Italy. 474 006 and 011 are now with Hector Rail in Sweden as 441 001 and 002.

Built: 2004.
Systems: 15 kV AC 16.7 Hz, 3000 V DC.
Builder: Siemens.
Continuous Rating: 6400 kW.   **Maximum Tractive Effort:** 300 kN.
Wheel Diameter: 1250 mm.   **Weight:** 86 tonnes.
Length over Buffers: 19.58 m.   **Maximum Speed:** 140 km/h.

All locomotives are with SBB.

Number	Livery	Sector	Depot		Number	Livery	Sector	Depot
474 002	C	C	BE		474 013	C	I	BE
474 003	C	I	BE		474 014	C	I	BE
474 004	C	I	BE		474 015	C	I	BE
474 005	C	I	BE		474 016	C	I	BE
474 009	C	I	BE		474 017	C	I	BE
474 012	C	I	BE		474 018	C	C	BE

CLASS Re 475   VECTRON MS   Bo-Bo

BLS Cargo has ordered 15 Vectron MS locos in order to renew its fleet (we assume withdrawing some Class 425) and expand traffic. The locos will be type D-A-CH-I-NL for operations right through from the Netherlands to Italy. They will be delivered in three batches from 2016 to 2018.

SBB Cargo International was also hiring two Vectrons in 2015 (193 209 and 210) but they were only used in Germany so are not included in this book. See German Railways Part 2 for details. Other Vectrons may visit Basel on workings from Germany.

Built: 2016–
Builder: Siemens, München Allach.
Systems: 15 kV AC 16.7 Hz, 25 kV AC 50 Hz, 1500/3000 V DC.
Power Rating: 6400 kW.   **Maximum Tractive Effort:** 300 kN.
Wheel Diameter: 1250 mm.   **Weight:** 87 tonnes.
Length over Buffers: 18.98 m.   **Maximum Speed:** 200 km/h.

Number	Company		Number	Company
475 401	BLS		475 409	BLS
475 402	BLS		475 410	BLS
475 403	BLS		475 411	BLS
475 404	BLS		475 412	BLS
475 405	BLS		475 413	BLS
475 406	BLS		475 414	BLS
475 407	BLS		475 415	BLS
475 408	BLS			

CLASS Re 482   TRAXX AC   Bo-Bo

When SBB Cargo started to expand northwards into Germany, it needed more than just its two dozen Class 421. So the company ordered ten Class Re 482 locomotives, almost identical to the German Class 185 (see above), then added 40 more locos to take the total to 50. The main difference compared with Class 185 was the addition of rear-facing mini cameras behind the cab doors to allow the driver to back onto a train without opening the window in the Swiss winter. Like Class 185, the locos have 25 kV AC equipment as standard but this is not used. Class 482 are used throughout Switzerland and into Germany, mainly northwards along the Basel–Köln corridor but also to many other places including Aachen and Hamburg daily. The last batch also works to Wien in Austria. In contrast, the class usually come off freights over the Gotthard route at Basel. Many locos have been hired to other operators.

Built: 2002–04.
Builder: Bombardier Transportation, Kassel.
Traction Motors: Nose-suspended.   **Systems:** 15 kV AC 16.7 Hz, 25 kV AC 50 Hz.
Continuous Rating: 5600 kW.   **Maximum Tractive Effort:** 300 kN.
Wheel Diameter: 1250 mm.   **Weight:** 84 tonnes.
Length over Buffers: 18.90 m.   **Maximum Speed:** 140 km/h.

All locomotives are multiple working fitted within class and with Classes 420 and 620. All locos are with SBB Cargo, some hired to other operators as shown.

b   Authorised to operate to Brennero in Italy.

TRAXX 1 Locomotives.

Number	Livery	Sector	Depot/Hired to		Number	Livery	Sector	
482 000	C	I	BS		482 021	C	I	BS
482 001	C	I	BS		482 022	A	I	BS
482 002	C	I	BS		482 023	C	I	BS
482 003	C	I	BS		482 024	C	I	BS
482 004	C	I	BS		482 025	C	I	BS
482 005	C	I	BS		482 026	A	I	BS
482 006	C	I	BS		482 027	C	I	BS
482 007	C	I	BS		482 028	A	I	BS
482 008	C	I	BS		482 029	C	I	BS
482 009	C	I	BS		482 030	C	C	HSL
482 010	C	I	BS		482 031	C	C	TXL
482 011	C	I	BS		482 032	C	C	HSL
482 012	A	I	BS		482 033	C	C	HSL
482 013	A	I	BS		482 034	C	C	HSL
482 014	C	I	BS		482 035	C	C	b	Raildox
482 015	C	I	BS		482 036	C	C	b	Raildox
482 016	C	I	BS		482 037	C	C	b	Railpool/
482 017	C	I	BS						InfraLeuna
482 018	A	I	BS		482 038	C	C	Locon
482 019	C	I	BS		482 039	C	C	Locon
482 020	C	I	BS					

Names:

482 000	Köln		482 033	Basler Rheinhäfen
482 008	Ökotrans		482 034	Duisburg

TRAXX 2 Locomotives. Authorised for use in Austria.

Number	Livery	Sector		Hired to		Number	Livery	Sector		
482 040	C	C		Locon		482 045	A	C		Railpool/
482 041	C	C		Railpool/Metrans						Lokomotion
482 042	C	C		Railpool/Metrans		482 046	C	C		HSL
482 043	C	C	b	Railpool		482 047	C	C	b	TXL
482 044	C	C		HSL		482 048	C	C	b	TXL
						482 049	A	C	b	Locon

CLASS Re 484   TRAXX MS   Bo-Bo

In order to expand into Italy, SBB Cargo's Italian subsidiary ordered 18 Class Re 484 locomotives from Bombardier, plus 30 options, in late 2002. Three options have been taken up. These were the first TRAXX locomotives designed to operate under 3000 V DC as well as 15 kV AC. The locos are also pre-equipped to operate off 1500 V DC and 25 kV AC but only have signalling for Switzerland and Italy. The locos are used south of Bellinzona and Chiasso, taking over from straight 15 kV AC machines, running mainly to points such as Novara, Gallarate, Ollegio and Milano.

Five Class 484 were also built for leasing company MRCE. Originally numbered E.484.901 to 905, 903 to 905 were later renumbered E.484.103 to 105. Although two were previously used in Switzerland by Crossrail, all were only operating in Italy at the time of writing.

Built: 2003/04.
Builder: Bombardier Transportation, Kassel.
Traction Motors: Nose-suspended.
Continuous Rating: 5600 kW.
Wheel Diameter: 1250 mm.
Length over Buffers: 18.90 m.

Systems: 15 kV AC 16.7 Hz, 3000 V DC.
Maximum Tractive Effort: 300 kN.
Weight: 85.6 tonnes.
Maximum Speed: 140 km/h.

All are with SBB; some may be hired. Hired out locos are still maintained at BE depot.

E   Equipped with ETCS Level 2.

Number	Livery	Sector		Depot/Company		Number	Livery	Sector	Depot/Company
484 001	C	I	E	BE		484 012	C	I	BE
484 002	C	I	E	BE		484 013	C	I	BE
484 003	C	I	E	BE		484 014	C	I	BE
484 004	C	I	E	BE		484 015	C	C	BE
484 005	C	I	E	BE		484 016	C	C	BE
484 006	C	I	E	BE		484 017	C		FuoriMuro
484 007	C	I	E	BE		484 018	C		Captrain IT
484 008	C	I	E	BE		484 019	C		FuoriMuro
484 009	C	I	E	BE		484 020	C		Captrain IT
484 010	C	I	E	BE		484 021	C		Captrain IT
484 011	C	I		BE					

Name:

484 021   Gottardo

CLASS Re 485   TRAXX AC   Bo-Bo

These BLS Cargo locos are Bombardier TRAXX F140 AC locomotives which are identical to DB Schenker Class 185 and SBB Class Re 482. These were the first locos in the new BLS livery of grey and apple green. The locos haul freight from Basel to the Italian border over both the Lötschberg and Gotthard routes and as far north as Mannheim in Germany. They also work over several other routes in Switzerland. All are equipped with ETCS Level 2. BLS Cargo hires additional locos of this type – numbered as Class 185 – from Alpha Trains, when necessary.

Built: 2003/04.
Builder: Bombardier Transportation, Kassel.
Electric Brake: Regenerative.
Maximum Rating: 5600 kW.
Wheel Diameter: 1250 mm.
Length over Buffers: 18.90 m.
Multiple Working: Within class and with Class Re 486.

Systems: 15 kV AC 16.7 Hz, 25 kV AC 50 Hz.
Maximum Tractive Effort: 300 kN.
Weight: 84 tonnes.
Maximum Speed: 140 km/h.

All locomotives are with BLS Cargo.

▲ SBB Cargo International 484 012 and another of the class pass through Arth-Goldau station with a soutbound intermodal train on 24 September 2014. The class is not often seen north of Bellinzona.
Mario Stefani

▼ BLS 485 012 pilots a Class 486 loco with a train of containers on the Gotthard route on 30 June 2015.
Brian Denton

Number	Names		Number	Names
485 001	Haltingen		485 011	Weil-am-Rhein
485 003			485 013	
485 004			485 014	
485 005			485 015	
485 006			485 016	
485 008			485 018	
485 009			485 019	
485 010			485 020	

CLASS Re 486   TRAXX MS   Bo-Bo

In 2007 BLS Cargo ordered ten TRAXX MS multi-voltage electric locomotives numbered 486 501–510. Locos are the D-A-CH-I version, equipped to operate in Germany, Austria, Switzerland and Italy and have the relevant national signalling systems plus ETCS Level 2. Locos carry numbers 486 501 upwards on the front end as well as 501 upwards in large blue numbers, inviting confusion with BLS Class 420. Locos work HUPAC and Ambrogio trains in particular through Switzerland to Novara and Gallarate in Italy. In 2014 some were on hire and working deep into Germany.

Details as Class Re 485 except:

Systems: 15 kV AC 16.7 Hz, 3000 V DC.
Weight: 85 tonnes.
Multiple Working: Within class and with Class Re 485.

Number	Company	Names		Number	Company
486 501	BLS	Beura Cardezza		486 506	BLS
486 502	BLS/Lokomotion			486 507	BLS
486 503	BLS/Lokomotion			486 508	BLS
486 504	BLS			486 509	BLS
486 505	BLS/Lokomotion			486 510	BLS/Lokomotion

CLASS Rem 487   TRAXX AC3 LM   Bo-Bo

Class Rem 487 is identical to Class 187 (see above), being a third generation Bombardier TRAXX loco with a "last mile" diesel engine. The loco was built for SRT in 2015. Livery is yellow and grey.

Details as Class 187.

Number	Company
487 001	SRT

CLASS Re 620 (ex Re 6/6)   Bo-Bo-Bo

An SBB class, effectively an enlarged and uprated version of the Re4/4ⁱⁱ, this class was built to work on the mountain routes, but also appears elsewhere. The wheel arrangement was selected to provide a total adhesion weight similar to Co-Co Class Ae 6/6, but with a better ability to run through curves, and to reduce weight transfer. Four prototypes were built, the first two having a hinged body with the axis of the hinge horizontal; the rigid body design was adopted for the production version. The entry into service of the Re 460 Class saw a reduction in Re 620 workings on the Gotthard route, and the class now appears over a much wider area than previously. 11638 was withdrawn following an accident. Locos in SBB Cargo livery are all renumbered.

Built: 1975–80 (* 1972).
Builder–Mechanical Parts: SLM.
Builder–Electrical Parts: BBC/SAAS (* BBC).
Traction Motors: Six single-phase commutator type, fully suspended with BBC spring drive.
One Hour Rating: 7850 kW.   **Maximum Tractive Effort:** 398 kN (* 394 kN).
Wheel Diameter: 1260 mm.   **Weight:** 120 tonnes.
Length over Buffers: 19.31 m.   **Maximum Speed:** 140 km/h.

E   Equipped with ETCS.

All locomotives are multiple working fitted within class and with SBB Classes Re 420 and 430. All locos are with SBB.

Number	Livery	Sector		Names
11601	R	C	*	WOLHUSEN
11602	R	C	*	MORGES
11603	R	C	*	WÄDENSWIL
11604	R	C	*	FAIDO
11605	R	C	E	USTER
11606	R	C	E	TURGI
11607	R	C	E	WATTWIL
11608	R	C	E	WETZIKON
11609	R	C	E	UZWIL
11610	R	C	E	SPREITENBACH
11611	R	C	E	RÜTI ZH
620 012	C	C	E	REGENSDORF
11613	R	C	E	RAPPERSWIL
11614	R	C	E	MEILEN
11615	R	C	E	KLOTEN
11616	R	C	E	ILLNAU-EFFRETIKON
11617	R	C	E	HEERBRUGG
11618	R	C	E	DÜBENDORF
11619	R	C	E	ARBON
11620 (U)	R	C	E	WANGEN-BEI-OLTEN
11621	R	C	E	TAVERNE-TORRICELLA
11622	R	C	E	SUHR
11623	R	C	E	RUPPERSWIL
11624	R	C	E	ROTHRIST
11625	R	C	E	OENSINGEN
11626	R	C	E	ZOLLIKOFEN
11627	R	C	E	LUTERBACH-ATTISHOLZ
11628	R	C	E	KONOLFINGEN
11629	R	C	E	INTERLAKEN
11630	R	C	E	HERZOGENBUCHSEE
11631	R	C	E	DULLIKEN
11632	R	C	E	DÄNIKEN
620 033	C	C	E	MURI AG
11634	R	C	E	AARBURG-OFTRINGEN
11635	R	C	E	MUTTENZ
11636	R	C	E	VERNIER-MEYRIN
11637	R	C	E	SONCEBOZ-SOMBEVAL
11639	R	C	E	MURTEN
11640	R	C		MÜNCHENSTEIN
11641	R	C		MOUTIER
620 042	C	C		MONTHEY
11643	R	C		LAUFEN
11644	R	C		CORNAUX
11645	R	C		COLOMBIER
11646	G	C		BUSSIGNY
620 047	C	C		BEX
11648	R	C		AIGLE
11649	R	C		AARBERG
11650	R	C		SCHÖNENWERD
620 051	C	C		DORNACH-ARLESHEIM
11652	R	C		KERZERS
11653	R	C		GÜMLINGEN
11654	R	C		VILLENEUVE
620 055	C	C		COSSONAY
11656	R	C		TRAVERS
11657	R	C		ESTAVAYER-LE-LAC
620 058	C	C		AUVERNIER
620 059	C	C		CHAVORNAY
620 060	C	C		TAVANNES
620 061	C	C	E	GAMPEL-STEG
620 062	C	C	E	REUCHENETTE-PÉRY
11663	G	C	E	EGLISAU
11664	R	I	E	KÖNIZ

620 065	C	I	E	ZIEGELBRÜCKE
11666	R	I	E	STEIN AM RHEIN
11667	R	I	E	BODIO
11668	R	I	E	STEIN-SÄCKINGEN
620 069	C	I	E	HÄGENDORF
11670	R	I	E	AFFOLTERN AM ALBIS
11671	R	I	E	OTHMARSINGEN
11672	R	I	E	BALERNA
11673	R	I	E	CHAM
620 074	C	C	E	MURGENTHAL
620 075	C	I	E	GELTERKINDEN
11676	R	I	E	ZURZACH
11677	R	C	E	NEUHAUSEN AM RHEINFALL
11678	R	I	E	BASSERSDORF
11679	R	I	E	CADENAZZO
11680	R	I	E	MÖHLIN
11681	R	I	E	IMMENSEE
11682	R	I	E	PFÄFFIKON SZ
11683	R	I	E	AMSTEG-SILENEN
11684	R	I	E	UZNACH
11685	R	I	E	SULGEN
620 086	C	I	E	HOCHDORF
620 087	C	I	E	BISCHOFSZELL
620 088	A	C	E	LINTHAL
11689	R	I	E	GERRA-GAMBAROGNO

▲ Class Re 620 11668 and an Re 4/4 head an intermodal service over the Gotthard route at Wassen on 15 August 2014. **Laurence Sly**

1.3. ELECTRIC MULTIPLE UNITS

Newer EMUs operate in fixed formations. Older railcars (now only Class 560, 565, 566, 567, 576 and 578) are single motor coaches which are coupled to driving and intermediate trailer cars to make up push-pull trains, although their formations are now normally fixed, too. Trailers for the above are numbered in the carriage series and are not shown here. All units can operate only under 15 kV AC 16.7 Hz in Switzerland unless otherwise shown. Many classes of unit are common user and depot codes are not usually shown. SBB also owns one of the Lyria single-deck TGV sets – train 4406.

Under "accommodation" are shown the number of first and second class seats, followed by the number of toilets. "TD" indicates a disabled toilet. Tip-up seats are shown in brackets. Example: 16/32(8) 1T indicates 16 first class seats, 32 second class seats, 8 tip-up seats and one toilet.

All EMUs have EVNs in the 94 85 0xxx xxx-c series. Power cars which can be formed with coaches (from Class 560) are numbered 94 85 7xxx xxx-c.

CLASS Rabde 500   "ICN"   7-CAR TILTING UNITS

These tilting train sets are known as ICN – Intercity *Neigezug* (tilting train). Sets are named after famous personalities, either Swiss or with a strong connection to the country. All sets are equipped with ETCS Level 2, bogies with steerable axles and electric tilt, disc, regenerative and magnetic track brakes. Sets are used on the Basel–Biel/Bienne–Genève Aéroport, Basel–Biel/Bienne–Lausanne, St. Gallen–Zürich–Biel/Bienne–Genève Aéroport and Lausanne–Biel/Bienne–Zürich–St. Gallen services plus since 2008 Zürich/Basel–Lugano. All sets are now receiving a mid-life overhaul and have a cross logo when on the nose when outshopped.

Built: 1998–2005.
Builder–Mechanical Parts: Schindler/FIAT-SIG.
Builder–Electrical Parts: ABB.
Wheel Arrangement: 1A-A1 + 1A-A1 + 2-2 + 2-2 + 2-2 + 1A-A1 + 1A-A1.
Length over Couplers: 27.4 + 26.8 + 26.8 + 26.8 + 26.8 + 26.8 + 27.4 m.
Accommodation: –/70 (3) 1T + –/93 1T + 24/– 26 restaurant + 60/– 1TD + 47/– 1T + –/93 1T + –/70 (3) 1T.
Traction Motors: 8 x 650 kW.   **Total Weight:** 355 tonnes.
Maximum Speed: 200 km/h.

Sets are known as 500 0xx, and numbered 94 85 2500 0xx + 3500 0xx + 4500 0xx + 5500 0xx + 6500 0xx + 7500 0xx + 1500 0xx and so on.

Number	Depot	Names	Number	Depot	Names
500 000	GE	Le Corbusier	500 022	GE	Expo.02
500 001	GE	Jean Piaget	500 023	GE	Charles Ferdinand Ramuz
500 002	GE	Annemarie Schwarzenbach	500 024	GE	Ernest von Stockalper
500 003	GE	Germaine de Staël	500 025	GE	Xavier Stockmar
500 004	GE	Mani Matter	500 026	GE	Alfred Escher
500 005	GE	Heinrich Pestalozzi	500 027	GE	Henry Dunant
500 006	GE	Johanna Spyri	500 028	GE	Francesco Borromini
500 007	GE	Albert Einstein	500 029	GE	Eduard Spelterini
500 008	GE	Vincenzo Vela	500 030	GE	Louis Chevrolet
500 009	GE	Friedrich Dürrenmatt	500 031	GE	Louis Favre
500 010	GE	Robert Walser	500 032	GE	Henri Dufaux
500 011	GE	Blaise Cendrars	500 033	GE	Gallus Jakob Baumgartner
500 012	GE	Jean Rudolf von Salis	500 034	GE	Gustav Wenk
500 013	GE	Denis de Rougemont	500 035	GE	Niklaus Riggenbach
500 014	GE	Max Frisch	500 036	GE	Minister Kern
500 015	GE	Jean-Jacques Rousseau	500 037	GE	Grock
500 016	GE	Alice Rivaz	500 038	GE	Arthur Honnegger
500 017	GE	Willi Ritschard	500 039	GE	Auguste Piccard
500 018	GE	Adolf Wölfli	500 040	GE	Graf Zeppelin
500 019	GE	Friedrich Glauser	500 041	GE	William Barbey
500 020	GE	Jeanne Hersch	500 042	GE	Steivan Brunies
500 021	GE	Jeremias Gotthelf	500 043	GE	Harald Szeemann

▲ 500 039 "Auguste Piccard" stands in Delémont station on 17 April 2014. **David Haydock**

▼ One of the new Class 502 double-deck EMUs is seen on test at Bettlach on 6 January 2016.
Mario Stefani

CLASS RABDe 501   "GIRUNO"
11-SECTION ARTICULATED UNITS

These 29 trains are on order for use on the Zürich–Milano line and will be capable of 249 km/h once the Gotthard base tunnel is open. This will be the first time Stadler has built high speed trains; the first units will enter service in 2019. The trains will be nicknamed "Giruno" – buzzard in Romansch, and will be decorated with shields and names, mainly of cantons, but also three tunnels.

Built:
Builder: Stadler
Wheel Arrangement: .
Length: 22.25 + 17.5 x 9 + 22.25 m.
Formation:
Accommodation: 34/– + 31/– 3T + 37/– + 15/– 1TD 1T + 17 restaurant + 14/18 1TD + –/48 + –/48 3T + –/54 + –/44 3T + –/52.
Power Rating: 6000 kW.   **Total Weight:** 382 tonnes.
Maximum Speed: 249 km/h.

Number	*Names*		
501 001	Ticino	501 016	Glarus
501 002	Uri	501 017	Fribourg
501 003	Schwyz	501 018	St. Gallen
501 004	Luzern	501 019	Appenzell I.R.
501 005	Nidwalden	501 020	Appenzell A.R.
501 006	Obwalden	501 021	Grigioni
501 007	Aargau	501 022	Vaud
501 008	Solothurn	501 023	Valais / Wallis
501 009	Basel Land	501 024	Neuchâtel
501 010	Basel Stadt	501 025	Genève
501 011	Zug	501 026	Jura
501 012	Zürich	501 027	San Gottardo
501 013	Schaffhausen	501 028	Sempione
501 014	Bern / Berne	501 029	Ceneri
501 015	Thurgau		

CLASS RABDe 502   4- & 8-CAR DOUBLE-DECK UNITS

These new units (known variously as "Duplex", Twindexx" or "FV-Dosto") were ordered in May 2010 for delivery in 2012 and service from December 2013 on St Gallen–Zürich–Genève, Romanshorn–Zürich–Brig IC and Zürich–Luzern IR services. They are running late and are now not expected to be in service until 2017. There was a problem with disabled groups lobbying over accommodation, but the main hitch has been with building the bodies. In November 2014 SBB agreed a new delivery schedule with Bombardier, in exchange for three extra sets and free spares. All sets will be delivered by 2020. The original order was for 20 Class 502.0 8-car IC 200 InterCity sets, 30 502.2 8-car IR 200 InterRegio sets and nine 502.4 4-car IR 200 sets; the extra three sets will be Class 502.0. The units have bogies that allow slight tilt which allows higher speeds on lines between Bern and Lausanne.

Built: 2014–
Builder: Bombardier (Görlitz and Villeneuve).
Wheel Arrangement: 8-car: B-B + Bo-Bo + 2-2 + 2-2 + Bo-Bo + Bo-Bo + Bo-Bo + Bo-Bo; 4-car Bo-Bo + Bo-Bo + 2-2 + Bo-Bo.
Length:
Formation:
Accommodation: Class 502.0: 40/– + 65/– 3T + 65/– 3T + 8/– 32 restaurant + –/108 3T + –/108 3T + –/108 3T + –/69 3T.
Class 502.2: 45/– + 65/– 3T + 65/– 3T + –/88 (14) + –/108 3T + –/108 3T + –/108 3T + –/77 3T.
Class 502.4: 45/– + –/108 3T + –/96 (8) + –/77 3T.
Power Rating: 8-car 7500 kW; 4-car 3750 kW.   **Weight:**
Maximum Speed: 200 km/h.

Number

502 001	502 209
502 002	502 210
502 003	502 211
502 004	502 212
502 005	502 213
502 006	502 214
502 007	502 215
502 008	502 216
502 009	502 217
502 010	502 218
502 011	502 219
502 012	502 220
502 013	502 221
502 014	502 222
502 015	502 223
502 016	502 224
502 017	502 225
502 018	502 226
502 019	502 227
502 020	502 228
502 021	502 229
502 022	502 230
502 023	
	502 401
502 201	502 402
502 202	502 403
502 203	502 404
502 204	502 405
502 205	502 406
502 206	502 407
502 207	502 408
502 208	502 409

▲ ETR.610 set 5 tilts through the Wattinger Kurve in the legendary photo spot at Wassen. A minute or two later the train would be seen passing the church in the background.　**Laurence Sly**

CLASS RABe 503 (ETR.610) PENDOLINO DUE
7-CAR TILTING UNITS

These trains operate EuroCity services from Genève, Basel and Zürich to Milano in Italy. A first batch of 14 ETR.610 sets was built from 2007 for the Swiss-Italian joint venture Cisalpino, but at about this time SBB and Italian Railways fell out and the class was split in two, SBB recovering sets 5, 6, 7, 9, 10, 13 and 14. After initial teething problems, SBB decided it liked the trains and ordered eight more, then a further four. These will be almost identical but will be numbered RABe 503 011 to 022. The main difference between the newer and the older versions is the removal of two seats from each second class coach to give more luggage space, cutting total seating from 304 to 296. The older sets will now be modified. Units are maintained by Alstom in Genève. All have ETCS Level 2.

Built: 2007–10/2016.
Builder–Mechanical Parts: Alstom Ferroviaria.
Builder–Electrical Parts: Alstom Ferroviaria.
Continuous Rating: 5500 kW.
Systems: 15 kV AC 16.7 Hz, 25 kV AC 50 Hz, 3000 V DC.
Wheel Arrangement: Bo-Bo + 2-2 + Bo-Bo + 2-2 + Bo-Bo + 2-2 + Bo-Bo.
Length over Couplers: 27.2 + 26.2 x 5 + 28.2 m.
Formation:
Accommodation: 44/– 1T + 54/– + –/28 1T + –/80 2T + –/80 2T + –/80 1T + –/64.
Total Weight: 417 tonnes.
Maximum Speed: 250 km/h.

Class 503 sets are numbered 93 85 1503 xxx + 7503 xxx + 6503 xxx + 5503 xxx + 4503 xxx + 3503 xxx + 2503 xxx. Class ETR.610 sets are numbered 93 85 5610 1xx + 5610 2xx + 5610 3xx + 5610 4xx + 5610 5xx + 5610 6xx + 5610 7xx. It is not known if the ETR.610 sets will be renumbered.

Number	Depot	Names		Number	Depot
ETR.610.005	GE			503 014	GE
ETR.610.006	GE			503 015	GE
ETR.610.007	GE			503 016	GE
ETR.610.009	GE			503 017	GE
ETR.610.010	GE			503 018	GE
ETR.610.013	GE			503 019	
ETR.610.014	GE			503 020	
				503 021	
503 011	GE			503 022	
503 012	GE	Ticino			
503 013	GE	Valais			

CLASS RABDe 511 DUPLEX REGIO
4- & 6-CAR DOUBLE-DECK UNITS

These were Stadler's first double-deck EMUs and are branded "KISS". The first were built for the Zürich S-Bahn and entered service from March 2011. The initial order was for 50 6-car sets with options for 160 more. There then followed an order for 24 511.1 4-car sets for Lausanne–Genève and Basel–Zürich RE services, then 29 more 511.0 sets for Zürich. In July 2014 SBB ordered a further 19 6-car sets for the Zürich area, all to be delivered by the end of 2018 to allow service expansion. Zürich units also operate RE services to Chur, although they have the same interiors.

The units are able to operate in multiple with Class 514 but in reality this never happens. Set 511 001 has individual coaches numbered 1511 001, 2511 001 and so on to 6511 001.

Built: 2010–
Builder: Stadler Altenrhein.
Wheel Arrangement: Bo-Bo + 2-2 + 2-2 (+ 2-2 + 2-2) + Bo-Bo.
Length over Couplers: 25.36 + 24.82 + 24.82 (+ 24.82 + 24.82) + 25.36 m.
Accommodation: 4-car: –/70 + –/95 1TD + 60/42 + –/70.
6-car: –/70 + 60/42 + –/96 1T + –/92 (3) 1TD + 60/42 + –/70.
Traction Motors: 8 x 500 kW.   **Total Weight:** 297.6 tonnes.
Maximum Speed: 160 km/h.

Class 511.0. 6-car units for Zürich. Sets are numbered 94 85 6511 xxx + 5511 xxx + 4511 xxx + 3511 xxx + 2511 xxx + 1511 xxx.

Number	Depot	Names
511 001	OW	Berlin
511 002	OW	Zürich
511 003	OW	
511 004	OW	
511 005	OW	
511 006	OW	
511 007	OW	
511 008	OW	
511 009	OW	
511 010	OW	URDORF
511 011	OW	Dietikon
511 012	OW	
511 013	OW	
511 014	OW	WETTINGEN
511 015	OW	
511 016	OW	
511 017	OW	Schaffhausen
511 018	OW	
511 019	OW	
511 020	OW	
511 021	OW	
511 022	OW	St Gallen
511 023	OW	Graubünden
511 024	OW	
511 025	OW	
511 026	OW	
511 027	OW	
511 028	OW	
511 029	OW	
511 030	OW	
511 031	OW	Bezirk Affoltern
511 032	OW	
511 033	OW	WINTERTHUR
511 034	OW	
511 035	OW	

Number	Depot
511 036	OW
511 037	OW
511 038	OW
511 039	OW
511 040	OW
511 041	OW
511 042	OW
511 043	OW
511 044	OW
511 045	OW
511 046	OW
511 047	OW
511 048	OW
511 049	OW
511 050	OW
511 051	OW
511 052	
511 053	
511 054	
511 055	
511 056	
511 057	
511 058	
511 059	
511 060	
511 061	
511 062	
511 063	
511 064	
511 065	
511 066	
511 067	
511 068	
511 069	

Class 511.1. 4-car units mainly for Lausanne–Genève. Equipped with ETCS Level 2. Sets are numbered 94 85 6511 xxx + 4511 xxx + 2511 xxx + 1511 xxx.

Number	Depot
511 101	GE
511 102	GE
511 103	GE
511 104	GE
511 105	GE
511 106	GE
511 107	GE
511 108	GE
511 109	GE
511 110	GE
511 111	GE
511 112	GE

Number	Depot
511 113	GE
511 114	GE
511 115	GE
511 116	GE
511 117	GE
511 118	GE
511 119	GE
511 120	ZU
511 121	ZU
511 122	ZU
511 123	ZU
511 124	ZU

▲ 511 021 heads away from the camera with a train from Chur to Zürich while an RhB metre gauge train approaches Zizers station between Landquart and Chur on 14 June 2014.　**David Haydock**

▼ The Seetal line is something of a "light" railway, often running beside roads. As the Lenzburg–Luzern train leaves Beinwil am See on 21 June 2012, 520 010 has to cross a roundabout.

Jan Lundstrøm

CLASS RABde 514   DTZ   4-CAR DOUBLE-DECK UNITS

Recent air-conditioned double-deck EMUs (known as *Doppelstocktriebzüge* – DTZ – or double-deck EMUs) for the Zürich S-Bahn built by Siemens – the company's first double-deck EMUs. Can operate in multiple with Class 450. Used on S-Bahn Lines S7, S8 & S15.

Built: 2006–09.
Builder: Siemens.
Wheel Arrangement: Bo-Bo + 2-2 + 2-2 + Bo-Bo.
Length over Couplers: 25 + 25 + 25 + 25 m.
Accommodation: –/84 + –/118 (12) + –/112 1T + 74/–.
Traction Motors: 8 x 400 kW.   **Weight:** 218 tonnes.
Maximum Speed: 140 km/h.

Sets are numbered 94 85 0514 1xx + 0514 2xx + 0514 3xx + 0514 4xx.

Number Depot

514 001	OW	514 022	OW	514 042	OW
514 002	OW	514 023	OW	514 043	OW
514 003	OW	514 024	OW	514 044	OW
514 004	OW	514 025	OW	514 045	OW
514 005	OW	514 026	OW	514 046	OW
514 006	OW	514 027	OW	514 047	OW
514 007	OW	514 028	OW	514 048	OW
514 008	OW	514 029	OW	514 049	OW
514 009	OW	514 030	OW	514 050	OW
514 010	OW	514 031	OW	514 051	OW
514 011	OW	514 032	OW	514 052	OW
514 012	OW	514 033	OW	514 053	OW
514 013	OW	514 034	OW	514 054	OW
514 014	OW	514 035	OW	514 055	OW
514 015	OW	514 036	OW	514 056	OW
514 016	OW	514 037	OW	514 057	OW
514 017	OW	514 038	OW	514 058	OW
514 018	OW	514 039	OW	514 059	OW
514 019	OW	514 040	OW	514 060	OW
514 020	OW	514 041	OW	514 061	OW
514 021	OW				

Names:

514 006	Hans Künzi	514 027	Lufingen
514 007	Bülach	514 043	Neuhausen am Rheinfall
514 012	Russikon	514 050	Züri West
514 016	Schaffhausen	514 059	Elsau
514 017	Wetzikon	514 060	Oerlikon
514 022	Frauenfeld/Weinfelden		

CLASS RABe 515 "MUTZ" (KISS) 4-CAR DOUBLE-DECK UNITS

These are similar to SBB KISS EMUs, but have the most recent, flatter, Stadler front-end design and are nicknamed "MUTZ" by BLS – "bear", making a reference to Bern and its S-Bahn network, where the units are used. They are mainly used on Lines S1 and S6.

Built: 2012–14.
Builder: Stadler.
Wheel Arrangement: Bo-Bo + 2-2 + 2-2 + Bo-Bo.
Length over Couplers: 102.24 m.
Accommodation: –/74 + –/86 (2) 1TD + 58/34 1T + –/74.
Continuous Rating: 4000 kW.   **Total Weight:** 216 tonnes.
Maximum Speed: 160 km/h.

Number	Company	Names			
515 001	BLS	Stadt Bern	515 015	BLS	
515 002	BLS		515 016	BLS	
515 003	BLS	Düdingen	515 017	BLS	
515 004	BLS	Ville de Neuchâtel	515 018	BLS	
515 005	BLS		515 019	BLS	
515 006	BLS	Köniz	515 020	BLS	Schwarzenburg
515 007	BLS		515 021	BLS	
515 008	BLS		515 022	BLS	
515 009	BLS	Muri bei Bern	515 023	BLS	
515 010	BLS		515 024	BLS	
515 011	BLS		515 025	BLS	
515 012	BLS	Lyss	515 026	BLS	
515 013	BLS	Fribourg/Freiburg	515 027	BLS	
515 014	BLS		515 028	BLS	

CLASS RABe 520   GTW   3-SECTION ARTICULATED UNITS

This is a version of Stadler's GTW 2/8 EMU with a body 2.65 metres wide, compared with 3.00 metres as normally used on standard gauge units, for the Luzern–Lenzburg *Seetal* line. The unit has two doors per car – more than the usual units of this type.

Built: 2001/02.
Builder: Stadler.
Wheel Arrangement: 2-Bo-2-2.
Length over Couplers: 53.434 m.
Accommodation: 12/32 (1) + –/36 (8) 1T + –/48 (2).
Traction Motors: 2 x 260 kW.   **Total Weight:** 78.5 tonnes.
Maximum Speed: 115 km/h.

Number	Depot	Names			
520 000	LZ	Seon	520 009	LZ	Schloss Heidegg
520 001	LZ	Beinwil am See	520 010	LZ	Staufen
520 002	LZ	Hochdorf	520 011	LZ	Ballwil
520 003	LZ	Emmen	520 012	LZ	Hallwil
520 004	LZ	Mosen	520 013	LZ	Lenzburg
520 005	LZ	Eschenbach	520 014	LZ	Gelfingen
520 006	LZ	Hitzkirch	520 015	LZ	Ermensee
520 007	LZ	Boniswil	520 016	LZ	Birrwil
520 008	LZ	Stadt Luzern			

CLASS RABe 521.0   FLIRT   4-SECTION ARTICULATED UNITS

FLIRT (Flinker Leichter Innovativer Regional Triebzug – faster, lighter, innovative regional unit) was the first EMU – low floor, air conditioned and articulated – to be built by Stadler for city suburban services and was ordered by SBB in five versions. Class 521 (now Class 521.0) was built for Line S3 of the Basel S-Bahn network and for operation into Germany. SBB has the contract with Baden-Württemberg Land to operate services from Basel Bad to Zell (Wiesenthal) via Lörrach and Lörrach to Weil am Rhein. Normally 521 001–012 are used on this service, but all can be used in Germany if necessary. FLIRT EMUs have become a big success and have been turned out in many different, but similar versions, for SBB and other companies, numbered as Classes 521, 522, 523, 524, 526.0 and 527.

Built: 2005–07.
Builder: Stadler.
Wheel Arrangement: Bo-2-2-2-Bo.
Length over Couplers: 74.078 m.
Accommodation: 20/16 (6) + –/28 (14) 1TD + –/40 (8) + –/48.
Traction Motors: Four of 500 kW.   **Weight:** 120 tonnes.
Floor Height (entrance): 570 mm.   **Maximum Speed:** 160 km/h.

Number	Names		Number	Names
521 001	Regio TriRhena		521 016	Sissach
521 002	Riehen		521 017	
521 003	Weil am Rhein		521 018	
521 004	Lörrach		521 019	
521 005			521 020	Porrentruy
521 006			521 021	
521 007			521 022	Lausen
521 008			521 023	Ajoie
521 009			521 024	
521 010			521 025	
521 011	Oberdorf-Weissenstein		521 026	
521 012	Olten		521 027	Gilberte de Courgenay
521 013	Delémont		521 028	Liestal
521 014			521 029	
521 015			521 030	République et Canton du Jura

▲ Class 522.2 units have a modified front end compared with the other Swiss FLIRT units – they were redesigned to French crashworthiness standards. 522 211 stands in Delémont station on 17 April 2014. From 2017 they will work from here to Belfort in France. **David Haydock**

CLASS RABe 521.2 FLIRT 4-SECTION ARTICULATED UNITS

This version of the FLIRT was delivered to SBB subsidiary SBB GmbH (Deutschland) for the "Seehas" service operated by the company from Konstanz to Engen in Germany, under contract with the Baden-Württemberg Land. The units are therefore very similar to those used on the Basel S-Bahn but have only one door instead of two in the outer cars and more space for bikes. They were originally numbered 526 651 to 659 but were renumbered to avoid confusion with completely different THURBO Class 526.6.

Details as Class 521.0 except:

Built: 2006.
Builder: Stadler, Pankow.
Accommodation: 16/32 + –/30 1T + –/32 + –/52.

Number		Names		Number	
521 201	(521 651)	Konstanz		521 206	(521 656)
521 202	(521 652)			521 207	(521 657)
521 203	(521 653)			521 208	(521 658)
521 204	(521 654)			521 209	(521 659)
521 205	(521 655)				

CLASS RABe 522.2 FLIRT 4-SECTION ARTICULATED UNITS

The first Class 522 – originally numbered 522 001 to 012 – were basically the same as Class 521.0 but equipped to operate with 25 kV AC in France instead of with 15 kV AC in Germany. However, when tests started, the French pointed out that they did not meet the latest crashworthiness standards! So SBB ordered Class 522.2 with slightly different front ends to its other FLIRTs. 522 001 to 012 became 523 032 to 043.

Class 522.2 will be used on the Biel/Bienne–Delémont–Delle–Belfort (France) service when the Delle–Belfort line reopens in December 2017. They will also probably take over the Neuchâtel–Frasne shuttle financed by Lyria and may work other services to be financed by France's Franche-Comté region. In the meantime they are used mainly in the Basel/Delémont area, although four were transferred to work Genève–La Plaine–Bellegarde services in summer 2014. In June 2014 SBB announced that it had ordered 18 more sets, plus one set for tests. These will be equipped with ETCS Level 2 for the Genève area – the first nine for an increase in frequencies in 2017, then nine more in 2019 for the opening of the CEVA line to Annemasse in France. SNCF has ordered Alstom Régiolis sets for CEVA services.

Details as Class 521.0 except:

Built: 2011/12.
Systems: 15 kV AC 16.7 Hz/25 kV AC 50 Hz.
Accommodation: 24/16 (6) + –/24 (18) 1TD + –/48 (12) + –/40 (12).
Weight: 132.5 tonnes.

Number	Depot	Number	Depot	Number	Depot
522 201	GE	522 212	BS	522 223	
522 202	GE	522 213	GE	522 224	
522 203	BS	522 214	GE	522 225	
522 204	BS	522 215		522 226	
522 205	BS	522 216		522 227	
522 206	BS	522 217		522 228	
522 207	BS	522 218		522 229	
522 208	BS	522 219		522 230	
522 209	BS	522 220		522 231	
522 210	BS	522 221		522 232	
522 211	BS	522 222		522 233	

CLASS RABe 523   FLIRT   4-SECTION ARTICULATED UNITS

These units are basically the same as Class 521.0 but are not equipped to operate in Germany. They also have a slightly different livery. Originally, the first 12 were used on the Zug S-Bahn network, and are marked as such, but now they seem to be common user. A further 12 were ordered in 2007, then a further seven. 520 013 to 031 have a special leather-seated first class area and are used on the RER Vaudois network around Lausanne. 523 032 to 043 are former 522 001 to 012 (see above) and are normally used on the Luzern S-Bahn. 523 044–056 were built for the Olten/Luzern area, then 523 057–066 for expansion in Lausanne and Zug. 523 067–073 are to compensate the use of Class 522.2 on Delémont–Belfort from December 2017.

Details as Class 521.0 except:

Accommodation: –/44 + –/44 + –/28 (14) 1TD + 20/19.

Number		*Depot*	*Names*
523 001	E	LZ	
523 002	E	LZ	
523 003	E	LZ	
523 004	E	LZ	
523 005		LZ	
523 006		LZ	
523 007		LZ	
523 008		LZ	
523 009		LZ	
523 010		LZ	
523 011	E	LZ	
523 012	E	LZ	
523 013	E	GE	La Brine
523 014	E	GE	
523 015	E	GE	
523 016	E	GE	
523 017	E	GE	
523 018	E	GE	
523 019	E	GE	
523 020	E	GE	
523 021	E	GE	La Veveyse
523 022	E	GE	
523 023	E	GE	
523 024	E	GE	
523 025	E	GE	
523 026	E	GE	
523 027	E	GE	
523 028	E	GE	
523 029	E	GE	
523 030	E	GE	
523 031	E	GE	

Number		Depot	Names
523 032	(522 001)	LZ	
523 033	(522 002)	LZ	
523 034	(522 003)	LZ	Wohlen
523 035	(522 004)	LZ	Lindenberg
523 036	(522 005)	LZ	Sins
523 037	(522 006)	LZ	Ebikon
523 038	(522 007)	LZ	
523 039	(522 008)	LZ	
523 040	(522 009)	LZ	
523 041	(522 010)	LZ	
523 042	(522 011)	LZ	
523 043	(522 012)	LZ	
523 044			
523 045			
523 046			
523 047			
523 048			
523 049			
523 050			
523 051			
523 052			
523 053			
523 054			
523 055			
523 056			
523 057			
523 058			
523 059			
523 060			
523 061			
523 062			

CLASS RABe 524   FLIRT   4- & 6-SECTION ARTICULATED UNITS

These units are very similar to Class 521.0 but have only one entrance door instead of two in the outer cars and are equipped for operation under 3000 V DC in Italy as well as 15 kV AC in Switzerland. The units are being used on services around Bellinzona and into Italy under the branding TILO, which combines the letters representing TIcino canton and the LOmbardia region. A few services reach Milano Centrale. The main cross-border service will be from Bellinzona to Malpensa airport when the new line from Mendrisio to Varese is complete, in principle in December 2017. The late opening has allowed some 4-car sets to be used on Neuchâtel–Le Locle. Units 524 201–204 are owned by Italian operator FNM. All sets are fitted with ETCS Level 2.

Details as Class 521.0 except:

Built: 2007/08.
Systems: 15 kV AC 16.7 Hz, 3000 V DC.
Accommodation: 28/16 + –/32 (14) 1T + –/48 (+ –/46 + 36/–) + –/40 (8).
Weight: 133 tonnes (4-car); 175 tonnes (6-car).

▲ Two TILO FLIRT EMUs led by 6-car 524 108 skirt Lago Lugano near Capolago on 9 July 2015.
Laurence Sly

▼ RegionAlps (formerly Martigny-Orsières) "NINA" EMU 525 039 (formerly 527 513) stands at Sembrancher on 16 April 2014. **David Haydock**

Class 524.0. 4-Section Units. Sets are numbered 94 85 2524 xxx + 3524 xxx + 4524 xxx + 1524 xxx.

Number	Depot	Names		Number	Depot
524 001	BE	Lombardia		524 011	BE
524 002	BE	Ticino		524 012	BE
524 003	BE	Tre Valli		524 013	BE
524 004	BE	Gambarogno		524 014	BE
524 005	BE			524 015	BE
524 006	BE	Valli del Luinese		524 016	BE
524 007	BE	Locarnese		524 017	BE
524 008	BE			524 018	BE
524 009	BE	L'Allondon		524 019	BE
524 010	BE				

Class 524.1. 6-Section Units. Sets are numbered 94 85 2524 xxx + 3524 xxx + 6524 xxx + 5524 xxx + 4524 xxx + 1524 xxx.

Number	Depot	Names		Number	Depot
524 101	BE	Arbedo-Castione		524 110	BE
524 102	BE	San Gottardo/Gotthard		524 111	BE
524 103	BE	Mendrisio		524 112	BE
524 104	BE			524 113	BE
524 105	BE			524 114	BE
524 106	BE			524 115	BE
524 107	BE			524 116	BE
524 108	BE			524 117	BE
524 109	BE				

Class 524.2. 4-Section Units; owned by Italian operator FNM.

Number	Depot		Number	Depot
524 201	BE		524 203	BE
524 202	BE		524 204	BE

CLASS RABe 525   "NINA"
3- & 4-SECTION ARTICULATED UNITS

Articulated EMUs originally ordered by BLS with an 80% low floor for the Bern S-Bahn, Class 525 are known as "NINA" meaning *Niederflür NAhverkehr* – low-floor local services. Following a BLS tradition for stock with number 13, 525 013 is "NINO". The first batch of eight work Line S5 Bern–Neuchâtel whilst the 18 in the second batch were ordered to take over Lines S1 and S3 from SBB Class 560 EMUs when BLS took over the whole of the Bern S-Bahn. The first batch was supplied without toilets but retrofitted in 2002. The names are mainly rivers, lakes and streams on Bern S-Bahn lines. NINA units have now been replaced on Bern Line S1, so have been cascaded to more minor BLS services, replacing Class 566. 525 037 and 038 were former TRN sets 527 321 and 322; 525 038 has since been sold to RegionAlps, which already had the three Martigny-Orsières units, which have been renumbered. All BLS sets are to be modernised from mid 2015 to late 2018.

Built: 1998/99 001–008, 2003–06 009–036.
Builder–Mechanical Parts: Vevey/Talbot 001–008, Bombardier 009–036.
Builder–Electrical Parts: Traxis 001–008, Alstom 009–036.
Wheel Arrangement: Bo-2-2-Bo.
Accommodation: 3-car 16/32 + –/54 + –/46 1T, 4-car 16/32 + –/54 + –/54 + 16/32 1TD.
Refurbished sets –/50 + 20/14 (+ –/50) + –/46 1TD.
Continuous Rating: 1000 kW.   **Maximum Tractive Effort:**
Driving Wheel Diameter: 750 mm.   **Total Weight:** 31 + 17 (+ 17) + 31 tonnes.
Length: 16.785 + 14.17 (+ 14.17) + 16.785 m.   **Maximum Speed:** 140 km/h.

525 015–027 are 4-car units, others 3-car. BLS units carry numbers NINA 01 to 37 on their front ends. RegionAlps units carry RA 38 to 41 on their front ends.

Number	Company	Livery	Names/Notes		Number	Company		Names/Notes
525 001	BLS		Thielle/Zihl		525 005	BLS		Aare
525 002	BLS		Schwarzwasser		525 006	BLS		Gürbe
525 003	BLS		Emme		525 007	BLS		Gäbelbach
525 004	BLS		La Broye		525 008	BLS		La Sarine/Saane

▲ SOB 526 044 plus a second set form an Uznach–Sargans srrvice via St Gallen near Sevelen on 18 July 2014. **Robin Ralston**

▼ Despite still being in RM red livery, 526 283 is now part of the SBB fleet and is seen at Crémines with a Moutier–Solothurn service on 17 April 2014. **David Haydock**

525 009	BLS		Schwarzsee
525 010	BLS		Gerzensee
525 011	BLS		
525 012	BLS		
525 013	BLS		Konolfingen
525 014	BLS		Wohlensee
525 015	BLS	**A**	
525 016	BLS		
525 017	BLS		Grabenbach
525 018	BLS		Thunersee
525 019	BLS		
525 020	BLS		Scherlibach
525 021	BLS		
525 022	BLS		Worble
525 023	BLS		
525 024	BLS		
525 025	BLS		
525 026	BLS		Chräbsbach
525 027	BLS		Glütschbach
525 028	BLS		La Bibera/Bibere
525 029	BLS		
525 030	BLS		
525 032	BLS		
525 033	BLS		Wankdorf
525 034	BLS		
525 035	BLS		
525 036	BLS	**A**	
525 037	BLS	**A**	Ex TRN
525 038	RA		Ex BLS, ex TRN; Anton
525 039	RA		Ex 527 513
525 040	RA		Ex 527 512
525 041	RA		Ex 527 511

CLASS RABe 526.0 SOB FLIRT 4-SECTION ARTICULATED UNITS

More Stadler FLIRT EMUs, acquired in two batches and now in charge of almost all SOB local services.

Details as SBB Class 521.2 except:

Built: 2007/08 526 041–051, 2013 526 052–063.
Accommodation: –/48 (10) + –/48 (10) + –/36 (15) 1TD + 24/16 (8).

Number	*Names*
526 041	Mythen
526 042	Chrüzberg
526 043	Churfirsten
526 044	Morgartenberg
526 045	Federispitz
526 046	Ringelspitz
526 047	Rossberg
526 048	Kronberg
526 049	Hochstuckli
526 050	Alvier
526 051	Zimmerberg
526 052	Schnabelsberg
526 053	Etzel
526 054	Hoher Kasten
526 055	Mürtschenstock
526 056	Pizol
526 057	Gonzen
526 058	Speer
526 059	St. Anton
526 060	Hundwiler Höhi
526 061	Rigi Kulm
526 062	Chapfenberg
526 063	Alpstein

CLASS RABe 526.2 SBB GTW 3-CAR UNITS

These units were originally ordered by RM, were taken over by BLS then moved to SBB in a special deal in 2013. They are used on lines around Solothurn. 526 260–265 were originally 2-car sets, but were extended to 3-car in 2009. See THURBO Class 526.7 for technical details except:

Built: 2003/04.
Accommodation: 15/38 (4) + –/56 (4) + –/43 (2) 1T.
Length: 53.37 m. **Weight**: 84.2 tonnes

Number	*Livery*	*Names*
526 260	**R**	Luzerner Hinterland
526 261	**R**	Gotthelf
526 262	**R**	Weissenstein
526 263	**R**	Emme
526 264	**R**	Napf
526 265	**R**	Wankdorf
526 280	**R**	Aare
526 281	**R**	Pierre Pertuis
526 282	**R**	Oberaargau
526 283	**R**	Willisau
526 284	**R**	
526 285	**R**	
526 286	**R**	

CLASS RABe 526.6   THURBO GTW   2-CAR UNITS

This small class is the earliest version of the Stadler GTW 2/6 EMU. They differ from the later series units in having a rather flat front end but have the same short, central two-axle power unit with a driving trailer supported on each side by just one bogie. The units operate mainly Lines S5 and S55 from Gossau to St Gallen and Weinfelden, sometimes with an extra driving trailer.

Built: 1998/99.
Builder: Stadler/FIAT-SIG/Adtranz.
Wheel Arrangement: 2-Bo-2.
Accommodation: –/56 (8) + 12/44 (8) 1T.
Traction Motors: Two of 380 kW.   **Weight:** 57 tonnes.
Overall Length: 18.90 + 18.90 m.   **Maximum Speed:** 130 km/h.

Number	Names	Number	Names
526 680		526 685	Ostwind
526 681	Weinfelden	526 686	
526 682	Amriswil	526 687	
526 683		526 688	
526 684		526 689	

CLASS RABe 526.7   THURBO GTW   2- & 3-CAR UNITS

Used on almost all regional services in north-east Switzerland, the name THURBO is derived from the fact these mainly cover Thurgau canton. 3-car sets are employed on S29 Winterthur–Stein am Rhein, S33 Winterthur–Schaffhausen and S35 Winterthur–Wil. The original order was altered several times and eventually 51 2-car (526 701–751) and 29 3-car sets (526 752–780) were delivered. 526 709–718 were then converted to 3-car in 2008 and renumbered in order as 526 781–790. Units 720 to 751 were fitted with pantographs and safety equipment to work in Germany from 2005. The first unit to be dealt with, 526 706, became 526 720 and the original 526 720 became 526 706. The others were not renumbered. 12 more units were delivered for the St Gallen S-Bahn which was inaugurated in December 2013, then three for the Schaffhausen S-Bahn. One set works the Olten–Sissach service – well out of the THURBO area!

Built: 2003–07 526 701–790, 2012/13 526 791–805.
Builder: Stadler.
Wheel Arrangement: 2-Bo-2 (2-car); 2-Bo-2-2 (3-car).
Accommodation: –/56 (6) (+ –/56 (6)) + 16/34 (6) 1T.
Traction Motors: Two of 350 kW.   **Weight:** 63 tonnes (2-car); 82 tonnes (3-car).
Overall Length: 39.40 m (2-car); 54.447 m (3-car).   **Maximum Speed:** 140 km/h.

Number	Names	Number	Names
526 701	Kanton Thurgau	526 732	
526 702	Frauenfeld	526 733	
526 703	Kanton St. Gallen	526 734	
526 704	Der Scharfe Maxx	526 735	Rumikon AG
526 705	slowUp	526 736	
526 706	Simone Niggli	526 737	
526 707	TOP-Blitz	526 738	
526 708	Steinach	526 739	
526 719		526 740	
526 720	Spieleland Express/Ravensburger Spieleland	526 741	
		526 742	Flawil
526 721		526 743	
526 722	Märwil	526 744	Säntis-Express
526 723		526 745	Stein am Rhein
526 724	CONNY-LAND Express	526 746	Sirnach
526 725	Theater St. Gallen	526 747	Elgg
526 726	Rorschach/Rorschacherberg	526 748	Elsau
526 727	Napoleon III	526 749	
526 728	Läufelfingerli	526 750	Zürcher Weinland
526 729	Kanton Aargau	526 751	
526 730	Wil	526 752	
526 731	Waldshut-Tiengen	526 753	Schiffahrtsgesellschaft

526 754		526 780	Bussnang
526 755	Rheinfall	526 781	Schaffhausen
526 756		526 782	Alstätten
526 757	St. Galler Rheintal	526 783	Bodensee
526 758	Sargans	526 784	slowUp
526 759		526 785	Eschlikon
526 760	myblueplanet	526 786	Bad Zurzach
526 761		526 787	Barockes Bischofszell
526 762	Stadler Rail	526 788	Romanshorn
526 763	Thurgau	526 789	Aadorf
526 764		526 790	Zihlschacht-Sitterdorf
526 765		526 791	Spieleland Express
526 766	Insel Mainau	526 792	
526 767	Kreuzlingen	526 793	
526 768	Säntispark	526 794	Chur
526 769	Maienfeld	526 795	
526 770	Batzenheid	526 796	
526 771	Kanton Luzrn	526 797	
526 772	TCS	526 798	
526 773		526 799	
526 774	Säntis	526 800	
526 775		526 801	
526 776		526 802	
526 777	Turbenthal	526 803	
526 778	S Bahn St Gallen	526 804	
526 779		526 805	

CLASS RABe 527   TPF and transN FLIRT
4-SECTION ARTICULATED UNITS

Details mainly as SBB Class 521.1. TPF units operate mainly between Bulle and Fribourg. transN units operate the Buttes–Neuchâtel service and since December 2015 the Neuchâtel–Le Locle service, for which three more sets have been ordered. Details as SBB Class 521.1 except:

Built: 2007 527 331, 2009 527 332, 2011 527 333, 2012–14 527 191–198.
Accommodation: TPF: 24/16 (8) + –/24 (24) 1TD + –/48 (8) + –/48 (8).
transN: 24/23 (8) + –/38 (14) 1TD + –/48 (8) + –/48 (8).

Number	Company		Number	Company
527 191	TPF		527 331	TRN
527 192	TPF		527 332	TRN
527 193	TPF		527 333	TRN
527 194	TPF		527 334	
527 195	TPF		527 335	
527 196	TPF		527 336	
527 197	TPF			
527 198	TPF			

CLASS RABe 535   BLS "Lötschberger"
4-SECTION ARTICULATED UNITS

These are a modified version of the Class 525 "NINA" design with larger windows for use on the Brig–Spiez Lötschberg summit line plus Spiez–Zweisimmen, with trains eventually all being extended from Spiez to Bern. They now also work Bern–Luzern. Plans to build more units were scotched; the units do not meet new TSI collision standards.

Built: 2008/09.
Builder: Bombardier/Alstom.
Accommodation: –/44 (3) + –/44 (3) + 28/– + –/32 (11) 1T.
Wheel Arrangement: Bo-2-2-2-Bo.   **Power Rating:** 1000 kW.
Driving Wheel Diameter: 750 mm.   **Weight:** 107 tonnes.
Length over Couplers: 62.70 m.   **Maximum Speed:** 160 km/h.

▲ Brand new SZU EMU Be 552 514 is seen at Triemli station with a service to Zürich HB on 12 June 2014. Note the characteristic offset pantograph. **David Haydock**

▼ Travys (PBr) EMU 560 384 is seen with a Vallorbe–Le Brassus train soon after leaving Le Pont station on 9 October 2014. **David Haydock**

Number	Names
535 101	Züri West
535 102	
535 103	
535 104	Naters
535 105	
535 106	
535 107	
535 108	
535 109	
535 110	
535 111	
535 112	

Number	Names
535 113	
535 114	
535 115	
535 116	
535 117	
535 118	
535 119	
535 120	
535 121	
535 122	
535 123	
535 124	Eggerberg
535 125	

CLASS Abde 537   SINGLE CARS

A typical 1960s design for private lines, similar in outline to SBB Class RBe 540. RA, formerly Martigny-Orsières, still has three units used to haul works trains.

Built: 1965.
Builder–Mechanical Parts: SIG/SWS.
Builder–Electrical Parts: BBC/MFO/SAAS.
Wheel Arrangement: Bo-Bo.   **Accommodation:** 6/47 1T.
One Hour Rating: 1100 kW.   **Weight:** 64 tonnes.
Length over Buffers: 24.30 m.   **Maximum Speed:** 100 km/h.

All are push-pull & multiple working fitted (can mw with Re4/4^{II}, Re4/4^{III}, Re4/4^{IV} & Re6/6 Classes).

Number	Company	Name	Notes
537 506	RA	ORSIERES	Ex 6
537 507	RA	BAGNES	Ex 7
537 509	RA	SEMBRANCHER	Ex 9

CLASS Be 552   SZU UETLIBERG LINE   3-CAR UNITS

These sets were delivered in 2013 to the Uetlibergbahn (originally numbered 556 511 to 516) and are dual-voltage – the pantographs can be moved from the middle (for the Sihltalbahn) to the side (Uetlibergbahn) – in anticipation of removing the 1200 V DC wire over the common section. This suggests that there will be further orders in future to produce a common fleet.

Built: 2013.
Builder: Stadler.
Accommodation: –/40 (6) + –/43 (4) + –/40 (6).
Wheel Arrangement: 2-Bo-Bo-2.   **Systems:** 1200 V DC/15 kV AC 16.7 Hz.
Maximum Rating: 1400 kW.   **Weight:** 91.7 tonnes.
Length: 50 m.   **Maximum Speed:** 120 km/h.

Number			
552 511	552 513	552 515	552 516
552 512	552 514		

CLASS Be 556   SZU UETLIBERG LINE   POWER CARS

These power cars are used in 3-car formation with a trailer between; 521 + 221 + 522, 523 + 222 + 524 and so on. The new units are longer so these will probably be used less in future.

Built: 1992/93.
Builder: SWS/Siemens.
Accommodation: –/40 (12).
Power Rating: 800 kW.   **Weight:** 44 tonnes.
Length: 21.71 m.   **Maximum Speed:** 70 km/h.

Number			
556 521	556 523	556 525	556 527
556 522	556 524	556 526	556 528

CLASS Bem 558 (Bem 4/6)

TL LINE M1
2-SECTION ARTICULATED UNITS

These bi-directional articulated light rail vehicles, used on the TL line from Lausanne Flon to Renens, incorporate an 88 kW diesel engine since the depot area is not electrified. They are numbered in the national computerised system for railway stock, although operation is self-contained. They usually operate in pairs. Units are very similar to SBB Class 550 EMUs and at one time TL planned to buy the latter. However, adapting them for urban use proved too difficult so TL bought new units instead.

Built: 1990/91; * 1995, § 2013/14.
Builder–Mechanical Parts: ACMV/Duewag, § Bombardier.
Builder–Electrical Parts: ABB; § Kiepe.
Accommodation: –/28 (4) + –/28 (4).
Wheel Arrangement: B-2-B.
Traction Motors: 2 x 188 kW.
Length over Couplers: 31.00 m.

Weight: 42.6 tonnes.
Maximum Speed: 80 km/h.

Number

558 201	558 209	558 216	*
558 202	558 210	558 217	*
558 203	558 211	558 218	§
558 204	558 212	558 219	§
558 205	558 213 *	558 220	§
558 206	558 214 *	558 221	§
558 207	558 215 *	558 222	§
558 208			

▲ SBB Class 560 EMUs are still numerous and can be found across the country. The 16 units in the 560.4 series operate for RegionAlps ariund Martigny and can be distinguished by their red window band, instead of black. This is 560 412 at Sion on 16 April 2014. **David Haydock**

CLASSES Rbde 560, 561 & 562   POWER CARS

This power car design for local services is formally known as the "NPZ" – *Neue Pendel Zug* or "new shuttle train" – and informally, though officially, as *Kolibri* or "humming bird". Four prototypes 2100 to 2103 (later 560 000 to 003) were delivered in 1984 with series production beginning in 1987. Units were originally numbered 2100–2183 and were first renumbered 560 000 to 083 in order, then in the 560 200 series, out of order, from 2008. They are equipped with solid state control. Operating in sets of varying length, with driving and intermediate trailers, they can also multiple with other members of the class. Gangwayed at the non-driving end only. Operate throughout Switzerland. Classes 565, 566 and 567, operated by private companies, are similar.

Prototypes 560 000 to 003 were withdrawn in 2007/8. 560 001 and 003 were sold to the Montafonerbahn in Austria, 560 000 to OeBB and 560 002 to CJ.

In 2008, the units started to be refurbished, with air conditioning, and receiving one or more new, central low-floor coaches. The resulting units are known as "Domino" and carry a livery of white with red front ends, window bands and doors. Refurbished 3-car units for RegionAlps were renumbered in the 560 400 series and other units in the 560 200 series. The first of these were 6-car units for Glarus Sprinter services, but are now in normal formations. The Bombardier "Inova" centre cars were built in three versions: four Type AB 24/37 1T, 95 Type B with toilet –/61 1T and 41 Type B without toilet –/68. Non-standard 2-car set 560 141 was rebuilt as standard. PBr also has two Class 560 units.

560 223 to 234 have Schwab-Enotrac auto-couplers which can be controlled from the cab.

The RegionAlps units have a slightly different livery, with more red.

Six Class 560 were modified as 561 000–005 for use on the Basel–Zell line in Germany, but then replaced by Class 521. They were converted back to standard as 560 298–303.

561 081–084 are power cars used by SOB on the Voralpern Express and are almost identical to SBB sets. They were previously 566 077–080. 561 174 is the last of four former MThB units (566 631 to 634, later 561 171 to 174), also almost identical, absorbed by SBB. 561 174 has now been purchased by SOB as a spare for the Voralpen Express service.

Six Class 560 were rebuilt in 1997 as Class 562 for dual voltage (15/25 kV AC) operation for use on through local services from Basel to Mulhouse in France. They now only normally operate the Neuchâtel–Frasne service, paid for by Lyria, and connecting with the latter's Lausanne–Paris TGV service, and will shortly be replaced by Class 522.

Built: 560 000–003 1984, 560 004–083 1987–90, 560 101–135 1993–96, 561 081–084 1995, 561 174 1994.
Builder–Mechanical Parts: FFA/SIG/SWP/ABB (560 101–135 SWG-A/SWG-P/SIG).
Builder–Electrical Parts: BBC (ABB).
Accommodation: –/48 (6).
Wheel Arrangement: Bo-Bo.
One Hour Rating: 1714 kW.   **Weight:** 70 tonnes.
Length over Couplers: 25.00 m.   **Maximum Speed:** 140 km/h.
EVN: 94 95 7560 000-c and so on.

Class 560.0. Ex SBB.

Number	Company	Names/Notes		Number		Names/Notes
560 000	OeBB 207	"Balsthal"	|	560 141	CJ	Ex SBB 560 002

Class 560.2. Owned by SBB. AC: Equipped with auto couplers controlled by driver from cab.

Number		Names/Notes		Number		Names/Notes
560 201	(560 029)		|	560 212	(560 027) E	
560 202	(560 007)		|	560 213	(560 028)	
560 203	(560 005)		|	560 214	(560 030) E	
560 204	(560 006)		|	560 215	(560 031) E	
560 205	(560 012)		|	560 216	(560 032) E	La Broye
560 206	(560 013)		|	560 217	(560 033) E	
560 207	(560 014)		|	560 218	(560 034) E	
560 208	(560 018)		|	560 219	(560 035)	
560 209	(560 024) E		|	560 220	(560 036)	
560 210	(560 025) E		|	560 221	(560 037)	
560 211	(560 026) E		|	560 222	(560 038)	Glarus Sud

560 223	(560 039) AC		560 264	(560 080)	
560 224	(560 040) AC	La Glâne	560 265	(560 081)	La Neirigue
560 225	(560 041) AC		560 266	(560 082)	
560 226	(560 042) AC		560 267	(560 083)	Nebikon
560 227	(560 043) AC		560 268	(560 100)	
560 228	(560 044) AC	La Versoix	560 269	(560 101)	
560 229	(560 045) AC		560 270	(560 102)	
560 230	(560 046) AC		560 271	(560 103)	
560 231	(560 047) AC		560 272	(560 104)	
560 232	(560 048) AC		560 273	(560 106)	
560 233	(560 049) AC		560 275	(560 108)	
560 234	(560 050) AC	Le Doubs	560 277	(560 110)	
560 235	(560 051)		560 278	(560 111)	
560 236	(560 052)		560 279	(560 112)	
560 237	(560 053)		560 280	(560 113)	
560 238	(560 054)		560 281	(560 114)	
560 239	(560 055)		560 282	(560 115)	
560 240	(560 056)		560 283	(560 116)	
560 241	(560 057)		560 284	(560 117)	
560 242	(560 058)		560 285	(560 118)	Glarus Nord
560 243	(560 059)		560 286	(560 119)	
560 244	(560 060)		560 287	(560 120)	
560 245	(560 061)		560 288	(560 121)	
560 246	(560 062)	Le Seyon	560 289	(560 122)	
560 247	(560 063)		560 290	(560 123)	
560 248	(560 064)		560 291	(560 124)	
560 249	(560 065)		560 292	(560 125)	
560 250	(560 066)		560 293	(560 126)	
560 251	(560 067)		560 295	(560 130)	
560 252	(560 068)		560 296	(560 131)	
560 253	(560 069)		560 297	(560 132)	
560 254	(560 070)		560 298	(561 000)	
560 255	(560 071)	Avenches/Aventicum	560 299	(561 001)	
560 256	(560 072)		560 300	(561 002)	
560 257	(560 073)		560 301	(561 003)	
560 258	(560 074)		560 302	(561 004)	
560 259	(560 075)		560 303	(561 005)	
560 260	(560 076)				
560 261	(560 077)		560 384		Travys (PBr)
560 262	(560 078)		560 385		Travys (PBr)
560 263	(560 079)				

Class 560.4. 3-car SBB units for RegionAlps services around Martigny.

Number

560 401	(560 004) E	560 407	(560 021) E	560 412	(560 010) E
560 402	(560 008) E	560 408	(560 022) E	560 413	(560 011) E
560 403	(560 019) E	560 409	(560 020) E	560 414	(560 109) E
560 404	(560 015) E	560 410	(560 016) E	560 415	(560 107) E
560 405	(560 009) E	560 411	(560 017) E	560 416	(560 129) E
560 406	(560 023) E				

Class 561. Owned by SOB, for Voralpern Express service.

Number

561 081	(566 077)	561 083	(566 079)	561 174	(566 631)
561 082	(566 078)	561 084	(566 080)		

Class 562. 5-car SBB units for operation into France.

Number   *Livery*

562 000	(560 136)	N	562 003	(560 139)	N	562 005	(560 141)	N
562 001	(560 137)	N	562 004	(560 140)	N			

CLASS RBDe 565 (RBDe 4/4)   POWER CARS

Modern BLS railcars, very similar to SBB Class 560, found on Bern S-Bahn services S2 and S3. Fitted with thyristor control. They have recently been equipped with pairs of articulated low-floor centre cars known as "Jumbo". Units carry the 721–742 series numbers on the front end but the number of the driving trailer is carried on the other end of sets.

Built: 1982–85 565 721–738, 1991 565 739–742.
Builder–Mechanical Parts: SIG/SWP.
Builder–Electrical Parts: BBC 565 721–738, ABB 565 739–742.

Wheel Arrangement: Bo-Bo.	**Accommodation:** –/54 (1).
One Hour Rating: 1700 kW.	**Maximum Tractive Effort:** 186 kN.
Driving Wheel Diameter: 940 mm.	**Weight:** 69.7 tonnes.
Length over Couplers: 25.00 m.	**Maximum Speed:** 125 km/h.

Number	Livery	Names
565 721		
565 722		
565 723		
565 724		
565 725		
565 726		
565 727		
565 728		
565 729		
565 731	BUMPLITZ/HOLLIGEN	
565 732	ERLENBACH	

Number	Names
565 733	BOLTIGEN
565 734	INS/ANET
565 735	BELP
565 736	TOFFEN
565 737	FERENBALM/MÜHLEBERG
565 738	KERZERS/RIED
565 739	WIMMIS
565 740	UETENDORF
565 741	MARIN-ÉPAGNIER
565 742	ST-BLAISE

ASS RBDe 566.0   SOB NPZ   POWER CARS

These ex-BT power cars are coupled to trailers to form 2-car EMUs. Some names have been removed recently. They are very similar to BLS Class 565, the main (minor) difference being gear ratio, and therefore tractive effort. Details as BLS Class 565 except:

Built: 1982 by FFA/SIG/BBC.   **Accommodation:** –/48.

Number	Names
566 071	Muolen
566 072	Haggenschwil
566 073	Roggwil-Berg

Number	Names
566 074	Mogelsberg
566 075	Brunnadern
566 076	Lichtensteig

CLASS RBDe 566.2   POWER CARS

Very similar to Class 565, but formerly with RM. Many of the names have been removed; it is not known whether they will be restored. The earlier units, 566 220–227, have all now been withdrawn. Most sets are 3-car and are candidates for early withdrawal. Details as BLS Class 565 except:

Built: 1984/85.

Number	
566 230	(EBT 230)
566 231	(EBT 231)
566 232	(EBT 232)
566 233	(EBT 233)
566 234	(EBT 227)
566 235	(EBT 228)
566 236	(EBT 229)

Number	
566 237	(VHB 262)
566 238	(VHB 263)
566 239	(VHB 264)
566 240	(VHB 265)
566 241	(SMB 282)
566 242	(SMB 283)

CLASS RBDe 567.170 POWER CARS

These power cars were built for several small railways and look like a more angular version of SBB Class RBDe 540. Their technical details are very similar to Class 565 but the front end is completely different. They can be used in various formations but usually in 3-car sets. Travys 567 174 was formerly 567 315 at TRN, previously RABDe 4/4 105.

Built: 1983.
Builders: SIG/SWS/BBC.
Wheel Arrangement: Bo-Bo.
One Hour Rating: 1700 kW.
Wheel Diameter: 940 mm.
Length over Couplers: 20.30 m.

Accommodation: –/48; 567 171 –/43.
Weight: 70 tonnes.
Maximum Speed: 125 km/h.

Number	Company	Names	Notes
567 171	TPF	LA SARINE	
567 172	TPF	VULLY	
567 173	TPF	LA GLÂNE	
567 174	Travys (PBr)	FLEURIER	Ex TRN 567 315

CLASS RBDe 567.180 & 567.3 POWER CARS

Very similar to Class 565. Details as BLS Class 565 except:

Built: 1985 567 316, 1991 567 180 & 567 317.
Accommodation: –/55 567 180, –/54 567.3.

Builders: SWP/SIG/ABB.
Weight: 71 tonnes 561.180, 69 tonnes 567.3.

Number	Company	Names			
567 181	TPF	CRESSIER	(567) 316 transN	(COUVET)
567 182	TPF	COURTEPIN	(567) 317 transN	MÔTIERS (NE)

CLASS 576 POWER CARS

Similar to SBB Class 540, but even more powerful! Now used for hauling trains of gravel. 577 049 has a rounder body like Class 540, while 577 055 to 059 have a boxier body like TPF Class 567. 576 057 now has an auxiliary diesel engine for shunting. 576 059 is now only used for shunting by SOB.

Built: 1959 576 049, 1978/79 567 055–059.
Builders: SIG/BBC.
Wheel Arrangement: Bo-Bo.
Wheel Diameter: 1040 mm.
Length over Couplers: 23.70 m.

One Hour Rating: 2100 kW.
Weight: 72 tonnes.
Maximum Speed: 110 km/h.

Number	Company	Names	Notes
576 049	Makies	Mabette	Ex SOB BDe 4/4 81
576 055	Makies		Ex SOB Bde 4/4 83; for spares
576 056	Makies	Elisi	Ex SOB BDe 4/4 84
576 057	Makies	Jeanette	Ex SOB BDe 4/4 85
576 058	SOB	WOLLERAU	Ex BDe 4/4 86
576 059	SOB	FREIENBACH	Ex Bde 4/4 87

CLASS BDe 577 POWER CARS

More railcars which look similar to those with RA (MO). These now haul works trains on the CJ Bonfol line, and occasionally carry passengers if other stock is out of action.

Built: 1968 577 101, 1980 568 102.
Builders: SWS/MFO/BBC.
Wheel Arrangement: Bo-Bo.
Wheel Diameter: 940 mm.
Length over Buffers: 22.35 m.

One Hour Rating: 640 kW.
Weight: 51 tonnes.
Maximum Speed: 70 km/h.

Number	Company	Names			
577 101	CJ	BONFOL	577 102	CJ	ALLE

CLASS ABe 578   POWER CAR

Similar in looks to Class RBe 540. 578 016 is ex MThB 16 (later 538 316) and originally GFM 171.

Built: 1966.
Builders: SWS/BBC/MFO/SAAS.
Wheel Arrangement: Bo-Bo.
Accommodation: 12/31.
Wheel Diameter: 1040 mm.
Length over Couplers: 19.80 m.

One Hour rating: 1100 kW.
Weight: 64 tonnes.
Maximum Speed: 100 km/h.

Number   Company   Notes
578 016   Travys (PBr)   Ex 538 316, MThB 16

Some other vehicles in the 500 series are not included in this section: 570 001 is Gmeinder diesel loco "HUSKY" with Scheuchzer; 580 009 is a Gmeinder D100BB (5733, 1996, ex VPS 1302) with Müller Technologie; 587 111 is a locomotive with CJ; 588 721 and 722 (21 and 22) are locos with RHB; 591 021 is the preserved "Churchillpfeil" EMU Rae 4/8 1021.

▲ transN unit 567 316 is seen at Auvergnier on 24 March 2015.   **Mario Stefani**

1.4. DIESEL LOCOMOTIVES

In this new edition, we have added a number of diesel locomotives owned by industrial users. In early 2016, numbering was a little anarchic and some numbers are likely to change. All diesel locomotives have EVNs in the series 98 85 5xxx xxx-c except where shown.

CLASS Bm 4/4 (Bm 840.4)   Bo-Bo

SBB locos for shunting and trip working on non-electrified tracks. Several have now been withdrawn and are operated by other companies, renumbered as Class 840. SBB locos still carry their 184xx numbers. Infrastructure locos are used for fire-fighting and rescue trains.

Built: 1960–70.
Builder–Mechanical Parts: SLM.
Builder–Electrical Parts: SAAS.
Engine: SLM 12YD20TrTH of 895 kW.
Wheel Diameter: 1040 mm.
Length over Buffers: 12.65 m. († 13.15 m).

Transmission: Electric.
Maximum Tractive Effort: 216 kN.
Weight: 72 tonnes.
Maximum Speed: 75 km/h.

§ Fitted with signalling and radio for operation over RBS dual gauge lines.
z Equipped with ZUB/ETM signalling.

Number		Livery	Company/Sector		Depot	Notes/Names
840 402	(18402)		SRT			
840 403	(18403)		SRT			
18405		R	C		S	
18406		P	I		RW	
18407		R	C		O	
18408		R	C		W	
18410		P	C		W	
840 411	(18411)		Stauffer			840 111 "Rosi I"
18412		P	C			
18413		P	C		W	
18414		P	C	§	W	

▲ Bm 4/4 18446 heads a short infrastructure train at Immensee on 10 April 2014.   **Mario Stefani**

18415		**P**	P		BS
840 416	(18416)		SRT		
840 420	(18420)		Stauffer		For spares
18422		**R**	C		O
18423		**P**	C		O
18424		**R**	C		O
18425		**P**	I		SG
840 426	(18426)		SRT		
18427		**R**	C	†	O
18428		**P**	C	z†	O
840 430	(18430)		Stauffer		
18431		**R**	C	†	O
18432		**R**	C	z†	W
18433		**R**	C	†	O
18434		**R**	C	†	S
18435		**R**	P	†	S
18436		**R**	I	†	LS
18437		**R**	I	†	GO
18438		**R**	I	†	GE
18440		**R**	I	†	BS
18441		**R**	I	†	W
18442		**R**	I	†	ER
18443		**R**	I	†	BI
18444		**R**	C	†	BS
18446		**R**	I	†	ER

CLASS Bm 6/6 (Bm 860) — Co-Co

Centre cab diesels used for yard shunting and trip working. Each bonnet contains its own engine and generator set. SBB only has one remaining loco, used at Brig. All the others still in service are owned by Schorno. Schorno Locomotive Management (Mr Schorno has craftily revived SLM!)

Built: 1954–61.
Builder–Mechanical Parts: SLM.
Builder–Electrical Parts: BBC/SAAS.
Engine: Two Sulzer 6LDA25 of 635 kW each.
Wheel Diameter: 1040 mm.
Length over Buffers: 17.00 m. (* 17.56 m).
Transmission: Electric.
Maximum Tractive Effort: 334 kN.
Weight: 106 tonnes.
Maximum Speed: 75 km/h.

Number	Livery	Company		Number	Livery	Company
18501		Schorno		18508		Schorno
18503		Schorno		18509		Schorno
18504		Schorno		18510		Schorno
18505	**R**	SBB H		18511		Schorno
18506		Schorno		18512		Schorno
18507		Schorno		18513	*	Schorno

CLASS Bm 6/6 (Am 861) — Co-Co

SBB heavy shunting locos, built specifically for use in Limmattal Yard near Zürich. They have three-phase traction motors supplied from a fixed frequency alternator via frequency conversion equipment tested on the Henschel DE 2500 prototype. The engine is the same as that in SNCF's Class BB 67400. EVNs are 92 85 5861 5xx-c.

Built: 1976.
Builder–Mechanical Parts: Thyssen Henschel.
Builder–Electrical Parts: BBC.
Engine: SEMT Pielstick 16 PA4 V-185 VG of 1840 kW.
Wheel Diameter: 1260 mm.
Length over Buffers: 17.40 m.
Transmission: Electric.
Maximum Tractive Effort: 393 kN.
Weight: 111 tonnes.
Maximum Speed: 85 km/h.

Number	Livery	Sector	Depot		Number	Livery	Sector	Depot
18521	**P**	I	ZU		18525	**P**	I	ZU
18522	**P**	I	ZU		18526	**P**	I	ZU
18523	**P**	I	ZU					

▲ Schorno loco Bm 6/6 18508 is seen at Boudry hauling a preserved Ae 6/6 electric loco to Genève on 12 September 2014. **Mario Stefani**

▼ Em 831 000 is seen being hauled by Stauffer electric shunter 936 154 at Sion on 26 November 2014. **Charles-André Fluckiger**

CLASS Em 3/3 (Em 830)   C

General purpose shunting locomotives found throughout the system. SBB now has few left, but others are turning up elsewhere, Travys having taken three. 18832 is used to supply spares.

Built: 1962–63.
Builder–Mechanical Parts: SLM.
Builder–Electrical Parts: BBC/SAAS.
Engine: SLM 6VD20TrTH of 450 kW.
Transmission: Electric.   **Maximum Tractive Effort:** 124 kN.
Wheel Diameter: 1040 mm.   **Weight:** 49 tonnes.
Length over Buffers: 10.02 m.   **Maximum Speed:** 65 km/h.

Number	Livery	Company/Sector	Depot
18808	R	P	NW
18815	P	P	OW
830 816	(18816)	Travys (OC)	
18824	R	P	OL
830 830		Travys (OC)	
18831	R	P	NW
18838	P	I	BU
830 840	(18840)	Travys (OC)	

Name:

18824   EMMA

CLASS 580   TYPE D100 BB   B-B

These locomotives were bought second-hand from VPS in Germany, which works the internal network of Peine/Salzgitter steel works. The locos have retained their German EVNs in the 98 80 0xxx xxx-c series.

Built: 1993/96.   **Transmission:** Hydraulic. Voith L520rzU2.
Builder: Gmeinder Type D100 BB.
Maximum Tractive Effort: 235kN.   **Engine:** MTU 12V4000R20 of 1320 kW.
Wheel Diameter: 1000 mm.   **Weight:** 80 tonnes.
Length over Buffers: 13.09 m.   **Maximum Speed:** 90 km/h.

Number	Company	Builder/Type	Works No	Built	Notes
580 008	Müller Gleisbau	Gmeinder D100BB	5708	1993	Ex VPS 1301
580 009	Müller Gleisbau	Gmeinder D100BB	5733	1996	Ex VPS 1302
580 010	Müller Gleisbau	Gmeinder D100BB	5734	1996	Ex VPS 1303

CLASS Em 831   Co

The prototypes of a new generation of diesel shunters for SBB of which series production never took place. Now all sold to Stauffer.

Built: 1992.
Builder–Mechanical Parts: RACO.
Builder–Electrical Parts: ABB.
Engine: Cummins of 895 kW.   **Transmission:** Hydraulic.
Wheel Diameter: **Maximum Tractive Effort:** 175 kN.
Length over Buffers: 9.84 m.   **Weight:** 60 tonnes.
                                                Maximum Speed: 80 km/h.

Number	Company	Notes		Number	Company	Notes
831 000	Stauffer	Ex SBB		831 002	Stauffer	Ex SBB
831 001	Stauffer	Ex SBB				

"CLASSES Em 836 & 837"

Not really classes, but a variety of largish shunters of which we can only include technical details for the most common:

HENSCHEL TYPES DH 500 Ca & DHG 500 C   C

The DH 500 Ca was a typical Henschel loco from the company's third generation of shunters. The DHG 500 C is from the fourth generation and is very similar, especially from the outside.
Built: DH 500 Ca: 89 built 1957–71; DHG 500 C: 63 built 1963–76.
Engine: DH 500 Ca Mercedes-Benz MB836Bb of 365 kW;
DHG 500 C Henschel 12V 1416 of 368 kW.
Transmission: Hydraulic. Voith.   **Maximum Tractive Effort**: 190 kN.
Wheel Diameter: 1250 mm.   **Weight**: 54 tonnes.
Length over Buffers: DH 500 Ca 8.90 m; DHG 500 C 9.90 m.
Maximum Speed: DH 500 Ca 30/60 km/h; DHG 500 C 30/50 km/h.

HENSCHEL TYPE DHG 700 C   C

A more powerful version of the DHG 500 C, the 500 and 700 indicating horsepower.
Built: 93 built 1965–85.
Engine: MTU of 507 kW.
Transmission: Hydraulic. Voith.   **Maximum Tractive Effort**: 190 kN.
Wheel Diameter: 1000 mm.   **Weight**: 60 tonnes.
Length over Buffers: 9.84 m.   **Maximum Speed**: 37 km/h.

Number	Company	Builder/Type	Works No	Built	Notes/Names
836 361	GGRB	Henschel DH500Ca	29725	1958	Ex BLS, ex EBT 15
836 908	LBA, Bronschhofen	Stadler	112	1961	
836 914	LBA, Rynächt Arsenal, Altdorf	Stadler	148	1976	
836 915	LBA, Oberburg	Stadler	156	1979	
837 084	TPF	Krupp 440PS	4395	1963	Ex Shell, Hamburg 3
837 601	WRS	Krupp V60	3995	1960	Ex DB 360 572
837 800	Holcim, Eclépens	Henschel DH500Ca	31083	1965	"2003"
837 801	Sersa	Henschel DH500Ca	30303	1961	Ex Rheinstahl
837 802	Florin, Muttenz	KM M350C	19399	1969	
837 803	Travys (OC)	Henschel DHG700C	32724	1985	Em 3/3 3
837 804	Panlog	MaK DE502	700081	1986	Ex Krupp MaK hire loco; "3"
837 811	Rhenus, Basel	Deutz MG600C	58164	1968	
837 813	SFS, Schweizerhalle	Jung R30C	12998	1957	
837 814	Makies	Henschel DH500Ca	30710	1965	Ex PTT "6"
837 815	Ultra-Brag, Kleinhüningen	Henschel DH500Ca	30515	1963	"3"
837 816	Makies	Henschel DH500Ca	30590	1964	Ex GSW 10; "1"
837 818	Schnyder Gotthard, Emmen	Jung RC43C	14163	1974	
837 819	Sappi Schweiz, Biberist	Henschel DH500Ca	31078	1964	"1"
837 820	Sappi Schweiz, Biberist	Henschel DH500Ca	31309	1968	"2"
837 821	Tensol, Giornico	Henschel DH500Ca	30506	1962	
837 822	Migros, Neuendorf	Henschel DHG700C	31993	1977	
837 823	Perlen Papier, Perlen	KM M500C	19405	1968	"9"
837 824	Holcim, Eclépens	Henschel DH500Ca	31082	1965	"2001"
837 825	Makies	Henschel DHG500C	30858	1965	Ex Rheinstahl 56; "2"
837 826	ASm	Henschel DHG500C	31111	1965	Ex SNB Em 326
837 827	Constellium, Chippis	Henschel DHG700	32749	1981	
837 828	Varo Energy, Birsfelden	MaK G763C	700072	1983	
837 829	Sersa	Gmeinder DHG700C	32514	1980	
837 831	LSB/Züdzucker, Frauenfeld	KM M700C	19765	1973	
837 852	Vanoli	Henschel DH500Ca	30258	1960	Lok Immensee
837 853	LSB/Juracime, Cornaux	Henschel DHG500C	31236	1968	

837 862	GGRB	Henschel DH440Ca	30592	1965	Ex BLS, ex VHB 57; "VIVIENNE"
837 900	GGRB, Birmensdorf	Henschel DH500Ca	31079	1964	
837 901	Stauffer	Henschel DH500Ca	30511	1963	Monika
837 902	Juracime, Cornaux	MAK G500C	500052	1970	
837 903	Solvay, Bad Zurzach	Moyse CN60EE500D	3537	1973	
837 905	AMA, Amsteg	Moyse CN60EE500D	3548	1975	
837 907	Lonza, Visp	Henschel DHG500C	31232	1968	"162"
837 908	LSB	Henschel DH360Ca	30703	1963	Ex LONZA; "VIKTOR" "162"
837 909	Loacker, Emmen	Henschel DHG500C	31184	1967	
837 910	LSB	Henschel DHG500C	31239	1968	Ex Lonza 163
837 911	Holcim, Untervaz	MaK DE501C	700041	1981	
837 950	Sersa	Henschel DH440Ca	30261	1960	
837 951	Sersa	Henschel DH500Ca	31193	1966	ex Raffinerie Cornaux 4; "KARIN"
837 952	Sersa	KM ML700C	19089	1963	"SVENJA"
837 953	AMA, Amsteg	Moyse CN54EE500C	3523	1972	
837 954	AMA, Amsteg	Moyse CN60EE500Ba	3546	1974	

▲ Em 837 853, a Henschel DHG500C owned by LSB and seen here whilst on hire to Lonza, shunts container wagons at Visp on 12 July 2013. **Charles-André Fluckiger**

CLASS Am 840.0   VOSSLOH G2000   B-B

Class Am 840 is a standard Vossloh Type G2000-2. SBB Cargo used them to work freight into northern Italy, then sold them to Scheuchzer in 2014. EVNs: 92 85 8 840 xxx-c

Built: 2003.
Builder: Vossloh. Type G2000-2.
Engine: Caterpillar 3516 B-HD of 2240 kW.
Transmission: Hydraulic. Voith L620 re U2.   **Maximum Tractive Effort:** 282 kN.
Wheel Diameter: 1000 mm.   **Weight:** 87.3 tonnes.
Length over Buffers: 17.40 m.   **Maximum Speed:** 120 km/h.

Number	Company	Works No	Name				
840 001	Scheuchzer	1001453	RHINO 1	840 003	Scheuchzer	5001482	RHINO 3
840 002	Scheuchzer	5001481	RHINO 2				

CLASS Am 841   Bo-Bo

A centre-cab diesel locomotive with SBB for use on shunting and trip work. Similar on the outside to RENFE Class 311 and SNCF Class BB 60000. Five locos are equipped with ETCS Level 2. All have been transferred from SBB Cargo to SBB Infra. They will be replaced by new Class 940 electro-diesels then sold.

Built: 1996–97.
Builder: GEC-Alsthom. Type GA-DE 900 AS.
Engine: One MTU 8V 396 TB14 of 920 kW at 1800 rpm.
Transmission: Electric. Four 6 FRA 3055 asynchronous traction motors.
Maximum Tractive Effort: 190 kN.
Wheel Diameter: 1100 mm.   **Weight:** 72 tonnes.
Length over Buffers: 14.12 m.   **Maximum Speed:** 80 km/h.

E   Fitted with ETCS.
f   Equipped with particle filter.

Number	Livery	Sector	Depot		Number	Livery	Sector	Depot
841 000	R	I	W		841 020	R	I	W
841 001	R	I	W		841 021	R	I	W
841 002	R	I	W		841 022	R	I	Ef	S
841 003	R	I	W		841 023	R	I	S
841 004	R	I	W		841 024	R	I	S
841 005	R	I	Ef	S	841 025	R	I	S
841 006	R	I	Ef	S	841 026	R	I	S
841 007	R	I	Ef	S	841 027	R	I	S
841 008	R	I	S		841 028	R	I	S
841 009	R	I	S		841 029	R	I	S
841 010	R	I	O		841 030	R	I	O
841 011	R	I	O		841 031	R	I	O
841 012	R	I	O		841 032	R	I	S
841 013	R	I	W		841 033	R	I	S
841 014	R	I	W		841 034	R	I	f	S
841 015	R	I	S		841 035	R	I	S
841 016	R	I	S		841 036	R	I	S
841 017	R	I	S		841 037	R	I	W
841 018	R	I	Ef	S	841 038	R	I	W
841 019	R	I	S		841 039	R	I	GE

▲ Travys (Orbe-Chavornay) Em 837 803, a Henschel DHG700C, heads a freight for Chavornay, just after leaving a factory at Les Granges on 9 October 2014. **David Haydock**

▼ Scheuchzer Vossloh G2000 RHINO 2 (840 002) is seen at Bulle on 16 September 2014.
Mario Stefani

CLASS Am 842 B-B

The first of these locos are MaK Type G1204 BB – a pair of diesel locomotives purchased in 1993/94 by SBB from permanent way contractor Sersa. They were formerly known as "Corinne" and "Daniela" respectively – MaK works numbers 1001878 and 1001879. Only 18 of this type were built, of which these were the last two. A third Sersa G1204 "Bettina" numbered Am 847 953 was sold to a German operator and is now owned by Vossloh and hired out in Germany.

The second batch is similar, but is the more recent Vossloh G1000 BB. SBB Cargo hired 842 011–014, and 842 101–102 from Alpha Trains but has now returned them all. 842 704 and 705 are also Vossloh G1000 BBs, owned by Tamoil and used at the St Triphon refinery. There is another G1000 BB in Switzerland, but it is numbered 845 002! This may be "corrected" during the currency of this book. The loco was first hired by Alpha Trains to BLS, then to Sersa.

Last but not least, Sersa has leased yet another G1000 BB, but this has retained its German EVN, the shortened version of which is 271 023.

MaK Type G 1204

Built: 1991.
Engine: MTU 12V 396 TC13 of 1120 kW.
Transmission: Hydraulic. Voith L5r4U2.
Wheel Diameter: 1000 mm.
Length over Buffers: 12.50 m.

Maximum Tractive Effort:
Weight: 80 tonnes.
Maximum Speed: 90 km/h.

Number	Livery	Sector	Depot
842 000	R	I	ZU
842 001	R	I	ZU

Vossloh Type G1000 BB (also see Class Am 845)

Engine: MTU 8V 4000 R41L of 1100 kW.
Transmission: Hydraulic. Voith L4r4.
Length over Buffers: 14.13 m.

Maximum Tractive Effort: 259 kN.
Maximum Speed: 100 km/h.

Number		Company	Works No	Built	Names
842 704	TAM 6	Tamoil	5001897	2010	
842 705	TAM 5	Tamoil	5001533	2004	
845 002		AT/Sersa	1001323	2003	MICHAELA
271 023		MRCE/Sersa	5001577		

▲ SBB Infra Am 843 022 is seen at Steinen with a works train on 4 June 2015. **Laurence Sly**

CLASS Am 843 G 1700-2 BB B-B

In July 2002, SBB ordered 59 Class Am 843 diesel-hydraulic locos based on Vossloh's G1700-2 design. This was followed by options taking the total to 73 locos. The locos are split between the Infrastructure and Cargo divisions, the Infra locos being all red and the Cargo locos red and blue. Infra locos originally had the name of the activity in big letters on the bonnet side but this was changed to the SBB logo in 2009. Originally, five locos (843 031–035) were ordered for the Passenger activity but there was a change of heart and these became Cargo's 843 091–095 which can work in Germany. Infra locos are used for yard shunting and rescue trains whilst Cargo locos work mainly trip freights and some shunting. 843 015 was renumbered from 840 051 in autumn 2005. In May 2008, SBB's Passenger division ordered three more locos to be numbered 843 041–043. Two went to Basel and one to Chiasso. Note that 277 015 carries an EVN in the German series 98 80 1xxx xxx-c.

Sersa has five locomotives for track work. 843 151–153 were bought new in 2004, but the other two were hired to various companies before being acquired in 2009. Sersa has a sixth G1700 which still carries its German EVN.

BLS bought three locos (843 501–503) in 2006, then a fourth in 2012. They are equipped with ETCS Level 2 for rescue and maintenance work in the Lötschberg base tunnel.

Built: 2003–05.
Engine: Caterpillar CAT 3512 B of 1500 kW.
Transmission: Hydraulic. Voith L5r4zseU2. **Maximum Tractive Effort:** 250 kN.
Wheel Diameter: 1000 mm. **Weight:** 80 tonnes.
Length over Buffers: 15.20 m. **Maximum Speed:** 100 km/h.

843 026–28 are equipped with ETCS Level 2 for use on the Rothrist–Mattstetten line.

d   equipped to operate in Germany.
E   Equipped with ETCS.

Number	Livery	Sector		Depot	Base					
843 001	R	I		ZU	Altstetten	843 050	C	C	O	
843 002	R	I		BS	Sursee	843 052	C	C	O	
843 003	R	I		BS	Muttenz	843 053	C	C	O	
843 004	R	I		RK	Buchs	843 054	C	C	W	
843 005	R	I		OL	Olten	843 055	C	C	O	
843 006	R	I		CH	Chiasso	843 056	C	C	O	
843 007	R	I		CH	Chiasso	843 057	C	C	O	
843 008	R	I		CH	Chiasso	843 058	C	C	W	
843 009	R	I		BS	Muttenz	843 059	C	C	W	
843 010	R	I	E	CH	Chiasso	843 060	C	C	W	
843 011	R	I	E	BS	Muttenz	843 061	C	C	W	
843 012	R	I	E	CH	Chiasso	843 062	C	C	O	
843 013	R	I	E	BS	Muttenz	843 063	C	C	W	
843 014	R	I	E	BS	Muttenz	843 064	C	C	O	
843 015	R	I	E	ZU	Limmattal	843 065	C	C	W	
843 016	R	I	E	CH	Chiasso	843 066	C	C	W	
843 017	R	I	E	BU	Buchs	843 067	C	C	O	
843 018	R	I	E	BS	Muttenz	843 068	C	C	O	
843 019	R	I	E	BS	Muttenz	843 069	C	C	O	
843 020	R	I	E	BS	Muttenz	843 070	C	C	O	
843 021	R	I	E	OL	Olten	843 071	C	C	W	
843 022	R	I	E	CH	Chiasso	843 072	C	C	W	
843 023	R	I	E	OL	Limmattal	843 073	C	C	W	
843 024	R	I	E	BN	Neuchâtel	843 074	C	C	O	
843 025	R	I	E	ZU	Limmattal	843 075	C	C	S	
843 026	R	I	E	BN	Bern	843 076	C	C	O	
843 027	R	I	E	OL	Olten	843 077	C	C	O	
843 028	R	I	E	OL	Olten	843 078	C	C	S	
						843 079	C	C	O	
843 041	R	P		BS		843 080	C	C	O	
843 042	R	P		BS		843 081	C	C	E	W
843 043	R	P		CH		843 082	C	C	O	
						843 083	C	C	O	

843 084	C	C	O		843 090	C	C		O
843 085	C	C	O		843 091	C	C	d	O
843 086	C	C	O		843 092	C	C	d	O
843 087	C	C	W		843 093	C	C	d	O
843 088	C	C	O		843 094	C	C	d	O
843 089	C	C	O		843 095	C	C	d	O

Name:

843 074 Uristei

Number	Company	Works No	Built	Names
843 151	Sersa	5001492	2004	TRUDY
843 152	Sersa	5001493	2004	BARBARA
843 153	Sersa	5001494	2004	CINDERELLA
843 154	Sersa	1001210	2003	BETTINA
843 155	Sersa	5001488	2004	AMELIE
843 501	E	BLS	5001645	
843 502	E	BLS	5001646	
843 503	E	BLS	5001647	
843 504	E	BLS	5001922	
277 015			5001592	Julia

CLASS Am 845   B-B

For some reason Vossloh G1000BB locos have two class numbers. See Class Am 842.

OeBB also has a loco numbered Am 845 001. This is former DB V60D loco 345 164, formerly used by BLS and numbered "20" by OeBB.

▲ CFD loco 847 011 is seen at the Holcim Untervaz-Trimmis cement works on 23 August 2012.
Sylvain Meillasson

CLASSES Am 846.4 & 846.6   Bo-Bo

These are MaK Type DE 1003, of which only four were built, originally delivered to RAG as 661–664 in 1988. They are very similar in looks to other Vossloh and MaK diesels, but have electric transmission, so are closely related to former NS Class 6400 and Eurotunnel's five Krupp/MaK diesels which are classified DE 1004. They are unusual in having two engines, one of which shuts off when not needed for heavy traction. Of the four locos, 662 was withdrawn after an accident, whilst the others were acquired by Railconsult in Italy. After use by SRT, two locos are now with Stauffer.

846 601 is a Brissonneau & Lotz loco, very similar to SNCF Class BB 63500 and formerly with northern France coal producer HBNPC. Formerly numbered 80 85 9770 002-6.

846 633 is former SOB loco Am 4/4 61 (later 846 033). This was Krupp-AEG DE 1500 prototype (works number 4400), tested by DB as 201 001 then becoming WLE 0901.

Built: 1988.
Builder: MaK/BBC.
Engine: 2 x MWM TBD234V12 of 510 kW each.
Transmission: Electric.
Wheel Diameter: 1000 mm.   **Weight:** 88 tonnes.
Length: 15.00 m.   **Maximum Speed:** 40 km/h.

Number		Company	Works No	Built	Names
846 401	(RAG 664)	Stauffer/SRT	1000846		
846 402	(RAG 663)	Railconsult/SRT	1000845		
846 601	(HBNPC 29)	Scheuchzer		1960	GAZELLE
846 633	(SOB Am 4/4 61)	SRT	KRUPP 4400	1964	

CLASS Em 847.0   GRAVITA 10BB   B-B

These are Gravita 10BB diesel-hydraulics, built by Voith during its brief foray into producing diesel locos in competition with arch-rivals Vossloh. All are used in steelworks and can be seen in sidings near the main line when exchanging freights with SBB – at Emmenbrücke and Gerlafingen/Biberist.

Built: 2009/10.
Builder: Voith Turbo Lokomotivtechnik, Kiel.
Engine: MTU 8V 4000 R3 of 1000 kW.
Transmission: Hydraulic. Voith L4r4zseU2.   **Maximum Tractive Effort:** 337 kN.
Wheel Diameter: 1000 mm.   **Weight:** 80 tonnes.
Length: 15.72 m.   **Maximum Speed:** 100 km/h.

Number	Company	Works No	Names
847 001	Panlog	L04-10031	Emmen
847 002	Panlog	L04-10033	Luzern
847 003	Panlog	L04-10034	Littau
847 004	Stahlwerk Gerlafingen	L04-10029	Biberist
847 005	Stahlwerk Gerlafingen	L04-10032	Gerlafingen

CLASS Bm or Em 847.1 to 847.9   B-B or Bo-Bo

A wide variety of other B-B or Bo-Bo diesel locos are numbered in the 847 series. Of the Henschel DHG1200BB locos, two were originally with Danish private operators. The two former DR V100 locos are used on main line movements of track maintenance trains by WRS and still carry their Connex liveries. See Class 203 below for details. Sersa has three former DB V100 locos (ex Class 211) but had several more which have now been sold to other countries.

Number	Company	Builder & Type	Works No	Built	Notes/Names
847 011	Holcim, Untervaz	CFD BB700HR		1997	
847 101	Scheuchzer	CFD BB 1500 HV	152-001	2004	"BISON"
847 851	Holcim, Untervaz	CEM		1968	Ex WM Em 4/4 151
847 852	Sersa	Vossloh G1206	1001019	1999	Ex Panlog; "ALINA"
847 853	Vanoli	Henschel DHG1200BB	31948	1977	Ex VNJ DL 14 (DK); "Lok Goldau"

847 855	Vanoli	Henschel DHG1200BB	31949	1977	Ex HP 16 (DK); "Lok Meggen"
847 856	VARO, Birsfeld Hafen	ART DH440	180	1997	
847 900	Stauffer	MTE BB800H	6174	1982	
847 901	LSB	Faur (U23) LDH370	23879	1979	
847 902	Greuter	Faur (U23) LDH45	24122	1980	
847 903	Perlen Papier, Perlen	MaK G1204BB	1000819	1983	"Füchsli"
847 904	LSB	Henschel DHG1200BB	31575	1973	Ex HGK V25
847 905	WRS	LEW V100D	15381	1976	Ex DR 110 863
847 906	WRS	LEW V100D	12834	1971	Ex DR 110 325
847 908	OeBB	LEW V60D	12246	1969	Ex industrial; "22"
847 909	Vanoli	Gmeinder D180BB	5764	2011	
847 951	Sersa	Krupp V100	4359	1962	Ex DB 211 249; "GRETLI II"
847 954	Eberhard, Recycling, Kloten	MaK 850D	800112	1958	Ex HFHJ M9
847 957	ASm	Henschel V100	30564	1962	Ex DB 211 215; "LOTTI"
847 958	Sersa	Deutz V100	57355	1961	Ex DB 211 118; "NICOLE"
847 959	Sersa	MaK 1200D	1000250	1964	Ex WBHE V15; "FRIEDA"
847 960	Vanoli	MaK 1000D	100009	1958	Ex RStE V101; "Iris"

CLASSES 1275 & 1276   TYPE G1206   B-B

This type is now ubiquitous across Europe but most of the locos used in Switzerland are hired from MRCE, registered in Germany, and carry German EVNs. The only G1206 registered in Switzerland is 847 852. The MWB loco is on long-term hire to SBB and is used to serve branches into France around Basel, especially from St Johann. 1275 625 is owned by SBB Cargo International, but is only used in Germany. EVNs 92 80 1xxx xxx-c

Built: 1997–
Builder: MaK, SFT, VSFT, VL.
Engine: Caterpillar 3512B DI-TA, of 1500 kW.
Transmission: Hydraulic, Voith L5r4 zU2.
Maximum Tractive Effort: 267 kN.

Wheel Diameter: 1000 mm.
Weight: 87.3 tonnes.
Length over Buffers: 14.70 m.
Maximum Speed: 100 km/h.

Number		Company	Works No	Base	Names
1275 008		MRCE/Sersa	5001676		Lea
1275 615		MRCE/Sersa	5001508		
1275 618		MRCE/Sersa	5001553		
1275 628		MRCE/Sersa	5001648		
1276 005	V 2106	MWB/SBB Cargo	5001726	Basel St Johann	

CLASS 2143   ex-ÖBB, now RTS   B-B

These are former Austrian Railways Class 2143 locos, owned by Austrian track maintenance company RTS and in the company's orange livery, but on hire to SBB Infra.

Built: 1965–77.
Builder–Mechanical Parts: SGP.
Engine: SGP T12c of 1100 kW (1475 hp) plus 224 kW (300 hp) for train heating.
Transmission: Hydraulic. Voith L830rU2.   **Maximum Tractive Effort:** 197 kN.
Wheel Diameter: 950 mm.   **Weight:** 67 tonnes.
Length Over Buffers: 15.76 m.   **Maximum Speed:** 100 km/h.
EVN: 93 81 2143 xxx-c

Number	Company		Number	Company
2143 007	RTS/SBB Infra		2143 025	RTS/SBB Infra
2143 012	RTS/SBB Infra		2143 077	RTS/SBB Infra
2143 014	RTS/SBB Infra			

▲ Two steel companies in Switzerland have bought Voith Gravita diesels, one of them being Panlog, whose loco 847 002 is seen at Emmenbrücke on 3 February 2015. **Mario Stefani**

▼ Em 847 901 is of Romanian origin (Faur) and is seen at Visp on 28 January 2013.
Charles-André Fluckiger

1.5. ELECTRIC AND ELECTRO-DIESEL SHUNTING LOCOMOTIVES

Switzerland has a long tradition of using electric shunting locomotives, the latest also have an auxiliary diesel engine. EVNs are 97 85 1xxx xxx-c

CLASS Ee 922   Bo

In mid 2009, SBB received the first of 21 new two-axle dual-voltage shunting locomotives from Stadler for shunting passenger stock. These were supposed to replace all of the 38 Ee 3/3 and seven Ee 3/3^{II} in passenger use around Switzerland. Only the eight Class Ee 934 used in Genève and Chiasso were to remain from the old classes. Four more locos were delivered in 2015.

Built: 922 001–021 2009/10; 922 022–025 2015.
Builder: Stadler.
Systems: 15 kV AC 16.7 Hz, 25 kV AC 50 Hz.
Power Rating: 600 kW.   **Maximum Tractive Effort:** 120 kN.
Wheel Diameter: **Weight:** 44 tonnes.
Length over Buffers: 8.80 m.   **Maximum Speed:** 100 km/h; shunting 40 km/h.

Number	Sector	Depot						
922 001	P	ZU	922 010	P	BI	922 018	P	ZU
922 002	P	ZU	922 011	P	BR	922 019	P	BR
922 003	P	ZU	922 012	P	BR	922 020	P	BN
922 004	P	BS	922 013	P	CH	922 021	P	BR
922 005	P	LZ	922 014	P	BN	922 022	P	BS
922 006	P	BS	922 015	P	LZ	922 023	P	GE
922 007	P	ZU	922 016	P	BS	922 024	P	GE
922 008	P	RO	922 017	P	CH	922 025	P	SG
922 009	P	BN						

▲ Eem 923 025 heads a train of empty timber wagons from Neuchâtel to Les Verrières and is seen at Travers on 5 February 2016.   **Sylvain Meillasson**

CLASS Eem 923   Bo

These locos are a development of Class Ee 922 with the inclusion of a diesel engine to allow shunting in non-electrified sidings. The locos were branded "BUTLER" by Stadler.

Built: 2012/13.
Builder: Stadler.
Engine: Deutz TCD2015 V6 of 360 kW.
One Hour Rating: 300 kW.
Wheel Diameter: 1100 mm.
Length over Buffers: 9.10 m.

Systems: 15 kV AC 16.7 Hz/25 kV AC 50 Hz.
Maximum Tractive Effort: 150 kN.
Weight: 45 tonnes.
Maximum Speed: 120 km/h.

Number		Name	Sector	Base
923 001		Heitern	C	Zofingen
923 002		Brestenegg	C	Suhr
923 003		Stählibuck	C	Frauenfeld
923 004		Roggen	C	Oensingen
923 005		Oberberg	C	Gossau
923 006		Born	C	Däniken
923 007		Schoren	C	Lüpfig
923 008		Schäflisberg	C	St Margarethen
923 009		Alvier	C	Buchs SG
923 010		Suhrerchopf	C	Suhr
923 011			C	Reserve
923 012		Chaumont	C	Marin-E
923 013	E	Le Moléson	C	Romont
923 014	E	Dents de Midi	C	St Maurice
923 015		Mont Vully	C	Payerne
923 016		Le Jorat	C	Donges
923 017		Frienisberg	C	Biel
923 018			C	Reserve
923 019		La Berra	C	Fribourg
923 020		Stockhorn	C	Thun
923 021		Tourbillion	C	Sion
923 022			C	Frauenfeld
923 023	E	Dent de Vaulion	C	Langenthal
923 024		Fronalpstock	C	Ziegelbrücke
923 025		Schlossberg	C	Romanshorn
923 026		Hofberg	C	Wil SG
923 027		Bözingenberg/Montagne de Boujean	C	Möhlin
923 028		Geissberg	C	Menznau
923 029		Rossberg	C	Thun
923 030		Chestenberg	C	Suhr

CLASS Ee 3/3 (CLASS Ee 930)   C

This is a development of the standard SBB Ee 3/3 electric shunter of the 1930s, featuring a single motor, geared to a layshaft and driving through a jack and coupling rods. It has a centre cab and shunter's platforms at both ends. The last ones will shortly be withdrawn.

Built: 1932–47.
Builder–Mechanical Parts: SLM.
Builder–Electrical. Parts: BBC.
Traction Motors: 1 single-phase frame mounted with jackshaft/side rod drive.
One Hour Rating: 428 kW.
Wheel Diameter: 1040 mm.
Length over Buffers: 9.75 m.

Maximum Tractive Effort: 88 kN.
Weight: 45 tonnes.
Maximum Speed: 40 km/h.

Number	Company	Livery	Sector	Depot
16362		R	P	ZU
16365		R	P	BS
16383		R	P	ZU
16388		R	P	CHUR

16393		R	P	YW
16396		R	I	Däniken
16403	RUWA, Sumiswald			
16406		P	P	LS
16408		P	P	BI
16410		R	P	CHUR

CLASS Ee 3/3 (CLASS Ee 930)   C

The final development of the Ee 3/3.

Built: 1951–66.
Builder–Mechanical Parts: SLM.
Builder–Electrical. Parts: BBC/MFO/SAAS.
Traction Motors: 1 single-phase frame mounted with jackshaft/side rod drive.
One Hour Rating: 502 kW.   **Maximum Tractive Effort:** 118 kN.
Wheel Diameter: 1040 mm.   **Weight:** 45 tonnes (* 44 tonnes).
Length over Buffers: 9.51 m.   **Maximum Speed:** 45 km/h.

Number	Livery	Sector		Depot		Number	Livery	Sector		Depot
16422	R	I		LT		16448	R	P	*	BE
16430	P	P		ZU		16451	R	P	*	BN
16440	R	P		BI		16454	P	P	*	O
16445	P	I	*	OL		16456	R	I	*	BI
16447	P	P	*	BE		16460	R	P	*	W

▲ Ee 3/3 16408 soldiers on after 70 years service and is seen at Biel/Bienne on 13 September 2013.   **Mario Stefani**

CLASS Ee 3/3ᴵᴵ (CLASS Ee 932)   C

The dual-voltage version of the Ee 3/3, which can be used under the 25 kV AC 50 Hz wires in Basel where the SNCF AC electrification extends into the SBB station. 16511–9 were built for SNCF (C 20151–9) for use around Basel, but were sold to the SBB in 1971. The last of the class now shunts at Yverdon works.

Built: 1957–63.
Builder–Mechanical Parts: SLM.
Builders–Electrical. Parts: SAAS.
Systems: 15 kV AC 16.7 Hz, 25 kV AC 50 Hz.
Traction Motors: 1 single-phase frame mounted with jackshaft/side rod drive.
One Hour Rating: 506 kW.   **Maximum Tractive Effort**: 132 kN.
Wheel Diameter: 1040 mm.   **Weight**: 52 tonnes.
Length over Buffers: 9.42 m.   **Maximum Speed**: 45 km/h.

Multiple working fitted.

Number	Livery	Sector	Depot
16515	**R**	P	YW

CLASS Ee 934 (CLASS Ee 3/3ᴵⱽ)   C

The four-voltage version of the Ee 3/3, for use at border stations. It differs from the others in having two DC motors, one geared directly to the centre and one to the end axle, there being no intermediate jackshaft. The last three were in reserve in early 2016 and will be withdrawn shortly.

Built: 1962–63.
Builder–Mechanical Parts: SLM.
Builder–Electrical. Parts: SAAS.
Systems: 15 kV AC 16.7 Hz, 25 kV AC 50 Hz, 1500 V DC, 3000 V DC.
Traction Motors: 2 DC series wound, axle suspended with side rod drive.
One Hour Rating: 390 kW.   **Maximum Tractive Effort**: 118 kN.
Wheel Diameter: 1040 mm.   **Weight**: 48 tonnes.
Length over Buffers: 10.02 m.   **Maximum Speed**: 60 km/h.

Number		Livery	Sector	Depot	Number		Livery	Sector	Depot
934 553	(16553)	**R**	P	GE	934 556	(16556)	**R**	P	GE
934 555	(16555)	**R**	P	GE					

CLASS Eea 935 & Ee 936   Co

Electric shunters with auxiliary batteries for use in non-electrified sidings. 936 151–154 were built in 1985 for the Swiss post office (PTT) and were originally Ee 3/3 8–11 (SLM 5286 to 5289); they have been renumbered in reverse order.

BLS 402 (SLM 5468, ex GBS) was allocated the new number 935 402 but this is not carried. The loco is a version of the design with accumulator batteries and is thus classified Eea. The loco's name "Susi" has been painted out.

936 132–135 were built in 1991 for EBT (Ee 3/3 132–134) and VHB 151 (SLM works numbers 5469 to 5472), both of which were later absorbed by RM, then BLS. Stadler started using 936 133 on the main line in late 2015 to deliver trains from its Erlen plant.

In late 2015, Stadler acquired ex PTT 14, but it had not been put into service by the time this book was completed.

Built: 1985 936 151–154; 1991/92 others.
Builder–Mechanical Parts: SLM.
Builder–Electrical Parts: ABB.
Continuous Rating: 663 kW.   **Maximum Tractive Effort**: 130 kN.
Driving Wheel Diameter: 1040 mm.   **Weight**: 48 tonnes (402 50 tonnes).
Length over Buffers: 11.20 m.   **Maximum Speed**: 75 km/h.

▲ CJ loco 936 151 is seen at Tavannes on 18 October 2012 pushing shunter 237 480 (now 231 180) onto a metre gauge wagon so it can be moved to CJ's workshops at Tramelan. **Mario Stefani**

▼ SBB electric shunter 16814 is seen at Lausanne yard on 17 August 2015. These locos are unreliable and SBB has considered drafting in ÖBB locos to help out. **Mario Stefani**

Number (935) 402	Company BLS	Livery R	Notes/Names		936 135	BLS		Ex VHB 151
936 131	Stadler		Ex PTT 14		936 151	CJ		Ex PTT 11
936 132	BLS		Ex EBT 132		936 152	CJ		Ex PTT 10
936 133	Stadler		Ex EBT 133		936 153	CJ		Ex PTT 9
936 134	BLS		Ex EBT 134		936 154	Stauffer		Ex PTT 8; "Sabine"

CLASS Aem 940   Bo-Bo

In 2015 SBB Infra ordered 47 dual-mode Bo-Bo locomotives, with an off centre cab supporting a pantograph. They will also have two small diesel engines. They will be used to haul track maintenance trains and will shunt in Lausanne and Limmattal yards. Alstom calls the design Prima H4 although the only components they have in common with previous designs are the bogies – like SNCF Class BB 75000. They will be built in Belfort and delivered in 2017/18. In 2015 SBB tested Alstom's three-axle H3 hybrid design – loco 1002 006.

Built: 2017–
Builder: Alstom.
Continuous Rating: **Maximum Tractive Effort:**
Driving Wheel Diameter: **Weight:**
Length over Buffers: **Maximum Speed:** 120 km/h.

Number

940 001	940 017	940 033
940 002	940 018	940 034
940 003	940 019	940 035
940 004	940 020	940 036
940 005	940 021	940 037
940 006	940 022	940 038
940 007	940 023	940 039
940 008	940 024	940 040
940 009	940 025	940 041
940 010	940 026	940 042
940 011	940 027	940 043
940 012	940 028	940 044
940 013	940 029	940 045
940 014	940 030	940 046
940 015	940 031	940 047
940 016	940 032	

CLASS Ee 6/6ᴵᴵ (CLASS Ee 962)   C-C

A modern design of heavy yard loco which replaced some converted "Crocodiles" previously used for such work; fitted with three-phase traction motors supplied through an inverter. They can be radio controlled and are to be found in the yard at Denges (Lausanne).

Built: 1980.
Builder–Mechanical Parts: SLM.
Builder–Electrical. Parts: BBC.
Traction Motors: Six three-phase axle-hung, nose suspended.
One Hour Rating: 730 kW.   **Maximum Tractive Effort:** 360 kN.
Wheel Diameter: 1260 mm.   **Weight:** 111 tonnes.
Length over Buffers: 17.40 m.   **Maximum Speed:** 85 km/h.

Number	Livery	Sector	Depot		Number	Livery	Sector	Depot
16812	P	I	LT		16816	P	I	LT
16813	P	I	LT		16817	P	I	LT
16814	P	I	LT		16820	P	I	LT
16815	P	I	LT					

2. OTHER RAILWAYS

Switzerland has many "private" railways ranging from short branch lines such as the Orbe-Chavornay to BLS Lötschbergbahn which owns one of the two main lines across the Alps and now operates most of the Bern S-Bahn network. Under an open access regime, there is an increasing tendency for stock from the standard gauge railways to work on SBB main lines. The term "private" is used, although most railways are majority-owned by local authorities, particularly the cantons.

Many Swiss railways have now been grouped together; some have continued to use the familiar traditional names, but others have adopted completely new branding and the old names have disappeared. A list of former railways and the groups into which they have been absorbed can be found in Appendix I.

In this section railways are listed in alphabetical order of railway name. Groups of railways can be found at the appropriate point within the alphabetical listing; individual railways making up a group are listed in alphabetical order within their group. An index to railways by abbreviation is given on the following pages.

In the details given for each railway, main depots are shown in bold. Other places listed are often "sheds" for overnight/winter stabling and may be very small. The numbers given in brackets after the railway name are table numbers in the Swiss Timetable.

INDEX TO OTHER RAILWAYS BY ABBREVIATION

2.1. AAR bus + bahn (643, 644)   AAR (WSB)

Once separate lines, the Wynental and Suhrental Bahn lines were linked in the station south of the SBB platforms at Aarau in 1967. Trains now usually run through Schöftland–Aarau–Menziken and return. Both lines are mainly a mixture of roadside and street running and both traverse the Lenzburg–Zofigen SBB line on the level! In 2002 the line to Menziken-Burg was relaid on the trackbed of the former SBB line from Beinwil then the section from Aarau to Suhr diverted onto another former SBB trackbed. Units 15–27 are being modernised (during which they gain two seats) by WSB and mated with new Stadler driving trailers Bt 51–61. Class Be 4/8 are very similar to units with RBS. In 2010 WSB bought similar sets 21–25 from BDWM, converted their shorter coaches to first/second class, combining each with a second class coach from Be 4/8 28 to 32 – forming new ABe 4/4 sets 28–32 and 35–39.

The lines did carry some freight and had transfer facilities at Suhr and Unterentfelden. This has now finished and locos were withdrawn. 49 carries no numbers. Livery is virtually the same as the BDWM – the two railways are both in Aargau canton, and the same tariff area.

Gauge: 1000 mm.
Electrical System: 750 V DC.
Routes:
• Aarau–Schöftland (9.6 km).
• Aarau–Menziken-Burg (22.0 km).
Depots: Aarau, Menziken, Schöftland.

h   historic stock.
§   12/24 (8) + –/61 (2).
*   12/32 (8) + –/61 (2).

Class	No.	Names	Builder	Seats	km/h	tonnes	kW	Built
Be 4/4	15	Aarau	SWS/BBC	52	80	31	448	1979
Be 4/4	16	Suhr	SWS/BBC	50	80	31	448	1979
Be 4/4	17	Gränichen	SWS/BBC	50	80	31	448	1979
Be 4/4	19 (U)	Unterkulm	SWS/BBC	50	80	31	448	1979
Be 4/4	20	Oberkulm	SWS/BBC	50	80	31	448	1979
Be 4/4	21	Gontenschwil	SWS/BBC	50	80	31	448	1979
Be 4/4	22	Reinach	SWS/BBC	50	80	31	448	1979
Be 4/4	23	Menziken	SWS/BBC	50	80	31	448	1979
Be 4/4	24	Unterentfelden	SWS/BBC	50	80	31	448	1979
Be 4/4	25	Oberentfelden	SWS/BBC	50	80	31	448	1979
Be 4/4	26	Muhen	SWS/BBC	50	80	31	448	1979
Be 4/4	27	Schöftland	SWS/BBC	50	80	31	448	1979
ABe 4/4	28		SWA/SIG/ABB	§	80	57	600	1993
ABe 4/4	29		SWA/SIG/ABB	§	80	57	600	1993
ABe 4/4	30		SWA/SIG/ABB	§	80	57	600	1993
ABe 4/4	31		SWA/SIG/ABB	§	80	57	600	1993
ABe 4/4	32		SWA/SIG/ABB	§	80	57	600	1993
ABe 4/4	33		SWA/SIG/ABB	*	80	57	600	1993
ABe 4/4	34		SWA/SIG/ABB	*	80	57	600	1993
ABe 4/4	35		SWA/SIG/ABB	§	80	57	600	1993
ABe 4/4	36		SWA/SIG/ABB	§	80	57	600	1993
ABe 4/4	37		SWA/SIG/ABB	§	80	57	600	1993
ABe 4/4	38		SWA/SIG/ABB	§	80	57	600	1993
ABe 4/4	39		SWA/SIG/ABB	§	80	57	600	1993
Te 2/2	49 h	S'FARBIG BÄHNLI	SWS/MFO/WSB	-	55	14	107	1957

▲ ABe 4/4 30 (left) and Be 4/4 22 stand at Mentziken Burg station on 11 June 2014.

David Haydock

▼ BTI (ASm) GTW 2/6 EMU 5012/11 comes out of the sidings at Taüffelen to form a train to Biel/ Bienne on 17 April 2014. **David Haydock**

2.2. AARE SEELAND mobil Asm

This group combined the RVO, SNB and BTI plus bus company OAK. The BTI is completely separate from the other two in the area south of Biel known as Seeland. There is now a common numbering system. BTI stock is in the 500 series although units from the other network can be used there. Some of the operation of the Solothurn–Niederbipp–Langenthal line is on street. A 1.7 km extension from Niederbipp to Oensingen opened in December 2012. This is alongside the SBB line – not over the former OSST route here. There is significant freight around Langenthal hauled by Asm with standard gauge wagons on metre gauge "skates". BTI carries stone between a quarry at Siselen and a cement plant at Sutz, usually returning with infill material. Trains are formed of three tipping hoppers topped-and-tailed by electric railcars. The standard gauge locos Em 837 826 and Am 847 957 (ex DB 211 115) work tanks from Niederbipp to Oberbipp. ASm bought FW Be 4/4 14 plus Bt 112 in 2014. Unit 102 was sold to BLM and 103 plus 104 are for sale. Ge 4/4 126 has been preserved. 301 and 303 went to the MOB. 101 was scrapped in 2014 and 304 transferred to the BTI.

Gauge: 1000 mm.
Electrical System: 1200 V DC.
Routes:
• Solothurn–Niederbipp–Oensingen (16.2 km).
• Niederbipp–Langenthal (11.0 km).
• Langenthal–St. Urban Ziegelei (7.0 km).
• Biel–Täuffelen–Ins (21.2 km).
Depots: Langenthal (former RVO), **Täuffelen** (BTI), **Wiedlisbach** (SNB).

2.2.1. BIEL–TÄUFFELEN–INS BAHN (290) BTI

CLASS Be 2/6 3-SECTION ARTICULATED UNITS

These are early Stadler GTW 2/6 EMUs formed of a short central power unit with a driving trailer either side. They operate all passenger services between Biel/Bienne and Ins. The name is carried on the power unit. The confusion reported in the previous edition is no longer the case – formations normally stay the same, but 5080 is a spare power unit which can be swapped when necessary. A project to convert this line into a tramway have been shelved and now the BTI will receive three more GTW units from CEV. A large new depot was under construction at Sisselen in 2015.

Built: 501–508 1997; 509/510 2007.
Builder: 501–508 Stadler/SLM/Adtranz; 509/510 Stadler.
Wheel Arrangement: 2-Bo-2. **Power Rating:** 320 kW.
Accommodation: –/36 (4) + –/36 (4). **Weight:** 33.5 tonnes.
Length over Couplers: 30.00 m. **Maximum Speed:** 80 km/h.

5011	5010 Ipsac	5012	5061	5060 Ins		5062
5021	5020 Mörigen	5022	5071	5070		5072
5031	5030 Nidau	5032		5080		
5041	5040	5042	5091	5090		5092
5051	5050 Sutz - Lattrigen	5052	5101	5100		5102

OTHER BTI STOCK

§ Restaurant railcar, nicknamed "Ankerstube". Originally BTI BDe 4/4 6. Stored at Biel/Bienne.

Class	No.	Name	Builder	Seats	km/h	tonnes	kW	Built
Be 4/4	304	WIEDLISBACH	SWS/MFO	40	65	32	368	1978
BRe 4/4	516§	SEELAND	SWS/MFO	40	60	26	282	1947
Be 4/4	523		SWS/MFO	48	65	33.7	368	1965
Be 4/4	525		SWS/MFO	48	65	33.7	368	1970
Tm	541		RACO/DZ	-	75	19	177	1985
Tm	542		RJ/RACO/ZÜR	-	45	5	22	1929 (92)

2.2.2. REGIONALVERKEHR OBERAARGAU (413)   RVO

2.2.3. SOLOTHURN–NIEDERBIPP BAHN (413)   SNB

CLASS Be 4/8   3-SECTION ARTICULATED UNITS

ASm received six 3-section low-floor EMUs nicknamed STAR (*Schmalspur Triebzug für Attraktiven Regionalverkehr*) in 2008 and 2011. The units work the Solothurn–Niederbipp–Langenthal and Langenthal–St. Urban lines.

Built: 110–112 2008, 113–115 2011.
Wheel Arrangement: Bo-2-2-Bo.
Length over Couplers: 39.00 m.
Power Rating: 660 kW.

Builder: Stadler/Bombardier.
Accommodation: –/26 (5) + –/48 (6) + –/27 (5).
Weight: 54 tonnes.
Maximum Speed: 80 km/h.

110	JUPITER	112	VENUS	114	SATURN
111	MERKUR	113	MARS	115	NEPTUN

OTHER STOCK

§   Former FW Be 4/4 14, acquired in 2014, with FW Bt 112.
*   103 and 104 are ex BTI 502 and 501 respectively.
h   Historic railcar "Buffetwagen".

Class	No.	Name	Builder	Seats	km/h	tonnes	kW	Built
Be 4/4	14 §		FFA/BBC	40 (7)	75	35	620	1985
Be 4/4	103*		SWS/MFO	48	65	33.7	368	1970
Be 4/4	104*		SWS/MFO	48	65	33.7	368	1970
BRe 4/4	116 h		RING/ALIOTH/MFO	40	40	23.2	216	1907
De 4/4	121		STAD/SIG/BBC	-	65	45	620	1987
Tm 2/2	141		RACO/DZ	-	60	19	177	1985
Tm 2/2	142		RACO/PER	-	28	5.3	41	1933
Be 4/4	302		SWS/MFO	40	65	32	368	1966
De 4/4	321		SZB/MFO	-	50	30.1	264	1957 (69)

2.3. APPENZELLER BAHNEN GROUP

The Appenzeller Bahnen group was formed in 2006 by the merger of Appenzellerbahnen, the RHB, RhW and the Trogenerbahn. The RHB and RhW are geographically separate, but the AB and TB are to be linked in 2017.

2.3.1. APPENZELLERBAHNEN (854, 855, 856)   AB

The Appenzellerbahn (AB) and St. Gallen–Gais–Appenzell (SGA) merged in 1989 to form Appenzellerbahnen. Power cars 11–15, working in 3-car sets, have the Riggenbach system and work St. Gallen–Gais–Appenzell. Units 16/17 have Strub rack and work Gais–Altstätten Stadt in 2-car sets. 41–45 are adhesion only and work Gossau–Appenzell–Wasserauen in 3-car sets.

A new line is to be built by autumn 2017 to avoid the rack section on the St. Gallen–Appenzell line, then the latter will be connected with the former TB to form a cross-St. Gallen S-Bahn suburban line with a 15-minute service frequency. AB has ordered seven 133 passenger (of which 12 in first class), 62-tonne, 1200 kW Tango 5-section light rail vehicles for the line. There are five options, which AB will take up as it will sell the former TB Stadler sets to transN for the Neuchâtel tramway.

Gauge: 1000 mm.
Electrical System: 1500 V DC.
Rack Systems: St. Gallen–Riethüsli: Riggenbach; Stoss–Altstätten: Strub.
Routes:
• St. Gallen–Gais–Appenzell (20.1 km). Maximum gradient 10%.
• Wasserauen–Appenzell–Herisau–Gossau SG (32.1 km).
• Gais–Altstätten Stadt (7.7 km). Maximum gradient 16%.
Depots: Gais (main works), Herisau, Wasserauen, Appenzell.

h	Historic cars.
§	Formerly ABe 4/4 43.
†	Formerly numbered 31–35.
[1]	46 and 47 now only operate works trains.
[2]	49 and 89 (formerly 51) were converted from SB/AWW CFe 2/2 1 and 2 respectively.
[3]	ex WSB Tm 1.
[4]	Ex RAG 159, then via RBW, CGS, RhB, LSB and DFB.
[5]	Acquired in 1998. Type CFL 200 DCL, built for 900 mm gauge as DL16 for Arlberg road tunnel project, Austria. Works No. 3325.

Class	No.	Names	Builder	Seats	km/h	tonnes	kW	Built
Ge 4/4	1		STAD/SLM/ABB	-	75	43	1000	1994
BCFeh 4/4	5 h		SLM/SIG/BBC	6/39	40/24	40	440	1931
ABDeh	6	ALTSTÄTTEN	SLM/BBC	6/32	55/30	36	470	1953
BDeh 4/4	11	ST. GALLEN	FFA/SLM/BBC	40	65/40	44	820	1981
BDeh 4/4	12	TEUFEN	FFA/SLM/BBC	40	65/40	44	820	1981
BDeh 4/4	13	(BÜHLER)	FFA/SLM/BBC	40	65/40	44	820	1981
BDeh 4/4	14	GAIS	FFA/SLM/BBC	40	65/40	44	820	1981
BDeh 4/4	15	(APPENZELL)	FFA/SLM/BBC	40	65/40	44	820	1981
BDeh 4/4	16		SWA/SLM/ABB	40	65/40	45	820	1993
BDeh 4/4	17		SWA/SLM/ABB	40	65/40	45	820	1993
BCe 4/4	30 h §		SIG/MFO	12/40	65	34.2	450	1933
BDe 4/4	41 †	GOSSAU	FFA/SIG/BBC	39	75	36	820	1986
BDe 4/4	42 †	HERISAU	FFA/SIG/BBC	39	75	36	820	1986
BDe 4/4	43 †	GONTEN	FFA/SIG/BBC	39	75	36	820	1986
BDe 4/4	44 †		SWA/SIG/ABB	39	75	37	820	1993
BDe 4/4	45 †		SWA/SIG/ABB	39	75	37	820	1993
BDe 4/4	46 [1]	WALDSTATT	FFA/SIG/MFO	-	65	43	510	1968 (96)
BDe 4/4	47 [1]	URNÄSCH	FFA/SIG/MFO	-	65	43	510	1968 (98)
Te 2/2	49 [2]		SWS/MFO/AB	-	45	12	100	1912 (55)
BCFm 2/4	56 h		SIG/SZ/MFO	6/24	45	32	136	1929
Xm 1/2	89 [2]		SWS/SIG/SAU/AB	-	45	15	75	1912 (62)
Tm 2/2	91 [3]		ROBEL/DEUTZ	-	63	7.5	67	1969
Tm 2/2	97 [4]		O&K	-	30	23	150	1959
Tm 2/2	98 [5]	Schorsch	SCHÖMA	-		35	180	1972
Xrotm 2/2	99		RACO/BEIL/DZ	-	30	18	150	1974

2.3.2. BERGBAHN RHEINECK WALZENHAUSEN (858) (RhW)

Once a tramway with a connecting funicular, the whole line was converted to rack and adhesion operation in 1958. This is one of the smallest Swiss railways, less than 2 km long with just one item of motive power.

Gauge: 1200 mm.
Electrical System: 600 V DC.
Rack System: Riggenbach.
Route: Rheineck–Walzenhausen (1.9 km).
Depot: Ruderbach (but car normally stables overnight in Walzenhausen station).

Class	No.	Builder	Seats	km/h	tonnes	kW	Built
BDeh1/2	1	SLM/FFA/BBC	28	30/20	14.7	215	1958

2.3.3. RORSCHACH-HEIDEN-BERGBAHN (857) (RHB)

A short rack and adhesion line running into the hills above Rorschach, with through running over SBB tracks from Rorschach to Rorschach Hafen. Good views over the Bodensee (Lake Constance) from the top. Stadler unit No. 25 works most services, and often has open vehicles coupled to it in good weather. The new numbers are not carried by the electric stock. The line operates steam specials with Eurovapor's loco Eh 2/2 3 "Rosa".

Gauge: 1435 mm.
Electrical System: 15 kV AC 16.7 Hz.
Rack System: Riggenbach.
Route: Rorschach–Heiden (5.5 km). Maximum gradient 9%.
Depot: Heiden.

* Ex Maschinenfabrik Rüti in 2006. Previously carried number 237 916, but this is now carried by another loco.
§ Named Rorschach and Heiden on one side plus Lutzenberg and Rorschacherberg on the other!

No.	Class	Old No.	Builder	Seats	km/h	tonnes	kW	Built
*	Thm 2/2	20	SLM/BBC	-				1962
(DZeh 588 721)	DZeh 2/4	21	SLM/MFO	-	25	42.8	420	1930
(DZeh 588 722)	DZeh 2/4	22	SLM/MFO	-	25	42.8	420	1930
(BDeh 538 723)	ABDeh 2/4	23	SLM/BBC/FFA	8/49	25	42.3	550	1953
(BDeh 578 724)	ABDeh 2/4	24	SLM/BBC/FFA	8/49	25	42.3	550	1966
-	BDeh 3/6	25 §	STAD/SLM/AD	86		57.3	700	1998

▲ Trogenerbahn Be 4/8 32 arrives leaves Trogen on 13 June 2014. These units will be sold to transN when the line is connected to the AB line to Appenzell in 2017. **David Haydock**

2.3.4. TROGENER BAHN (859) (TB)

Originally an interurban tramway running from St. Gallen to Trogen, the TB has been upgraded to a light railway, mostly with roadside running, although there is still street running in St. Gallen. The line is soon to be linked to the AB Appenzell line – see above. 21, 23 and 24 were sold to the Rittnerbahn in Italy (22 is to follow) and 25 scrapped.

Gauge: 1000 mm.
Electrical System: 1000 V DC.
Route: St. Gallen–Trogen (9.8 km). Maximum gradient 7.5%.
Depot: Speicher.

h   historic unit.
§   31 is named Der St Galler / Die St Gallerin. 32 is Der Appenzeller / Die Appenzellerin.

Class	No.	Names	Builder	Seats	km/h	tonnes	kW	Built
BDe 4/4	7 h		SWP/MFO	30	65	27	385	1952
BDe 4/8	22		FFA/BBC/SWP	40+34	65	39	405	1975
Be 4/8	31 §		STAD/BOMB	86 (6)	80	43	640	2004
Be 4/8	32 §		STAD/BOMB	86 (6)	80	43	640	2004
Be 4/8	33	Speicher	STAD/BOMB	86 (6)	80	43	640	2008
Be 4/8	34	Trogen	STAD/BOMB	86 (6)	80	43	640	2008
Be 4/8	35	Teufen	STAD/BOMB	86 (6)	80	43	640	2008
Xrotm 2/2	72		RACO/BEIL/DZ	-	30	15	150	1974

2.4. BDWM TRANSPORT (654) BDWM

The Bremgarten–Dietikon metre gauge line is a light railway with mostly roadside running. The company recently received 14 new EMUs from Stadler which now work all services. Of the older BDe 8/8 articulated sets, no. 7 has been preserved by IG BDe 8/8. Be 4/8 units 21 to 25 went to AAR bus + bahn. The remains of the mixed gauge from Bremgarten West to Wohlen were removed in 2015.

Gauge: 1000 mm.
Electrical System: 1200 V DC.
Route: Dietikon–Bremgarten–Wohlen (18.9 km). Maximum gradient 5.4%.
Depot: Bremgarten.

CLASS ABe 4/8 3-SECTION ARTICULATED UNITS

Built: 2009–11.
Overall Length: 37.50 m.
Continuous Rating: 800 kW.
Accommodation: 20/– + –/40 (8) + –/27 (1).

Builder: Stadler.
Weight: 59 tonnes.
Wheel Arrangement: Bo-2-2-Bo.
Maximum Speed: 80 km/h.

5001	Kanton Aargau	5006	Berikon	5011	
5002	Kanton Zürich	5007	Widen	5012	
5003	Bremgarten	5008	Zufikon	5013	
5004	Dietikon	5009	Rudolfstetten-Friedlisberg	5014	
5005	Wohlen	5010	Waltenschwil		

OTHER ROLLING STOCK

h   Historic stock.

Class	No.	Names	Builder	Seats	km/h	tonnes	kW	Built
BDe 8/8	7 h	WIDEN	SWS/MFO	93	70	50	588	1969
BDe 4/4	10 h	Mutschellen-Zähni	SWS/MFO/BD	40	45	32	216	1932
Tm 2/2	51		STAD/BBC/SAU	-	50	13	88	1967
Tm 2/2	52		STAD/BBC/SAU	-	50	13	88	1968

2.5. BLS LÖTSCHBERGBAHN — BLS

The BLS group of railways is second only in route mileage to the metre gauge RhB among Swiss private railways. The Lötschberg route forms part of the Basel–Bern–Milano main line, and extensive joint through working occurs with SBB. In 2007, a partially completed base tunnel opened on this route, considerably accelerating long-distance passenger trains. The base tunnel is equipped with ETCS Level 2 cab signalling and all trains used on long-distance services have therefore been equipped.

In 1997 the former subsidiaries Bern Lötschberg Simplon (BLS), Bern Neuenburg (BN), Gürbetal Bern Schwarzenburg (GBS), Moutier–Lengnau Bahn (MLB) and Spiez Erlenbach Zweisimmen (SEZ) were integrated into the whole and the company was renamed BLS Lötschbergbahn. Then in 2006, Regionalverkehr Mittelland (RM, itself the merger of EBT, SMB and VHB in 1997) became part of BLS. The freight arm of RM became Crossrail. The "new" BLS adopted a livery of light grey, highlighted in apple green and dark blue. At the same time the company was divided into passenger, cargo and infrastructure subsidiaries.

BLS Cargo was initially part-owned by DB but this cooperation stopped in 2013. BLS Class 485 and 486 locos operate deep into Germany while DB Schenker Class 185 operate from Basel to Domodossola over the BLS main line. BLS Cargo also operates over the Gotthard route to Chiasso as well as across the rest of Switzerland.

Another major change was a "swap" of responsibility for certain services between BLS and SBB. The latter has taken over long-distance passenger trains and wagonload freight in exchange for BLS running the entire standard gauge part of the Bern S-Bahn. BLS now operates no express passenger services, being limited to regional and S-Bahn services.

In 2015 BLS had four Class Re 420, 30 Re 425, two Re 456, 18 Re 465, 20 Re 485 and ten Re 486 electric locos, mainly used on freight. The EMU fleet consists of 28 Class 515, 36 Class 525, 25 Class 535, 21 Class 565 and 13 Class 566. Most are used on the Bern S-Bahn. BLS also owns Class Tem 225, Tm 235, Tm 236 and Tea 245 shunters, Am 843 and Am 845 diesel locos, Eea 935 and 936 electric shunters. In the last two years, BLS has pioneered the use of Railpool Class 187, a TRAXX 3 electric loco with last mile diesel engine. BLS is currently using hired Class 186 locos to operate container trains through from Germany to Melzo, near Milano in Italy. In 2015 BLS Cargo ordered 15 Vectron MS electric locos from Siemens. They will be known as Class 475.

▲ BDWM units 5005 and 5007 arrive at Bremgarten Obertor with a service to Bremgarten on 11 June 2014.
David Haydock

Routes:
- Thun–Spiez–Kandersteg–Brig (73.8 km).
- Wengi–Raron (Lötschberg base tunnel) (34.6 km).
- Bern–Neuchâtel (42.9 km).
- Bern–Schwarzenburg (20.9).
- Bern–Belp–Thun (34.5 km).
- Lengnau–Moutier (13.0 km).
- Spiez–Interlaken Ost (28.0 km).
- Spiez–Zweisimmen (34.9 km).

Ex RM network:
- Moutier–Solothurn (22.1 km).
- Solothurn–Burgdorf–Hasle-Rüegsau–Ramsei–Obermatt (39.5 km).
- Hasle-Rüegsau–Konolfingen–Thun (34.5 km).
- Ramsei–Sumiswald-Grünen (4.6 km).
- Langenthal–Huttwil (14.1 km).
- Huttwil–Wohlhusen (25.2 km).

Works: Bönigen (Interlaken), Spiez, Oberburg (ex EBT).
Depots: Bern Holligen, Brig, Huttwil (ex VHB).
All motive power is, in principle, allocated to Spiez, the works and principal depot.

Liveries:
The standard livery is now grey with apple green front ends and blue highlights. All BLS stock is in this livery unless indicated otherwise.

A	Advertising livery.		K	Dark blue.	
B	Brown.		0	Orange.	
G	Dark green.		R	Red (mainly former RM stock)	

All stock is shown in the standard gauge lists in section 1.

2.6. BRIENZ-ROTHORN BAHN (475)   BRB

One of the few non-electrified lines in Switzerland, the BRB was entirely steam operated until diesels were introduced to augment the fleet in the 1970s. However, most trains remain steam, and the railway purchased three new oil-fired steam locos from SLM in 1992 and 1996. These usually operate, together with just two of the other, coal-fired locos. The line is pure rack, and boasts the greatest height difference between lowest (566 m) and highest (2244 m) stations of any Swiss railway. At the time of writing No. 3 was being exhibited in Thun. Kanaya is a partner town in Japan.

Gauge: 800 mm.
Rack System: Abt.
Route: Brienz–Rothorn Kulm (7.6 km). Maximum gradient 25%.
Depot: Brienz.

*   ex FMG 7, 1962.
†   ex WAB 1, 1911.
§   ex MTGN 1.

Class	No.	Name	Builder	Seats	km/h	tonnes	kW	Built
H 2/3	1 *		SLM	-	9.5	17	175	1891
H 2/3	2		SLM	-	9.5	17	175	1891
H 2/3	3		SLM	-	9.5	17	175	1892
H 2/3	4		SLM	-	9.5	17	175	1892
H 2/3	5 †		SLM	-	9.5	17	175	1891
H 2/3	6		SLM	-	9.5	20	225	1933
H 2/3	7		SLM	-	9.5	20	225	1936
Hm 2/2	9		STECK/MTU	-	14	13.5	485	1975
Hm 2/2	10		STECK/MTU	-	14	13.5	485	1975
Hm 2/2	11		STECK/MTU	-	14	13.5	485	1987
H 2/3	12	KANTON BERN	SLM	-	14	15.7	300	1992
H 2/3	14	GEMEINDE BRIENZ	SLM	-	14	15.7	300	1996
H 2/3	15	STADT KANAYA	SLM	-	14	15.7	300	1996
H 2/3	16 §		SLM	-	14	16	300	1992

2.7. CHEMINS DE FER DU JURA (236, 237, 238) CJ

The CJ comprises two separate systems, a short standard gauge branch linking Porrentruy and Bonfol, and a lengthy metre gauge system meeting the SBB at La Chaux de Fonds, Tavannes and Glovelier. The metre gauge network still hauls standard gauge freight stock on transporter wagons. CJ has acquired Be 4/4 11, 12, 13 and 15 from the FW. CJ has ordered five new Be 4/4 power cars numbered 651–655 from Stadler and will mate them with existing stock to form new units. They should bring about withdrawal of 603 and 608. There is a long term project to add extra rails to the standard gauge Glovelier–Delémont line so that CJ can extend metre gauge trains.

Gauge: 1435/1000 mm.
Electrical System: 15 kV AC 16.7 Hz (1435 mm), 1500 V DC (1000 mm).
Routes:

1435 mm gauge:
• Porrentruy–Bonfol (10.9 km).
1000 mm gauge:
• Tavannes–Le Noirmont–La Chaux de Fonds (44.0 km.) Maximum gradient 5%.
• Le Noirmont–Glovelier (30.3 km).

Depots: Bonfol (1435 mm), Tramelan, Saignelégier, Le Noirmont (1000 mm).

METRE GAUGE STOCK:

h   Restored as museum car from Xe 2/4 no. 503.
*   Ex SBB 9455.
+   Ex Frauenfeld-Wil Bahn 13, 12 and 11 respectively in 2014/15.
‡   Ex FW 207 in 1991. Previously BTI no. 5.
§   Ex RhB ABe 4/4 487. Used for freight.
o   On order 2015.

Class	No.	Name	Builder	Seats	km/h	tonnes	kW	Built
BCe 2/4	70 h		SWS/BBC	4/32	45	22	124	1913
De 4/4^{I}	401		SIG/SAAS	-	60	36	544	1952
De 4/4^{II}	411		SIG/BBC/FFA	-	90	41	820	1953
Tm 2/2	501		Moyse/Deutz	-	34	24	120	1967
Te 2/2	504		BBC	-	45	15	126	1913
Xm	509		Beilhack/Deutz	-	60	26	263	1985
Tm	511 *		RACO/SAURER	-	60	28	165	1981
ABDe 4/4^{I}	603		SIG/SAAS	9/16	70	26.5	332	1953
BDe 4/4^{I}	608		SIG/SAAS	32	70	26.5	332	1953
BDe 4/4^{II}	611		FFA/BBC/SIG	39	90	36	820	1985
BDe 4/4^{II}	612		FFA/BBC/SIG	39	90	36	820	1985
BDe 4/4^{II}	613		FFA/BBC/SIG	39	90	36	820	1985
BDe 4/4^{II}	614		FFA/BBC/SIG	39	90	36	820	1985
Be 4/4	615 +		FFA/BBC	40 (7)	75	35	620	1985
Be 4/4	616 +		FFA/BBC	40 (7)	75	35	620	1985
Be 4/4	617 +		FFA/BBC	40 (7)	75	35	620	1985
BDe 4/4	621 ‡		SWS/SIG/SAAS/CJ	16	60	35	528	1947
ABe 2/6	631	Pouillerel	STAD/AD	9/68 (5) 1T	90	43	320	2001
ABe 2/6	632	Mont-Soleil	STAD/AD	9/68 (5) 1T	90	43	320	2001
ABe 2/6	633	La Gruère	STAD/AD	9/68 (5) 1T	90	43	320	2001
ABe 2/6	634	Le Tabeillon	STAD/AD	9/68 (5) 1T	90	43	320	2001
Bef 4/4	641 §		SWS/BBC/SAAS/CJ	24	65	45	720	1973
Be 4/4	651 o		Stadler					
Be 4/4	652 o		Stadler					
Be 4/4	653 o		Stadler					
Be 4/4	654 o		Stadler					
Be 4/4	655 o		Stadler					

STANDARD GAUGE STOCK: See the lists in section 1.

CJ owns four shunters of Classes 225, 231 and 232, Class 560 and 577 EMUs and Class 936 electric locos. 587 111 was built in 1910 for the MO and was completely rebuilt by the CJ.

Class	No.	Name	Builder	km/h	tonnes	kW	Built
De	587 111 (U)	VENDLICOURT	SWS/BBC/SAAS/CJ	100	48	1064	1980

2.8. CROSSRAIL   XRAIL

When Regionalverkehr Mittelland's (the merger of EBT, SMB and VHB) passenger operations were merged with those of BLS, RM's freight operations, which had been using the branding Crossrail since 2004, were put up for sale. In 2007 Belgian company DLC merged with Crossrail and is now Crossrail Benelux. The company also has an Italian subsidiary. German company Rhenus took a controlling share in the company in 2014, the other shares being with LKW Walter, HUPAC, Bertschi and MSC Belgium.

Only locomotives which can be seen in Switzerland are included in this book. Crossrail has its headquarters and a terminal in Wiler. Crossrail Italia has a terminal in Domodossola. Crossrail Benelux has its offices near Antwerpen in Belgium and manages a fleet of Class 66 diesels which do not reach Switzerland. Most of the Crossrail fleet is hired – the company had two Class 185.1, 16 185.2, six 186 and two 484 in 2015. The five Class Re 430 locos are owned by the company. 430 113 has been stored for some time after an accident.

2.9. DOLDERBAHN (732)   Db

Owned by Dolderbahn Betriebs AG but managed by Zürich tramway operator VBZ. Converted from a funicular in 1973, this rack railway connects with Zürich tram routes 3, 8 and 15 at Römerhof. The only two points are for a loop in the middle of the line.

Gauge: 1000 mm.
Electrical System: 600 V DC.
Rack System: Strub.
Route: Römerhof–Bergstation (1.328 km). Maximum gradient 19%.
Depot: Both upper and lower stations have closing doors and pits for stabling and maintenance, with room for one set at the top and one at the bottom!

Class	No.	Name	Builder	Seats	km/h	tonnes	kW	Built
Bhe 1/2	1		SLM/GANG/BBC	26	25	22.2	150	1973
Bhe 1/2	2		SLM/GANG/BBC	26	25	22.2	150	1973

▲ FART ABe 4/8 47 crosses SSIF ABe 4/6 64 at S. Maria Maggiore on 7 June 2015.   **Mario Stefani**

2.10. EISENBAHNDIESTLEISTER GmbH   EDG

A small company in Thayngen which supplies railway staff and services, with a few shunters.

2.11. FERROVIE AUTOLINEE REGIONALI TICINESE (620)   FART
SOCIETÀ SUBALPINA DI IMPRESE FERROVIARIE (620)   SSIF

This international light railway links Locarno in Switzerland with Domodossola in Italy, traversing spectacular scenery, which gives the line its nickname "Centovalli" – a hundred valleys. It is also known as the "Vigezzina" in Italy. The SSIF is an Italian company operating the western half of the line. Through services, using mainly panoramic units 81–87 but also 21–24, are jointly operated and the stock is numbered in a common series. Local services at each end are operated by units 45–64. The route into Locarno was rebuilt on a new underground alignment in 1990. Since the last edition, ABe 4/6 55 to 58 received an extra section and became ABe 4/8 45 to 48.

Gauge: 1000 mm.
Electrical System: 1200 V DC.
Routes:
• Domodossola–Camedo (SSIF 32.2 km).
• Camedo–Locarno (FART 18.3 km). Maximum gradient 6%.
Depots: Ponte Brolla (works), **Locarno (FART); Domodossola Vigezzina,** Camedo, Re (SSIF).

t   Ex Tranvie Elettriche Locarnesi.
h   Historic cars.
p   Rebuilt in 2007 as panoramic train.
*   Departmental unit.

Class	No.	Co.	Name	Builder	Seats	Km/h	tonnes	kW	Built
Be 2/2	7 th	FART		MAN/BBC	18	40	11	60	1908
Tm 2/2	9	FART		RACO/DZ	-		21		1989
ABDe 4/4	16 h	SSIF		CET/BBC/SSIF	6/30	45	33	310	1923 (75)
ABFe 4/4	17 h	SSIF		CET/BBC	6/30	45	33	310	1923
ABDe 4/4	18	SSIF		CET/BBC	-	45	33	310	1923
Abe 8/8	21	SSIF	ROMA	SWP/TIBB	24/80	60	60	725	1959
Abe 8/8	22	SSIF	TICINO	SWP/TIBB	24/80	60	60	725	1959
Abe 8/8	23	SSIF	OSSOLA	SWP/TIBB	24/80	60	60	725	1959
Abe 8/8	24 p	SSIF	VIGEZZO	SWP/TIBB	24/80	60	60	725	1959
ADe 6/6	31	FART	TICINO	SWP/TIBB	53/–	60	45	540	1963
ABDe 6/6	32	FART	VALLESE	SWP/TIBB	18/48	60	45	540	1963
Abe 6/6	33	SSIF	SEMPIONE	SWP/TIBB	10/72	60	45.5	545	1968
Abe 6/6	34 *	SSIF	PIEMONTE	SWP/TIBB	10/72	60	45.5	545	1968
Abe 6/6	35	SSIF	VERBANO	SWP/TIBB	10/72	60	45.5	545	1968
Abe 4/8	45	FART	VALLEMAGGIA	ACMV/SIG/ABB	31/88	70	60	640	1993
Abe 4/8	46	FART	LAGO MAGGIORE	ACMV/SIG/ABB	31/88	70	60	640	1993
Abe 4/8	47	FART	CITTÀ DI BERNA	ACMV/SIG/ABB	31/88	70	60	640	1993
Abe 4/8	48	FART	LOSANNA	ACMV/SIG/ABB	31/88	70	60	640	1993
Abe 4/6	52	FART	MURALTO	ACMV/SIG/ABB	18/64	80	45.9	640	1992
Abe 4/6	53	FART	ASCONA	ACMV/SIG/ABB	18/64	80	45.9	640	1993
Abe 4/6	54	FART	INTRAGNA	ACMV/SIG/ABB	18/64	80	45.9	640	1993
Abe 4/6	61	SSIF	S. MARIA MAGGIORE	ACMV/SIG/ABB	18/64	80	45.9	640	1992
Abe 4/6	62	SSIF	RE	ACMV/SIG/ABB	18/64	80	45.9	640	1992
Abe 4/6	63	SSIF	MALESCO	ACMV/SIG/ABB	18/64	80	45.9	640	1992
ABe 4/6	64	SSIF	DRUOGNO	ACMV/SIG/ABB	18/64	80	45.9	640	1992

▲ A pair of Forchbahn Stadler Be 4/6 sets arrive at Forch with a train for Zürich Stadelhofen on 12 June 2014. The depot is on the left. **David Haydock**

▼ On 27 August 2014 new FW Stadler ABe 4/8 set 7001 "Frauenfeld" approaches Murkart with a train to Wil. **Quintus Vosman**

CLASS ABe 12/16 (SSIF)   4-CAR UNITS

These are panoramic EMUs which operate most end-to-end services and incur a small supplement. ABe 4/4 Pp 81–86 are driving power cars, Be 4/4 Pp 87–89 intermediate power cars and Rimorchiata P 810–812 intermediate trailers.

Built: 2007.   **Builders:** OFV/CORIFER.
Length: 16.25 + 15.55 + 15.55 + 16.25 m.   **Power Rating:** 1020 kW.
Accommodation: 17/19 1T + –/51 1T + –/51 1T + –/54 1T.
Weight: 31.8 + 30.2 + 30.2 + 31.8 tonnes.   **Maximum Speed:** 70 km/h.

OFV = Officine Ferroviarie Veronesi

81	Domodossola	811	88	84	Craveggia
82	Toceno	810	87	83	Masera
85	Trantano	812	89	86	Villette

2.12. FERROVIE LUGANESI (635)   FLP

Formerly known as Ferrovia Lugano-Ponte Tresa. The only survivor of several light railways in the Lugano area, the FLP has been modernised and new cars purchased. Be 4/12 units were delivered as Be 4/8 but received low floor centre cars from Stadler in 2002/3. They are very similar to the old RBS EMUs.

Gauge: 1000 mm.
Electrical System: 1000 V DC.
Route: Lugano–Ponte Tresa (12.2 km).
Depot: Agno.

*   Ex FART 41/42 in 1993.
§   Also carries "Collina d'oro"

Class	No.	Name	Builder	Seats	km/h	tonnes	kW	Built
Tm 2/2	1		GLEIS/IVECO	-	60	20	200	1994
Be 4/12	21	LEMA	SIG/BBC	184	60	62.9	330	1978
Be 4/12	22	MALCANTONE	SIG/BBC	184	60	62.9	330	1979
Be 4/12	23	VEDEGGIO	SIG/BBC	184	60	62.9	330	1979
Be 4/12	24	MAGLIASENA	SIG/BBC	184	60	62.9	330	1979
Be 4/12	25	CERESIO	SIG/BBC	184	60	62.9	330	1979
Be 4/8	41*	PEDEMONTE §	SIG/BBC	112	60	46	335	1979
Be 4/8	42*	MELEZZA	SIG/BBC	112	60	46	335	1979

2.13. FORCHBAHN (731)   FB

Run by Zürich tramway operator VBZ. Once a tramway basically operated as a rural extension of the Zürich system, this light railway over the Forch Pass has been upgraded mostly to roadside running, but with some sections of private right-of-way and the section through Zumikon in tunnel. The cars run (limited stop) over the Zürich tram tracks from the terminus at Stadelhofen (adjacent to the SBB station) to Rehalp. When the Stadler sets were introduced, BDe 4/4 11–16 were sold to Madagascar! Units 21–32 and 51–58 are tramway-style vehicles. 51–58 run with driving trailers BT 201–204. The Stadler "Tango" units 61–73 are 2-section low-floor articulated Bo-Bo-2 half trains (very similar to those on the Trogenerbahn) with a cab at one end. These usually operate in back-to-back pairs 61+62 and so on, although half trains are added in the peaks, making trains too long for the Zürich tram stations. The FB passes the Zürich tram museum at Burgwies. CFe 2/2 4 is a vintage tram in VBZ blue and white livery which operates with trailer 11 (former 111). Xe 4/4 9 is for works trains and snow clearing. BDe 4/4 10 is for charters. Units were being named in 2014.

Gauge: 1000 mm.
Electrical System: 1200 V DC (600 V over VBZ tram tracks).
Route: Zürich Rehalp–Forch–Esslingen (13.0 km). Maximum gradient 6.7%.
Depot: Forch.

h   Historic cars.
*   Named Aesch Scheuren

Class	No.	Name	Builder	Seats	km/h	tonnes	kW	Built
CFe 2/2	4 h		SWS/MFO	24	36	20.2	150	1912 (35)
Xe 4/4	9		SWS/MFO/VBZ	-	70	26	300	1948 (82)
BDe 4/4	10 h		SWS/MFO	40	65	26.5	300	1948 (67)
Be 8/8	21+22		SWS/SWP/BBC	86	65	42	610	1976
Be 8/8	23+24		SWS/SWP/BBC	86	65	42	610	1976
Be 8/8	25+26		SWS/SWP/BBC	86	65	42	610	1976
Be 8/8	27+28		SWS/SWP/BBC	86	65	42	610	1981
Be 8/8	29+30		SWS/SWP/BBC	86	65	42	610	1981
Be 8/8	31+32		SWS/SWP/BBC	86	65	42	610	1986
Be 4/4	51		SWP/SIG/ABB	46	65	24.5	500	1993
Be 4/4	52		SWP/SIG/ABB	46	65	24.5	500	1993
Be 4/4	53		SWP/SIG/ABB	46	65	24.5	500	1993
Be 4/4	54		SWP/SIG/ABB	46	65	24.5	500	1993
Be 4/4	55		SWP/SIG/ABB	46	65	24.5	500	1993
Be 4/4	56		SWP/SIG/ABB	46	65	24.5	500	1993
Be 4/4	57		SWP/SIG/ABB	46	65	24.5	500	1993
Be 4/4	58		SWP/SIG/ABB	46	65	24.5	500	1993
Be 4/6	61		STAD/BOMB	34+25(3)	80	33.3	400	2003
Be 4/6	62		STAD/BOMB	34+25(3)	80	33.3	400	2003
Be 4/6	63		STAD/BOMB	34+25(3)	80	33.3	400	2003
Be 4/6	64		STAD/BOMB	34+25(3)	80	33.3	400	2003
Be 4/6	65		STAD/BOMB	34+25(3)	80	33.3	400	2003
Be 4/6	66 *		STAD/BOMB	34+25(3)	80	33.3	400	2004
Be 4/6	67	Hinteregg	STAD/BOMB	34+25(3)	80	33.3	400	2004
Be 4/6	68	Egg	STAD/BOMB	34+25(3)	80	33.3	400	2004
Be 4/6	69	Zumikon	STAD/BOMB	34+25(3)	80	33.3	400	2004
Be 4/6	70	Zollikon	STAD/BOMB	34+25(3)	80	33.3	400	2004
Be 4/6	71	Küsnacht	STAD/BOMB	34+25(3)	80	33.3	400	2004
Be 4/6	72	Maur	STAD/BOMB	34+25(3)	80	33.3	400	2004
Be 4/6	73	Zürich	STAD/BOMB	34+25(3)	80	33.3	400	2004

2.14. FRAUENFELD–WIL BAHN (841)　　FW

This light railway has mostly roadside running, with street running in Frauenfeld. Now managed by the Appenzellerbahnen. The FW received new 3-car EMUs in 2014 and sold units 11, 12, 13 and 15 to the CJ while 14 went to the ASm. The most recent units, 16 and 17 have been modified to form a permanently coupled reserve unit.

Gauge: 1000 mm.
Electrical System: 1200 V DC.
Route: Frauenfeld–Wil (16.9 km).
Depot: Wil.
§　　12/20 (4) + –/48 (6) + –/39 (4).

Class	No.	Name	Builder	Seats	km/h	tonnes	kW	Built
Be 4/4	16	KUFSTEIN IM TIROL	STAD/ABB/SIG	40(7)	75	35	620	1992
Be 4/4	17	TUTTWIL	STAD/ABB/SIG	40(7)	75	35	620	1992
ABe 4/8	7001	Frauenfeld	Stadler	§	100	64	800	2014
ABe 4/8	7002	Matzingen	Stadler	§	100	64	800	2014
ABe 4/8	7003	Wängi	Stadler	§	100	64	800	2014
ABe 4/8	7004	Münchwilen	Stadler	§	100	64	800	2014
ABe 4/8	7005	Wil	Stadler	§	100	64	800	2014

2.15. GLEIS-GENOSSENSCHAFT RISTET-
BERGERMOOS　　　　　　　　　　GGRB

A small company with two Em 837 shunters for carrying out track work, based in Birmensdorf, near Zürich.

▲ FLP EMU Be 4/12 22 "Malcantone" and another unit are seen at Ponte Tresa station on 12 February 2016. **Gordon Wiseman**

▼ Gornergratbahn EMU Bhe 4/8 3041 is seen at Riffelberg on 10 February 2015. **Mario Stefani**

2.16. GORNERGRAT BAHN (142) GGB

Managed by the MGB with a short connection with the latter at Zermatt. A pure rack mountain railway climbing 1484 metres in 9.4 km, finishing at the highest open air station in Europe, at 3089 metres a.s.l. Views at the summit, especially of the Matterhorn, are astonishing. This line and the Jungfraubahn are the only Swiss railways electrified on the three-phase system which requires two overhead wires. 3061/62 are mainly used for freight.

Gauge: 1000 mm.
Electrical System: 725 V 50 Hz three-phase.
Rack System: Abt.
Route: Zermatt–Gornergrat (9.4 km). Maximum gradient 20%.
Depot: Zermatt. Some stock is stabled in a tunnel around 1500 metres out of Zermatt.

f	Converted to carry supplies to hotels on line.
h	Historic train. On display at Stalden-Saas on roundabout.
*	Converted to breakdown train.

Class	No.	Builder	Seats	km/h	tonnes	kW	Built
He 2/2	3001	SLM/SIG/BBC	-	8.5	14.7	132	1898 (1966)
He 2/2	3002 h	SLM/SIG/BBC	-	8.5	13.3	132	1898 (1966)
He 2/2	3003	SLM/SIG/BBC	-	9	14.7	132	1898 (1975)
Dhe 2/4	3015 f	SLM/BBC/MFO/GGB	-	15	17.5	190	1954 (2004)
Xhe 2/4	3017*	SLM/BBC/SIG/GGB	-	15	18	190	1959
Bhe 2/4	3019	SLM/BBC/SIG	56	15	18	190	1961
Bhe 2/4	3020	SLM/BBC/SIG	56	15	18	190	1961
Bhe 2/4	3021	SLM/BBC/SIG	56	15	18	190	1961
Bhe 2/4	3022	SLM/BBC/SIG	56	15	18	190	1961
Bhe 4/8	3041	SLM/BBC	120	15	35.3	380	1965
Bhe 4/8	3042	SLM/BBC	120	15	35.3	380	1965
Bhe 4/8	3043	SLM/BBC	120	15	35.3	380	1975
Bhe 4/8	3044	SLM/BBC	120	15	35.3	380	1975
Bhe 4/8	3051	SLM/ABB	124	28	49.8	804	1993
Bhe 4/8	3052	SLM/ABB	124	28	49.8	804	1993
Bhe 4/8	3053	SLM/ABB	124	28	49.8	804	1993
Bhe 4/8	3054	SLM/ABB	124	28	49.8	804	1993
Bhe 4/4	3061	SLM/BBC	28	15.3	27.2	380	1981
Bhe 4/4	3062	SLM/BBC	28	15.3	27.2	380	1981
Bhe 4/6	3081	STAD	120	30	51	880	2006
Bhe 4/6	3082	STAD	120	30	51	880	2006
Bhe 4/6	3083	STAD	120	30	51	880	2006
Bhe 4/6	3084	STAD	120	30	51	880	2006
Xrote	3931	SLM/BEIL/MFO	-	15	13.8	221	1944
Xrote	3932	SLM/BEIL/MFO	-	15	14.2	264	1970

RIFFELALP TRAM

There is a 675 m-long 800 mm gauge tram line which connects Riffelalp station on the Gornergrat Bahn to the 5-star Riffelalp Hotel. It was opened in 1899, but closed in 1959 when the hotel was closed after a fire. It reopened in June 2001. The two four-wheeled trams of Class Ce 2/2 were built in 1899 as overhead electric and rebuilt as battery vehicles in 2001. It is thought that there is very little of the original vehicles remaining.

CLASS Ba 2/2

Built: 1899 as overhead electric. Rebuilt 2001 as battery electric.
Battery: 80 V 320 Ah.
Traction Motors: 2 x 10 kW.
Length: 5.30 m.
Weight: 3.3 tonnes.
Seats: 12.

2.17. JUNGFRAUBAHNEN GROUP

The Jungfraubahnen group is a private company with subsidiaries BLM, JB and WAB plus Harderbahn and Firstbahn. The company owns 7% of shares in, and works closely with, the BOB which is mainly owned by the Swiss Federation and the Bern canton. SPB is run by the BOB.

2.17.1. BERGBAHN LAUTERBRUNNEN–MÜRREN (313)
BLM

The BLM runs from Grütschalp (where there is a cable car from Lauterbrunnen – the funicular was replaced in 2006) along a mountain ledge, to Mürren where road vehicles are banned.

Gauge: 1000 mm.
Route: Grütschalp–Mürren (4.3 km). Maximum gradient 5%.
Depot: Grütschalp.
Electrical System: 550 V DC.

h   Historic car.

Class	No.	Name	Builder	Seats	km/h	tonnes	kW	Built
CFe 2/4	11 h		SIG/Alioth	40	25	17.5	100	1913
Be 4/4	21		SIG/BBC/SAAS	48 (8)	30	25	200	1967
Be 4/4	22		SIG/BBC/SAAS	48 (8)	30	25	200	1967
Be 4/4	23		SIG/BBC/SAAS	48 (8)	30	25	200	1967
Be 4/4	31	Lisi	SWS/MFO/BBC	40 (8)	65	32	368	1966
Xrotm	25		PETER/FORD	-	25	5	125	1956

Be 4/4 31 is ex ASm 102.

2.17.2. BERNER OBERLAND BAHN (311, 312)   BOB

This line runs from Interlaken to Lauterbrunnen and Grindelwald, at both of which connections are made with the WAB. At Wilderswil, the line connects with the Schynige Platte Bahn. There are rack sections south of Zweilütschinen on both routes. The BOB being the "main line" out of Interlaken, trains are often formed of 2 x six cars as far as Zweilütschinen where trains divide and join. BOB has ordered six new ABDeh 8/8 3-car EMUs to be delivered from December 2016 to May 2017. HGe 3/3 29 has moved to the Blonay-Chamby line. 309 was sold to the BZB in Germany

Gauge: 1000 mm.
Rack System: Von Roll.
Routes:
Electrical System: 1500 V DC.
Depots: Zweilütschinen (2).

• Interlaken Ost–Wilderswil–Zweilütschinen–Lauterbrunnen (12.3 km). Maximum gradient 9%.
• Zweilütschinen–Grindelwald (11.2 km). Maximum gradient 12%.

h   Historic stock.
s   Used as a snowplough.
w   Used for works trains.

Shunters 1 and 31 are nicknamed but the names are not carried.

Class	No.	Name	Builder	Seats	km/h	tonnes	kW	Built
Tm 2/2	1	Chrigel	STAD/SAU/BBC/MFO/SIG	-	30	15	120	1946
Tm 2/2	2		Donelli	-	45	10	-	1983
Xrote	5		SIG/BBC/Peter/BOB	-	30	13	170	1954
Xm 1/2	21		P+T/Saurer	-	20	-	123	1979
HGe 3/3	24 h		SLM/BBC/MFO	-	40/15	35.6	294	1914
HGm 2/2	31	Ferdinand	STECK/SLM/DZ	-	60/30	19.5	296	1985
Deh 4/4	302 w		SLM/BBC	-	60/40	40	632	1949
Deh 4/4	303 s		SLM/BBC	-	60/40	40	632	1949
ABeh 4/4	304	BERN	SLM/SIG/BBC	12/32 1T	70/30	44	1000	1965
ABeh 4/4	305	GUNDLISCHWAND	SLM/SIG/BBC	12/32 1T	70/40	44	1000	1965

ABeh 4/4	306	LÜTSCHENTAL	SLM/SIG/BBC	12/32 1T	70/40	44	1000 1965
ABeh 4/4	307	WILDERSWIL	SLM/SIG/BBC	12/32 1T	70/40	44	1000 1965
ABeh 4/4	308	GSTEIGWILER	SLM/SIG/BBC	12/32 1T	70/40	44	1000 1979
ABeh 4/4	310	MATTEN b. INTERLAKEN	SLM/SIG/BBC	12/32 1T	70/40	44	1000 1979
ABeh 4/4ᴵᴵ	311	GRINDELWALD	SLM/BBC	12/24 1T	70/40	44.5	1256 1986
ABeh 4/4ᴵᴵ	312	INTERLAKEN	SLM/BBC	12/24 1T	70/40	44.5	1256 1986
ABeh 4/4ᴵᴵ	313	LAUTERBRUNNEN	SLM/BBC	12/24 1T	70/40	44.5	1256 1986
ABDeh 8/8	321		Stadler	12/95 (28)			3600 2016
ABDeh 8/8	322		Stadler	12/95 (28)			3600 2016
ABDeh 8/8	323		Stadler	12/95 (28)			3600 2016
ABDeh 8/8	324		Stadler	12/95 (28)			3600 2016
ABDeh 8/8	325		Stadler	12/95 (28)			3600 2016
ABDeh 8/8	326		Stadler	12/95 (28)			3600 2016

2.17.3. JUNGFRAUBAHN (311, 312) JB

This rack line starts at Kleine Scheidegg, where it connects with the WAB, and climbs in tunnel from Eigergletscher through the Eiger and Mönch to Jungfraujoch, the highest railway station in Europe (3454 m), below the summit of the Jungfrau (4158 m). There are superb views at the top but the trip is very expensive, even with the 25% reduction given with the Swiss Pass. JB has ordered four new 3-car trains and is expected to withdraw all Class BDhe 2/4 when they are delivered in 2016. He 2/2 9 and Xrote 51 were sold to Steck.

Gauge: 1000 mm.
Electrical System: 1125 V 50 Hz three-phase AC.
Rack System: Strub.
Route: Kleine Scheidegg–Jungfraujoch (9.3 km). Maximum gradient 25%.
Depots: Eigergletscher, Kleine Scheidegg (2).

▲ BLM's most recent arrival is Be 4/4 31 "Lisi", formerly ASm 102, seen here on 15 July 2014.

Ian Francis

CLASS BDhe 2/4 — SINGLE CARS

Operate with driving trailers.

Built: 1955–66.
Builder: SLM/BBC (* SLM/BBC/JB).
Wheel Arrangement: Bo-2.
Traction Motors: 2 x 220 kW.
Accommodation: –/41 (4).

Length over Couplers:
Weight: 24 (* 25) tonnes.
Maximum Speed: 24 km/h.

201	203	205	207	209 *	210
202	204	206	208		

Name:

209   EUROTUNNEL

CLASS BDhe 4/8 — 2-CAR UNITS

Built: 1992/2002.
Builder: SLM/ABB (211–214); Stadler/Bombardier (215–218).
Wheel Arrangement: Bo-2 + 2-Bo.
Traction Motors: 4 x 201 kW.
Accommodation: 56 (3) + 48 (3).

Length over Couplers: 15.675 + 15.675 m.
Weight: 22.4 + 22.4 tonnes.
Maximum Speed: 27 km/h.

211	213	215	216	217	218
212	214				

Names:

211   Adolf Guyer-Zeller | 218   Trem do Corcovado

CLASS Bhe 4/8 — 3-SECTION ARTICULATED UNITS

Built: 2016.
Wheel Arrangement: A1-A1-A1-A1.
Length over Couplers: 16.225 + 15.410 + 16.225 m.
Traction Motors: 4 x 350 kW.
Accommodation: 56 (4) + 56 (6) + 56 (4).

Builder: Stadler.

Weight: 61 tonnes.
Maximum Speed: 33 km/h.

219	220	221	222

OTHER STOCK

h   Historic locomotive.

Class	No.	Name	Builder	Seats	km/h	tonnes	kW	Built
He 2/2	8		SLM/BBC	-	18.5	16	280	1912
He 2/2	10		SLM/BBC	-	18.5	15	280	1912
He 2/2	11 h		SLM/BBC	-	18.5	15	280	1912

2.17.4. SCHYNIGE PLATTE BAHN (314) — SPB

This pure rack mountain line connects with the BOB at Wilderswil near Interlaken. Trains are still operated with open sided stock powered by four-wheel electric locomotives dating from the time of electrification. The line also has steam loco H 2/3 no. 5 built in 1894 and looked after by Verein Lok 5. Name plates seem to be added, removed and swapped between locos. The service runs only from early June to mid October.

Gauge: 800 mm.
Rack System: Riggenbach.
Route: Wilderswil–Schynige Platte (7.3 km), Maximum gradient 25%.
Depot: Wilderswil.

Electrical System: 1500 V DC.

CLASS He 2/2   ELECTRIC LOCOMOTIVES   B

Built: 1910–12 (* 1914).
Length over Couplers:
Weight: 16 tonnes.

Builder: SLM/ALIOTH (* SLM/BBC).
Traction Motors: 2 x 110 kW.
Maximum Speed: 12 km/h.

11 *	WILDERSWIL	16	ANEMONE	61	ENZIAN
12 *		18	GÜNDLISWAND	62	ALPENROSE
13 *	MATTEN	19	FLUHBLUME	63	
14 *		20	GSTEIGWILER		

Note: SPB 16–20, 61–63 were originally WAB 56–63.

2.17.5. WENGERNALPBAHN (311, 312)   WAB

This railway operates the middle section of the route to Jungfraujoch, connecting with the BOB at Lauterbrunnen and Grindelwald and the JB at Kleine Scheidegg. In 2014/15, WAB received six more BDhe 4/8 sets, to be used on Lauterbrunnen–Kleine Scheidegg services, to allow withdrawal of the oldest BDhe 4/4 units.

Gauge: 800 mm.
Electrical System: 1500 V DC.
Rack System: Riggenbach. Maximum gradient 25%.
Routes:
• Lauterbrunnen–Wengen–Kleine Scheidegg (11.3 km).
• Grindelwald–Kleine Scheidegg (8.6 km).
Depots: Lauterbrunnen (2), Grindelwald Grund (2).

CLASS He 2/2   ELECTRIC LOCOMOTIVES   B

Locomotives, similar to those on the SPB, normally used only for works trains.

Built: 1909 (* 1926, † 1929).
Builder: SLM/ALIOTH (* SLM/BBC, † SLM/MFO).
Traction Motors: 2 x 110 (*† 118) kW.
Maximum Speed: 12 km/h.

Length over Couplers:
Weight: 16 (* 16.5, † 17) tonnes.

51	52	53	54	64 *	65 †

CLASS BDhe 4/4   SINGLE CARS

Ageing, spartan units, used both on passenger trains, with trailers, and works trains.

Built: 1947–64.
Builder: SLM/BBC.
Wheel Arrangement: Bo-Bo.
Traction Motors: 4 x 220 kW.
Accommodation: –/38 (2).

Length over Couplers: 12.20 m.
Weight: 24 tonnes.
Maximum Speed: 25 km/h.

* Equipped with AC traction motors and GTO thyristors.

104 *	108	111	113	115	117
106	109	112	114	116	118
107	110				

CLASS BDhe 4/4   SINGLE CARS

Built: 1970.
Builder: SLM/SIG/BBC/SAAS.
Wheel Arrangement: Bo-Bo.
Traction Motors: 4 x 220 kW.
Accommodation: –/40 (8).

Length over Couplers: 13.11 m.
Weight: 25.7 tonnes.
Maximum Speed: 25 km/h.

119	120	121	122	123	124

CLASS BDhe 4/8   2-CAR UNITS

All this class carry plates with a very long phrase celebrating local anniversaries.

Built: 1988.
Builder: SLM/ABB.
Wheel Arrangement: Bo-2 + 2-Bo.   **Length over Couplers:**
Traction Motors: 4 x 200 kW.   **Weight:** 43.1 tonnes.
Accommodation: 40 (6) + 48 (6).   **Maximum Speed:** 28 km/h.

131 | 132 | 133 | 134

CLASS BDhe 4/8   3-SECTION ARTICULATED UNITS

These units have low-floor entrances (350 mm) and panoramic centre cars. Additional units, almost identical and for the Wengen route, were delivered in 2014/15.

Built: 141–144 2004; 145–150 2014/15.
Builder: Stadler/Bombardier.
Wheel Arrangement: 1A-1A-1A-1A.   **Length over Couplers:** 41.83 m.
Traction Motors: 4 x 220 kW.   **Weight:** 47.5 tonnes.
Accommodation: 32 (6)+64+32 (6).   **Maximum Speed:** 28 km/h.

| 141 | 143 | 145 | 147 | 149 | 150 |
| 142 | 144 | 146 | 148 | | |

OTHER STOCK

As cars are banned from Wengen, goods are moved from Lauterbrunnen by train. Tractors 31 and 32 and EMU power cars work these.

Class	No.	Builder	Seats	Km/h	tonnes	kW	Built
Xrote	11	SLM/MFO/BEIL	-	11	13.5	138	1928
Xrote	12	SLM/MFO	-	11	15	290	1945
Xrote	21	Zaugg	-	17.5	16	400	2008
He 2/2	31	STAD/SLM/ABB	-	22	16	460	1995
He 2/2	32	STAD/SLM/ABB	-	22	16	460	1995

2.18. LAUSANNE–ECHALLENS–BERCHER (101)
LEB

A light railway serving the area to the north of Lausanne. The railway was extended in 2000 from the inconveniently located terminus at Lausanne Chauderon to a new terminus at Flon, nearer the town centre and with an interchange with Lausanne's two "metro" lines, operated by TL, which took over responsibility for LEB in 2014. The new Stadler units have allowed an increase in frequency on the southern section. They are used in multiple with the Be 4/8 sets in the peaks, to ensure some low floor access. The company also has a preserved steam loco for heritage trains.

Gauge: 1000 mm.   **Electrical System:** 1500 V DC.
Route: Lausanne Flon–Echallens–Bercher (23.7 km). Maximum gradient 6%.
Depots: Echallens.

h   Historic cars (22 is now with NStCM).
*   ex Deutschen Kraftfutterwerke, Düsseldorf in 1984.

Class	No.	Name	Builder	Seats	Km/h	tonnes	kW	Built
Tm 2/2	1 *		DIEMA/DEUTZ	-	40	5	25	1966
Tm 2/2	2		RACO/CUMM	-	50/80	22	336	1988
BDe 4/4	21 h	ROPRAZ	SWS/SAAS	40	60	30	324	1935
Are 4/4	25 h	GROS-DE-VAUD	SWS/SAAS	32	60	30	324	1947
Be 4/4	26	JOUXTENS-MEZERY	SWS/SAAS	40 (4)	80	35	588	1966
Be 4/4	27	ETAGNIÈRES	SWS/SAAS	40 (4)	80	35	588	1966

Be 4/8	31	LAUSANNE	ACMV/SIG/BBC	56+64	80	33.5 + 21	808	1985
Be 4/8	32	ECHALLENS	ACMV/SIG/BBC	56+64	80	33.5 + 21	808	1985
Be 4/8	33	BERCHER	ACMV/SIG/BBC	56+64	80	33.5 + 21	808	1985
Be 4/8	34	PRILLY	ACMV/SIG/ABB	58+68	80	33.5 + 21	808	1991
Be 4/8	35	ROMANEL	ACMV/SIG/ABB	58+68	80	33.5 + 21	808	1991
Be 4/8	36	CHESEAUX	ACMV/SIG/ABB	58+68	80	33.5 + 21	808	1991
RBe 4/8	41		Stadler	55+55	80	63		1400	2009
RBe 4/8	42		Stadler	55+55	80	63		1400	2009
RBe 4/8	43		Stadler	55+55	80	63		1400	2009
RBe 4/8	44		Stadler	55+55	80	63		1400	2009
RBe 4/8	45		Stadler	55+55	80	63		1400	2009
RBe 4/8	46		Stadler	55+55	80	63		1400	2009

2.19. LOCO SERVICE BURKHARDT   LSB

A company with a depot in Hinwil which maintains and overhauls locos, as well as selling and hiring them. The "fleet" is likely to change as sales and purchases are made.

2.20. MAKIES   MAKI

A small quarrying firm based in Gettnau on the Huttwil–Wolhusen line between Bern and Luzern. Makies uses former SOB Class BDe 576 electric railcars to haul trains of sand from Briseck (between Zell and Gettnau) to Stalden Industrie (between Gettnau and Willisau), a distance of 3.6 km. Trains of gravel also run from Gettnau to Luzern. Trains are operated under SRT's licence. Also has three Am 837 Henschel shunters.

2.21. MARTI   MARTI

A large building holding company with a subsidiary carrying out track maintenance work. One depot is on the OeBB line north of Oensingen.

▲ SPB He 2/2 no. 20 "GSTEIGWILER", now over a century old, is seen near Breitlauenen on 28 August 2014.   **Mario Stefani**

2.22. MATTERHORN GOTTHARD BAHN   MGB

This railway was formed in 2003 through the merger of two mountain railways with similar features which met in Brig:

BRIG–VISP–ZERMATT (139, 140, 141) BVZ
FURKA OBERALP (142, 143) FO

The former BVZ provides the transport link to Zermatt where "normal" road traffic is not permitted. In addition to the main service from Brig, the frequent "Zermatt Shuttle" runs from Täsch, the end of the valley road. Through coaches from Zermatt also operate as the Glacier Express to Chur and St. Moritz over the MGB to Disentis/Muster then via the RhB.

Forming the only east–west rail link across the south of the country, for many years the FO line over the Furka pass, from which the Rhône glacier could be seen, was only open during the summer. However, in 1982 the Furka base tunnel was opened, facilitating all-year-round operation, but eliminating the spectacular section over the pass itself which is now operated by the DFB with steam. Several stretches of rack remain on this scenic line. A winter car carrier shuttle is operated through the base tunnel, and there are less frequent winter car carrier trains eastwards from Andermatt.

Stock now operates in a pool. Names of locos are confusing, often being different on each side.

In 2015 MGB issued tenders for seven new two-axle shunters – three electric locos for adhesion operation and four electro-diesels equipped for rack/adhesion operation.

Electrical System: 11 kV 16.7 Hz AC.
Rack System: Abt.
Routes:
• Brig–Visp–Zermatt (44.0 km) (ex BVZ).
• Brig–Andermatt–Disentis/Muster (96.9 km) (ex FO).
• Andermatt–Göschenen (3.7 km) (ex FO).
Depots: Andermatt (ex FO), Brig Glisergrund (BVZ and FO).

ELECTRIC LOCOMOTIVES

CLASS HGe 4/4ᴵᴵ   Bo-Bo

These rack-fitted locos are very similar to ZB Class HGe 101. They are mainly used on Glacier Express trains from Zermatt via Brig and Andermatt to Disentis-Muster but also power some Zermatt–Brig services. 1–5 are ex BVZ while 101–108 are ex FO. 104 and 105 were SBB Brünig line 1951 and 1952 respectively, acquired in 1990. 108 was originally named "Nufenen" but was renamed in an "exchange" with Eurotunnel whose loco 9026 is named "FURKATUNNEL 1982".

Built: 1986 (101–103), 1989 (106–108), 1990 (1–5, 104, 105).
Builder–Mechanical Parts: SLM.
Builder–Electrical Parts: BBC/ABB.
One Hour Rating: 1932 kW.   **Tractive Effort:** 140 kN.
Wheel Diameter: 943 mm.   **Weight:** 64 tonnes.
Length over Couplers: 14.78 m.   **Maximum Speed:** 90 km/h (35 km/h on rack).

Number	Names		
1	MATTERHORN	103	CHUR/MARCAU DE CUERA
2	MONTE ROSA	104	Furka
3	DOM	105	Oberalp/Alpsu
4	TÄSCHHORN	106	St. Gotthard/S. Gottardo
5	MOUNT FUJI	107	Grimsel
101	SITTEN/VILLE DE SION	108	CHANNEL TUNNEL
102	ALTDORF		

▲ WAB shunter He 2/2 no. 32 is seen at Wengernalp on 12 February 2015. **Mario Stefani**

▼ MGB HGe 4/4ᴵᴵ 101 passes Oberalppass with Glacier Express train 903 from St Moritz to Zermatt on 2 February 2016. **Laurence Sly**

CLASSES Deh 4/4, 4/4ᴵ & 4/4ᴵᴵ   Bo-Bo

These are not locomotives but motor luggage vans which power all local push-pull trains from Visp to Brig, Andermatt and Göschenen plus Andermatt to Disentis/Mustér. Ex BVZ Deh 4/4 † and former FO Deh 4/4ᴵ § look very similar but have slightly different technical details. Deh 4/4 § and Deh 4/4ᴵᴵ, both ex FO, have almost identical technical details but the later units look very different due to their ribbed sides. The 60 or 65 km/h limit is a handicap to improving services over the Visp–Andermatt section which has many quite level, straight sections.

Built: 1972–75 §, 1975 †, 1980–84.
Builder–Mechanical Parts: SLM plus SIG Deh 4/4 & 4/4ᴵ.
Builder–Electrical Parts: ABB (†SAAS).
One Hour Rating: 1032 kW (†1095 kW).   **Maximum Tractive Effort:** 120 kN (†104 kN).
Wheel Diameter: 790 mm.   **Weight:** 48–49 tonnes.
Length over Couplers: 11.59 m (†§12.79 m)
Maximum Speed: 65 km/h (35 km/h on rack) †, 60/30 km/h rest.

*   52 has names TAVETSCH and TUJETSCH on opposite sides, plus SEDRUN on both sides.

Number	Names		
21 †	STALDEN	55 §	BRIG
22 †	ST. NIKLAUS	91	GÖSCHENEN
23 †	RANDA	92	REALP
24 †	TÄSCH	93	OBERWALD
51 §	DISENTIS/MUSTER	94	FIESCH
52 §	SEDRUN/TAVETSCH/TUJETSCH*	95	ANDERMATT
53 §	URSEREN	96	MÜNSTER
54 §	GOMS		

ELECTRIC MULTIPLE UNITS

CLASSES Abdeh 4/8 & Abdeh 4/10
3- & 4-CAR ARTICULATED UNITS

These units are the Stadler "Komet" (Komfortabler Meterspur Zug) design. The central power car has all four axles powered, a high floor and no access doors. The end cars have only one bogie, at the outer end. The intermediate trailer in the 4-car version also has just one bogie. These units have only one pair of doors in each outer car and first class accommodation.

They were ordered to operate an upgraded service on the Brig–Visp–Zermatt line in connection with the opening of the Lötschberg base tunnel and the new station at Visp. They share these duties with Class HGe 4/4 plus hauled stock.

Built: 2007/8, (2011–13, 2021/22); 2014 (2014, 2023–28).   **Builders:** Stadler/Bombardier.
Continuous Rating: 1000 kW.
Wheel Arrangement: 2-Bo-Bo(-2)-2.
Accommodation: –/36 (3) 1T + –/72 (+ 15/27) + 26/– (4) 1T.
Length over Couplers: 18.607 + 18.869 (+18.064) + 18.607 m.
Weight: 17 + 45 (+ 16) + 17 tonnes.
Maximum Speed: 80 km/h (adhesion); 35 km/h (rack).

4-car units

2011	2012	2013	2014

3-car units

2021	2023	2025	2027
2022	2024	2026	2028

▲ MGB diesel loco HGm 4/4 61 heads a special train over the DFB-run summit line between Realp and Oberwald on 14 September 2014.　　　　**Andrew Thompson**

▼ MIB unit Be 4/4 8 is seen at Aarenschlucht Ost on 2 June 2015.　　　　**Mario Stefani**

CLASS Bdseh 4/8   3-CAR UNITS

These "Komet" units were delivered before the above class and are a second class only version for the "Zermatt Shuttle" between Täsch and Zermatt. They have two pairs of doors in the outer cars which only have seats in the outer end, the rest being space for standees and baggage. Details as for ABDeh 4/8 except:

Built: 2003 2051/52; 2005 2053/54.
Accommodation: −/20 + −/80 + −/20.
Length: 52.104 m.
Weight: 70.5 tonnes.

Number	Names		Number	Names
2051	Castor		2053	Albatros
2052	Pollux		2054	Eagle

OTHER ROLLING STOCK

n   81 and 82 are officially WALLIS and URI but actually only carry shields from these cantons. They both mainly work from Andermatt.

†   73 ex Tauern Scheiteltunnel DL 11 in 1980.

‡   4971 and 4972 ex Itzehoe cement works 11 and 12 in 1980.

*   74 and 4973 ex DB 333 901 and 902 respectively, originally Kerkerbachbahn 18 and 19. 74 acquired in 1991, 4973 in 1984.

Class	No	Names	Former Rly	Builder	Seats	km/h	tonnes	kW	Built
HGe 4/4^I	15		BVZ	SLM/SWS/MFO	-	45/25	47	736	1930
HGe 4/4	32		FO	SLM/MFO	-	55/30	49	911	1941
HGe 4/4	36		FO	SLM/MFO	-	55/30	49	911	1948
HGm 4/4	61		FO	SLM/BBC/MFO	-	50/30	54	708	1968
HGm 4/4	62		FO	SLM/BBC/MFO	-	50/30	54	708	1968
Gm 3/3	72		BVZ	MOY/Asper	-	45	26	191	1975
Tm 2/2	73 †		BVZ	SCH/DZ	-	40	21	177	1972
Tm 2/2	74 *		BVZ	RUHR/MWM	-	30	25	180	1958
HGm 2/2	75	NIKLAUS	BVZ	STAD/MTU/ABB	-	60/30	23	550	2002
HGm 2/2	76			STAD/MTU/ABB	-	60/03	18	550	2010
Ge 4/4^{III}	81 n		FO	SLM/BBC	-	90	50	1700	1980
Ge 4/4^{III}	82 n		FO	SLM/BBC	-	90	50	1700	1980
Tm 2/2	4971 ‡		FO	SCH/ASPER	-	45	21.8	170	1961
Tm 2/2	4972 ‡		FO	SCH/DZ	-	45	21.8	170	1961
Tm 2/2	4973 *		FO	RUHR/MWM	-	45	23.3	176	1958
Ta 2/2	4982		FO	SIG	-	20	16	75	1994

2.23. MEIRINGEN–INNERTKIRCHEN BAHN (474) MIB

Originally built in 1926 as a construction railway for a hydro-electric scheme, this line was opened to the public in 1946. Initially the line was battery operated, and was only electrified in 1977, but not at 15 kV AC which means a change with ZB at Meiringen is necessary. The line is still owned by the local electricity generator KWO and the terminus is surrounded by power station buildings. It runs through the Aare gorge, but mostly in tunnel. Alight at Alpbach, cross the bridge and take the Reichenbachfallbahn to see where Sherlock Holmes and Moriarty fell to their deaths! Tm 10 has been preserved by La Traction.

Gauge: 1000 mm.   **Electrical System:** 1200 V DC.
Route: Meiringen–Innertkirchen KWO (4.8 km).
Depot: Innertkirchen KWO.

†   Ex CJ BDe 4/4 604 in 2005.

§   Ex CJ 402, fitted with diesel generator.

Class	No.	Names	Builder	Seats	km/h	tonnes	kW	Built
Be 4/4	8	Oberhasli/Innertkirchen	STAD/SIG/ABB	40	75	25	360	1996
BDe 4/4	11 †		SIG/SAAS	32	70	26.5	332	1953
Gem 4/4	12 §		SIG/SAAS	-	60	36	544	1953

2.24. MONTE GENEROSO (636) MG

The only mountain rack line south of the Gotthard Pass, the MG was electrified as late as 1982. For many years prior to this, the line was diesel operated. Some of the old diesel stock still remains on the line, either stored or for works or reserve use. The line is closed until spring 2017 to allow rebuilding of the hotel at Monte Generoso Vetta.

Gauge: 800 mm.
Electrical System: 800 V DC.
Rack System: Abt.
Route: Capolago–Generoso Vetta (9.0 km). Maximum gradient 22%.
Depot: Capolago.

* Built on the frames of steam locos 5/6 (new 1890).

Class	No.	Name	Builder	Seats	km/h	tonnes	kW	Built
Thm 2/3	1*		SLM/MG/VM	-	14	13	400	1953 (93)
Thm 2/2	7		BÜH/CAT/MG	-	14	10.2	300	1975 (89)
Bhe 4/8	11	Mendrisio	SLM/SE	48+48	14	34.1	810	1982
Bhe 4/8	12	Mendrisio	SLM/SE	48+48	14	34.1	810	1982
Bhe 4/8	13	Salorino	SLM/SE	48+48	14	34.1	810	1982
Bhe 4/8	14	San Gallo	SLM/SE	48+48	14	34.1	810	1982

▲ Soon to be withdrawn – MOB EMU ABDe 8/8 4002 VAUD/WAADT is seen at Rossinière on 25 September 2013. **Mario Stefani**

2.25. MONTREUX OBERLAND BERNOIS (120)
MOB

The MOB is a lengthy metre gauge railway linking Montreux with Zweisimmen, where connections can be made with BLS for Interlaken, plus a branch from Zweisimmen to Lenk. There are connections with the Blonay–Chamby (BC) preserved line at Chamby and with the TPF at Montbovon. The climb out of Montreux is one of the world's steepest adhesion-worked lines, and excellent views can be had over Lac Léman (Lake Geneva). The company also manages CEV and MTGN (MVR). Exchanges of stock between the MOB and CEV are made over the Blonay–Chamby preserved line.

Most of the company's trains are now marketed as "Golden Pass" and most trains on the regular Montreux–Zweisimmen service are formed of luxury panoramic or heritage coaches. A project to convert the line from Zweisimmen to Interlaken (BLS owned) to mixed gauge to enable through trains to operate to Luzern over the Brünig line was dropped in 2008. The plan is now to fit stock with gauge-changing bogies by 2018.

Class 3000 are now used on works trains; 3004–3006 are in dark blue livery. Class 4000 are 2-car EMUs which haul other coaches on the less prestigious Montreux–Zweisimmen trains. Class 5000 are now centre cars with a driving trailer on each side. They were completely rebuilt in 2004/5 and work only services from Zweisimmen to Lenk and Gstaad. CEV's Class 7000 units are used on the Montreux suburban service. Class 8000 are identical to RhB 641–652 and are all in advertising liveries. The numbers are tiny and only on the left-hand snowplough.

MOB has ordered eight powerful new ABe 8/8 EMUs from Stadler to be known as Class 9000. They can be used as 2-car EMUs but can also be used as power cars for long trains. MOB wishes to replace Class 8000 locos with them and sell the latter to RhB. The new units will also replace Class 4000.

MOB has also ordered three Gem 2/2 electro-diesel locos from Stadler for track work.

Gauge: 1000 mm.
Electrical System: 900 V DC.
Routes:
• Montreux–Chamby–Montbovon–Zweisimmen (62.4 km).
• Zweisimmen–Lenk (12.9 km). Maximum gradient 7%.
Depots: Chernex, Montreux, Zweisimmen.
* No. 3 ex Verkehrsbetriebe Grafschaft Hoya (Germany) V121 in 1984. Converted from standard gauge. Works shunter at Chernex.
a 5 and 6 Gmeinder Type 300B ex Halberger Hütte, Brebach (Germany) 25 and 26 in 2008.
b 7 ex RhB Xm 2/2 9914 in 2008.
c 1001 ex LCD 9 in 1972. 1002 ex BA 4 in 1973.
d ex FLP Be 4/4 no. 5.
e 1006, 1007 ex ASm 301 and 303 respectively in 2012.
§ Ex TPF 101 and 102 in 2007. Identical to 6001–6004.
† Formation is Be 4/4 9201 + ABe 4/4 9301 etc.

Class	No.	Name	Builder	Seats	km/h	tonnes	kW	Built
Tm 2/2	3*		Deutz	-	30	16	88	1954
Tm 2/2	5 a		Gmeinder	-		29	220	1977
Tmf 2/2	6 a		Gmeinder	-		29	220	1977
Tm 2/2	7 b		RhB/SAU/MFO	-	55	19	112	1950
Be 4/4	1001 c		ACMV/BBC/SWS/MFO	64	45	30.4	308	1955
Be 4/4	1002 c	SAANEN	SWS/SAAS	56	60	29	176	1951
Be 4/4	1003 d		SWS	56	60	31	244	1958
Be 4/4	1006 e		SWS/MFO	40	65	32	368	1966
Be 4/4	1007 e		SWS/MFO	40	65	32	368	1971
Gm 4/4	2003	MONTBOVON	MOY/CFD/POY	-	80	44	485	1976
Gm 4/4	2004	ALBEUVE	MOY/CFD/Scania	-	80	44	632	1982
BDe 4/4	3002	(CHÂTEAU D'OEX)	SIG/BBC	-	75	35.7	440	1944
BDe 4/4	3004		SIG/BBC	-	75	35.7	440	1944
BDe 4/4	3005		SIG/BBC	-	75	36	440	1946
BDe 4/4	3006		SIG/BBC	-	75	36	440	1946
ABDe 8/8	4001	SCHWEIZ	SIG/BBC/SAAS	22/68	70	60	880	1968

ABDe 8/8	4002	VAUD/WAADT	SIG/BBC/SAAS	22/68	70	60	880	1968
ABDe 8/8	4003	BERN/BERNE	SIG/BBC/SAAS	22/68	70	60	880	1968
ABDe 8/8	4004	FRIBOURG/						
		FREIBURG	SIG/BBC/SAAS	22/69	70	60	880	1968
Be 4/4	5001		SIG/SAAS	48	80	32	448	1976
Be 4/4	5002		SIG/SAAS	48	80	32	448	1976
Be 4/4	5003		SIG/SAAS	48	80	32	448	1979
Be 4/4	5004		SIG/SAAS	48	80	32	448	1979
GDe 4/4	6001	VEVEY	SLM/BBC	-	90	48.2	1053	1983
GDe 4/4	6002	ROSSINIÈRE	SLM/BBC	-	90	48.2	1053	1983
GDe 4/4	6003	SAANEN	SLM/BBC	-	90	48.2	1053	1983
GDe 4/4	6004	INTERLAKEN	SLM/BBC	-	90	48.2	1053	1983
GDe 4/4	6005 §	VILLE DE BULLE	SLM/BBC	-	90	48.2	1053	1983
GDe 4/4	6006 §	NEIRIVUE	SLM/BBC	-	90	48.2	1053	1983
Ge 4/4	8001		SLM/ABB	-	120	62	2000	1995
Ge 4/4	8002		SLM/ABB	-	120	62	2000	1995
Ge 4/4	8003		SLM/ABB	-	120	62	2000	1995
Ge 4/4	8004		SLM/ABB	-	120	62	2000	1995
ABe 8/8	9201 + 9301 †		Stadler					
ABe 8/8	9202 + 9301 †		Stadler					
ABe 8/8	9203 + 9301 †		Stadler					
ABe 8/8	9204 + 9301 †		Stadler					
ABe 8/8	9205 + 9301 †		Stadler					
ABe 8/8	9206 + 9301 †		Stadler					
ABe 8/8	9207 + 9301 †		Stadler					
ABe 8/8	9208 + 9301 †		Stadler					

2.26. MONTREUX-VEVEY-RIVIERA   MVR

MVR is a grouping of the railways formerly known as CEV and MTGN plus the Vevey–Mont
Pélerin, Territet–Glion and Les Avants–Sonloup funiculars. The lines are managed by MOB.

2.26.1. CHEMINS DE FER ÉLECTRIQUES VEVEYSANS (112)   CEV

Once a much larger system, two sections remain in operation – the adhesion line from Vevey to
Blonay and the rack line from Blonay to Les Pléiades. 71 was rebuilt by SWP/R&J in 1998 with
a modern body and only one cab and works as a 2-car set with Bt 224. 72 had a similar rebuild
in 2002 but is still a single car with two cabs. 73 to 75 operate with driving trailers Bt 221 and
222. The Blonay–Chamby museum line was once part of the CEV and is still used to move stock
between CEV and the MOB. Class 7000 units also work on the MOB. Units 103 and 105 has been
preserved. CEV has ordered nine new Class 7500 2-car EMUs from Stadler for delivery from
2015. Some will be used on Montreux–Les Avants and 7001–7004 will be sold to ASm for the
BTI line (three) and the MIB (one). Class 7500 will work all services throughout and cause the
withdrawal of 73 to 75. 71 and 72 will initially be retained in reserve. The CEV will also receive
one HGem 2/2 electro-diesel loco from Stadler.

Gauge: 1000 mm.
Electrical System: 850 V DC.
Rack System: Strub. Maximum gradient 20%.
Route: Vevey–Blonay–Les Pléaides (10.5 km).
Depots: Vevey, Blonay.

+   Bt 224 is coupled to Beh 2/8
*   SAINT LÉGIER-LA CHIESAZ (two EMUs with the same name).
§   Class 7500 seating is 12/32 (6) + -/46 (8)

Class	No.	Name	Builder	Seats	km/h	tonnes	kW	Built
He 2/2	1		SLM/MFO/SIG	-	20	17.4	390	1911 (51)
He 2/2	2		SLM/MFO/SIG	-	20	17.4	390	1911 (51)
Beh 2/8	71 +		SWP/SAAS/MOB	51+46 (4)	50/16	33.8	428	1969
Beh 2/4	72		SWP/SAAS/MOB	48	50/16	33.8	428	1970
BDeh 2/4	73		SWP/SAAS	48 (8)	50/16	33.8	428	1970
BDeh 2/4	74		SWP/SAAS	48 (8)	50/16	33.8	428	1970
BDeh 2/4	75		SWP/SAAS	48	50/16	33.8	428	1983
Te 2/2	81		SWS/MFO/CEV	-	30	12	62	1921
Te 2/2	82		CEV/MFO	-	25	9.3	60	1938
Be 2/6	7001	VEVEY	STAD/SLM/AD	32 (4)+32 (4)	80	33.5	592	1997
Be 2/6	7002	*	STAD/SLM/AD	32 (4)+32 (4)	80	33.5	592	1997
Be 2/6	7003	BLONAY	STAD/SLM/AD	32 (4)+32 (4)	80	33.5	592	1998
Be 2/6	7004	MONTREUX	STAD/SLM/AD	32 (4)+32 (4)	80	33.5	592	1998
ABeh 2/6	7501	*	Stadler	§	60/40	51.5	850	
ABeh 2/6	7502		Stadler	§	60/40	51.5	850	
ABeh 2/6	7503		Stadler	§	60/40	51.5	850	
ABeh 2/6	7504		Stadler	§	60/40	51.5	850	
ABeh 2/6	7505		Stadler	§	60/40	51.5	850	
ABeh 2/6	7506		Stadler	§	60/40	51.5	850	
ABeh 2/6	7507		Stadler	§	60/40	51.5	850	
ABeh 2/6	7508		Stadler	§	60/40	51.5	850	
ABeh 2/6	7509		Stadler	§	60/40	51.5	850	

▲ MVR HGe 2/2 no. 2, built in 1909 and still wearing MTGN markings, powers a rotary snowplough at Jaman (1742 metres asl) on 10 March 2014. **Pierre Julien**

2.26.2. MONTREUX–TERRITET–GLION–NAYE (121) MTGN

The MTGN was formed in 1992 by the merger of the Montreux Glion Naye (MGN) rack line with the Territet–Glion funicular. The MGN itself was the result of a 1987 merger between the Montreux–Glion (MGI) and Glion–Naye (GN) railways which had been operated as a single entity for almost 50 years. A pure rack line giving fantastic views over Lac Léman.

Gauge: 800 mm.
Electrical System: 850 V DC.
Rack System: Abt. Maximum gradient 22%.
Route: Montreux–Glion–Rochers-de-Naye (10.3 km).
Depot: Glion.

‡   ex BRB No. 8 in 1996.

Class	No.	Name	Builder	Seats	km/h	tonnes	kW	Built
HGe 2/2	2		SLM/MFO	-	13	14.2	162	1909
Hm 2/2	4 ‡	BRIENZ	RC/BÜH/CAT/PLEI/MG	-	14	12.3	415	1973
Bhe 2/4	201 (S)	SLM/BBC		52	18	15.5	150	1938
Bhe 2/4	203		SLM/BBC	52	18	15.5	150	1938
Bhe 2/4	204		SLM/BBC	52	18	15.5	150	1938
Bhe 2/4	207		SLM/BBC	52	18	15.5	150	1949
Bhe 4/8	301	Montreux	SLM/SE	48+48	25	34	800	1983
Bhe 4/8	302	(Veytaux)	SLM/SE	48+48	25	34	800	1983
Bhe 4/8	303	(Villeneuve)	SLM/SE	48+48	25	34	800	1983
Bhe 4/8	304	La Tour-de-Peilz	SLM/SE	48+48	25	34	800	1992

2.27. (TRANSPORTS DE LA RÉGION) MORGES-BIÈRE-COSSONAY MBC

2.27.1. BIÈRE–APPLES–MORGES (156) BAM

BAM is part of Transports de la Région Morges-Bière-Cossonay (MBC) which also includes bus companies TPM and MBC which carry the same green and white livery. One of the few narrow gauge lines in Switzerland electrified at high voltage AC. Car 14 was originally 13, renumbered for superstitious reasons! 11, 12 and 14 usually operate with driving trailers Bt 51, 52 and 53 respectively. MBC ordered three 2-car EMUs, which will receive existing modern intermediate trailers, plus one new 3-car EMU, in time for introducing a half-hourly service from Morges to Apples and Bière in December 2015.

This is the only narrow gauge line in Switzerland where freight receipts can exceed those from passengers – the line serves an important army base near Bière as well as autumn sugar beet traffic. The two electric locos are basically the same as RhB Class Ge 4/4 III but also have standard gauge buffer beams. BAM has two ex SBB standard gauge tractors as the latter pulled out of shunting at Morges. MBC also has two standard gauge electric shunters for work in Morges plus Re 420 506 for new stone traffic: see main standard gauge section. This loco is actually taken to Bière on skates for maintenance!

Gauge: 1000 mm.
Electrical System: 15 kV AC 16.7 Hz.
Routes:
• Morges–Apples–Bière (19.1 km). Maximum gradient 3.5%.
• Apples–L'Isle (10.7 km), junction–Bière Casernes (1.9 km).
Depots: Bière, L'Isle.

h   Historic unit.
§   Centre cars are B 2065–2068 respectively.

Class	No.	Name	Builder	Seats	km/h	tonnes	kW	Built
BCFe 4/4	2 h		SWS/SAAS	40	65	36	500	1943
BDe 4/4	5 h		SWS/SAAS	40	65	36	500	1949
Be 4/4	11		ACMV/SIG/SAAS	40 (5)	75	46	780	1981
Be 4/4	12		ACMV/SIG/SAAS	40 (5)	75	46	780	1981
Be 4/4	14		ACMV/SIG//SAAS	40 (5)	75	46	780	1981
Ge 4/4	21	LA MORGES	SLM/ABB	-	100	62.2	2400	1994
Ge 4/4	22	LA VENOGE	SLM/ABB	-	100	62.2	2400	1994
ABe 8/12	31+32 §	LE JORAN	Stadler					2015
ABe 8/12	33+34 §		Stadler					2016
ABe 8/12	35+36 §		Stadler					2016
ABe 8/12	37+38 §		Stadler					2016
Tm 2/2	41	PASSE-PARTOUT	RACO/Cummins	-	50/75	22	336	1990

2.28. MÜLLER GLEISBAU & M-RAIL   MFAG

A company involved in track maintenance, based in Frauenfeld. The company has an associate called Müller Technologie, which itself has a department called M-Rail which may hire out locos. The company has about ten locos – shunters plus three Gmeinder locos which carry German EVNs, the short versions being 580 008 to 010. In spring 2015, M-Rail was hiring 456 142 from BLS for trains on behalf of SBB Cargo.

2.29. NYON–ST. CERGUE–MOREZ (155)   NStCM

Once an international line linking Nyon on Lac Léman (Lake Geneva) with Morez in France, the French section was closed in 1958. Now part of Transport Publics de la region Nyonnaise (TPN). The new Stadler units allowed a 15-minute service Nyon–Genolier from December 2015. NStCM has ordered one Gem 2/2 electro-diesel loco from Stadler for track work. A new depot is planned at Asse, between Nyon and Trelex. NStCM is studying the possibility of extending the line 3 km from La Cure to Les Rousses in France.

Gauge: 1000 mm.   **Electrical System:** 1500 V DC.
Route: Nyon–St. Cergue–La Cure (27.0 km). Maximum gradient 6.0%.
Depots: Nyon Les Plantaz, St. Cergue.

‡ Ex LEB 22 in 1991. Departmental use.
§ Ex CJ 606 in 2003 and 607 in 2007 respectively.
* Can be fitted with rotary snowplough in winter.

Class	No.	Builder	Seats	km/h	tonnes	kW	Built
Be 4/4	201	ACMV/BBC/SAAS	40	65	33	752	1985
Be 4/4	202	ACMV/BBC/SAAS	40	65	33	752	1985
Be 4/4	203	ACMV/BBC/SAAS	40	65	33	752	1985
Be 4/4	204	ACMV/BBC/SAAS	40	65	33	752	1985
Be 4/4	205	ACMV/BBC/SAAS	40	65	33	752	1986
BDe 4/4	211	ACMV/ABB	24	65	33	752	1991
BDe 4/4	221 ‡	SWS/SAAS	40	60	30	324	1935
BDe 4/4	231 §	SIG/SAAS	40	70	26.5	332	1952
BDe 4/4	232 §	SIG/SAAS	40	70	26.5	332	1952
Xtm 2/2	251*	Beilhack	-	50	22.1	149	1984
Tm 2/2		O&K	-	15	16	35	1958
ABe 4/4	401+402	Stadler	78 (14)	100	63	1160	2015
ABe 4/4	403+404	Stadler	78 (14)	100	63	1160	2015
ABe 4/4	405+406	Stadler	78 (14)	100	63	1160	2015
ABe 4/4	407+408	Stadler	78 (14)	100	63	1160	2015

2.30. OENSINGEN BALSTHAL BAHN (412)   OeBB

A short branch line connecting with the SBB Olten–Solothurn line at Oensingen. From December 2015 OeBB stopped supplying the (vintage) rolling stock and the line's service is now operated by an SBB Class 560 EMU. The company has close links with the Seetalbahn and runs its preserved stock there. 15301 is known as the "Seetalkrokodil". OeBB also owns 0-6-0T steam locos E 3/3 1 (ex KLB) and E 3/3 2, and often accommodates and repairs other people's steam locos. The line has significant freight traffic at the Oensingen end. OeBB has sold its two ex SBB RBe 540 sets for preservation but still uses one for freight. Its ex SBB RBDe 560 EMU is kept in reserve.

Gauge: 1435 mm.
Route: Oensingen–Balsthal (4 km).
Electrical System: 15 kV AC 16.7 Hz.
Depot: Balsthal.

a   LEW 17690, V60D, ex DB 345 164, ex BLS Em 845 001.
b   LEW 12246, V60D, delivered to VEB Kalibetrieb Zielitz, East Germany, later Conserves Estavayer.
c   ex Von Roll, Kluz. RACO 1699.
d   ex SBB in 1974. "Roter Pfeil", similar to RAe 2/4 1001 in SBB Historic fleet.

Class	Old SBB No.	OeBB No.	Builder	Seats	km/h	tonnes	kW	Built
Em 4/4		20 a	LEW	-	30/60	60	478	1982
Em 4/4		22 b	LEW	-	30/60	60	478	
Tm		24 c	RACO	-	45	28	150	1966
Ce 2/2		102 (S)	SLM/SAAS	-	60	28	257	1944
Ce 2/2		103 (S)	SLM/SAAS	-	60	28	257	1944
RBe 2/4	1007	202 d	SLM/BBC/MFO/SAAS	–/67	125	38	394	1938

2.31. PANLOG   PLAG

Serves a steelworks near Emmenbrücke (Luzern) plus local trips. Received two Voith Gravita diesels in autumn 2009.

2.32. PILATUS BAHN (473)   PB

The world's steepest rack railway, requiring the "Locher" rack system, comprising a double-sided horizontal rack rail, the railcars having two pinions, one on each side of the rack. Opened in 1889, electrified in 1937. Although there is a published timetable, many extras run and trains arrive from Pilatus at Alpnachstad in short succession. There is a traverser here as the single platform can only hold two trains. Operates May to November only.

Gauge: 800 mm.
Rack System: Locher.
Route: Alpnachstad–Pilatus Kulm (4.6 km). Maximum gradient 48%.
Depot: Alpnachstad.
Electrical System: 1550 V DC.

Note: Only one underframe exists for cars 29 & 31, the bodies being exchanged as required. Hence, only one of these two cars can be in use at any one time.

Class	No.	Builder	Seats	km/h	tonnes	kW	Built
Bhe 1/2	21	SLM/MFO	40	12	9.65	155	1937
Bhe 1/2	22	SLM/MFO	40	12	9.65	155	1937
Bhe 1/2	23	SLM/MFO	40	12	9.65	155	1937
Bhe 1/2	24	SLM/MFO	40	12	9.65	155	1937
Bhe 1/2	25	SLM/MFO	40	12	9.65	155	1937
Bhe 1/2	26	SLM/MFO	40	12	9.65	155	1937
Bhe 1/2	27	SLM/MFO	40	12	9.65	155	1937
Bhe 1/2	28	SLM/MFO	40	12	9.65	155	1937
Bhe 1/2	29	SLM/MFO	40	12	9.6	155	1962
Bhe 1/2	30	SLM/MFO	40	12	10.5	175	1968
Ohe 1/2	31	SLM/MFO	-	12	8.3	155	1954
Xhm 1/2	32	SLM/STAD/BBC	-	12	11.3	320	1981

▲ OeBB 205 (former SBB 540 019) is seen at Balsthal on 13 May 2014. The unit has now been preserved but is still used to haul freight on the line. **David Haydock**

▼ Pilatusbahn units 25 and 26 are seen stabled at Alpnachstad station, behind the line's splendid administration building, on 7 July 2014. **Ian Francis**

2.33. POST TELEPHON TELEGRAPH   PTT

Not a private railway, the Swiss Post Office is included since it uses shunting locos at a few locations. However, it seems that the locos have gradually been sold off. P16 and P17, now 237 916 and 917, are now owned by leasing company Serfahr but are still used at Daillens and Härkingen.

2.34. RAILCARE   RLC

A company based in Härkingen and owned by the Swiss Co-op supermarket chain. Railcare operates container trains, mainly carrying goods for the Co-op within Switzerland. The company initially hired Class 186 locos but from December 2013 swapped its 186s with 465 015 to 018 from BLS. The main bases are at Niederbottingen and Oensingen.

2.35. REGIONALVERKEHR BERN–SOLOTHURN (295, 307, 308)   RBS

The former SZB (Solothurn Zollikofen Bern) and VBW (Vereinigte Bern Worb Bahnen) merged as the RBS in 1985. The railway provides frequent suburban services from Bern, at one time all routes entering the town over the urban tram tracks, which explains the right-hand running on most sections. A new line, terminating in an underground station below Bern HB was opened in 1965, and is used by all Solothurn line trains, plus those on the ex VBW route from Worb via Bolligen. The station was designed for 16 000 passengers a day but now handles 60 000. A new station will be built from 2017.

The other ex VBW route to Worb via Muri enters Bern over the urban tram tracks, and for many years terminated at the inconveniently-located Helvetiaplatz. Due to the width and weight of the existing rolling stock, the cars could not continue further. Therefore, new tramway type cars were purchased for this route which was extended to Bern Zytglogge in 1997. The voltage of this line was lowered from 800 to 600 V DC to be fully compatible with the tramways then, in 2010, Line G became part of Bernmobil tramway Line 6, which RBS stock shares with Combino trams. The voltage on the Solothurn line is eventually expected to be boosted to 1500 V DC.

The RBS network represents 13% of Bern's S-Bahn in length but carries 50% of traffic – 18.2 million passengers a year. In 2015 RBS was expected to order a further 16 new 4-car tram-style trains to replace Be 4/8 and 4/12 sets on Line S7 in 2018.

Gauge: 1000 mm.
Electrical System: Line G 600 V DC; Lines J, W and Z 1250 V DC.
Routes:
• Line G Worb Dorf–Gümlingen–Bern Egghölzli (9.7 km).
• Line J Bern HB–Worblaufen–Solothurn (33.6 km).
• Line W Worblaufen–Boll-Utzigen–Worb Dorf (11.2 km).
• Line Z Worblaufen–Unterzollikofen (1.4 km).
Depots: Solothurn, Worblaufen, Worbboden; Worb Dorf (Line G).

1250 V DC STOCK

CLASS RABe 4/12   "NExT"   3-CAR UNITS

These units are known as NExT (*Niederflur Express Triebzug*) by Stadler, or "*Orangen*" being all orange, by the locals. They operate on the Solothurn–Bern service. The fastest narrow gauge trains in Switzerland.

Built: 21–26 2009; 27–34 2012/13.
Wheel Arrangement: 2-2 + Bo-Bo + 2-2.
Accommodation: 18/20 (3) + –/64 + –/52.
Continuous Power Rating: 1160 kW.

Builder: Stadler, Altenrhein.
Length: 19.835 + 20.330 + 19.835 m.
Weight: 83.5 tonnes.
Maximum Speed: 120 km/h.

21	24	27	29	31	33	
22	25	28	30	32	34	
23	26					

CLASS Be 4/8 & Be 4/12 "MANDARINLI" 2- OR 3-CAR UNITS

These units were delivered as 2-car but extended by the addition of a Stadler/Bombardier low-floor car from 2001 to 2009. They operate all trains on S-Bahn Lines S7 (Line W) and S9 (Line Z) plus short workings to Urtenen and Jegenstorf on S8 (Line J).

Built: 1974 (units 41–52); 1978 (53–61).
Wheel Arrangement: Bo-Bo (+ 2-2) + 2-2.
Accommodation: –/64 (+ –/56) + –/64.
Power Rating: 326 kW.

Builders: SIG/BBC.
Length: 59.50 m (*40 m 2-car).
Weight: 62.7 tonnes (*48.7 tonnes 2-car).
Maximum Speed: 75 km/h.

43	51	54	56	58 *	60
47	52	55	57	59	61
50	53 Lugano				

CLASS Be 4/12 3-CAR UNITS

These modern light rail vehicles are very similar to those used on the WSB. Built as 2-car sets they received a low-floor centre car with a central first class section labelled "Prima" in 1994–2001 to work the fast Bern–Solothurn service on S-Bahn Line S8. This has been taken over by NExT sets so the first class was downgraded in 2013 and units reclassified from ABe to Be 4/12. They now operate short workings on Line S8. Names were removed during refurbishment.

Built: 1992/93.
Builders: SWA/SAG/ABB.
Wheel Arrangement: Bo-2 + 2-2 + 2-Bo.
Accommodation: –/60 + 18/40 + –/60 (6).
Power Rating: 640 kW.

Length: 59.73 m.
Weight: 80 tonnes.
Maximum Speed: 90 km/h.

62	64	66	68	70	72
63	65	67	69	71	

▲ Brand new RBS "NExT" EMU RABe 4/12 28 is seen at Solothurn on 17 April 2014. **David Haydock**

600 V DC STOCK

CLASS Be 4/10   4-SECTION TRAM

These vehicles work over Bern tramway Line 6. They were repainted from the older white, blue and orange livery into a less attractive all-over blue in 2009 and received an additional low-floor section built by Stadler in 2009/10.

Built: 1987/88.
Builders: SWP/SIG/ABB.
Wheel Arrangement: B-2-2-2-B.
Accommodation: –/88.
Power Rating: 300 kW.

Length: 39.80 m.
Weight: 45.6 tonnes.
Maximum Speed: 65 km/h.

81	84	Muri / Gümlingen	87
82	85		88
83	86		89

OTHER STOCK

§   1 and 11 are historic cars. 11 is ex BDe 4/4 24.
†   Dual voltage stock.
*   161 and 162 are former Brünig line Tm 596 and 999 respectively.

Class	No.	Name	Builder	Seats	km/h	tonnes	kW	Built
Bre 4/4	1 §	PENDLER-PINTLI	SWS/MFO/SZB	44	75	40	512	1916 (87)
CFe 4/4	11 §		SWS/MFO/SZB	36	75	34	256	1916 (91)
Ge 4/4	111 †		AEG/VBW	-	40	32	470	1927 (57)
Ge 4/4	112 †		AEG/VBW	-	40	34	470	1927 (67)
Tm 2/2	161*		RACO	-	40	13	70	1966 (02)
Tm 2/2	162*		RACO/DZ	-	30	3.2	37	1932 (67)
Tmf 2/2	165		SCHÖMA	-	60	25	336	1996
Tmf 2/2	166		SCHÖMA	-	60	25	336	1996
Tmf 2/2	167	MAX	SCHÖMA	-	75	28	330	2010
Tmf 2/2	168	MORITZ	SCHÖMA	-	75	28	330	2010

2.36. RHÄTISCHE BAHN   RhB

In terms of route mileage the RhB is the largest of the Swiss private railways. It operates all the lines in south east Switzerland (mainly in the Graubünden canton), connecting with the SBB at Chur and Landquart, and serving the major tourist centres of St. Moritz, Davos and Klosters. Branches also serve Disentis-Mustér (where there is an end-on connection with the MGB allowing through Glacier Express trains to Zermatt), Arosa, Scuol-Tarasp and Tirano (Italy). The main system is electrified at 11 kV AC 16.7 Hz whilst the Berninabahn (St. Moritz–Tirano), once a separate company, is 1000 V DC. The Chur–Arosa line was converted from 2000 V DC to 11 kV AC in 1997.

All the lines of the RhB are very scenic, particularly the Berninabahn and the Albula pass. The Romantsch language (as well as German) is used in this region and this explains some of the double place names. The network carries a remarkable amount of freight. There is significant works traffic at present as RhB is building a new Albula tunnel parallel to the old one.

In 2015 RhB announced it would order 27 4-car "Retica" EMUs, to be delivered in 2018/19. This will inevitably mean fewer loco-hauled trains in future.

Routes:
- Landquart–Chur–Reichenau-Tamins–Disentis-Mustér (72.9 km).
- Reichenau-Tamins–Filisur–Bever–Samedan–St. Moritz (79.4 km).
- Samedan–Pontresina (5.4 km).
- Landquart–Klosters–Davos Platz–Filisur (69.3 km).
- Klosters–Vereinatunnel–Sagliains (22 km).
- Scuol-Tarasp–Sagliains–Bever (39.4 km); maximum gradient 3.5%.
- Chur–Arosa (25.7 km); maximum gradient 6%.
- St. Moritz–Pontresina–Tirano (60.7 km); maximum gradient 7%. (1000 V DC).

Depots: 11 kV AC system: Landquart (depot and works), Chur, Samedan; Berninabahn: Poschiavo.

2.36.1. BERNINABAHN STOCK (1000 V DC)

CLASS ABe 4/4   Bo-Bo

The survivors, all much rebuilt, of the original Berninabahn stock. Used on works duties and as reserve power. Fitted with track brakes for street running in Tirano. 35 is preserved on the Blonay–Chamby. 38 and 37 were rebuilt as rescue units 9922 and 9924. 30 and 34 are in the old yellow livery.

Built: 1908–11; rebuilt 1986/87.
Builder–Mechanical Parts: SIG/RhB.
Builder–Electrical Parts: SAAS.
One Hour Rating: 382 kW.
Maximum Tractive Effort: 55 kN.   **Wheel Diameter:** 850 mm.
Weight: 30 tonnes (†31 tonnes).   **Length over Couplers:** 13.93 m (†14.66 m).
Maximum Speed: 55 km/h.   **Accommodation:** 12/27 († 12/29).

30 †		32		34

CLASS ABe 4/4   Bo-Bo

These railcars together with 51–56, hauled most trains on the Berninabahn before the arrival of the new EMUs. Their use is now restricted to works trains. Multiple and track brake fitted. 49 has been converted into breakdown vehicle 272 01 and 48 into service unit 232 01.

Built: 1964–65 (* 1972).
Builder–Mechanical Parts: SWS.
Builder–Electrical Parts: BBC/MFO/SAAS (*BBC/SAAS).
One Hour Rating: 680 kW.
Maximum Tractive Effort: 156 kN.   **Wheel Diameter:** 920 mm.
Weight: 41 tonnes (*43 tonnes).   **Length over Couplers:** 16.54 m (16.89 m *).
Maximum Speed: 65 km/h.   **Accommodation:** 12/24.

46		47 *

CLASS ABe 4/4ᴵᴵ   Bo-Bo

Railcars with three-phase motors built to supplement 41–49. Multiple & track brake fitted.

Built: 1988 (51–53), 1990 (54–56).
Builder–Mechanical Parts: SWA.
Builder–Electrical Parts: ABB.
One Hour Rating: 1016 kW.   **Maximum Tractive Effort:** 178 kN.
Wheel Diameter: 920 mm.   **Weight:** 47 tonnes.
Length over Couplers: 16.90 m.   **Maximum Speed:** 65 km/h.
Accommodation: 12/16.

51	Poschiavo	53	Tirano	55	Diavolezza
52	Brusio	54	Hakone	56	Corviglia

CLASS De 2/2   Bo

A former B-B motor luggage van, much rebuilt and used for shunting.

Built: 1909, rebuilt 1980.
Builder–Mechanical Parts: SIG.
Builder–Electrical Parts: Alioth.
One Hour Rating: 147 kW.   **Maximum Tractive Effort:**
Wheel Diameter: 850 mm.   **Weight:** 13 tonnes.
Length over Couplers: 7.15 m.   **Maximum Speed:** 45 km/h.

151

CLASS Ge 2/2   Bo

Former B-B centre cab electric locos, normally used for shunting around Poschiavo and Tirano.

Built: 1911.
Builder–Mechanical Parts: SIG.
Builder–Electrical Parts: Alioth.   **One Hour Rating:** 242 kW.
Maximum Tractive Effort: 35 kN.   **Wheel Diameter:** 975 mm.
Weight: 18 tonnes.   **Length over Couplers:** 7.73 m.
Maximum Speed: 45 km/h.

161 | 162

2.36.2. 11 kV ELECTRIC & DIESEL LOCOMOTIVES

CLASS Ge 3/3   C

Modern electric shunting locos, a single motor drives all wheels through cardan shafts.

Built: 1984.
Builder–Mechanical Parts: RACO.
Builder–Electrical Parts: BBC.
Traction Motor: 1 single-phase frame-mounted with cardan shaft drive.
One Hour Rating: 425 kW.   **Maximum Tractive Effort:** 102 kN.
Driving Wheel Diameter: 920 mm.   **Weight:** 33 tonnes.
Length over Couplers: 8.64 m.   **Maximum Speed:** 40 km/h.

214 | 215

CLASS Ge 2/4   1B1

Historic electric locomotive in old brown livery, based at Samedan. Originally part of the same class as 212, but when rebuilt from 204 for shunting in 1945/46 retained the original box cab.

Built: 1913, rebuilt 1945/46.
Builder–Mechanical Parts: SLM.
Builder–Electrical Parts: BBC/RhB.
Traction Motor: 1 single-phase frame-mounted with side rod drive.
One Hour Rating: 428 kW.   **Maximum Tractive Effort:** 59 kN.
Driving Wheel Diameter: 1070 mm.   **Pony Wheel Diameter:** 710 mm.
Weight: 31.8 tonnes.   **Length over Couplers:** 8.70 m.
Maximum Speed: 30 km/h.

222

CLASS Gm 3/3   C

Diesel shunters used at Landquart and Chur, they have a two-speed transmission giving different characteristics for shunting and line operation.

Built: 1975–76.
Engine: MTU of 396 kW.
Maximum Tractive Effort: 153 kN.
Weight: 34 tonnes.
Maximum Speed: 35/55 km/h.

Builder: Moyse Type CL; works nos. 3553–3555.
Transmission: Hydraulic.
Wheel Diameter: 920 mm.
Length over Couplers: 7.96 m.

231 | 232 | 233

CLASS Gm 4/4   B-B

A unique diesel loco (although similar to DB V 51 and V 52 narrow gauge designs), originally built to 860 mm gauge for a cement works in Itzehoe, Germany, then had three other owners. Converted to metre gauge by Schöma in 1967 and purchased in 1988 from the Brohltalbahn in Germany (loco D4) for use on construction work on the Vereina Tunnel. Usually shunts Untervaz cement works.

Built: 1958. Rebuilt by RhB Landquart works in 1999.
Builder: MaK (Type 400 BB, works number 400029).
Engine: Two Cummins KT 19-L of 136 kW.
Maximum Tractive Effort: 86 kN.
Weight: 36 tonnes.
Maximum Speed: 50 km/h.

Transmission: Hydraulic.
Wheel Diameter: 850 mm.
Length over Couplers: 9.68 m.

241

CLASS Gmf 4/4ᴵ   B-B

First used on construction work on the Vereina Tunnel and now used on general ballast work.

Built: 1992.
Builder: Gmeinder/Kaelble/RhB (Gmeinder Type D75 BB).
Engine: Caterpillar of 560 kW.
Maximum Tractive Effort: 165 kN.
Weight: 50 tonnes.
Maximum Speed: 60 km/h.

Transmission: Hydraulic. Voith.
Wheel Diameter:
Length over Couplers: 11.70 m.

242 | 243

CLASS 234 (Gmf 4/4ᴵᴵ)   Bo-Bo

These are four new diesel locos ordered in 2009 for heavy works trains. 234 01 (originally 287 01) was delivered in 2013 for trials, but delivery of the others did not take place as planned in 2014 and 287 02 (now 234 02) arrived in 2015, also for tests. The bogies are of a special design to allow the loco to operate over curves as low as 45 metre radius. The locos are also numbered D1 to D4.

Built: 2013.
Engine: MTU 12V 4000 R43L of 1800 kW.
Maximum Tractive Effort: 230 kN.
Weight: 64 tonnes.
Maximum Speed: 100 km/h.

Builder: Schalke Eisenhütte, Germany.
Transmission: Electric.
Wheel Diameter: 1070 mm.
Length over Couplers: 16.69 m.

234 01 | 234 02 | 234 03 | 234 04

CLASS Ge 4/6   1D1

Historic locomotive in brown livery, based at Samedan. The last survivor of an assortment of locos of this wheel arrangement dating from the time of electrification. It has been retained as a historic loco. The body contains two traction motors geared to a single layshaft driving through an additional layshaft and coupling rods.

Built: 1914.
Builder–Mechanical Parts: SLM.   **Builder–Electrical Parts:** MFO.
Traction Motors: 2 single-phase frame-mounted with side rod drive.
One Hour Rating: 588 kW.   **Maximum Tractive Effort:** 106 kN.
Driving Wheel Diameter: 1070 mm.   **Pony Wheel Diameter:** 710 mm.
Weight: 56.3 tonnes.   **Length over Couplers:** 11.10 m.
Maximum Speed: 55 km/h.

353

CLASS Ge 6/6   C-C

The last survivors of "Baby Crocodiles" 401–415 built in the 1920s to the same configuration as their SBB counterparts. They no longer have any regular work, being retained at Samedan and Landquart as reserve locos and for specials. 402, 406, 407 and 411 are preserved, but none in operating order.

Built: 1929.
Builder–Mechanical Parts: SLM.   **Builder–Electrical Parts:** BBC/MFO.
Traction Motors: 2 single-phase frame-mounted with jackshaft/side rod drive.
One Hour Rating: 794 kW.   **Maximum Tractive Effort:** 172 kN.
Wheel Diameter: 1070 mm.   **Weight:** 66 tonnes.
Length over Couplers: 13.30 m.   **Maximum Speed:** 55 km/h.

414 | 415

▲ RhB Ge 6/6 (a very rare class of metre gauge Bo-Bo-Bos) 701 "Raetia" is seen between Ems Werk and Domat Ems with a works train on 5 September 2013.   **Gordon Wiseman**

CLASS Ge 4/4   Bo-Bo

Mixed traffic locos, extensively refurbished with new cabs. All equipped with regenerative brakes and for push-pull and multiple operation. The last three locos, having filled in usefully on passenger trains in previous years, were downgraded to infrastructure duties in late 2014. 602 returned from static exhibition in 2015 and is back in service.

Built: 1947 (601–604), 1953 (605–610); rebuilt 1986–92.
Builder–Mechanical Parts: SLM.
Builder–Electrical Parts: BBC/MFO.
Traction Motors: 4 single-phase fully suspended with BBC spring drive.
One Hour Rating: 1176 kW.   **Maximum Tractive Effort:** 142 kN.
Wheel Diameter: 1070 mm.   **Weight:** 48 tonnes.
Length over Couplers: 12.10 m.   **Maximum Speed:** 80 km/h.

| 602 | Bernina | 605 | SILVRETTA | 610 | Viamala |
| 603 | Badus | | | | |

CLASS Ge 4/4^{II} Bo-Bo

The standard RhB electric, used throughout the AC system, fitted with thyristor control and DC motors. Resembles a mini version of an SBB Re 4/4^{II}. The name on 615 is in metal.

Built: 1973 (*1984–85).
Builder–Mechanical Parts: SLM.   **Builder–Electrical Parts:** BBC.
Traction Motors: 4 pulsating current fully suspended with BBC spring drive.
One Hour Rating: 1648 kW.   **Maximum Tractive Effort:** 179 kN.
Wheel Diameter: 1070 mm.   **Weight:** 50 tonnes.
Length over Couplers: 12.96 m.   **Maximum Speed:** 90 km/h.

All equipped with regenerative brakes and for push-pull operation.

611	Landquart	619	Samedan	627 *	Reichenau–Tamins
612	Thusis	620	Zernez	628 *	S-chanf
613	Domat/Ems	621 *	Felsberg	629 *	Tiefencastel
614	Schiers	622 *	Arosa	630 *	Trun
615	Klosters	623 *	Bonaduz	631 *	Untervaz
616	Filisur	624 *	Celerina/Schlarigna	632 *	Zizers
617	Ilanz	625 *	Küblis	633 *	Zuoz
618	Bergün/Bravuogn	626 *	Malans		

CLASS Ge 4/4^{III} Bo-Bo

A general purpose locomotive used mainly on Chur–St Moritz RE trains. 650–652 were added to operate car-carrying trains through the Vereina tunnel. Push-pull equipped. All are in advertising liveries.

Built: 1993–94/1997.
Builder-Mechanical Parts: SLM.
Builder-Electrical Parts: ABB.
Traction Motors: Four 3-phase.   **One Hour Rating:** 2500 kW.
Maximum Tractive Effort: 200 kN.   **Wheel Diameter:** 1070 mm.
Weight: 61 tonnes.   **Length over Couplers:** 16.00 m.
Maximum Speed: 100 km/h.

641	Maienfeld	647	Grüsch
642	Breil/Brigels	648	Susch
643	Vals	649	Lavin
644	Savognin	650	Seewis im Prättigau
645	Tujetsch	651	Fideris
646	Sta. Maria/Val Müstair	652	Vaz/Obervaz Lenzerheide-Valbella

CLASS Ge 6/6ᴵᴵ   Bo-Bo-Bo

Articulated locos, mainly used on freight trains between Chur and St. Moritz, but with some passenger work. The two halves of the body are joined by a hinge with its axis horizontal; the centre bogie has some sideplay. 704 has its name in metal letters.

Built: 1958 *, 1965 †.
Builder–Mechanical Parts: SLM.
Builder–Electrical Parts: MFO/BBC.
Traction Motors: Six single-phase fully suspended with BBC spring drive.
One Hour Rating: 1764 kW.   **Maximum Tractive Effort:** 214 kN.
Wheel Diameter: 1070 mm.   **Weight:** 65 tonnes.
Length over Couplers: 14.50 m.   **Maximum Speed:** 80 km/h.

701 *	Raetia		705 †	Pontresina/Puntraschigna
702 *	Curia		706 †	Disentis/Mustér
703 †	St. Moritz		707 †	Scuol
704 †	Davos			

▲ RhB Allegra EMU ABe 4/16 3104 is caught at Bonaduz on 2 October 2013.   **Mario Stefani**

2.36.3. ELECTRO-DIESEL LOCOMOTIVES

CLASS Gem 4/4   Bo-Bo

These electro-diesels operate as electrics on the Berninabahn (1000 V DC) and as diesel elsewhere. Replaced by the new EMUs on the Bernina Express between Samedan and Tirano, they are now mainly used on snowplough duties, and on works trains. The locos are known as "Steinbock" (ibex) and "Murmeltier" (marmot) but carry stylised images rather than names.

Built: 1968.   **Rebuilt:** 2001/03 by RhB.
Builder–Mechanical Parts: SLM.   **Builder–Electrical Parts:** BBC/MFO/SAAS.
Diesel Engines: Two Cummins VT12-825B1 of 463 kW each.
Traction Motors: 4 axle-hung nose-suspended.
One Hour Rating: 680 kW (electric), 926 kW (diesel).
Maximum Tractive Effort: 192 kN.   **Wheel Diameter:** 920 mm.
Weight: 50 tonnes.   **Length over Couplers:** 13.54 m.
Maximum Speed: 65 km/h.

Fitted for multiple operation; can also multiple with ABe 4/4 41–49 and 51–56 under electric traction.

801 | 802

2.36.4. 11 kV AC ELECTRIC RAILCARS

CLASS ABe 4/4   Bo-Bo

Operates with driving trailers BDt 1721–3. Now historic stock, based at Samedan.

Built: 1939; rebuilt by RhB in 1983/84.   **Builder–Mechanical Parts:** SWS.
Builder–Electrical Parts: BBC/MFO.   **One Hour Rating:** 440 kW.
Maximum Tractive Effort: 78 kN.   **Wheel Diameter:** 850 mm.
Weight: 39 tonnes.   **Length over Couplers:** 18.00 m.
Maximum Speed: 70 km/h.   **Accommodation:** 12/28 1T.

501

CLASS Be 4/4   Bo-Bo

Single-ended motor coaches (gangwayed at the non-driving end), used on Klosters–Landquart–Chur–Filisur local services , operating as 2-, 3- or 4-car sets with driving trailers ABDt 1711–16 and intermediate trailers B 2411–20. They have thyristor control, DC motors and electropneumatic brakes.

Built: 1971 (* 1979).   **Builder–Mechanical Parts:** FFA/SIG.
Builder–Electrical Parts: SAAS.   **One Hour Rating:** 776 kW.
Maximum Tractive Effort: 112 kN.   **Wheel Diameter:** 750 mm.
Weight: 44.6 tonnes.   **Length over Couplers:** 18.70 m.
Maximum Speed: 90 km/h.   **Accommodation:** –/40 1T.

511 | 512 | 513 | 514 | 515 * | 516 *

CLASS ABe 4/16   "ALLEGRA"   4-CAR UNITS

These units followed the 3-car dual-voltage versions and are used on the Chur area suburban service running Thusis–Chur–Landquart–Schiers. All Allegra units are named after local personalities.

Built: 2012/13.
One Hour Rating: 1400 kW.
Driving Wheel Diameter: 685 mm.
Wheel Arrangement: Bo-Bo + 2-2 + 2-2 + 2-2.
Length over Couplers: 74.75 m.
Maximum Speed: 100 km/h.
Accommodation: 12/32 (3) + –/56 (4) + –/52 (6) 1TD + 12/24 (3).

Builder: Stadler.
Maximum Tractive Effort: 130 kN.
Weight: 113 tonnes.
Systems: 11 kV 16.7 Hz AC; 1000 V DC.

3101	Meta von Salis	3104	Achilles Schucan
3102	Richard la Nicca	3105	Angelika Kauffmann
3103	Hortensia von Gugelberg		

CLASS ABe 8/12   "ALLEGRA"   3-CAR UNITS

These units have replaced some loco-hauled trains and electric railcars on both the 11 kv AC system and the Berninabahn. The sets are dual-voltage and operate on the Bernina and Arosa lines plus Landquart–Davos. They often haul long rakes of loose coaches and freight wagons. Set 3501 is numbered 35001 + 35601 + 35101 and so on.

Details as ABe 4/16 except:

Built: 2009–11.
One Hour Rating: 2600 kW (AC); 2400 kW (DC).
Weight: 106 tonnes.
Wheel Arrangement: Bo-Bo + 2-2 + Bo-Bo.
Length over Couplers: 49.50 m.
Accommodation: 12/24 (4) + –/36 (8) 1TD + 12/16 (4).

Maximum Tractive Effort: 260 kN.
Systems: 11 kV 16.7 Hz AC; 1000 V DC.

3501	Willem Jan Holsboer	3509	Placidus Specha
3502	Friedrich Hennings	3510	Alberto Giacometti
3503	Carlo Janka	3511	Otto Barblan
3504	Dario Cologna	3512	Jörg Jenatsch
3505	Giovanni Segantini	3513	Simeon Bavier
3506	Anna von Planta	3514	Steivan Brunies
3507	Benedetg Fontana	3515	Alois Carigiet
3508	Richard Coray		

2.36.5. TRACTORS, SNOWPLOUGHS, ETC

As with other Swiss railways, the RhB owns a selection of tractors and snowploughs, plus an assortment of other departmental motive power. 9213 is a self-propelled steam rotary snowplough, still occasionally used at times of severe weather, but also used on specials!

§   16–26 renumbered from, 65–67, 62/3, 57–61, 56 respectively.
+   93 was former Tauern Scheiteltunnel no. DL 2.
*   ex BDe 4/4 38 in 1992.
#   ex ABe 4/4 37 in 2008.
‡   Former ABe 4/4 48 and 49 respectively.

Class	Number	Builder	Max Speed	Tonnes	kW	Built
Tm 2/2	16 §	RACO/SLM	30	9	37	1957
Tm 2/2	20 §	RACO/SLM	30	9	41	1962
Tm 2/2	22 §	RACO/SLM	30	9	41	1965
Tm 2/2	25 §	RACO/SLM	30	9	41	1965
Tm 2/2	26 §	RACO/SLM	30	9	41	1969
Te 2/2	71	SLM/SAAS	30	13	97	1946
Te 2/2	72	SLM/SAAS	30	13	97	1946
Te 2/2	73	SLM/SAAS	30	13	97	1946
Te 2/2	74	SE/GSEG	50	24	216	1969
Te 2/2	75	SE/GSEG	50	24	216	1969

▲ RhB tractors Tm 2/2 83 and Tm 2/2 86 are seen stabled at Bergün on 8 September 2014.
Matthias Müller

▼ Rigibahnen historic railcar BDhe 2/4 no. 7, plus an historic trailer stand at Rigi Staffel on 28 June 2015. **Andrew Thompson**

Ta 1/2	80	WIND	3.9	9.2	6	1980
Tm 2/2	81	RACO/RhB	80	22	336	1987
Tm 2/2	83	RACO/RhB	80	22	336	1987
Tm 2/2	84	RACO/RhB	80	22	336	1987
Tm 2/2	85	RACO/RhB	60	24	336	1990
Tm 2/2	86	RACO/RhB	60	24	336	1990
Tm 2/2	87	RACO/RhB	60	24	336	1990
Tm 2/2	88	RACO/RhB	60	24	336	1990
Tm 2/2	89	RACO/RhB	60	24	336	1990
Tm 2/2	90	RACO/RhB	60	24	336	1994
Tm 2/2	93 +	SCH/DZ	35	21	172	1971
Tm 2/2	95	WIND	60	22	336	1998
Tm 2/2	96	WIND	60	22	336	1998
Tm 2/2	97	WIND	60	22	336	1998
Tm 2/2	98	WIND	60	22	336	1998
Tmf 2/2	111	SCH	16/50	24	317	2001
Tmf 2/2	112	SCH	16/50	24	317	2001
Tmf 2/2	113	SCH	16/50	24	317	2001
Tmf 2/2	114	SCH	16/50	24	317	2001
Tmf 2/2	115	SCH	16/50	24	317	2006
Tmf 2/2	116	SCH	16/50	24	317	2006
Tmf 2/2	117	SCH	16/50	24	317	2006
Tmf 2/2	118	SCH	16/50	24	317	2006
Tmf 2/2	119	SCH	16/50	24	317	2006
Tmf 2/2	120	SCH	16/50	24	317	2006
Xm 2/2	9912	RACO/SAU	30	10	41	1962
Xm 2/2	9915	PFING/SAU/MFO	55	20	112	1958
Xm 2/2	9916	RACO/NEN/DZ	40	13	100	1963
Xm 2/2	9917	STAD/RhB/DZ	55	27	224	1974
Xm 4/4	9918	WIND/CUMM	90		485	1994
Xm 4/4	9919	WIND/CUMM	90		485	1994
Xe 4/4	9920	SIG/Alioth	45	31	298	1908
Xmf 2/2	9921	RACO	50	25	283	1994
Xe 4/4	9922 *	SIG/SAAS	55	55	426	1911
Xe 4/4	9924 #	SIG/SAAS/MFO	55	55	429	1911
Xe 4/4	232 01 ‡	SWS/BBC/SAAS	65	43	680	1972
Xe 4/4	272 01 ‡	SWS/BBC/SAAS	65	43	680	1972

2.37. RIGIBAHNEN (602, 603)　　　　　　　RB

The RB was formed in 1992 by the merger of the Arth Rigi Bahn (ARB) and Vitznau Rigi Bahn (VRB). The VRB was the very first Swiss mountain rack line, pioneering the Riggenbach system, opened in 1871. It connects with the steamers on the Vierwaldstättersee (Lake Lucerne) at Vitznau, while the former ARB connects with the Gotthard main line at Arth Goldau. The two lines run side by side at the summit of the Rigi. Both lines are pure rack. Since the merger, the two lines have retained their separate liveries of red for the VRB and blue for the ARB. Numbers did not change with the merger. Readers should be warned that three items of stock carry number 1 and most numbers here are duplicated by non-powered historic stock. The RB also has two steam locos – vertical boilered no. 7 (SLM works number 1, 1873, now in the Verkehrshaus) plus VRB 16 and 17 built in 1923 and 1925. No. 17 was used for works trains in 2014! 11–15 are usually used on the ARB and are paired with driving trailers 21–25 in order. 1–5 plus 21 and 22 (plus trailers 31 and 32) are used on the VRB. It is possible to sit next to the driver on most units. The VRB still carries milk churns on a small wagon.

Gauge: 1435 mm.
Electrical System: 1500 V DC.
Rack System: Riggenbach.
Routes:
• Arth-Goldau–Rigi Kulm (8.6 km).
• Rigi Kulm–Vitznau (6.9 km).
Depots: Arth Goldau, Vitznau, Rigi Kulm.

† ex VRB
§ Number duplicated.
* ex ARB.
a Battery shunter used at Vitznau, built from parts of SBB Tm 540 (new 1949).
h Historic car.

Class	No.	Builder	Seats	km/h	tonnes	kW	Built
Ta 2/2	1 †§ a	RACO/STAD/MFO/BBC	-	8	7.5	7	1982
Xm	1 †§	RACO	-		17		1974
Bhe 2/4	1 †§	SLM/BBC	64 (4)	18	18.7	335	1937
Bhe 2/4	2 †	SLM/BBC	64 (4)	18	18.7	335	1937
Bhe 2/4	3 †	SLM/BBC	64 (4)	18	18.7	335	1937
Bhe 2/4	4 †	SLM/BBC	64 (4)	18	18.7	335	1953
Bhe 4/4	5 †	SLM/SIG/BBC	62	30	36.3	870	1965
Cfhe 2/3	6 * h	SLM/SWS/MFO	60	15	23.5	395	1911 (39)
BDhe 2/4	7 * h	SLM/SIG/MFO	60	15	25.5	455	1925 (39)
He 2/3	8 *	SLM/MFO	-	15	33.6	455	1930 (39)
BDhe 2/4	11 *	SLM/SAAS	60 (2)	21	29	485	1949
BDhe 2/4	12 *	SLM/SAAS	60 (2)	21	27.3	485	1949
BDhe 2/4	13 *	SLM/SAAS	60 (2)	21	26.5	485	1954
BDhe 2/4	14 *	SLM/SAAS	60 (2)	21	26.5	485	1967
BDhe 4/4	15 *	SLM/BBC	60 (2)	18.6	30.3	835	1982
He 2/2	18 †	SLM/BBC	-	18	14.9	335	1938
Bhe 4/4	21 †	SLM/BBC	74	30	30.5	824	1986
Bhe 4/4	22 †	SLM/BBC	74	30	30.5	824	1986

2.38. SCHEUCHZER   SCHEU

This is a track maintenance contractor, with a depot at Bussigny, near Lausanne, with a small number of interesting locos, all with names of animals. Livery, for some locos, is blue with white cabs – very similar to Alpha Trains.

2.39. SERSA & SERFAHR   SERSA

This is a big company with several sites in Switzerland, the main ones being Rumlang and Weinfelden, which mainly carries out track maintenance but ran its first test open access freight train in summer 2008. Its fleet includes several main line locos, including former DB V100s, five Vossloh G1700s (843 151 to 155) and several hired Vossloh G1206s.

In December 2014, the leasing company Serfahr was set up, and took over Tm 237 916 and 917 (ex PTT).

2.40. SIHLTAL ZÜRICH UETLIBERG (712, 713) SZU

Two lines whose management merged in 1973. The Sihltalbahn, which follows the river Sihl, provides a suburban service from Zürich to Langnau-Gattikon, with some trains continuing to Sihlwald (the line beyond to Sihlbrugg is no longer served) and is electrified on the same system as SBB. The shed at Sihlwald is now only used to house a steam loco and stock is stabled at Langnau-Gattikon.

The Uetlibergbahn is the steepest standard gauge line in Europe, climbing the hills above Zürich to a terminus at Uetliberg (814 m above sea level) and is electrified at 1200 V DC. To enable trains from both lines to use the common section from Zürich HB to Giesshübel, the DC wires are offset, resulting in the tracks on this section having two sets of overhead wires, and giving the DC stock an odd appearance with off-centre pantographs. From May 1990, both lines were extended from the inconveniently-located Selnau terminus to a new underground terminus at the Hauptbahnhof using platforms built for the never constructed U-Bahn. Traffic quickly quadrupled!

SZU took over two SBB Class 450 locos plus their double-deck trailers in 2008.

All trains carry their short numbers (without the class prefix) prominently, the longer numbers being less conspicuous. Trains on the Sihltalbahn are Class 450 sets or powered by Class 456 locos with a mix of double-deck trailers and single-deck driving trailers. Uetlibergbahn power cars 521–528 are used in pairs – 521 + 522 and so on, with a trailer between. 531 and 532 are 2-car sets used in the peaks only. The new 511 to 516 are 3-car sets. SZU also has shunters 233 911 and 238 507 plus Robel track trolley 236 508.

Gauge: 1435 mm.
Electrical Systems: Sihltalbahn 15 kV 16.7 Hz AC; Uetlibergbahn 1200 V DC.
Routes:
• Zürich HB–Uetliberg (9.1 km), Maximum Gradient 7.9%.
• Zürich HB–Sihlbrugg (17.4 km).
Depot: Giesshübel.

2.41. STAUFFER   JUST

This is a quite large company in Frauenfeld maintaining, overhauling and dealing in locomotives then hiring or selling them. While Stauffer locos may be found in any siding in Switzerland, locos listed in this book may be sold on, including to other countries.

2.42. SÜDOSTBAHN (670, 671, 672, 853, 870) SOB

This railway was formed in 2002 from the merger of the Bodensee Toggenburg (BT) and the Schweizerische Südost Bahn (SOB). The old BT formed the eastern section of the Romanshorn–Luzern route from Romanshorn to Wattwil. A joint SOB/THURBO Wil–Wattwil–Nesslau service also operates. The former SOB line runs from Rapperswil to Arth Goldau on the Gotthard line, providing the middle section of the Romanshorn–Luzern route. There are also branches to Einsiedeln and Wädenswil.

SOB's main service is the "Voralpen Express" (VAE) over the 147 km route from St Gallen to Luzern. This is worked by Class 446 or 456 locos or Class 561 power cars at each end.

SOB owns four Class Re 446 and six Class Re 456 electric locos, 23 Class 526 FLIRT EMUs plus five Class 561 (four former SOB Class 566 and one ex SBB, ex MThB) and six Class 566 power cars, plus a number of shunters. Sadly most names have been removed from locos and older EMUs.

SOB plans to buy 50 new EMUs – six 150 metre-long for the VAE, plus 14 options, five 75 metre-long for the VAE and S-Bahn plus 15 options, and six 100–120 metre-long for regional services, plus four options.

Routes:
• Romanshorn–St. Gallen–Wattwil (53.2 km).
• Ebnat-Kappel–Nesslau-Neu St. Johann (7.9 km).
• Rapperswil–Pfäffikon SZ–Samstagern–Biberbrugg–Arth-Goldau (38.6 km).
• Wädenswil–Samstagern (5.4 km).
• Biberbrugg–Einsiedeln (5.2 km).
Electrical System: 15 kV AC 16.7 Hz.
Depots: Herisau (ex BT), Samstagern (ex SOB).

2.43. SWISS RAIL TRAFFIC   SRT

This company, based in Glattbrugg, started operations on 1 May 2008 with a freight service between Basel and a paper plant at Biberist, near Solothurn. Initially the company hired traction but it now has its own – in particular a Class 487 TRAXX electric loco and three Class Bm 840.4 diesels. The company is allied to Rail-event, Bahn-Support and Bermane Logistics & Rail.

2.44. THURBO

THURBO was originally set up as a joint subsidiary of SBB, Mittel Thurgau Bahn (MThB) and the Thurgau canton for the operation of regional services in north-eastern Switzerland from December 2002. MThB then went bankrupt so the company is now basically a subsidiary of SBB, Thurgau canton owning just 10%. All services are operated by Stadler Class 526.6 and 526.7 2- or 3-car EMUs of the GTW type. Livery is white with doors of various colours and coloured blobs along the roof line. THURBO now operates virtually all local stopping services on the SBB network across north-east Switzerland – from the edge of the Zürich conurbation. Additional units have been received for new services, particularly for the St Gallen and Schaffhausen S-Bahn networks.

Depot: Weinfelden, but some work carried out at SBB's Oberwinterthur depot.

2.45. TRANSPORTS DE MARTIGNY ET RÉGIONS (RegionAlps) TMR

TMR is a body organising transport in a large area around Martigny. Its fleet includes SBB Class 560.4 EMUs plus the former MC and MO.

2.45.1. FORMER MARTIGNY–CHÂTELARD (132) MC

This rack and adhesion line possesses a number of unusual features. From Martigny to Vernayez overhead current collection is used, but the remainder of the line to Châtelard, which includes the rack sections, has third rail. The third rail is being gradually converted to overhead. At Châtelard, the MC links with the metre gauge SNCF line from St. Gervais, which uses a similar third rail system. The MC and the SNCF have purchased five EMUs to enable a joint through service to be operated. SNCF sets are numbered Z 801+802 to Z 805+806. The MC units 21 and 22 are Z 821+822 and 823+824. They are maintained jointly with SNCF. These work through services to France whilst other units work Swiss-only trains. Xemh 4/4 4 and 6 were converted from passenger units for use on works trains, both on the TMR line in Switzerland and on the SNCF extension in France. Services are marketed as "Mont Blanc Express".

Gauge: 1000 mm.
Electrical System: 800 V DC overhead and third rail.
Rack System: Riggenbach. Maximum Gradient 20%.
Route: Martigny–Le Châtelard (18.1 km).
Depots: Vernayaz, Finhaut, Le Châtelard.

† ex VBZ 1906 in 1974.
* Can be fitted with rotary snowplough.

Class	No.	Builder	Seats	km/h	tonnes	kW	Built
Xemh 4/4	4 "Bobby II"	SWP/SAAS	-	50/25	40	560	1957
BDeh 4/4	5	SWP/SAAS	52	50/25	40	560	1957
Xemh 4/4	6 "Bobby I"	SWP/SAAS	-	50/25	40	560	1957
BDeh 4/4	7	SWP/SAAS	52	50/25	40	560	1964
BDeh 4/4	8	SWP/SAAS	52	50/25	40	560	1964
BDeh 4/8	21	ACMV/SLM/AD	48+48	70/16	72	1000	1997
BDeh 4/8	22	ACMV/SLM/AD	48+48	70/16	72	1000	1997
Te 2/2	91 †	SWS/MFO/MC	-	40	16.6	108	1962(81)
Tmx 2/2	204 *	BEIL	-	50	16	149	1982
BDeh 4/4	501	SWP/SLM/BBC	44	65/24	41.1	716	1979

▲ TMR set 21 is seen at Martigny station with preserved former Martigny-Châtelard unit 32 with a charter train on 26 October 2013. **Christophe Masse**

▼ Former ASD EMU BDe 4/4 402, in the new TPC livery, is seen leaving Aigle on 16 March 2015. **Mario Stefani**

2.45.2. FORMER MARTIGNY ORSIÈRES (133)   MO

A standard gauge line serving an area to the south of the Rhône Valley. Buses connect at Orsières for the Grand St. Bernard Pass, of large rescue dog fame. Services were formerly marketed as "Saint Bernard Express". The NINA Class 527 3-car EMUs operate some services on the SBB main line. Most details for these are the same as BLS Class 525.

Gauge: 1435 mm.
Electrical System: 15 kV AC 16.7 Hz.
Routes:
* Martigny–Sembrancher–Orsières 19.3 km.
* Sembrancher–Le Chable (6.2 km). Maximum Gradient 3.7%.
Depot: Orsières.

2.46. TRANSPORTS PUBLICS DU CHABLAIS TPC

TPC has ordered three HGem 2/2 electro-diesel rack/adhesion locos from Stadler for track work.

2.46.1. AIGLE–LEYSIN (125)   AL

This line has street running in Aigle and then, after reversal, climbs steeply from Leysin dépôt with rack assistance. 101 was renumbered 1101 to avoid duplication with the AOMC unit 101. A 750 metre extension from Leysin to La Berneuse is under study.

Gauge: 1000 mm.
Rack System: Abt. Maximum Gradient 23%.

Electrical System: 1500 V DC.
Route: Aigle–Leysin Grand Hotel (6.2 km).

* To be restored as a monument.
+ Dining car, ex BDeh 201.
§ Formerly numbered 303–305.

Class	No.	Name	Builder	Seats	km/h	tonnes	kW	Built
He 2/2	12 (U) *		SLM/MFO/SIG	-	7.5	20.3	264	1915
ARseh 2/4	201 (U) +		SLM/BBC/AL	32	25/15	24.5	250	1946
BDeh 4/4	301		SIG/SAAS	48	40/24	33	596	1966
BDeh 4/4	302		SIG/SAAS	48	40/24	33	596	1966
BDeh 4/4	311 §	YVORNE	ACMV/SLM/BBC	32	40/25	36	836	1987
BDeh 4/4	312 §	OLLON	ACMV/SLM/BBC	32	40/25	36	836	1987
BDeh 4/4	313 §	LA BERNEUSE	ACMV/SLM/ABB	32	40/25	36	836	1993
Te 2/2	1101		ACMV/BBC/AL	-	20	11.5	82	1949

2.46.2. AIGLE–OLLON–MONTHEY–CHAMPÉRY (126) AOMC

The AOMC was formed by the merger of the Aigle–Ollon–Monthey and Monthey–Champéry–Morgins in 1946. Only the line to Champéry has rack sections so the former BLT railcars only work Aigle–Monthey shuttles. 501–503, 511–514 were previously 1–3 and 11–14.

The line is to be re-electrified at 1500 V DC and the rack system will be rebuilt as Abt, to allow interworking with the other lines as necessary. A new alignment will be built in Monthey to reduce journey times. Stadler will supply seven new 2-car EMUs which will replace all stock except 591/592 which will be converted. All except one old unit will be scrapped. 103 and 105 were converted in 2014 into "rolling art exhibitions".

Gauge: 1000 mm.
Electrical System: 850 V DC.
Rack System: Strub. Maximum Gradient 13%.
Routes:
* Aigle–Monthey Ville (11.2 km).
* Monthey Ville–Champéry (13.0 km).

* ex BLT (Birsigtalbahn) 14, 12, 13, 11 respectively in 1985/86.

Class	No.	Name	Builder	Seats	km/h	tonnes	kW	Built
Be 4/4	101 *	YVORNE	SWP/BBC	44	65	27	382	1966
Be 4/4	102 *	CHABLAIS	SWP/BBC	44	65	27	382	1966
Be 4/4	103 *	COLLOMBEY-MURAZ	SWP/BBC	44	65	27	382	1966
Be 4/4	105 *	AIGLE	SWP/BBC	44	65	27	382	1966
BDeh 4/4	501	VAUD	ACMV/SLM/BBC	32 (6)	65/30	40	656	1987
BDeh 4/4	502	VALAIS	ACMV/SLM/BBC	32 (6)	65/30	40	656	1987
BDeh 4/4	503	EUROPE	ACMV/SLM/ABB	32 (6)	65/30	40	656	1992
Xeh 4/4	512	VAL D'ILLIEZ	SWP/BBC	40	50/18	30.4	368	1954
BDeh 4/4	513	MONTHEY	SWP/BBC	40	50/18	30.4	368	1954
BDeh 4/4	514	TROISTORRENTS	SWP/BBC	40	50/18	30.4	368	1954
Beh 4/8	591		STAD/BOMB	48+48	70/30	53	1000	2001
Beh 4/8	592	Portes du Soleil	STAD/BOMB	48+48	70/30	53	1000	2001

2.46.3. AIGLE–SÉPEY–DIABLERETS (124)   ASD

The least used of the four lines in the group, serving a sparsely populated area.

Gauge: 1000 mm.
Electrical System: 1500 V DC.
Routes:
• Aigle–Les Planches–Le Sépey (13.8 km).
• Les Planches–Les Diablerets 8.5 km). Maximum Gradient 6%.
Depot: Les Diablerets.

h   Historic car.

Class	No.	Name	Builder	Seats	km/h	tonnes	kW	Built
BDe 4/4	1 h		SWS/BBC	8/32	50	25	240	1913
BDe 4/4	2 h		SWS/BBC	8/32	50	25	240	1913
BDe 4/4	401	ORM ONTS-DESSOUS	ACMV/SIG/SLM/BBC	32	65	32.5	820	1987
BDe 4/4	402	ORMONTS-DESSUS	ACMV/SIG/SLM/BBC	32	65	32.5	820	1987
BDe 4/4	403	OLLON	ACMV/SIG/SLM/BBC	32	65	32.5	820	1987
BDe 4/4	404	AIGLE	ACMV/SIG/SLM/BBC	32	65	32.5	820	1987

2.46.4. BEX–VILLARS–BRETAYE (127, 128)   BVB

This rack and adhesion line is run in two sections, Bex–Villars and Villars–Bretaye. The upper section is very heavily used by skiers in winter and operates up to quarter-hourly but in the low season is only three returns per day. The local "tram" service from Bex to Bévieux has been cut to one return per day with railcar 16 whilst 15 operates a couple of Villars–Gryon runs.

Gauge: 1000 mm.
Electrical System: 700 V DC.
Rack System: Abt. Maximum Gradient 20%.
Route: Bex–Villars-sur-Ollon (12.4 km), Villars-sur-Ollon–Col-de-Bretaye (4.7 km).
Depots: Bévieux, Villars.

*   ex VBZ 1225 in 1958.
h   Historic car.

Class	No.	Name	Builder	Seats	km/h	tonnes	kW	Built
Be 2/2	9* h		SWS/MFO	20	37	15	108	1915
Be 2/3	15		SWS/SLM/MFO	28	40	15	96	1948
Be 2/3	16		SWS/SLM/MFO	28	40	15	96	1948
BDeh 2/4	22		SLM/MFO	53	35/18	19	96	1940
BDeh 2/4	23		SLM/MFO	53	35/18	19	96	1941
BDeh 2/4	24		SLM/MFO	53	35/18	19	96	1941

Bdeh 2/4	25		SLM/MFO	53	35/18	19	96	1944
Bdeh 2/4	26		SLM/MFO	53	35/18	19	96	1945
Hge 4/4	31	LAVEY-MORCLES	SIG/MFO	-	35	24.4	368	1953
Hge 4/4	32	VILLARS	SIG/MFO	-	35	24.4	368	1964
Te 2/2	42		SIG/BVB/ACEC/MFO	-	35	8.5	108	1898
Bdeh 4/4	81	GRYON	SLM/SWP/SAAS	24	40/16	36.5	720	1977
Bdeh 4/4	82	OLLON	SLM/SWP/SAAS	24	40/16	36.5	720	1977
Bdeh 4/4	83	BEX	ACMV/SLM/BBC	24	40/25	36.1	720	1988
Beh 4/8	91	Bretaye	STAD/BOMB	40+40	45/30	54	1000	2000
Beh 4/8	92	LA BARBOLEUSE	STAD/BOMB	40+40	45/30	54	1000	2001
Beh 4/8	93	TUTTLINGEN	STAD/BOMB	40+40	45/30	54	1000	2001
Xrote	913		Rolba/Oehler/BVB/MFO	-		5.5	60	1952
Xrotm	920		Rolba/FFA	-		16.5	220	1971

2.47. TRANSPORTS PUBLICS FRIBOURGEOIS TPF

This system was formerly known as the Gruyère–Fribourg–Morat (GFM). There are two separate standard gauge branches, Fribourg–Murten–Ins and Bulle–Romont, plus an extensive metre gauge system centred on Bulle. The metre gauge connects with the SBB at Palézieux and with the MOB at Montbovon. The Bulle–Romont service has been boosted significantly, with an hourly Bulle–Fribourg operated by eight new Class 527 FLIRT EMUs, and an hourly Bulle–Fribourg–Bern, operated by SBB. The metre gauge branch to Broc serves the Cailler (Nestlé) chocolate factory and generates significant freight traffic with standard gauge wagons carried on skates. This line is to be converted to standard gauge and re-electrified by 2021 for this reason. TPF received six new 3-car metre gauge EMUs in 2015/16 and has ordered one Gem 2/2 electro-diesel loco from Stadler for track work. 141, 142, 151 and 152 are to be withdrawn. A new standard gauge depot will be built in Givisiez, near Fribourg, by 2019, and will be shared with BLS.

Gauges: 1435 mm, 1000 mm.
Electrical System: 15 kV AC 16.7 Hz (1435 mm), 900 V DC (1000 mm).
Routes:
Standard gauge:
• Fribourg–Ins (32.2 km).
• Bulle–Romont (18.2 km).

Metre gauge:
• Palézieux–Châtel St. Denis–Bulle–Montbovon (43.5 km).
• Bulle–Broc Fabrique (5.4 km). Maximum Gradient 3.2%.

Depots: Bulle, Fribourg (1435 mm); Châtel St. Denis, Montbovon (1000 mm).
Works: Planchy (both gauges).

*   Set 101 is formed of ABe 2/4 101.1 + B 101.3 + Be 2/4 101.2, and so on.
b   Ex Tavern Scheiteltunnel (900 mm gauge) No. DL6 in 1980.
h   Historic car.

Metre Gauge Stock:

Class	No.	Name	Builder	Seats	Km/h	tonnes	kW	Built
Te 2/2	11		MFO	-	30	16.5	88	1912
Te 2/2	12		CEG/ALIOTH	-	50	9	774	1913
Te 4/4	13		CEG/ALIOTH	-	30	25	148	1901 (27)
Te 4/4	14		CEG/ALIOTH	-	50	21.5	264	1901 (33)
Tm 2/2	15 b		SCHÖMA/DZ	-	35	24	168	1971
Tef 2/2	16		CFD/TPF	-	40	20	160	1986
Tmf 2/2	17		SCHÖMA	-	65	28	330	2011
ABe 4/12	101 *		Stadler	15/133(14)	100		1020	2015
ABe 4/12	102 *		Stadler	15/133(14)	100		1020	2015
ABe 4/12	103 *		Stadler	15/133(14)	100		1020	2015
ABe 4/12	104 *		Stadler	15/133(14)	100		1020	2015
ABe 4/12	105 *		Stadler	15/133(14)	100		1020	2015
ABe 4/12	106 *		Stadler	15/133(14)	100		1020	2015
Be 4/4	115 h		SWS/ALIOTH	44	60	29.5	296	1905 (59)
Be 4/4	116 h		SWS/MFO	58	75	35	486	1922
BDe 4/4	121	REMAUFENS	ACMV/ABB	32	90	36	640	1992
BDe 4/4	122	LA TOUR DE TRÊME	ACMV/ABB	32	90	36	640	1992
BDe 4/4	123	BROC	ACMV/ABB	32	90	36	640	1995
BDe 4/4	124	VUADENS	ACMV/ABB	32	90	36	640	1995

Be 4/4	131 h		SWS/BBC	48		75	33	408	1943
Bde 4/4	141	GRUYERES	SWP/SAAS	40 1T		70	38	648	1972
Bde 4/4	142	SEMSALES	SWP/SAAS	40 1T		70	38	648	1972
Be 4/4	151	LA GRUYÈRE	SIG/SAAS	48			80	32	448	1977
Be 4/4	152	CHÂTEL-ST.-DENIS	SIG/SAAS	48			80	32	448	1977

Standard Gauge Stock (also see main section):

TPF also has one Class 234 and one Class 837 shunter, plus eight Class 527 FLIRT and five Class 567 EMUs.

§   Moyse Type BN24HA150 works no. 1416, delivered new to CFD Montmirail.
*   Ex MThB RABDe 11 (536 611) in 2006. RABDe 12 (536 612) is now preserved.

Class	No.	Builder	km/h	tonnes	kW	Built
Tm 2/2	Tm 82	RACO/VR/MB	45	33	236	1964
Tm 2/2	Tm 85 §	Moyse	22	24	110	1977
Xe	537 161	SIG/BBC	100	56	736	1946
Xe	537 176 *	SIG/SWS/SAAS	100	64	1076	1965

2.48. TRANSPORTS PUBLICS NEUCHÂTELOIS
transN

transN was formed from the merger of Transports Régionaux Neuchâtelois (TRN) and the Neuchâtel tramway (see section 7).

2.48.1. CHEMINS DE FER DES MONTAGNES NEUCHÂTELOISES (214, 222)   CMN

This railway comprises two completely separate lines. The Italian built cars are unusual for Switzerland although they look very similar to domestic stock of the time. The chassis of railcar no. 1 now supports a very modern saloon car. All stock is used on the Ponts de Martel line (2 and 4 for works trains) except 3 and 5 on the Brenets line. Les Brenets is a backwater on the river Doubs, which forms the Swiss/French border, and is near the Saut-du-Doubs waterfall.

Gauge: 1000 mm.   **Electrical System:** 1500 V DC.
Routes:
• La Chaux-de-Fonds–Les Ponts-de-Martel (16.2 km). Maximum Gradient 4%.
• Le Locle–Les Brenets (4.1 km).
Depots: Les Brenets, Les Ponts-de-Martel.

Class	No.	Name	Builder	Seats	km/h	tonnes	kW	Built
Bde 4/4	2		REG/BBC/SAAS	44	60	23.5	244	1950
Bde 4/4	3	Edmée	REG/BBC/SAAS	41	60	23.5	244	1950
Bde 4/4	4		REG/BBC/SAAS	44	60	23.5	244	1950
Bde 4/4	5	Sophie	REG/BBC/SAAS	42	60	23.5	244	1950
Bde 4/4	6	La Chaux-de-Fonds	ACMV/ABB	48 (6)	80	35.5	752	1991
Bde 4/4	7	Les Ponts-du-Martel	ACMV/ABB	48 (6)	80	35.5	752	1991
Bde 4/4	8	La Sagne	ACMV/ABB	48 (6)	80	35.5	752	1996
Tm 2/2	11		RACO/DZ	-	75	19	177	1983

▲ Brand new TPF Stadler EMU ABe 4/12 103 crosses one of the units it is replacing, Be 4/4 152, at Vaulruz Sud on 28 January 2016. **Charles-André Fluckiger**

▼ On the rarely photographed line from Le Locle to Les Brenets, BDe 4/4 no. 3 stables the snowplough at Les Brenets after clearing the line on 9 February 2015. **Mario Stefani**

2.48.2 RÉGIONAL DE VAL DE TRAVERS (221) RVT

A secondary line in the west of the country, through services running over the SBB to Neuchâtel. The Fleurier to St. Sulpice branch is freight only, but sees occasional use for steam specials. The former RVT mainly uses 4-car FLIRT EMUs 527 331, 332 and 333 on services to Neuchâtel. In December 2015 transN started to operate an improved Neuchâtel–Le Locle service and is to receive three more FLIRTs in 2016. 567 315 has been sold to Travys (PBr line). The Val de Travers name is known in Britain thanks to the past production of asphalt in this region. RVT's historic stock is preserved by RVT Historique.

Gauge: 1435 mm.
Routes:
• Travers–Fleurier–Buttes (12.0 km).
• Fleurier–St. Sulpice (1.6 km).
Depot: Fleurier.

Electrical System: 15 kV AC 16.7 Hz.

No.	Old no.	Builder	Seats	km/h	tonnes	kW	Built
Be 417 301	Be 4/4 1	ACMV/SAAS	-	75	45	690	1952

2.49. TRAVYS

Travys stands for Transports Vallée du Joux Yverdon-les-Bains Sainte Croix, which covers two of the three constituents, the third being the Orbe Chavornay. These are three short, separate and heterogeneous lines (two standard, one metre gauge) in the west of Switzerland, near the French border.

2.49.1. CHEMIN DE FER PONT BRASSUS (201) PBr

A somewhat remote 13.3 km line in the west of the country, the PBr was for many years operated by the SBB and its predecessors. The PBr never owned any motive power until a tractor was purchased from SBB in 1982. Services have always run through to Vallorbe, but from 1989 these were extended to Lausanne using EMUs 2184–5, numbered in the SBB list and operated by them, but financed by the local canton and lettered for the PBr (Vallée de Joux) – these were numbered into PBr stock in 1996. These are now 560 384 and 385 (formerly 568 384/5) and no longer work to Lausanne. PBr also has EMU 567 174 for schools services, Re 420 503 for freight (mostly generated at Sentier Orient) plus a few shunters: see standard gauge section.

Gauge: 1435 mm.
Route: Le Pont–Le Brassus (13.0 km).

Electrical System: 15 kV AC 16.7 Hz.
Depot: Le Brassus.

2.49.2. ORBE CHAVORNAY (211) OC

A 4 km branch line north of Lausanne which is the only Swiss private standard gauge adhesion line with DC electrification. As a consequence, it has been used for testing stock built for export. Passenger trains are operated by unit 14 at weekends and in holidays and by 15 plus driving trailer 51 in the school term. The line generates significant freight around Les Granges and Chavornay including daily vans of Nespresso coffee to Payerne. The OC also has a Class 238 shunter, three Class 830 and one Class 837: see standard gauge section.

Gauge: 1435 mm.
Route: Chavornay–Orbe (3.9 km).

Electrical System: 750 V DC.
Depots: Orbe, Les Granges.

* Ex SZU BDe 4/4 513. Accompanies driving trailer Bt 51.

Class	New Number	Old No.	Name	Builder	Seats	km/h	tonnes	kW	Built
Ee 2/2	927 601	1		SIG/MFO	-	50	40	455	1970
Ee 2/2	927 602	2		SIG/MFO	-	50	40	455	1970
Be 2/2	-	14	Orbe/Chavornay	STAD/ABB	40	80	20.2	360	1990
BDe 4/4	-	15 *	La Sihl/L'Orbe	SWS/MFO	46	60	28.3	330	1960
Fe 2/2	-	32		SWS/MFO	-	45	15.4	106	1902

2.49.3. YVERDON–STE. CROIX (212)   YSteC

A light railway running from the SBB station at Yverdon into the mountains near the French border. The two Stadler units work most services. Ge 4/4 21 is a centre-cab "crocodile" and has a double-headed "croc" painted on its sides. The YSteC received three 3-car EMUs from Stadler in 2015/16. The Be 4/4 units will be retained for freight.

Gauge: 1000 mm.
Electrical system: 15 kV AC 16.7 Hz.
Route: Yverdon-les-Bains–Sainte Croix (24.2 km). Maximum Gradient 4.4%.
Depots: Yverdon, Ste. Croix.

h   Historic railcar.
§   Former YSteC no. 3.
*   Sets are Be 4/4 3001 + AB 3031 + Be 4/4 3002 etc.

Class	No.	Builder	Seats	km/h	tonnes	kW	Built
Be 4/4ᴵᴵ	1	ACMV/HESS/BBC	40 (4)	75	45	780	1981
Be 4/4ᴵᴵ	2	ACMV/HESS/BBC	40 (4)	75	45	780	1981
Be 4/4ᴵ	5 h	SIG/BBC	46	65	39	440	1945
Be 4/4	15 §	ACMV/HESS/BBC	40 (5)	75	44.5	780	1981
Ge 4/4	21	SIG/YStC/BBC	-	55	41	700	1950
Tm 2/2	22	Schöma	-	55	6.5	78	1971
Tm 2/2	23	Schöma	-	50	21	300	1988
Be 2/6	2000	Stadler	88 (9)	80	46.5	640	2001
Be 2/6	2001	Stadler	88 (9)	80	46.5	640	2001
ABe 8/12	3001+3031+3002 *	Stadler					2015
ABe 8/12	3003+3032+3004 *	Stadler					2016
ABe 8/12	3005+3033+3006 *	Stadler					2016

Names:

1	YVERDON-LES-BAINS		2000	L'ARNON
2	BAULMES		2001	La Thiéle

▲ Travys (formerly YSteC) railcar Be 4/4 2 leaves Essert-sous-Champvent for Yverdon with three standard gauge wagons loaded with sugar beet, on metre gauge chassis, on 9 October 2014. A year later this unit ran away, derailed and is now out of action.   **David Haydock**

2.50. VANOLI CVI

Another track maintenance company, based in Zofingen but with another site at Samstagern. The company had three shunters and three bigger locos (847 853, 855 and 960) in 2015.

2.51. WALDENBURGERBAHN (502) WB

Unique for Switzerland in being 750 mm gauge, the WB is a mainly roadside light railway with some street running, connecting with the SBB Basel–Olten line at Liestal. Power cars operate with driving trailers Bt 111–120: 11 + 111, and so on. The company runs steam heritage trains, one Sunday a month May to September, with G3/3 0-6-0T no. 5 "G. THOMMEN". The line is now to be converted to metre gauge by 2023, which means that steam workings will finish. BLT now manages the line.

Gauge: 750 mm.
Electrical System: 1500 V DC.
Route: Liestal–Waldenburg (13.1 km).
Depot: Waldenburg.

Class	No.	Name	Builder	Seats	km/h	tonnes	kW	Built
BDe 4/4	11	Niederdorf	SWP/SIG/BBC	33	75	24	446	1985
BDe 4/4	12	Oberdorf	SWP/SIG/BBC	33	75	24	446	1986
BDe 4/4	13	Hölstein	SWP/SIG/BBC	33	75	24	446	1986
BDe 4/4	14	Ramlinsburg	SWP/SIG/BBC	33	75	24	446	1986
BDe 4/4	15	Bubendorf	SWP/SIG/ABB	33	75	24	446	1993
BDe 4/4	16	Liestal	SWP/SIG/ABB	33	75	24	446	1993
BDe 4/4	17	Waldenburg	SWP/SIG/ABB	33	75	24	446	1993

2.52. WIDMER RAIL SERVICES WRS

An emerging company based at Glarus, but with most locos at Sursee. The initial fleet consisted of two former East German V100 diesels acquired from Connex in Germany (Am 847 905/6) plus a couple of shunters. The company then bought nine ÖBB Class 1042 electric locos and gained approval for three of them in late 2014. They will be used to move track maintenance trains around but are available for other work, including passenger trains. Their first operation was with trains of cereals from Basel in May 2015.

2.53. ZENTRALBAHN ZB

In 2005 the Interlaken–Luzern Brünig line, operated by SBB (which holds 66% of shares in ZB), merged with the LSE, which already used the Hergiswil–Luzern section of the Brünig line. Both have the Riggenbach rack system and 15 kV AC electrification. Through trains on the Brünig line are operated by new Class 150 EMUs, while Class HGe 101 locos now mainly work Engelberg trains. Most "lowland" stopping services are now worked by Class 130 and 160 EMUs.

The LSE was once an isolated three-phase electrified line connecting the lake steamers at Stansstad with the towns of Stans and Engelberg. The line was modernised and upgraded in the 1960s. A link was built from Stansstad to join the SBB Brünig line at Hergiswil. At the same time, the electrical system was changed to 15 kV AC. A tunnel to avoid rack operation on the Engelberg line opened December 2010.

Electrical System: 15 kV AC 16.7 Hz.
Rack system: Riggenbach.
Routes:
• Luzern SBB–Hergiswil–Meiringen–Interlaken Ost (74.0 km), Maximum Gradient 12.1%.
• Hergiswil–Engelberg (24.8 km), Maximum Gradient 24.6%.
Depots: Ex SBB: Meiringen; ex LSE: Stansstad, Engelberg.

▲ Waldenburgerbahn units 13, 17 and 16 stand outside Waldenburg depot on 13 May 2014. This line is to be converted from its unusual 750 mm gauge to metre gauge. **David Haydock**

▼ Appenzellerbahnen loco Ge 4/4 1 heads train 1119 from Gossau as it approaches its destination, Wasserauen, on 7 September 2014. **Matthias Müller**

2.53.1. ELECTRIC LOCOMOTIVES

CLASS HGe 101 Bo-Bo

These locos are based on prototypes 1951/2, later sold to the FO, now part of the MGB. They are now mainly used on Luzern–Engelberg trains, but are maintained at Meiringen.

Built: 1989–90.
Builder–Mechanical Parts: SLM.
One Hour Rating: 1836 kW.
Driving Wheel Diameter: 965 mm.
Length over Couplers: 14.80 m.
Former Class: HGe 4/4.

Builder-Electrical Parts: ABB.
Continuous Tractive Effort: 130 kN.
Weight: 63 tonnes.
Maximum Speed: 100 km/h (40 km/h on rack).

101 961	Horw	101 964	Sachseln	101 967	Brienz
101 962	Hergiswil	101 965	Lungern	101 968	Ringgenberg
101 963	Alpnach	101 966	Brünig-Hasliberg		

CLASS De 110 Bo-Bo

These motor luggage vans were rebuilt from Class Deh 4/4 (locos 901 to 916) dating from the electrification of the line. The rack equipment was removed and push-pull equipment fitted. Most of Class Deh 4/4 became Class 110 or 120 but 905 and 907 went to LSE (now part of ZB) and were renumbered 121 and 122, now 110 021 and 022. Workings are now very rare – 110 021 was stored at Stansstad in 2014 but 110 022 was serviceable at Meiringen. Former Deh 4/6 Bo-2-Bo loco 914 (120 011), which is still rack-equipped, is now with SBB Historic.

Built: 1941–42, rebuilt 1986–94 by SBB and Stadler.
Builder-Mechanical Parts: SLM.
One Hour Rating: 894 kW.
Driving Wheel Diameter: 900 mm.
Length over Couplers: 14.60 m.
Former Class: Deh 4/4.

Builder-Electrical Parts: BBC.
Maximum Tractive Effort: 102 kN.
Weight: 42 tonnes.
Maximum Speed: 75 km/h.

110 021 (U)	110 022

2.53.2. ELECTRIC RAILCARS

CLASS ABe 130 "SPATZ" 3-CAR UNITS

Recent adhesion-only "SPATZ" (*Schmalspur Panorama Triebzug*) EMUs with panoramic windows used mainly on the Luzern–Stans and Giswil services together with similar trailers. 130 001/010 are dedicated to Meiringen–Interlaken as they have track circuit brushes due to kerosene deposited on the rails by local military aircraft!

Built: 2004/05.
Length: 51.93 m.
Power Rating: 1150 kW.
Maximum Speed: 100 km/h.
Wheel Arrangement: 2-Bo-Bo-2.

Builder: Stadler.
Weight: 66 tonnes.
Maximum Tractive Effort: 100 kN.
Accommodation: 19/– (9) 1T + –/76 + –/39 (5).

130 001	Haslital	130 005		130 008	Mörlialp
130 002		130 006		130 009	
130 003	Brisen	130 007		130 010	Brienzer Rothorn
130 004	Stanserhorn				

▲ Zentralbahn "FINK" EMU ABeh 160 003 is seen at Sarnen with a Luzern–Sachseln service on 13 May 2014. **David Haydock**

▼ Zentralbahn shunter Te 171 202 shunts empty stock at Luzern on 30 June 2015. **Andrew Thompson**

CLASS BDeh 140   SINGLE RAILCARS

These units were inherited from LSE and still operate the odd service on the Engelberg line, with trailers. They are still numbered 4 to 8 although number 6 also carries 140 006 on the side. In 2014, 140 004 was being used to supply spares, 005 was preserved, 006 in reserve and 007 for sale. The others were stored or scrapped.

Built: 1964 (1–5); 1970 6/7; 1980 8.   **Builders:** SWP/SLM/BBC.
Accommodation: –/32 (2) 1T.
Maximum Speed: 75 km/h (adhesion); 20 km/h (rack).
Weight: 48 tonnes.   **One Hour Rating:** 736 kW.
Wheel Arrangement: Bo-Bo.   **Length over Couplers:** 17.84 m.

140 004 (S) | 140 005 | 140 006 | 140 007 (S)

CLASS ABeh 150 & 160 "ADLER & FINK"
3-CAR & 7-CAR ARTICULATED UNITS

In 2012/13 Stadler delivered four 7-car Class 150 "ADLER" and six 3-car Class 160 "FINK" to ZB. The units are very similar on the outside but, in principle, "ADLER" sets work all Luzern–Interlaken services while "FINK" sets only work local stopping services at each end of the line. In practice, Class 160 operate with 3-car or 4-car sections of Class 150 sets in winter. In the 3-car sets, there is one powered bogie under each outer car and two powered bogies under the centre car which carries the pantograph. The 7-car sets have only one non-powered coach, in the centre. ZB has ordered a further five 3-car sets to enter service at the end of 2016 on the Luzern S-Bahn.

Built: 2012/13.   **Builder:** Stadler Rail.
Accommodation: Class 150: 18/14 + –/56 1T + –/45 1TD + –/49 bar + –/43 (6) 1T + –/50 IT + 39/–.
    Class 160: 18/14 1TD + –/68 + –/43 (8).
Maximum Speed: 120 km/h adhesion; 40 km/h rack, upwards; 29 km/h rack downwards.
Weight: Class 160 92 tonnes.
Power Rating: Class 150 3200 kW; Class 160 1600 kW.
Wheel Arrangement: Class 150: Bo+1A-A1+Bo+2-2+Bo+1A-A1+Bo; Class 160: Bo+1A-A1+Bo.
Length: Class 150 126.00 m; Class 160 54.00 m.

Class 150

| 150 001 | Meiringen | 150 003 | | 150 004 |
| 150 002 | | | |

Class 160

160 001		160 005		160 009
160 002		160 006	Engelberg	160 010
160 003	Stansstad	160 007		160 011
160 004		160 008		

2.53.3. OTHER STOCK

171 201 to 203 are the narrow gauge equivalent of SBB's 139–179 electric tractors. Tm^{II} 172 101, 102, 597, 598, 982 and 983 are all similar track trolleys – the narrow gauge equivalent of the SBB 601–853 series. 980 (rebuilt from SBB 709 in 1987) was sold to the MIB. 985 and 986 were sold to the FO.

†   Ex SBB 734 in 1994 (rebuilt from standard gauge by SBB's Olten works).
§   Ex SWEG V22.01, Germany in 1981. Ex MEG.

Class	Number	Name	Builder	km/h	tonnes	kW	Built
HGm	104 001		STAD/MTU/TSA	60/25	23	550	2005
HGm	104 002		STAD/MTU/TSA	60/25	23	550	2011
Gm	105 001		STAD/MTU/TSA	80	20	450	2011
Te	171 201		SLM/MFO	60	26	260	1962
Te	171 202		SLM/MFO	60	26	260	1962
Te	171 203	MEIRINGEN	SLM/MFO	60	26	260	1962

Tmll	(172) 101 †	RACO/SAU	45	10	70	1964
Tmll	(172) 102 (S)	RACO/DZ/VR	45	10.4	80	1961
Tmll	172 103	RACO/DZ/VOITH	50	16	115	1967
Tmll	(172) 597	RACO/SAU	45	10	70	1959
Tmll	172 598	RACO/SAU	45	10	70	1959
Tmlll	172 599 §	Gmeinder	60	24	165	1957
Tmll	172 982	RACO/SAU	45	10	70	1964
Tmll	172 983	RACO/SAU	45	10	70	1967
Xtm	691 101	Deutz	25	17		1972
Xrotm	(791) 051	Beilhack	60	24		1986

3. OTHER COMPANIES' TRAINS SEEN IN SWITZERLAND

A growing number of freight operators work from Germany into Basel Muttenz yard. These are too numerous to mention and change over time. Most use hired Class 185, 186 and 189 electric locos.

Captrain

This subsidiary of SNCF operates freight between Basel and Chiasso with Class 185 and 189 electric locos, some of the former in Captrain grey/yellow livery.

DB (German Railways)

Class 101 electric locomotives work IC services and Class 111 electric locomotives work local services into Basel SBB.

A larger number of DB types work into Basel Bad Bf, including Class 143 electric locomotives plus Class 612 and 648 DMUs.

ICE 1 (Class 401 power cars) work into Basel SBB and several trains a day continue to Bern and Interlaken Ost.

A variety of DB Schenker freight locomotive types, particularly Classes 145, 151 and 185, work as far as Basel Muttenz yard. Class 185 electric locos passed for Switzerland – 185 095–149) also work throughout from Basel to Chiasso over the Gotthard route and to Domodossola over the Lötschberg route. Class 185 also operate over the Stuttgart–Singen route and into north-east Switzerland. DB Schenker Italia uses G2000 diesels from Chiasso into Italy.

ETF Services

This French company works sporadically with Class BB 37000 locos to Basel Muttenz.

Europorte

This French operator hauls trains of cereals with Class E 37500 electrics as far as Muttenz. An SBB diesel takes them forward to Rheinfelden.

ÖBB (Austrian State Railways)

ÖBB Class 1016 and 1116 Taurus electric locomotives operate into Buchs station on both passenger and freight trains. Class 1116 operate right through to Zürich with Railjet services from Wien. Class 4024 Talent EMUs work into St. Margrethen station on local services.

SNCF (French Railways)

A variety of SNCF trains work into Basel SBB station, particularly Class BB 26000 electric locos and B 82500 bi-mode multiple units.

A variety of train types operate into Genève Cornavin from the Lyon direction, particularly Class BB 22200 electric locos and B 82500 bi-mode multiple units.

A mixture of Lyria single-deck TGV sets 4401–4419 and TGV Duplex sets work services from Paris Gare de Lyon to Basel, Zürich, Bern, Lausanne and Genève, as well as Genève to the south of France.

X 73500 diesel railcars reach La Chaux-de-Fonds from Besançon.

Fret SNCF Class BB 37000 tri-voltage locomotives operate frequently into Basel Muttenz yard but also less frequently to Lausanne Denges yard.

TILO (Treni Regionali Ticino Lombardia)

TILO is an SBB/Trenord joint venture operating cross-border local services between the Ticino canton and the Lombardia region of Italy (the TI and LO of TILO). Cross-border services are all operated by the Class 524 EMUs shown in this book, except for Milano–Chiasso push-pull trains powered by Trenord Class E.464 electric locos. These can be found in the companion ITALIAN RAILWAYS book.

Trenitalia (Italian Railways)

Trenitalia operates tilting ETR.610 EMUs on the Milano–Zürich service.

Trenitalia Class E.444 and E.656 electric locomotives reach Chiasso station with IC/EC services. Class E.464 head TILO suburban trains from Milano.

Class E.656 and other classes also operate freight services into Chiasso yard but this is not visible from the passenger station.

▲ DB 185 095 and 185 124 head an Italy-bound intermodal train on the Gotthard route at Wassen on 14 April 2014.   **David Haydock**

4. SWISS TRAMWAY & METRO SYSTEMS

INTRODUCTION

Historically Switzerland had numerous urban tramways, almost all being built to metre gauge. In general, those in the smaller and medium sized towns closed down, many being replaced by trolleybuses. The larger systems have survived and have been modernised, but in Neuchâtel only a small part of a much larger system remains in use. Several systems have recently built or planned extensions, and there is one completely new standard gauge system at Lausanne.

It is often difficult to differentiate between tramways and light railways; the systems detailed in this section are those that are legally classified as tramways. In spite of this some have no street running, despite this being a feature of several railways.

Most of the systems have museum cars that are used for specials or tourist operations. These are not included in this publication and neither are works cars.

Note: In this section under "Accommodation" are shown the number of seats and an estimate of the amount of standing capacity (when known), e.g. 47/61 = 47 seats and room for 61 standees.

TRAMS

In the past most systems used the "Swiss Standard Tram" – a unidirectional bogie vehicle with four traction motors. Matching trailers were also built. In the 1970s and 1980s articulated vehicles from Schindler or Düwag were bought but Zürich went its own way with its "Tram 2000" design. Many trams have had low-floor centre sections added.

▲ BLT Be 4/8 tram 259 in the livery of the former BTB is seen near Basel Zoo with a Line 10 service on 25 May 2014. **Mario Stefani**

Recently, standard commercial products such as the Siemens "Combino" (Basel and Bern) and the Bombardier Cityrunner – now known as "Flexity Outlook" (Genève) have been ordered, but as usual Zürich decided to go its own way and specified the unique "Cobra" design. Unfortunately the Siemens Combino design ran into trouble with fatigue cracking in the body and all earlier examples had to be recalled by Siemens for rebuilding. Similarly the Cobra had a fairly disastrous introduction and the six prototypes have been effectively replaced by new vehicles, although classed as rebuilds. The Swiss firm of Stadler has now entered the fray with its new "Tango" design for Basel although BVB has ordered Bombardier Flexity trams, thus missing the chance to standardise designs.

All cars are unidirectional unless otherwise stated.

4.1. BASEL

The city of Basel in north-west Switzerland, close to the borders of France and Germany, is served by two tramway operators, both publicly owned. The green trams of the BVB serve the urban routes in accordance with the requirements of canton Basel Stadt. The yellow trams of the BLT serve the city and canton Basel-Landschaft on interurban routes that had their origin in separate light railways. A BVB line has been extended across the border to serve Weil-am-Rhein in Germany and another is being extended to St Louis in France. Fares are integrated through the *Tarifverbund Nordwestschweiz*.

4.1.1. BASELLAND TRANSPORT BLT

BLT was created in 1974 to operate or co-ordinate transport in the canton of Basel-Landschaft which excludes the city itself. Of the four tram routes that extend beyond the city boundary, two (to Aesch and Pratteln) were operated by the BVB, one (the Birseckbahn to Dornach) was an independent operation, and the other (the Birsigtalbahn to Rodersdorf) was a light railway. The last line (now Line 10) is unusual in that it passes through French territory at Leymen. The Pratteln route continues to be operated by the BVB in compensation for BTB trams carrying passengers within the city on the other routes. The BLT is also responsible for the Waldenburgerbahn; this is detailed separately as a railway. It may be completely absorbed in future. Since the last edition, the former Birseckbahn cars in the 101–115 series, BVB cars in the 123–158 series and Class B4 trailers have all been withdrawn.

Gauge: 1000 mm.
Electrical System: 600 V DC.
Depots: Hüslimatt, Ruchfeld, Rodersdorf, Aesch.
Livery: Yellow with orange stripes.

CLASS Be 6/10   TANGO   6-SECTION LOW-FLOOR CARS

These new cars feature air conditioning and are 75% low-floor. Four prototypes, 151 to 154, were followed by 15 series vehicles 155 to 169. 19 more – 170 to 188 – are on order for delivery in 2015/16.

Built: 2009–
Builder: Stadler.
Wheel Arrangement: Bo-2-Bo-2-Bo.
Traction Motors: 6 x 125 kW.
Weight: 57 tonnes.
Accommodation: 93 (1)/182.

Length over Couplers: 45.00 m.
Width: 2.30 m.
Maximum Speed: 80 km/h.

151	158	165	171	177	183
152	159	166	172	178	184
153	160	167	173	179	185
154	161	168	174	180	186
155	162	169	175	181	187
156	163	170	176	182	188
157	164				

CLASS Be 4/6 (*Be 4/8)   2(*3)-SECTION CARS

The cars indicated * have been lengthened with new low-floor centre sections; a few later had them removed.

Built: 1978–81 (*rebuilt 1987–95 by SWP). Some cars did not enter service until 1984.
Builder–Mechanical Parts: SWP.
Builder–Electrical Parts: Siemens.
Wheel Arrangement: Bo-2-Bo (*Bo-2-2-Bo).   **Length over Couplers:** 19.80 m (*25.40 m).
Traction Motors: 2 x Siemens Type 1KB 2021-7MCOZ of 150 kW.
Weight: 25 (*32) tonnes.   **Width:** 2.20 m.
Accommodation: 46/61 (*58 (8)/86).   **Maximum Speed:** 65 km/h.

§   259 is in BTB livery of blue and white.

201	*	212	*	223	*	234	*	245	*	257	*
202	*	213		224		235	*	246	*	258	
203	*	214	*	225		236	*	247	*	259 §	*
204	*	215	*	226		237	*	248	*	260	
205	*	216	*	227		238	*	249	*	261	
206	*	217	*	228		239	*	251	*	262	
207	*	218	*	229		240	*	252	*	263	
208	*	219	*	230		241	*	253	*	264	
209	*	220	*	231	*	242	*	254	*	265	
210	*	221	*	232	*	243	*	255	*	266	
211	*	222	*	233	*	244	*	256	*		

4.1.2. BASLER VERKEHRSBETRIEBE   BVB

Today this is the second largest tram system in Switzerland, and apart from some short sections across the borders into France and Germany, very little has been closed. Several new extensions are opening at present, including to Weil-am-Rhein in Germany and Saint Louis in France. The operation is complicated in that Baselland Transport operates over the BVB tracks into the city. BVB has ordered 61 Bombardier Flexity trams which are currently being delivered. Note that BVB was also used for the Bex–Villars–Bretaye metre gauge line, but this is now part of TPC.

Gauge: 1000 mm.
Electrical System: 600 V DC.
Depots: Allschwilerstrasse, Dreispitz, Klybeck (workshops), Wiesenplatz.
Livery: Green.

CLASS Be 6/8   COMBINO   7-SECTION CARS

These are Basel's longest trams but have been troublesome, so BVB is now buying Bombardier vehicles.

Built: 2001–02.
Builder: Siemens, Krefeld.
Wheel Arrangement: Bo-2-Bo-Bo.
Traction Motors: Six S-E ITB 1422-0GA03 2 of 100 kW each.
Length over Couplers: 42.868 m.
Weight: 47.87 tonnes.   **Width:** 2.30 m.
Accommodation: 90/163.   **Maximum Speed:** 65 km/h.

301	306	311	316	321	325
302	307	312	317	322	326
303	308	313	318	323	327
304	309	314	319	324	328
305	310	315	320		

CLASS Be 4/4 — SINGLE CARS

These are "Swiss Standard" bogie cars. They normally operate with bogie trailers.
Built: 1967–68.
Builder–Mechanical Parts: SWP.
Builder–Electrical Parts: Siemens.
Wheel Arrangement: Bo-Bo.
Traction Motors: Four BBC 0300a of 67 kW each.
Weight: 19.02 tonnes.
Accommodation: 28/67.
Length over Couplers: 13.745 m.
Width: 2.20 m.
Maximum Speed: 60 km/h.

457	465	467	469	472	475
463	466	468	470	473	476
464					

CLASS Be 4/4 — SINGLE CARS

These modern bogie cars are unusual in being asymmetric; the nearside taper is less severe than that on the offside to accommodate the wide doorways. They usually operate in multiple with the 659–686 series.
Built: 1986–87.
Builder–Mechanical Parts: SWP/ADtranz.
Builder–Electrical Parts: BBC/Siemens.
Wheel Arrangement: B-B.
Traction Motors: 2 Brown Boveri 4 ELO 2052T of 150 kW.
Weight: 19.50 tonnes.
Accommodation: 28/70.
Length over Couplers: 13.97 m.
Width: 2.20 m.
Maximum Speed: 60 km/h.

477	482	487	491	495	499
478	483	488	492	496	500
479	484	489	493	497	501
480	485	490	494	498	502
481	486				

CLASS Be 4/6 — 2-SECTION CARS

These cars are the standard Düwag design of articulated car that was adopted by Basel for financial reasons. All the Basel articulated cars normally operate with bogie trailers.
Built: 1967.
Builder–Mechanical Parts: Düwag.
Builder–Electrical Parts: Siemens.
Wheel Arrangement: B-2-B.
Traction Motors: Two BBC 4 ELG 2057 of 150 kW each.
Length over Couplers: 19.735 m.
Weight: 23.5 tonnes.
Accommodation: 40/113.
Width: 2.20 m.
Maximum Speed: 60 km/h.

* 627 and 628 now operate together as a "Party Tram".

624	628 *	639	646	651	655
626	629	644	647	653	656
627 *	637	645	650		

CLASS Be 4/6   "GUGGUMMERE"   3-SECTION CARS

Modern articulated cars, usually operated in multiple with the 477–502 series. New low-floor centre sections from SWG-P have been added to these cars. They are of lightweight fibreglass construction and have single axles at each inner end replacing the centre bogie.

Built: 1990–92.
Builder–Mechanical Parts: SWP/ADtranz.
Builder–Electrical Parts: BBC/Siemens.
Wheel Arrangement: B-1-1-B.
Traction Motors: 2 ABB 4 ELO 2052T of 150 kW.   **Length over Couplers:** 29.03 m.
Weight: 31.57 tonnes.   **Width:** 2.20 m.
Accommodation: 59/160.   **Maximum Speed:** 60 km/h.

659	664	669	674	679	683
660	665	670	675	680	684
661	666	671	676	681	685
662	667	672	677	682	686
663	668	673	678		

CLASS B4   BOGIE TRAILER

Built: 1961–72.
Builder: FFA.
Weight: 10.2 tonnes.   **Length over Couplers:** 13.80 m.
Accommodation: 26/70.   **Maximum Speed:** 60 km/h.

D   Dienstwagen (departmental use).
*   Fitted with low floor section.

1430		1450		1463	*	1474		1486	*	1497	*
1434		1451		1464	*	1475	*	1487	*	1498	
1435		1452		1465		1476	*	1488	*	1499	
1436		1453		1466	*	1477	*	1489	*	1500	
1439		1455		1467		1478		1490	*	1501	*
1441		1456	*	1468	*	1479	*	1491	*	1502	*
1442		1457		1469	*	1480	*	1492	*	1503	*
1444	D	1458		1470	*	1481	*	1493	*	1504	
1445		1459		1471		1483		1494	*	1505	*
1448		1460		1472	*	1484	*	1495	*	1506	*
1449	*	1461		1473	*	1485	*	1496	*		

CLASS Be 4/6 or Be 6/8   FLEXITYBasel   5- or 7-SECTION CARS

These are modern low-floor trams which are being delivered from 2012 to 2018. Be 6/8 are 7-section with four bogies of which three are powered, and numbered 5001–5044. Be 4/6 are 5-section with three bogies of which two are powered and are numbered 6001–6017.

Built: 2012–18.
Builder: Bombardier.
Wheel Arrangement: Be 4/6 B-1-B; Be 6/8 B-B-1-B.
Length over Couplers: Be 4/6 31.60 m; Be 6/8 42.90 m.
Weight: Be 4/6 42.6 tonnes; Be 6/8 56.9 tonnes.   **Width:** 2.30 m.
Accommodation: Be 4/6 55/127; Be 6/8 81/174.   **Maximum Speed:** 70 km/h.

5001	5009	5017	5024	5031	5038
5002	5010	5018	5025	5032	5039
5003	5011	5019	5026	5033	5040
5004	5012	5020	5027	5034	5041
5005	5013	5021	5028	5035	5042
5006	5014	5022	5029	5036	5043
5007	5015	5023	5030	5037	5044
5008	5016				

6001	6004	6007	6010	6013	6016
6002	6005	6008	6011	6014	6017
6003	6006	6009	6012	6015	

4.2. BERNMOBIL
(STÄDTISCHE VERKEHRSBETRIEBE BERN) SVB

The Swiss capital always operated a very traditional metre-gauge urban tramway, but in recent years there has been considerable rolling stock modernisation and a bold new red livery. The network has recently expanded with the *Tram Bern West* replacing two trolleybus routes, and an integration project with the interurban tramway to Worb (see RBS in "Other Railways" section). All tram services meet at the modern interchange station outside HB. Although Bernmobil is used as the branding, the company is still called SVB.

Gauge: 1000 mm.
Electrical System: 600 V DC.
Depots: Eigerplatz, Burgernziel, Weissenbühl.
Livery: Red.

CLASS Be 6/8   COMBINO XL   7-SECTION CARS

Recent low-floor cars. They were originally intended to be numbered 771 to 792.

Built: 2009–10.
Builder–Mechanical Parts: Siemens.
Wheel Arrangement: Bo-2-Bo-Bo.
Traction Motors: 6 x 100 kW.
Weight: 49.80 tonnes.
Accommodation: 59/116.
Floor Height at Doors: 300 mm.
Length over Couplers: 41.45 m.
Width: 2.30 m.
Maximum Speed: 70 km/h (60 km/h over SVB network).

651	655	659	663	667	670
652	656	660	664	668	671
653	657	661	665	669	672
654	658	662	666		

CLASS Be 4/8   3-SECTION CARS

These modern low-floor cars consist of a central two-bogie section and end sections with one bogie at the outer ends.

Built: 1989–90.
Builder–Mechanical Parts: ACMV/Duewag.
Builder–Electrical Parts: ABB.
Wheel Arrangement: Bo-2-2-Bo.
Traction Motors: 4 ELO Type 1860 B of 153 kW.
Weight: 34 tonnes.
Accommodation: 62 (2)/179.
Floor Height at Doors: 350 mm.
Length over Couplers: 31.03 m.
Width: 2.20 m.
Maximum Speed: 60 km/h.

731	733	735	737	739	741
732	734	736	738	740	742

CLASS Be 4/6 or *Be 6/8   COMBINO VL 5- or *7-SECTION CARS

New standard Siemens low-floor cars. VL means "Very Long"! They are used alongside RBS vehicles on Line 6 to Worb.

Built: 2002–04.
Builder–Mechanical Parts: Siemens.
Wheel Arrangement: Bo-2-Bo (*Bo-2-Bo-Bo).
Traction Motors: 4 (*6) of 100 kW.
Weight: 36 (*49) tonnes.
Accommodation: 59/116.

Floor Height at Doors: 300 mm.
Length over Couplers: 31.46 m (*42.9 m).
Width: 2.30 m.
Maximum Speed: 60 km/h.

*   Extended to 7-section cars in 2009.

751	*	754		757		760	*	762	*	764	*
752	*	755		758		761	*	763	*	765	*
753		756		759							

4.3. TRANSPORTS PUBLIQUES NEUCHÂTELOIS
transN

Previously known as Tramways de Neuchâtel, then Transports Publiques du Littoral Neuchâtelois, the company has been merged with heavy rail operated TRN to form transN (see transN in "Other Railways" section). Although the last urban tram route closed in 1976, the lakeside metre-gauge interurban tramway to Boudry was retained and modernised, with reserved track and automatic block signalling. The yellow bogie trams run solo, coupled or with a driving trailer. The existing stock will be replaced by former Trogenerbahn Be 4/8 31–35 around 2018.

Gauge: 1000 mm.
Electrical System: 630 V DC.
Depots: Neuchâtel Evole, Boudry.
Livery: Yellow with green stripes.

CLASS Be 4/4   SINGLE CARS

These are bi-directional light rail cars, and operate in various formations with driving trailers.

Built: 1981 (*1988).
Builder–Mechanical Parts: SWS (*SWP/SIG).
Builder–Electrical Parts: BBC.
Wheel Arrangement: Bo-Bo.
Traction Motors: 4 x 69 kW.
Weight: 18.5 tonnes.
Accommodation: 42/65.

Length over Couplers: 17.50 m.
Width: 2.40 m.
Maximum Speed: 75 km/h.

501	Boudry		503	Colombier		505	* NEUCHÂTEL
502	Auvernier		504	Cortaillod		506	*

CLASS Bt   BOGIE DRIVING TRAILER

Built: 1981.
Builder–Mechanical Parts: SWS.
Builder–Electrical Parts: BBC.
Weight: 17.3 tonnes.
Accommodation: 46.

Length over Couplers: 17.50 m.
Width: 2.40 m.
Maximum Speed:

551	552	553	554	

4.4. TRANSPORTS PUBLICS GENÈVOIS   TPG

After a period of closures reduced the metre-gauge tramway to one route, Genève is in expansion mode again, with new lines opened and more under construction (partly replacing trolleybuses). The whole fleet has been renewed, though the Duewag/Vevey articulated trams were the first low-floor cars to enter service anywhere, and feature a step entrance that current designs do not need.

Gauge: 1000 mm.
Electrical System: 600 V DC.
Depot: Bachet de Pesay
Liveries: Classes Be 4/6 and Be 4/8 were painted orange and white when delivered. Most have been re-liveried in the new blue and white livery (**B**) or carry advertising livery (**A**).

CLASS Be 4/6   TYPE "DAV"   2-SECTION CARS

The entire fleet of 'Swiss Standard' cars was replaced by these modern articulated cars.

Built: 1987–89 (†1984).
Builder–Mechanical Parts: ACMV/Duewag.
Builder–Electrical Parts: BBC.
Wheel Arrangement: B-2-B.
Traction Motors: 2 x 150 kW.
Weight: 27.9 tonnes.
Accommodation: 45/130.

Length over Couplers: 21.00 m.
Width: 2.30 m.
Maximum Speed: 60 km/h.

Number	Livery		Names				
801	B	†	GALLIARD	805	A		Thônex
802	B		Lancy	806	A		Chêne-Bourg
803	B		CAROUGE	807	B		CÉLIGNY
804	B		Chêne-Bougeries	808	A		Onex

▲ Recent Stadler "Tango" tram 1817 crosses Bombardier tram 890 at Etoile on Line 15 in Genève on 28 May 2013.
David Haydock

809	B	Aire-la-Ville	817	A	Dardagny
810	B	GENÈVE	818	B	Satigny
811	B	Collonge-Bellerive	819	B	Anières
812	B	AVULLY	820	B	Cartigny
813	B	AVUSY	821	B	Bernex
814	B	Bardonnex	822	B	Chancy
815	B	Bellevue	825	B	CHOULEX
816	B	Vernier	826	B	Confignon

CLASS Be 4/8   TYPE "DAV"   3-SECTION CARS

Class Be 4/6 lengthened with new centre sections.

Built: 1989. Rebuilt 1995–97, 2001.
Builder–Mechanical Parts: ACMV/Duewag.
Builder–Electrical Parts: BBC.
Wheel Arrangement: B-2-2-B.
Traction Motors: 2 x 150 kW.
Weight: 34.1 tonnes.
Accommodation: 70/200.

Length over Couplers: 30.90 m.
Width: 2.30 m.
Maximum Speed: 60 km/h.

Number	Old No	Livery	Names				
831		B	Gy	842		B	Pregny-Chambésy
832		B	Hermance	843			Presinge
833		B	Perly-Certoux	844		B	MEINIER
834			Jussy	845		B	SORAL
835		B	Grand-Saconnex	846		B	Vandoeuvres
836			Puplinge	847	(829)		GENTHOD
837			Meyrin	848	(830)	B	Corsier
838			Troinex	849	(828)	B	Veyrier
839			Russin	850	(827)	A	Colongy
840		B	Laconnex	851	(824)	B	VERSOIX
841		B	Plan-les-Ouates	852	(823)	B	Colle-Bossy

CLASS Be 6/8   FLEXITY OUTLOOK   7-SECTION CARS

These are new standard Bombardier low-floor cars, formerly known as "CityRunners".

Built: 2004–05, 2009–10.
Builder: Bombardier.
Wheel Arrangement: Bo-2-Bo-Bo.
Traction Motors: 6 x 85 kW.
Weight: 50.1 tonnes.
Accommodation: 66/171.

Length over Couplers: 42.00 m.
Width: 2.30 m.
Maximum Speed: 70 km/h.

861	B		874	B		887	B
862	A		875	B		888	B
863	B		876	A		889	B
864	A		877	B		890	B
865	B		878	B		891	B
866	B		879	A		892	B
867	B		880	B		893	B
868	B		881	B		894	B
869	B		882	B		895	B
870	A		883	B		896	B
871	B		884	B		897	B
872	B		885	B		898	B
873	B		886	B		899	B

CLASS Be 6/10   TANGO   6-SECTION LOW-FLOOR CARS

These new cars are similar to those in Basel but also have supercapacitors to store braking energy. 1821 to 1836 have been delayed due to late opening of certain extensions and will not arrive until later in 2016.

Built: 2011–16.
Builder: Stadler.
Wheel Arrangement: Bo-2-Bo-2-Bo.
Traction Motors: 6 x 125 kW.
Weight: 57 tonnes.
Accommodation: 80/228.

Length over Couplers: 45.00 m.
Width: 2.30 m.
Maximum Speed: 60 km/h.

1801	1807	1813	1819	1825	1831
1802	1808	1814	1820	1826	1832
1803	1809	1815	1821	1827	1833
1804	1810	1816	1822	1828	1834
1805	1811	1817	1823	1829	1835
1806	1812	1818	1824	1830	1836

4.5. TRANSPORTS PUBLICS DE LA REGION LAUSANNOISE   TL

TL operates bus and trolleybus services in the Lausanne area plus a light rail line (previously known as TSOL) and an automatic metro line which took over the trackbed of the former LG and LO rack lines. Line M1 Métro Ouest is the only standard-gauge tramway in Switzerland, built in 1990/91 to link a subway terminus at Flon (interchange with Line M2 and the LEB) with the south-east suburbs and the SBB at Renens. Much of the line is single-track with passing loops mostly with roadside running, but with a lengthy subway section at the Flon end. The university is a major traffic generator.

In October 2008 a French-style rubber-tyred metro M2 was opened, partly replacing the Lausanne-Ouchy rack line, but with new construction to the north-east suburbs. A third metro line the same features is planned as is a new tramway line from Flon to Renens.

LINE M1

Gauge: 1435 mm.
Electrical System: 750 V DC.
Depot: EPFL Dorigny.
Livery: White with blue highlights.
Length: 7.8 km.

The line's Class Bem 4/6 EMUs, 558 201 to 222, are included in the Standard Gauge EMU section of this book.

LINE M2

Gauge: 1435 mm.
Electrical System: 750 V DC third rail side contact.
Depot: Vennes.
Length: 5.9 km.

This is a fully-automatic standard gauge metro line, modelled on Paris Line 14 but with the steepest gradients of any adhesion-worked metro in the world – an average of 6% with sections at 12% (1 in 8.3). The line runs from Ouchy to Lausanne SBB station over the former LO single-track rack line (now doubled) then from Lausanne SBB to Lausanne Flon over the former LG rack line. Both of the latter were originally funiculars. From Flon northwards to Croisette the rest of the line was built new. The normal peak service from Ouchy to Croisettes is doubled over the central section between Lausanne SBB and Sarraz. To cope with the gradients, bogies are all powered and have rubber tyres as well as steel guide wheels. There are four types of brakes – regenerative, rheostatic, pneumatic tread brakes and magnetic shoes. Trains are worked by 15 2-car sets with four bogies each. The line has been a great success, with frequent overcrowding. Three more trains are on order.

▲ TL metro set 249 approaches Oulchy at the lower end of Line M2 in Lausanne on 6 October 2014. **David Haydock**

Built: 2005/06.
Builder: Alstom.
Power Rating: 1256 kW.
Weight: 57.3 tonnes.
Accommodation: 27/70 + 28/70.

Length over Couplers: 30.68 m.
Maximum Speed: 60 km/h.

241	244	247	250	253	256
242	245	248	251	254	257
243	246	249	252	255	258

4.6. VERKEHRSBETRIEBE DER STADT ZÜRICH (ZÜRI-LINIE) VBZ

Switzerland's largest city is served by a large and efficient metre-gauge tramway that has always been modernised in a restrained way. The last high-floor *Mirage* trams were replaced by *Cobra* low-floor cars, a design unique to Zürich that has not been without its teething troubles. Some of these are in the reversed livery (white with blue stripe) of the Glattalbahn system, a nominally independent but integrated tramway that has built new lines in the northern suburbs, including from Oerlikon to the airport. In November 2015, a vote approved the project to build the Limmattalbahn, a 13.4 km, 18 stop tramway from Altstetten via Dietikon (link to the BDWM) to Killwangen-Spreitenbach, to be electrified at 600/1200 V DC. The blue and white VBZ trams of the city system are expanding as well to reach western suburbs hitherto served only by bus or trolleybus. Fares are integrated under the Zürcher Verkehrsverbund. Burgwies depot is now a museum.

Gauge: 1000 mm.
Electrical System: 600 V DC.
Depots: Altstetten (workshops), Elisabethenstrasse, Hard, Kalkbreite, Irchel, Oerlikon, Wollishofen.
Livery: Blue & White (**G** Glattalbahn white with blue stripes).

CLASS Be 4/6   TRAM 2000   2-SECTION CARS

These trams, known as "Tram 2000" normally operate in pairs, or with the non-driving 2300 and 2400 series cars.

Built: 1976–78.
Builder–Mechanical Parts: SWS/SWP.
Builder–Electrical Parts: BBC.
Wheel Arrangement: B-2-B.
Traction Motors: 2 of 139 kW.
Weight: 26.5 tonnes.
Accommodation: 50/54.

Length over Couplers: 21.40 m.
Width: 2.20 m.
Maximum Speed: 65 km/h.

2001	Höngg	2016		2031	
2002	Seebach	2017		2032	
2003	Unterstrass	2018		2033	
2004	Höngg	2019		2034	
2005	Industriequartier	2020		2035	
2006	Fluntern	2021	Albisrieden	2036	
2007	Enge	2022		2037	Oberstrass
2008	Friesenberg	2023		2038	Witikon
2009	Triemli	2024		2039	Rennweg
2010	Wipkingen	2025		2040	Rechts der Limmat
2011	Orikon	2026		2041	Hottingen
2012	Wiedikon	2027		2042	Altstetten
2013		2028		2043	Rennweg
2014		2029		2044	Wollishofen
2015		2030	Hirslanden	2045	Fiesbach

CLASS Be 4/6   TRAM 2000   2-SECTION CARS

Development of 2000 series with higher-powered motors. 2060 was withdrawn after an accident.

Built: 1985–87.
Builder–Mechanical Parts: SIG/SWS/SWP.
Builder–Electrical Parts: BBC.
Wheel Arrangement: B-2-B.
Traction Motors: 2 of 154 kW.   **Length over Couplers:** 21.40 m.
Weight: 26.5 tonnes.   **Width:** 2.20 m.
Accommodation: 50/54.   **Maximum Speed:** 65 km/h.

2046	2055	2065	2074	2083	2091
2047	2056	2066	2075	2084	2092
2048	2057	2067	2076	2085	2093
2049	2058	2068	2077	2086	2094
2050	2059	2069	2078	2087	2095
2051	2061	2070	2079	2088	2096
2052	2062	2071	2080	2089	2097
2053	2063	2072	2081	2090	2098
2054	2064	2073	2082		

Names:

2070   Aussersihl and Hard | 2080   Schamendingen

CLASS Be 4/8   TRAM 2000   3-SECTION CARS

Built as Be 4/6. Development of 2046 series with 3-phase AC drive. Rebuilt 2001–2005 as Be 4/8. Known as "Sänfte" (Sedan Chairs). They have a low-floor centre section.

Built: 1991–92.
Builder–Mechanical Parts: SWS/SWP.
Builder–Electrical Parts: BBC.
Wheel Arrangement: B-2-2-B.
Traction Motors: 2 of 157 kW.   **Length over Couplers:** 28.00 m.
Weight: 31 tonnes.   **Width:** 2.20 m.
Accommodation: 68/75.   **Maximum Speed:** 65 km/h.

2099	2103	2107	2111	2115	2119
2100	2104	2108	2112	2116	2120
2101	2105	2109	2113	2117	2121
2102	2106	2110	2114	2118	

CLASS Be 4/6   TRAM 2000   2-SECTION CARS

These cars are similar to the 2000 series, but have no driving cabs, and are used as trailing units in multiple formations.

Built: 1978.
Builder–Mechanical Parts: SWS/SWP.
Builder–Electrical Parts: BBC.
Wheel Arrangement: B-2-B.
Traction Motors: 2 of 139 kW.   **Length over Couplers:** 21.40 m.
Weight: 26 tonnes.   **Width:** 2.20 m.
Accommodation: 50/57.   **Maximum Speed:** 65 km/h.

2301	2304	2307	2310	2312	2314
2302	2305	2308	2311	2313	2315
2303	2306	2309			

CLASS Be 2/4   TRAM 2000   SINGLE CARS

These bogie cars also have no driving cabs, and are used as trailing units in multiple formations with 2000 series cars. They are known as "ponies".

Built: 1985–87 (*1992).
Builder–Mechanical Parts: SWS/SWP.
Builder–Electrical Parts: BBC.
Wheel Arrangement: 2-B.
Traction Motor: 154 (*157) kW.
Weight: 18.5 (*16.5) tonnes.
Accommodation: 35/41.

Length over Couplers: 15.40 m.
Width: 2.20 m.
Maximum Speed: 65 km/h.

2401	2407	2413	2419	2425 *	2431 *
2402	2408	2414	2420	2426 *	2432 *
2403	2409	2415	2421 *	2427 *	2433 *
2404	2410	2416	2422 *	2428 *	2434 *
2405	2411	2417	2423 *	2429 *	2435 *
2406	2412	2418	2424 *	2430 *	

▲ VBZ "Tram 2000" car 2087 on Line 5 to Laubegg crosses a Type Be 5/6 "Cobra" tram on one of the busiest parts of the Zürich network near Bellevue on 14 June 2014.   **David Haydock**

CLASS Be 5/6   COBRA   5-SECTION CARS

These new trams were specially designed for Zürich and were originally ordered from SWS/SIG/Fiat/ADtranz. The original batch of six had many faults and have been completely "rebuilt" (renewed).

Built: 1999, 2002–10.
Builder: Bombardier.
Wheel Arrangement: The Cobra has separate stub axles on each side of the vehicle. Each has a motor drive, except that the centre two on the door side are unmotored.
Traction Motors: 10 of 62.5 kW.   **Length over Couplers:** 36.00 m.
Weight: 39.2 tonnes.   **Width:** 2.40 m.
Accommodation: 90/113.   **Maximum Speed:** 70 km/h.

G   Glattalbahn livery (white with a blue stripe).

3001	3016	3031	3046	3061	3075 G
3002	3017	3032	3047	3062 G	3076 G
3003	3018	3033	3048	3063 G	3077 G
3004	3019	3034	3049	3064 G	3078 G
3005	3020	3035	3050	3065 G	3079 G
3006	3021	3036	3051	3066	3080
3007	3022	3037	3052	3067	3081
3008	3023	3038	3053	3068	3082
3009	3024	3039	3054	3069	3083
3010	3025	3040	3055	3070	3084
3011	3026	3041	3056	3071 G	3085
3012	3027	3042	3057	3072 G	3086
3013	3028	3043	3058	3073 G	3087
3014	3029	3044	3059	3074 G	3088
3015	3030	3045	3060		

▲ Bernmobil Be 4/6 Combino 754 operates on Line 7 to Bümpliz on 22 August 2013. **Mario Stefani**

5. PRESERVED LOCOMOTIVES & RAILCARS

In this section, all preserved locomotives and railcars from Swiss public railways are shown, except for those shown earlier in this book. Not detailed are industrial locomotives and trams. Certain preserved locomotives may be found in the main section of the book as they are used on the main line. Many locos now have EVNs which means the loco is active and can operate on the national network – we show the the shortened six-figure version in brackets where known. The current status of the motive power is indicated as follows:

M	Museum, on display (not active).		MS	Museum, stored.
MA	Museum, active.		P	Plinthed.
MR	Museum, under repair.		S	Stored.

5.1. STEAM LOCOMOTIVES & RAILCARS

The Whyte notation is used for steam locomotives. The number of leading wheels are given, followed by the number of driving wheels and then the trailing wheels. Suffixes are used to denote tank locomotives as follows: T – side tank, RT – rack tank, WT, – well tank, VBT – vertical boiler tank. For example 2-6-2T.

Standard gauge

Rly.	Class	No.	Details	Status	Date	Location
SBB	B 3/4	1367	2-6-0	MA	1916	SBB H. Bahnpark Brugg
SBB	C 5/6	2958	2-10-0	S	1915	Locorama. Romanshorn
SBB	C 5/6	2965	2-10-0	M	1916	SBB H. VHS
SBB	C 5/6	2969	2-10-0	MR	1916	Eurovapor. Sulgen
SBB	C 5/6	2978	2-10-0	MA	1917	SBB H. Delémont
SBB	Eb 3/5	5810 (005 810)	2-6-2T	MA	1911	DBB. Konolfingen
SBB	Eb 3/5	5811 (005 811)	2-6-2T	MA	1912	SBB H/VDZ. Bahnpark Brugg
SBB	Eb 3/5	5819	2-6-2T	MR	1912	SBB H. Bahnpark Brugg
SBB	Eb 3/5	5886 (BT 6)	2-6-2T	MR	1910	CSG. Mendrisio
SBB	Eb 3/5	5889 (005 889)	2-6-2T	MA	1910	BT9. Herisau
SBB	E 3/3	8410 (SCB 41)	0-6-0WT	MR	1900	Balsthal (VHS)
SBB	E 3/3	8463 (008 463)	0-6-0WT	MA	1904	CSG. Mendrisio
SBB	E 3/3	8474	0-6-0WT	M	1907	Locorama. Romanshorn
SBB	E 3/3	8476 (008 476)	0-6-0WT	MA	1907	DVZO.
SBB	E 3/3	8479 (008 479)	0-6-0WT	MA	1907	ST. Triengen
SBB	E 3/3	8481	0-6-0WT	MS	1907	SBB H. Buchs
SBB	E 3/3	8483	0-6-0WT	S	1907	Eurovapor. Balsthal
SBB	E 3/3	8485	0-6-0WT	MR	1907	HEG. Delémont
SBB	E 3/3	8487	0-6-0WT	P	1909	Buchs
SBB	E 3/3	8492 (008 492)	0-6-0WT	MA	1909	VDZ
SBB	E 3/3	8494 (008 494)	0-6-0WT	MA	1909	CTVJ. Le Pont
SBB	E 3/3	8500	0-6-0WT	M	1910	OeBB. Balsthal
SBB	E 3/3	8501 (008 501)	0-6-0WT	MA	1910	CSG. Mendrisio
SBB	E 3/3	8507	0-6-0WT	P	1910	Sierre
SBB	E 3/3	8511 (008 511)	0-6-0WT	MA	1911	VVT. St. Sulpice
SBB	E 3/3	8512	0-6-0WT	S	1910	SBB H. St. Maurice
SBB	E 3/3	8516	0-6-0WT	MR	1910	Private. Zürich G depot
SBB	E 3/3	8518 "Bäretswil"	0-6-0WT	MA	1913	DVZO. Uster
SBB	E 3/3	8522 (ST 8522)	0-6-0WT	MA	1913	ST. Triengen
SBB	E 3/3	8523	0-6-0WT	MA	1915	CTVJ. Le Pont
SBB	E 3/3	8527	0-6-0WT	P	1914	Private. Chur, Spundisstr. 21
SBB	E 3/3	8532	0-6-0WT	MA	1916	Eurovapor. Kandern (Germany)
SBB	E 3/3	8551 (NOB 453)	0-6-0WT	M	1894	VDZ. Bahnpark Brugg
SBB	E 3/3	8554 (NOB 456)	0-6-0WT	MS	1894	HSTB. Balsthal
SBB	E 3/3	8573 (008 573)	0-6-0WT	MA	1890	DBB. Konolfingen
SBB	E 3/3	8575 (aka RVT no. 8)	0-6-0WT	M	1890	BMK. Kallnach
SBB	E 3/3	8651 (KLB 1)	0-6-0WT	MA	1909	OeBB. Balsthal
SBB	Xrotm	100	rotary	M	1896	VHS

BLS	E 2/2	72 "ZEPHIR"	0-4-0WT	MA	1874	SBB H. VHS. (Bödelibahn 3)
BSB	Ed 3/4	51 (007 451)	0-6-0T	MA	1906	DBB. Konolfingen
EB	Ed 3/3	3	0-6-0WT	M	1881	VHS
EB	Ed 4/5	8 (007 008)	2-8-0T	MA	1914	DBB. Konolfingen
GB	E 2/2	11	0-4-0WT	M	1881	VHS
GTB	Ed 3/3	77 (008 543)	0-6-0WT	MA	1901	BLS H. DBB. Konolfingen
HWB	Ec 3/3	5	0-6-0T	MA	1936	VHE
JS	Eb 2/4	35 (SBB 5469)	4-4-0T	M	1891	SBB H. Balsthal
JS	A 3/5	705[II] (ex 778)	4-6-0	MA	1908	SBB H. Bahnpark Brugg
MThB	Ec 3/5	3	2-6-2T	MA	1912	VHMThB. Romanshorn
NOB	D 1/3	1 "LIMMAT"	4-2-0	MA	1947	SBB H. Bahnpark Brugg (replica of 1847 loco)
OeBB	E 3/3	2	0-6-0WT	MA	1899	OeBB. Balsthal
RSG	Ed 3/4	2 "Hinwil"	2-6-0T	MA	1903	DVZO. Uster
SCB	Ec 2/5	28 "GENF"	0-4-6T	M	1858	SBB H. VHS.
SCB	Ed 2 x 2/2	196 (SBB 7696)	0-4-4-0T	MA	1893	SBB H. Balsthal
SiTB	E 3/3	2 "Hänsli"	0-6-0WT	MA	1893	ZMB. Sihlwald
SiTB	E 3/3	4	0-6-0WT	P	1897	Sihlwald
SiTB	E 3/3	5	0-6-0WT	MR	1899	ZMB. Horgen
SMB	Ec 3/4	1	2-6-0T	MS	1907	DVZO. Wald
SMB	Ed 3/4	2	2-6-0T	MA	1907	VHE. Huttwil
SMB	Ec 4/5	11 (006 811) "s'Eufsi"	2-8-0T	MA	1911	BLS H. DBB. Konolfingen
SOB	E 3/3	4 "SCHWYZ"	0-6-0WT	MA	1887	DVZO. Uster
STB	E 3/3	3 "BEINWYL"	0-6-0WT	MA	1884	HSTB. Hochdorf
UeBB	CZm 1/2	31 (railcar)	2-2-0	MR	1902	SBB H. Bahnpark Brugg
UeBB	Ed 3/3	401 "Bauma"	0-6-0WT	MA	1901	DVZO. Uster
VHB	Ed 3/4	11	2-6-0T	MA	1908	VHE. Huttwil
VRB	H I/2	7	2-2-0RVBT	MA	1873	VHS
VRB	H 2/3	16	0-4-2RT	MA	1923	RB. Vitznau
VRB	H 2/13	17	0-4-2RT	MA	1925	RB. Vitznau

▲ VVT's former SBB "Tigerli" 0-6-0T 8511 is seen at St Sulpice on 10 May 2014, with one of VVT's two ex DB Köf shunters on the right. **Pablo Hoya**

Narrow gauge

Rly.	Gauge	Class	No.	Details	Status	Date	Location
SBB	1000	G 3/3	6 (SBB 109)	0-6-0T	MA	1901	BS. Chaulin
SBB	1000	G 3/4	203	2-6-0T	S	1912	Volos (Greece). Scrapped?
SBB	1000	G 3/4	208	2-6-0T	MR	1913	BDB. Interlaken
SBB	1000	HG 3/3	1058	0-6-0T	P	1908	Lárissa (Greece)
SBB	1000	HG 3/3	1063	0-6-0RT	M	1909	VHS
SBB	1000	HG 3/3	1067	0-6-0RT	MA	1910	Interlaken
SBB	1000	HG 3/3	1068	0-6-0RT	MR	1926	BDB. Interlaken
RhB	1000	G 3/4	1	2-6-0T	MA	1889	Landquart
RhB	1000	G 3/4	11 "Heidi"	2-6-0T	MA	1902	RhB. Samedan
RhB	1000	G 3/4	14	2-6-0T	MR	1902	DLV AB. Herisau
RhB	1000	G 4/5	107	2-8-0	MA	1906	Landquart
RhB	1000	G 4/5	108	2-8-0	MA	1906	Landquart
RhB	1000	G 4/5	118 (RSR 340)	2-8-0	S	1912	Makkasan (Thailand)
RhB	1000	G 4/5	122 (RSR 338)	2-8-0	S	1913	Chiang Mai (Thailand) (Mr. Lim)
RhB	1000	G 4/5	123 (RES 336)	2-8-0	P	1913	Chiang Mai (Thailand)
RhB	1000	Xrotd	R12	rotary	MR	1913	DFB. Realp
RhB	1000	Xrotd 6/6	9214 (BB R 1052)	rotary	MA	1912	BC. Chaulin
FO	1000	HG 3/4	1 (DFB 1)	2-6-0RT	MA	1913	DFB. Realp
FO	1000	HG 3/4	3 (BFD 3)	2-6-0RT	MA	1913	BC. Chaulin
FO	1000	HG 3/4	4	2-6-0RT	MA	1913	DFB. Realp
FO	1000	HG 3/4	9 (DFB 9)	2-6-0RT	MA	1914	DFB. Realp
FW	1000	G 3/3	2	0-6-0T	P	1887	Wil, Kiesbachweg
GGB	1000	H 2/3	8	0-4-2RT	M	1892	Ribes de Freser, No. 6 (Spain)
LEB	1000	G 3/3	5	0-6-0T	MA	1890	BC. Chaulin
LEB	1000	G 3/3	8	0-6-0T	MA	1910	LEB. Echallens
MG	800	HII/3	2	0-4-2RT	MA	1890	Capolago
PB	800	Bhd 1/2	9	0-2-2RT	M	1889	VHS
PB	800	Bhd 1/2	10	0-2-2RT	M	1900	München (Germany)
RdB	1000	G 3/3	1	0-6-0T	MA	1890	BC. Chaulin
RdB	1000	G 3/3	2	0-6-0T	P	1890	Les Brenets
RdB	1000	G 3/3	3	0-6-0T	M	1892	Le Locle (incomplete)
SPB	800	HII/3	5	0-4-2RT	MA	1894	Wilderswil
VZ	1000	HG 2/3	6 "WEISSHORN"	0-4-2RT	MA	1902	DFB. Realp
VZ	1000	HG 2/3	7 "BREITHORN"	0-4-2RT	MA	1906	MGB. Realp
WB	750	G 3/3	5	0-6-0T	MA	1902	Waldenburg
WB	750	G 3/3	6	0-6-0T	M	1912	VHS
YStC	1000	G 4/4	4	Dh2t	P	1911	Lárissa (Greece)

▲ On 21 July 2013, SBB Historic railmotor CZm 1/2 no. 31 is seen at Ettenhausen-Emmetschloo between Hinwil and Bauma. Built in 1902 by Maschinenfabrik Esslingen for the Uerikon-Bauma-Bahn, the vehicle has a vertical boiler and one powered axle. **Andrew Thompson**

5.2. DIESEL & ELECTRIC LOCOMOTIVES & RAILCARS

Standard gauge

Rly.	Class	No.	Status	Date	Location
SBB	Re 4/4^I	10006	MS	1950	Centralbahn (D)
SBB	Re 4/4^I	10008	MS	1950	Centralbahn (D)
SBB	Re 4/4^I	10019	MS	1950	Centralbahn (D)
SBB	Re 4/4^I	10042	M	1951	Eisenbahnmuseum Horb (D)
SBB	Ae 3/5	10217	MA	1924	SBB H. Fleurier
SBB	Ae 3/6^{III}	10264	MA	1926	SBB H. St Maurice
SBB	Ae 3/6^{II}	10439^{II}	MA	1925	SBB H. Olten (ex 10452)
SBB	Ae 3/6^{II}	10448	MS	1925	Swisstrain. Neuchâtel
SBB	Ae 3/6^I	10639	M	1925	Swisstrain. Payerne
SBB	Ae 3/6^I	10650	M	1925	SBB H. Glarus
SBB	Ae 3/6^I	10664	M	1926	SBB H. Rapperswil
SBB	Ae 3/6^I	10693	M	1927	Swisstrain. Payerne
SBB	Ae 3/6^I	10700	M	1927	SBB H. Fleurier
SBB	Ae 4/7	10902	MA	1927	Swisstrain. Payerne
SBB	Ae 4/7	10905	MA	1927	SBB H. Buchs
SBB	Ae 4/7	10908	S	1928	Classic Rail. Locorama. Romanshorn
SBB	Ae 4/7	10948	S	1930	Swisstrain. Sissach
SBB	Ae 4/7	10949	M	1930	SBB H. Bahnpark Augsburg (Germany)
SBB	Ae 4/7	10950	MA	1930	Swisstrain. Payerne
SBB	Ae 4/7	10951	S	1930	Classic Rail. Sulgen
SBB	Ae 4/7	10961	S	1930	Classic Rail. Romanshorn
SBB	Ae 4/7	10976	M	1932	SBB H. Olten
SBB	Ae 4/7	10987	MA	1931	Verbano Express. Luino (IT)
SBB	Ae 4/7	10997	MA	1932	Swisstrain. Payern
SBB	Ae 4/7	10999	S	1932	Classic Rail. Glarus
SBB	Ae 4/7	11000	S	1932	Swisstrain. Le Locle
SBB	Ae 4/7	11001	S	1932	Classic Rail. Sissach
SBB	Ae 4/7	11002	S	1932	Classic Rail. Winterthur
SBB	Ae 4/7	11010	S	1931	Swisstrain. Payerne
SBB	Ae 4/7	11015	S	1931	Classic Rail. Sulgen
SBB	Ae 4/7	11022	M	1933	Eisenbahnmuseum. Horb (D)
SBB	Ae 4/7	11026	MA	1934	Mikado 1244. Bahnpark Brugg
SBB	Ae 6/6	11401	M	1951	SBB H. Eisenbahnmuseum. Horb (D)
SBB	Ae 6/6	11402	MA	1951	SBB H. Erstfeld
SBB	Ae 6/6	11404	S	1955	Romanshorn.
SBB	Ae 6/6	11407	MA	1955	SBB H. Mikado 1244. Bahnpark Brugg
SBB	Ae 6/6	11411	MA	1955	SBB H. Erstfeld
SBB	Ae 6/6	11413	M	1955	VHS (SBB Historic)
SBB	Ae 6/6	11416	S	1957	SBB H. Vallorbe (for spares)
SBB	Ae 6/6	11418	P	1957	Altishofen
SBB	Ae 6/6	610 420	M	1957	Private. Sissach
SBB	Ae 6/6	11421	MA	1957	SBB H. Erstfeld. Ae 6/6 VEhE.
SBB	Ae 6/6	11424	MA	1958	Swisstrain. La Chaux de Fonds
SBB	Ae 6/6	11425	MA	1957	SBB H. Olten
SBB	Ae 6/6	11456	MA	1957	SBB H. Olten
SBB	Ae 6/6	11501	M	1959	Swisstrain. La Chaux de Fonds
SBB	Ae 8/14	11801	MA	1931	SBB H. Erstfeld
SBB	Ae 8/14	11852	M	1940	SBB H. VHS.
SBB	Be 4/6	12320	M	1911	SBB H. Tram Be 4/6. Winterthur
SBB	Be 4/6	12332	S	1922	SBB H. Erstfeld
SBB	Be 4/6	12339	M	1920	Verbano Express. Luino (IT)
SBB	Be 4/7	12504	MA	1922	SBB H. Erstfeld
SBB	Be 6/8^{II}	13254	M	1920	SBB H. VHS
SBB	Be 6/8^{III}	13257	M	1920	Mürzzuschlag (Austria)
SBB	Be 6/8^{III}	13302	MA	1925	SBB H. Betriebsgruppe 13302. Rapperswil

SBB	Ce 4/4	13501	M	1904	(SW 1) VHS
SBB	Ce 4/4	13502	MS	1904	VHS. Olten
SBB	Ce 6/8ᴵ	14201	MS	1920	SBB H. Erstfeld
SBB	Ce 6/8ᴵᴵ	14253	MA	1921	SBB H. Erstfeld
SBB	Ce 6/8ᴵᴵ	14267	M	1921	Speyer (Germany)
SBB	Ce 6/8ᴵᴵ	14270	MR	1921	SBB H. Zürich Oerlikon
SBB	Ce 6/8ᴵᴵ	14276	MR	1922	CSG. Mendrisio
SBB	Ce 6/8ᴵᴵ	14282	M	1922	Sinsheim (Germany)
SBB	Ce 6/8ᴵᴵᴵ	14305	MR	1926	SBB H. Olten (Meiningen)
SBB	De 6/6	15301 (611 301)	M	1926	OeBB. Balsthal. Parts of BLS 316.
SBB	Ee 3/3	16313	M	1926	Swisstrain. Holderbank
SBB	Ee 3/3	16315	S	1926	Classic Rail. Holderbank
SBB	Ee 3/3	16316	S	1926	Classic Rail. Holderbank
SBB	Ee 3/3	16318	MA	1928	VHMThB. Locorama. Romanshorn
SBB	Ee 3/3	16326	S	1928	Classic Rail. Holderbank
SBB	Ee 3/3	16332	S	1930	Swisstrain. Le Locle
SBB	Ee 3/3	16351	MA	1932	Swisstrain. Payerne
SBB	Ee 3/3	16363	MA	1939	DVZO. Bauma.
SBB	Ee 3/3	16399	M	1943	SBB H. Olten
SBB	Ee 6/6	16801	M	1952	Swisstrain. Le Locle
SBB	Bm 4/4ᴵᴵᴵ	18451	MA	1939	SBB H. Olten.
SBB	Em 3/3	18814	MA	1963	SEHR&RS. Etzwilen
SBB	Em 3/3	18822	MA	1963	DSF. Koblenz
SBB	Teᴵ	44	MA	1941	BMK. Kerzers
SBB	Teᴵ	47	MA	1941	CSG. Mendrisio
SBB	Teᴵ	66	MA	1941	Verein Be 4/6. Winterthur
SBB	Teᴵᴵᴵ	130 (212 030)	MA	1948	DSF. Koblenz
SBB	Teᴵᴵᴵ	177	MS	1966	SBB H. Olten
SBB	Teᴵᴵᴵ	210	P	1927	Playground. Frenkendorf
SBB	Teᴵᴵᴵ	221	M	1927	Swisstrain. Payerne
SBB	Temᴵ	260	M	1955	Galleria Baumgartner, Mendrisio
SBB	Temᴵ	263 (66)	MS	1955	Verein Be 4/6. Winterthur
SBB	Temᴵ	270 (73)	M	1955	Eurovapor. Haltingen (D)
SBB	Temᴵ	273 (76)	MR	1957	Eurovapor. Sulgen
SBB	Temᴵ	275 (220 275)	MA	1957	DSF. Koblenz
SBB	Temᴵᴵ	277	MS	1967	SBB H. Olten
SBB	Temᴵᴵ	278	M	1967	Extrazug. Langnau
SBB	Temᴵᴵ	279 (220 279)	MA	1967	VEhE. Steinen
SBB	Temᴵᴵ	281	M	1967	SBB H. Rapperswil
SBB	Temᴵᴵ	285	M	1967	SBB H. Buchs
SBB	Temᴵᴵ	288	MA	1967	CTVJ. Le Pont
SBB	Temᴵᴵ	291	MA	1967	SBB H. Olten
SBB	Temᴵᴵ	292	MA	1967	RVT H. Travers
SBB	Temᴵᴵ	295	MA	1967	Locorama. Romanshorn
SBB	Temᴵᴵ	296 (220 296)	MA	1966	Trans Rail. Glis
SBB	Temᴵᴵ	298	MA	1967	Extrazug. Langnau
SBB	Temᴵᴵᴵ	324	MA	1956	DSF. Koblenz
SBB	Temᴵᴵᴵ	334	MA	1956	Association Club Bm 22-70. Schaffhausen
SBB	Temᴵᴵᴵ	344	MA	1957	Extrazug. Langnau
SBB	Temᴵᴵᴵ	351	MA	1962	SBB H. Winterthur
SBB	Temᴵᴵᴵ	354 (220 354)	MA	1958	DVZO. Bauma
SBB	Tmᴵ	413	MA	1960	Swisstrain. Le Locle
SBB	Tmᴵ	420	MA	1960	CTVJ. Le Pont (as Tmᴵ 102)
SBB	Tmᴵ	425 (230 425)	MA	1961	CSG. Mendrisio
SBB	Tmᴵ	453	S	1962	SBB H. Vallorbe
SBB	Tmᴵ	460 (230 460)	MA	1962	CSG. Mendrisio
SBB	Tmᴵ	462 (230 462)	MA	1962	Verein 241A65. Full
SBB	Tmᴵ	464	M	1931	SBB H. VHS
SBB	Tmᴵ	465 (230 465)	MA	1962	HSTB. Hochdorf
SBB	Tmᴵ	475	MA	1964	SBB H. Delémont
SBB	Tmᴵ	480	MA	1964	SBB H. St Maurice
SBB	Tmᴵ	485 (230 485)	MR	1964	VDZ. Zürich (Wolfhausen)
SBB	Tmᴵ	490	M	1964	CSG. Koblenz
SBB	Tmᴵ	511	MS	1935	DSF. Koblenz

SBB	Tm^I	531	MS	1937	Swisstrain (ex MO 511)
SBB	Tm^I	534	MS	1937	BMK. Kallnach
SBB	Tm^I	536 (230 536)	MA	1949	ZMB. ex SZU Tm 10
SBB	Tm^{II}	611	MA	1956	SBB H. Olten
SBB	Tm^{II}	617 (230 617)	MA	1956	DSF. Koblenz
SBB	Tm^{II}	620	M	1957	HEG. Delémont
SBB	Tm^{II}	631	P	1957	Sargans
SBB	Tm^{II}	633	M	1958	HEG. Delémont
SBB	Tm^{II}	663 (230 855)	MA	1959	VHMThB. Locorama. Romanshorn. Ex Tm 61
SBB	Tm^{II}	685 (230 685)	MA	1959	MJA. Emmenbrücke
SBB	Tm^{II}	706 (230 706)	MA	1961	DVZO. Uster (as "93")
SBB	Tm^{II}	717 (230 717)	MA	1962	Verein 241.A.65. Full. "Roger"
SBB	Tm^{II}	725 (230 725)	MA	1963	CSG. Mendrisio
SBB	Tm^{II}	758 (230 758)	MA	1952	VDZ. Bahnpark Brugg
SBB	Tm^{II}	769	MA	1953	CSG. Mendrisio
SBB	Tm^{II}	784 (230 784)	MA	1955	SEHR&RS. Ramsen
SBB	Tm^{II}	785 (230 785)	MA	1955	CSG. Mendrisio
SBB	Tm^{II}	797 (230 797)	MA	1955	DSF. Koblenz
SBB	Tm^{II}	801 (230 801)	MA	1964	SEHR&RS. Ramsen
SBB	Tm^{II}	813 (230 813)	MA	1965	Mikado 1244. Bahnpark Brugg
SBB	Tm^{II}	815	MA	1965	SEHR&RS. Ramsen
SBB	Tm	873	S	1933	Dampflokfreunde Langenthal
SBB	Tm	883 (723)	S	1925	Swisstrain. Le Locle
SBB	Tm	884	M	1930	Austria
SBB	Tm	899	MA	1930	RVT H. St. Sulpice
SBB	Te	955	M	1945	Au, Zürich
SBB	Te	959	M	1949	Au, Zürich (ex SOB 52)
SBB	Ta	960 (PBr 5)	P	1949	Galleria Baumgartner, Mendrisio
SBB	Ta	966	MA	1987	SBB H. Olten. "Tintenfisch"
SBB	Ta	969	MA	1911	SBB H. Olten.
SBB	Ta	970	MA	1924	SBB H. Olten.
SBB	Ta	971	M	1927	SBB H. VHS
SBB	Ta	972	M	1927	SBB H.

▲ Ae 3/6^{III} 10264, preserved by SBB Historic, is seen heading a charter train at Martigny on 9 April 2014. **Mario Stefani**

SBB	Ta	251 003	MA	1990	SBB H. Olten
SBB	RDe 4/4	601	MA	1938	Swisstrain. Payerne (ex BT 25, ex SZU 51, ex OeBB)
SBB	RAe 2/4	1001	MA	1935	SBB H. Olten
SBB	RCe 2/4	203 (1003)	M	1936	SBB H. VHS
SBB	RAe 4/8	1021 (591 021)	MA	1939	SBB Personenverkehr
SBB	RAe	1053	MA	1961	SBB H. Basel
SBB	RBe 4/4	1405	MA	1959	DSF. Koblenz
SBB	RBe 4/4	540 019	MA	1964	Private. Balsthal (205)
SBB	RBe 4/4	540 069	MA	1965	SBB H. Zürich
SBB	RBe 4/4	540 074	MA	1965	DSF. Balsthal (206)
SBB	BDe 4/4	1632	MS	1954	Swisstrain. Balsthal
SBB	BDe 4/4	1641 (570 641)	MA	1955	DSF. Koblenz
SBB	BDe 4/4	1643	MA	1955	SBB H. Team Be 4/6. Winterthur
SBB	BDe 4/4	1646	MA	1955	SBB H. Erstfeld
SBB	Fe 4/4	18518 (1678)	M	1928	VHS
SBB	De 4/4	1679	MA	1928	SBB H. Buchs
SBB	Tm^{III}	9527 (232 527)	MA	1986	VHE. Huttwil
SBB	Tm^{III}	9529 (232 529)	MA	1986	DVZO. Bauma
SBB	Tm^{III}	9571 (232 571)	MA	1975	VVT. Fleurier
SBB	Tm^{III}	9574	MA	1980	SBB H. Delémont
BLS	Te^{I}	11 (215 011)	MA	1950	BLS H.
BLS	Te^{I}	21	MA	1944	BLS H. ex Te 2/2 151, ex RM 216 321
BLS	Te 2/3	31^{II} (32)	MA	1956	VHE. Huttwil
BLS	Tem	41 (225 041)	MA	1960	BLS H. Spiez
BLS	Tem	42 (225 042)	MA	1960	DSF. Koblenz
BLS	Tem	43 (225 043)	MA	1965	DSF. Koblenz
BLS	Tm	61	MA	1974	DSF. Koblenz (ex Travys 238 304)
BLS	Tm	64 (235 064)	MA	1974	BLS H. Burgdorf
BLS	Tm 2/2	65 (235 065)	MA	1963	VPac 01 202
BLS	Tm 2/2	75	MA	1953	DBB. Konolfingen
BLS	Tm	85 (235 085)	MA	1980	VHMThB. Locorama. Romanshorn
BLS	Be 5/7	151^{II} (161)	M	1912	VHS
BLS	Ae 6/8	205 (015 205)	MA	1939	BLS H. Spiez.
BLS	Ae 6/8	206	S	1939	Swisstrain. Winterthur
BLS	Ae 6/8	208	MA	1943	Swisstrain. Payerne
BLS	Ae 4/4	251 (415 251)	MA	1944	BLS H. Langnau
BLS	Ae 4/4	258	MS	1955	BLS H. VHS
BLS	Ae 8/8	273 (485 273)	MA	1962	BLS H. Langnau
BLS	Ae 8/8	275	MS	1963	BLS H. Brig (converted from 255+256, spares)
BLS/BN	Ce 4/4	315	M	1920	Swisstrain. Biel/Bienne
BLS	BCFZe 4/6	731 (STB 103)	MA	1938	BLS H. Burgdorf
BLS	BCFZe 4/6	736	MA	1938	BLS H. Burgdorf
BLS	De 4/5	796	MS	1929	Classic Rail. Biasca
BN	Ce 2/4	727	M	1935	VHS
BN	Be 4/4	761 (545 761)	MA	1953	BLS H. Burgdorf
BT	Be 4/4	11 (416 011)	MA	1932	SOB. Bauma
BT	Be 4/4	13 (416 013)	M	1932	Eurovapor. Locorama. Romanshorn
BT	Be 4/4	14 (416 014)	MA	1932	Eurovapor. Sulgen
BT	Be 4/4	15 (416 015)	MA	1932	DVZO. Bauma
BT	Be 3/4	43 (556 043)	MA	1938	Eurovapor. Sulgen
BTB	De 2/2	1	M	1899	Lokwelt, Freilassing (Germany)
BTB	De 2/2	2	M	1899	VHS
BTB	Be 4/4	105	MS	1930	Swisstrain. Le Locle
EBT	Te^{I}	21	MA	1944	VHE. Huttwil
EBT	Te^{I}	22	M	1944	Mötschwil (BE)
EBT	BDe 4/4	82 (576 054)	MA	1966	VPM. Zell
EBT	Be 4/4	101	MS	1932	Swisstrain. Les Verrières
EBT	Be 4/4	102 (416 102)	M	1932	BLS H. Huttwil
EBT	Be 4/4	105	M	1932	Eisenbahnmuseum Horb (D)
EBT	Te 2/2	155	MA	1945	DBB. Konolfingen
EBT	Te^{I}	157	MA	1946	DBB. Konolfingen
EBT	BDe 2/4	240	MA	1932	VHE. Huttwil
EZB	Ce 4/6	307	MA	1920	BLS H. Spiez

GBS	Ce 4/4	312 (SZU 42)	MS	1920	BLS H. Mendrisio
GFM	ABDe 4/4	155	M	1931	BMK. Kerzers
MO	ABDe 4/4	5	M	1955	BMK. Kallnach
MThB	ABDe 4/4	12 (536 612)	MA	1965	VHMThB. Locorama. Romanshorn
MThB	Em 2/2	41	M	1972	VHMThB. Locorama. Romanshorn
OC	CFe 2/2	11	MS	1895	VHS
OC	BDe 4/4	13	M	1920	BMK. Kerzers
OeBB	RBe 2/4	202 (SBB 2007)	MA	1938	Swisstrain. Balsthal
OeBB	ABDe 2/8	203	P	1937	Balsthal (ex GBS 704)
OeBB	BDe 4/12	204	S	1935	Eisenbahnmuseum Horb (D). Ex DB 425 120
OeBB	ABDe 4/8	244	M	1945	BMK. Kallnach (ex GBS 742)
PTT	Tm	1	S	1930	Le Locle
RVT	Be 4/4	1 (417 301)	M	1952	VVT. Fleurier
RVT	BCm 2/5	9	M	1914	VHS
RVT	ABDe 2/4	102 (537 312)	MA	1945	RVT H. Fleurier
RVT	ABDe 4/4	313	S	1946	RVT H. St. Sulpice (ex BLS 743)
SiTB	CFe 2/4	84	MR	1924	ZMB. Sihlwald
SiTB	BDe 4/4	92	MA	1968	ZMB. Sihlwald.
SiTB	De 3/4	41	MA	1925	ZMB. Sihlwald
SMB	Be 4/4	171 (416 171)	MA	1932	Swisstrain. DBB Burgdorf
SOB	ABe 4/4	5	MS	1939	Arth Goldau
SOB	ABe 4/4	11 (526 290)	MA	1939	BLS. "Glaskasten"
SOB	Tm 2/2	32	MA	1958	Full
SOB	BDe 4/4	80	MA	1959	DSF. Koblenz
SZU	Em 3/3	6 (836 506)	MA	1962	CSG. Mendrisio "Leu"
SZU	Tm	8 (230 858)	MA	1975	SEHR&RS. Etzwilen "GIRAFF"
SZU	Ce 2/2	2	M	1923	Café. Winterthur
VHB	BDe 4/4	576 060 (51)	MA	1966	CSG. Mendrisio (576 021)
WM	BDe 4/4	2 (536 002)	MA	1966	DSF. Koblenz
WM	BDe 2/4	3 (STB 101)	MS	1938	Genève Aéroport
WM	Ta 2/2	31	MA	1917	BMK. Kallnach

▲ This early articulated EMU, BCFZe 4/6 736 has been preserved by BLS Historic and is seen operating a charter on 12 August 2014 at Marin-Epagnier. **Mario Stefani**

Narrow Gauge

Rly.	Gauge	Class	No.	Status	Date	Location
SBB	1000	Deh 4/6	914 (120 011)	MA	1942	ZB Historic. Meiringen
SBB	1000	Te	198	MA	1941	ZB Historic. Luzern
SBB	1000	Te	199	MS	1941	Luzerner Gartenbahn. Luzern
SBB	1000	Tmh	985	MA	1965	DFB. Realp
SBB	1000	G 3/3	6 (SBB 109)	MA	1901	BC. Chaulin
SBB	1000	HG 4/4	1992	MS	1954	ZB Historic. Stansstad
RhB	1000	Tm 2/2	15	MA	1957	CFBS. St Valéry sur Somme (F)
RhB	1000	Tm 2/2	21	MA	1965	CFBS. St Valéry sur Somme (F)
RhB	1000	BCe 4/4	30	MA	1953	RhB
RhB	1000	BCe 4/4	35 (BB 10)	MA	1908	BC. Chaulin
RhB	1000	Tm 2/2	68	MA	1948	DFB. Realp
RhB	1000	Tm 2/2	91	MA	1959	DFB. Realp
RhB	1000	Ge 4/4	181 (BB 81)	MA	1916	BC. Chaulin
RhB	1000	Ge 4/4	182 (BB 82)	MA	1928	RhB. Poschiavo
RhB	1000	Ge 2/4	205	MR	1913	BMA. Bergün
RhB	1000	Ge 2/4	207	M	1913	VHS
RhB	1000	Ge 2/4	212	M	1913	CF de Kaisersberg. Granges-Paccot
RhB	1000	Ge 4/6	391	M	1913	Deutschen Technikmuseum. Berlin
RhB	1000	Ge 6/6	402	M	1921	VHS
RhB	1000	Ge 6/6	406	M	1921	Meiningen, to Germany
RhB	1000	Ge 6/6	407	P	1922	BMA. Bergün
RhB	1000	Ge 6/6	411	M	1925	Deutsches Museum. München (Germany)
RhB	1000	ABe 4/4	484	MS	1958	La Mure (France)
RhB	1000	ABe 4/4	486	MR	1958	La Mure (France)
RhB	1000	BDe 4/4	491	MA	1958	SEFT. Grono
AB	1000	Tm 2/2	501	MA	1957	Albbähnle Amstetten (D)
AG	1000	CFeh 3/3	1 (SGA 16)	M	1911	VHS (false no. 3)
AG	1000	CFe 3/3	2 (SGA 17)	MA	1911	AG2. Gais
ASD	1000	ABDe 4/4	3	MS	1913	La Mure (France)
ASD	1000	ABDe 4/4	12	MS	1913	La Mure (France)
BA	1000	Be 4/4	5 (ASm 521)	MS	1963	SEFT. Grono
BOB	1000	HGe 3/3	29	MA	1926	BC. Chaulin
BTB	1000	BCe 4/4	7	S	1923	Pro BTB. Rudersdorf
BVB	1000	He 2/2	2	M	1899	BC. Chaulin
CEG	1000	Be 4/4	111	MA	1903	BC. Chaulin
CEV	1000	BDe 4/4	103	MR	1913	CEV. Vevey
CEV	1000	BDe 4/4	105	MR	1913	CEV. Vevey
CJ	1000	Tm	506	MA	1953	DFB. Realp
CJ	1000	CFe 4/4	601	MA	1953	La Traction. Pré Petitjean
ESZ	1000	CFe 4/4	3 (RVO 131)	MR	1913	ZDT. Zug
FO	1000	CFmh 2/2	21	MS	1927	Aarau (VHS)
FO	1000	XRote	2981	MA	1941	DFB. Realp
FO	1000	Xmh 1/2	4961	MA	1945	DFB. Realp
FW	1000	BCe 4/4	1	MS	1921	TVB. Attisholz
GFM	1000	Te 2/2	11	M	1913	Bulle
GFM	1000	Be 4/4	T 116	M	1922	Bulle
GFM	1000	Be 4/4	T 139	M	1943	Bulle
JB	1000	He 2/2	1	M	1898	VHS
JB	1000	He 2/2	9	M	1898	Steck, Bowil
LEB	1000	Te 2/2	2	MA	1896	BC. Chaulin
LJB	1000	Ce 2/2	12	MA	1907	BC. Chaulin
LLB	1000	ABFe 4/4	10	MA	1914	BC. Chaulin
LMB	1000	Ce 2/2	14	MR	1917	FSS. Ruefswil
LSE	1000	Gm 4/4	111	M	1955	Hartsfelder Eisenbahn, Neresheim (D)
LSE	1000	Tmᴵ	491 (100)	MS	1931	BNB. Alpnachstad
MC	1000	BCFeh 4/4	15	MA	1909	TNT. Martigny
MC	1000	ABDeh 4/4	32	MA	1921	TNT. Martigny
MCM	1000	BCFeh 4/4	6	MA	1909	BC. Chaulin
MGB	1000	Gm 4/4	70	MA	1966	DFB. Realp

MGB	1000	Tm 2/2	2922	MA	1959	DFB. REalp
MIB	1000	Ta 2/2	3 (T 46)	MS	1931	Museumbahn Bruchhausen Vilsen (D)
MIB	1000	CFa 2/2	4	M	1939	VHS
MIB	1000	CFa 2/2	5	P	1949	Innertkirchen
MIB	1000	Tm 2/2	10	MA	1961	La Traction. Pré Petitjean; Ex SBB 709
MOB	1000	Tm 2/2	1	M	1930	BC. Chaulin
MOB	1000	Tm 2/2	2	MA	1954	CFBS. St Valéry-sur-Somme (F)
MOB	1000	BCFe 4/4	16	MS	1905	Niederscherli
MOB	1000	ABDe 4/4	11	MR	1904	BC. Chaulin
MOB	1000	BCFe 4/4	20	MA	1905	BC. Chaulin
MOB	1000	BFZe 4/4	26	M	1912	MOS. Clubhouse. Saanen
MOB	1000	DZe 6/6	2002	MA	1932	BC. Chaulin
NStCM	1000	ABDe 4/4	1	MS	1916	La Mure (France)
NStCM	1000	ABDe 4/4	5	MS	1916	La Mure (France)
NStCM	1000	ABDe 4/4	10	MS	1916	NStCM
NStCM	1000	ABDe 4/4	11	MS	1916	La Mure (France)
OJB	1000	BDe 4/4	53	MS	1917	Niederscherli
OJB	1000	Ge 4/4	126	MA	1917	BMK. Kerzers
RBS	1000	Gem 4/4	122	MA	1916	La Traction. Pré Petitjean
SeTB	1000	BDe 2/2	4	MA	1928	BC. Chaulin
SGA	1000	BCFeh 4/4	5	MA	1930	AG2. Gais
StEB	1000	HGe 2/2	1	M	1898	VHS
SZB	1000	BDe 4/4	6	MS	1950	TVB. Aarberg
TB	1000	CFe 4/4	2	P	1903	Grüningen
VBW	1000	Be 4/4	30	MS	1910	TVB. Ungersheim (France)
VBW	1000	BDe 4/4	38	MS	1913	TVB. Ungersheim (France)
VBZ	1000	GM 3/3	71	MA	1975	DFB. Realp
WAB	800	HGe 2/2	55	P	1910	Münchenstein
WSB	1000	BSe 4/4	116	P	1901	Reinach (Aargau)
WT	1000	BDe 4/4	36	MA	1913	RBS. Solothurn
ZB	1000	Tm	984	P	1967	Aparthotel, Rotkreuz

MOS: Modelbahngruppe Obersimmental-Saanenland

▲ Former Martigny Châtelard railcar ABDeh 4/4 32 plus driving trailer Ct 21, preserved by the Train Nostalgique du Trient are seen at Martigny on 22 May 2014. **Pierre Julien**

5.3. FOREIGN LOCOMOTIVES PRESERVED IN SWITZERLAND (from State railways)

Standard gauge

Rly.	Class	No.	Details	Status	Date	Location
BDZ	01	01.22	2-8-2	MR	1935	Tabaklok. Full
DB	01	01 202 (001 202)	4-6-2	MA	1936	Verein Pacific 01 202. Lyss
DB	18	18 508	4-6-2	M	1924	Locorama. Romanshorn
DR	52.80	52 8055	2-10-0	MA	1943	DLM. Schaffhausen
DB	64	64 518	2-6-2T	MA	1940	VHE. Huttwil "Sybille"
DB	Köf II	322 175	B dh	MA	1951	Eurovapor. Full
DB	Köf II	323 782	B dh	MA	1950	VVT. St. Sulpice
DB	Köf II	323 967	B dh	MA	1944	VVT. St. Sulpice
ÖBB	152	52.221	2-10-0	MA	1944	VVT. St. Sulpice (52 7486)
PKP	TKt48	TKt48-188 (048 188)	2-8-2T	MR	1957	VVT. St. Sulpice
SNCF	141 R	141 R 73	2-8-2	MR	1945	Winterthur (in pieces)
SNCF	141 R	141 R 568	2-8-2	MA	1945	SCT. Vallorbe
SNCF	141 R	141 R 1207	2-8-2	MR	1947	Winterthur (in pieces)
SNCF	141 R	141 R 1244	2-8-2	MA	1947	Mikado 1244. Bahnpark Brugg
SNCF	241 A	241 A 65	4-8-2	MA	1931	Verein 241.A.65. Full
SNCF	241 P	241 P 30	4-8-2	MR	1951	VVT. St. Sulpice

Narrow gauge

Rly.	Gauge	Class	No.	Details	Status	Date	Location
CP	1000		E.164	0-4-4-0T	MA	1903	La Traction. Pré Petitjean
CP	1000		E.206	2-4-6-0T	MA	1913	La Traction. Pré Petitjean
DB	1000	99	99 193	0-10-0T	MR	1927	BC. Chaulin
DR	600	99	99 3311	0-8-0T	MA	1917	Baumschulbahn. Schinznach
PKP	600	Ty3	Ty3-194	0-6-0T	MA	1944	Baumschulbahn. Schinznach
SAR	600	NGG13	60	§	MA	1927	Baumschulbahn. Schinznach
Vietnam	1000	HG 4/4	40-304 (704)	0-8-0RT	MR	1924	DFB. Chur
Vietnam	1000	HG 4/4	40-308 (708)	0-8-0RT	MR	1930	DFB. Chur

§ 2-6-2+2-6-2 (Garratt)

▲ Ex SNCF 141 R 1244, together with ex DB 01 202 and DB Museum-owned 01 150 power a special towards the Gotthard line at Immensee on 27 June 2015. **Mario Stefani**

6. MUSEUMS, MUSEUM LINES AND PRESERVED STOCK OWNERS

There are few museum lines in Switzerland, due to the fact that very few lines have been closed by either the SBB or private railways. SBB Historic has a number of old electric locomotives retained as official museum locomotives that are used on specials, and appear at open days, etc. Several of the private railways have retained steam locomotives, or older examples of more modern traction, and these either operate at weekends, or are available for private hire.

The Swiss Transport Museum (*Verkehrshaus*) is located at Luzern, and is well worth a visit. It covers all aspects of communications, not just railways. The best known museum line operated by enthusiasts is perhaps the metre gauge Blonay–Chamby near Montreux, but there are a number of other operations, often over the lines of private railways.

The *Verband Öffentliche Verkehr* publishes each year on its website details of steam specials and public excursions (www.voev.ch/fr/Services/Agenda/Manifestations). Many of these trains also appear in the public timetable.

Also of interest are the paddle steamers operating on the Brienzersee, Lac Léman (Lake Geneva), Thunersee, Vierwaldstättersee (Lake Lucerne) and Zürichsee: see Section 7. These are also detailed in the SBB timetable.

It should be noted that all the above operations are summer only, usually from May to September.

The list below of museum operations is arranged in alphabetical order of associations.

Appenzellerbahnen (AG2)
www.appenzellerbahnen.ch
www.ag2.ch
The Appenzellerbahnen has one steam locomotive available in Herisau for charter and two historic EMUs preserved by AG2.

Chemin de fer Blonay-Chamby BC
www.blonay-chamby.ch
The Blonay Chamby metre gauge line is undoubtedly Switzerland's premier enthusiast-operated line, with excellent views over Lac Léman (Lake Geneva). Operates at weekends using both steam and electric traction. Some of the stock is stored at other locations.

Trains operate Blonay–Chamby–Chaulin depot Saturdays, Sundays and special holidays from early May to late October and also operate on selected weekends Vevey to Blonay.

11 steam, 3 electric, 1 diesel, 7 railcars, 9 trams.

Bahnmuseum Albula BMA
www.bahnmuseum-albula.ch
A small museum at Bergün station on the RhB Chur–St Moritz line.

2 electric.

Bahnmuseum Kerzers-Kallnach BMK
www.bahnmuseum-kerzers.ch
Aegertenstrasse 2, CH 3210 Kerzers.

Bahnmuseum Kerzers has stock at Kallnach, near Kerzers, but is to close by 2017. Some stock will move to Nordhausen in Germany.

1 steam, 6 electric, 15 diesel, 4 EMUs.

Bahnpark Brugg

www.bahnpark-brugg.ch

Unterwerkstrasse 11, CH 5200 Brugg.

A foundation looking after the old roundhouse in Brugg where SBB now keeps its Zürich area steam locomotives. Mikado 1244 and others also use the depot as their base.

Ballenberg-Dampfbahn   BDB

www.dampfbahnen.ch

The Ballenberg Dampfbahn has two steam locomotives based at Interlaken Ost and used on occasional excursions on the metre gauge line to Meiringen and also over the rack to Giswil. There are occasional trips on the BOB as well.

Baumschulbahn

www.schbb.ch

Degerfeldstrasse 4, CH 5107 Schinznach-Dorf.

A 600 mm gauge line operating at weekends around a garden centre in Schinznach Bad, on the Aarau–Brugg line. Access is easiest by bus from Brugg. Operating days are usually Saturdays and Sundays from mid-April until mid-October. Steam locos include a South African Garratt built by Hanomag.

9 steam, 5 diesel.

Berner Tramway-Gesellschaft

www.dampftram.ch

The Berner Tramway Gesellschaft operates steam tram G 3/3 no. 12 around the city once a month May to October but not in July.

Verein Pro Birsigthalbahn   Pro BTB

www.probirsigthalbahn.ch

A group which looks after preserved stock formerly with the Birsigthalbahn, which became part of Basel suburban tramway operator BLT. Some of the stock owned by BTB is stored at Ungersheim open air museum near Mulhouse in France.

BLS Stiftung   BLS H

www.bls-stiftung.ch

This foundation manages the BLS historic collection. Several items are based in the old depot at Burgdorf, others may be found at Spiez. As most are in working order they could be anywhere on the BLS system.

Verein Brünig Nostalgiebahn   BNB

www.verein-bnb.ch

An organisation which looks after stock from the former Brünigbahn which merged with the LSE to form Zentralbahn.

www.zbhistoric.ch

Closely linked seems to be Verein ZB Historic, which looks after stock from the former LSE as well as the Brünigbahn.

Brienz Rothorn Bahn   BRB

www.brienz-rothorn-bahn.ch

As detailed under the Brienz Rothorn Bahn, this railway still uses steam in regular service.

Chemin de Fer de Kaeserberg

www.kaeserberg.ch

This railway is a massive model railway layout at Granges-Paccot, a bus ride (route 9) from Fribourg. The railways also has real electric loco RhB Ge 2/4 212.

Classic Rail   (CR)

Classic Rail is a company run by Peter Hennig which owns several preserved locomotives – mainly main line electrics – which also offers maintenance to all-comers. It is not very clear whether the aim is to hire the locos and there is some overlap with Swisstrain and ownership of locos is sometimes difficult to determine. In 2014 Classic Rail's website disappeared and it seemed the organisation was in trouble.

Club Salon Bleu   CSB

A club which looks after former EBT electric railcar BDe 2/4 240, in connection with VHE.

▲ BFD (Brig–Furka–Disentis) 2-6-0T no. 3, preserved on the Blonay–Chamby line, operated a special train on the TPF line to Broc Fabrique in its centenary year on 23 June 2012. The factory (fabrique) in the background makes chocolates!   **Jan Lundstrøm**

Club San Gottardo CSG

www.clubsangottardo.ch

The Club San Gottardo operate regular excursions on the Mendrisio–Stabio–Valmorea (Italy) line. The line recently reopened to regular passenger services so the future of this operation may be in some doubt. Operational Ae 4/7 10997 is also based here but privately owned.

3 steam, 4 electric, 5 diesel, 1 railcar.

Compagnie du Train à Vapeur de la Vallee de Joux CTVJ

www.ctvj.ch

The CTVJ has two steam locomotives used between Le Pont (depot) and Sentier-Orient on public excursions over the Pont Brassus Bahn. Usually operates on two Sundays a month early June to early October.

2 steam, 1 diesel, 1 electro-diesel.

Dampfbahn-Bern DBB

www.dbb.ch

The Verein Dampfbahn Bern is now based in the old depot at Konolfingen and runs various public excursion trains May to October.

7 steam, 2 electric, 1 diesel.

Dampf-Loki-Club BT9

www.bt9.ch

Former Bodensee Toggenburg Bahn Eb 3/5 No. 9 (a.k.a. SBB 5889) steam locomotive is available for charter and operates the regular "Amor Express" from Herisau.

Dampfbahn Furka Bergstrecke DFB

www.dfb.ch
www.dieselcrew.ch

The DFB has restored the rack-equipped section of the metre gauge Furka Oberalp Bahn from Realp to Oberwald over the Furka Pass, abandoned when the Furka base tunnel opened. Three steam locomotives have been restored, including two repatriated from Vietnam! The terminus and depot at Realp, and the Oberwald station are close to the MGB stations on the Brig–Andermatt line. DFB carries out heavy work on its steam locos at Uzwil, near St Gallen. The diesel locos are looked after by "Diesel Crew". MGB also operates through trains over the summit line in summer with its diesel locos.

7 steam, 8 diesel.

Dampflokomotiv- und Maschinenfabrik DLM

www.dlm-ag.ch

Steam locomotive rebuild specialist DLM operates excursions from Schaffhausen several times a year using heavily modernised former DR 52 8055 which is also available for hire.

Dampfloki - Verein Appenzeller Bahnen DLV AB

www.dampfloki.ch

A group which looks after RhB tank G 3/4 14 plus coaches at Herisau, running special trains on the AB line there.

Draisine Sammlung Fricktal DSF

www.draisine.ch

Gütschhalde, CH 5322 Koblenz.

DSF, now known as Verein Depot und Schienenfahrzeuge Koblenz, uses the old depot at Koblenz for its collection of locomotives and railcars, but most of its draisines (track trolleys) are kept in its workshops in Laufenburg.

1 diesel, 4 electric railcars, 5 tractors.

Dampfverein Zürcher Oberland DVZO

www.dvzo.ch

The DVZO runs steam trains over the normally freight-only SBB line between Bauma and Hinwil on the first and third Sunday of the month May to October. The DVZO depot is at Uster; locos are based at Bauma as required.

7 steam, 1 electric, 1 electro-diesel, 3 diesel.

Eurovapor EV

www.eurovapor.ch
www.lokremise-sulgen.ch
www.appenzellerbahnen.ch
www.nostalgie-rhein-express.ch

Chaletstrasse 26a, CH 8583 Sulgen.

Eurovapor runs public excursions from Basel several times a year using a mixture of steam and electric traction. Destinations outside Switzerland are also featured. The company, which also has stock and runs trains in Germany, operates from the depot at Sulgen and runs steam on the Rorschach-Heiden Bahn (RHB, part of Appenzellerbahnen) with former industrial loco Eh 2/2 "Rosa", the latter usually on the first Sunday of the month May–October.

Extrazug

www.extrazug.ch

Verein Extrazug is a charter operator based at Langnau depot which hires preserved BLS electric locos and has four shunters of its own.

Feldschlösschen Brewery

Not really a museum operation, but the Feldschlösschen brewery near Rheinfelden station still owns active steam loco (ex SBB 8481), nowadays mainly for publicity. A diesel normally carries out the regular shunting. A set of coaches is available to take parties from the SBB station to the brewery.

1 steam (and another on a plinth!).

Freunde Schweizer Schmalspurbahnen FSS

www.fss-verein.ch

A group whose aim is to preserve Swiss narrow gauge stock. Based at Roggwil.

Genossenschaft Museumsbahn Emmentalbahn GME

www.emmentalbahn.ch

This organisation looks after the line from Huttwil to Sumiswald-Grünen, east of Bern. Works closely with both CSB and VHE.

Historische Eisenbahn Gesellschaft HEG

www.volldampf.ch

The old roundhouse in Delémont is now a listed monument. SBB Historic keeps some stock here and is represented by Historische Eisenbahn Gesellschaft. HEG donated 27 vehicles to SBB H in 2014.

5 steam, 1 electric, 3 diesel.

Verein Historische Seethalbahn HSTB

www.historische-seethalbahn.ch

Siedereistrasse 20, CH 6281 Hochdorf.

Verein Historische Seethalbahn operates excursions with steam loco E 3/3 no. 3 over the Lenzburg–Emmenbrücke (–Luzern) *Seethalbahn* line from Hochdorf depot, on this line. The group hopes to restore former NOB E 3/3 456 (SBB 8554) to working order and also has an ex SBB Tm[I].

1 steam, 1 tractor.

La Traction

www.la-traction.ch

La Traction has two steam locomotives, plus other stock, at Pré Petitjean, used on occasional public excursions over the CJ metre gauge system July–September.

2 steam, 2 electric, 1 EMU.

Lausanne Echallens Bercher LEB

www.leb.ch

The Lausanne–Echallens–Bercher railway has one steam loco and uses it between Cheseaux and Bercher on public excursions.

Locorama

www.locorama.ch

Egnacherweg 1, CH 8590 Romanshorn.

The old SBB depot at Romanshorn has been transformed into a museum. In 2015 opening was on Sundays 3 May to 25 October, 10.00–17.00.

3 steam, 4 electric, 2 diesel, 1 EMU.

Ferrovia Monte Generoso MG

www.montegeneroso.ch

The Ferrovia Monte Generoso has one steam locomotive used on occasional public excursions.

Museumsbahn Stein-Am-Rhein - Singen

www.etzwilen-singen.ch

Verein zur Erhaltung der Bahnlinie Etzwilen–Singen operates excursion trains over the former SBB non-electrified line from Etzwilen as far as Ramsen. They usually start from Stein am Rhein where stock is based.

1 steam, 3 diesel.

Mikado 1244

www.mikado1244.ch

Bahnpark Brugg.

Verein Mikado 1244 operates ex SNCF 2-8-2 steam loco 141 R 1244 on occasional public excursions over SBB main lines. The group now also has several other, more modern, locos.

1 steam, 2 electric, 1 tractor.

Militärmuseum Full

http://www.militaer-museum.ch

This museum has a shed which is used to house locomotives from several clubs. The museum is a 45 minute walk from Koblenz station, or a bus ride from the station to Full post office then 15 minutes' walk.

Oensingen Balsthal Bahn   OeBB

www.oebb.ch

The OeBB (see main section) has three steam locomotives used on public excursions over its own line several times a year. The depot at Balsthal is also home to museum locomotives owned by other organisations and awaiting overhaul.

5 steam, 1 electric, 2 diesel, 1 EMU.

▲ SBB Historic's electric railcar RAe 2/4 1001, built in 1935, is seen on a test run with loco Re 4/4¹ 10001 at Boudry on 17 June 2015.   **Mario Stefani**

Rhätische Bahn

RhB

www.rhb.ch

The Rhätische Bahn (see main section) continues to operate historic/nostalgic trains using steam or electric locomotives based at Landquart and Samedan. Watch out in winter for the operation of the steam rotary snow plough.

3 steam, 4 electric, 3 EMUs.

Rigibahnen

RB

www.rigi.ch

The Rigibahnen (see main section) runs regular steam trips often running Arth Goldau–Rigi Kulm–Vitznau and back.

RVT Historique

RVT H

This organisation looks after the historic stock owned by RVT, now part of TransN. The depot is at Fleurier – see also VVT.

SBB Historic

SBB H

www.sbbhistoric.ch

The old SBB depot in Olten is now one of the main holding points for the SBB Historic collection. However it is not a museum but a storage point and SBB day to day operations still take place at the facility. Other SBB Historic locos are based at Bahnpark Brugg, Erstfeld, St Maurice and other points.

7 electric, 1 diesel, 2 EMUs.

Società Esercizio Ferroviario Turistico

SEFT

www.seft-fm.ch

SEFT ran tourist trains over the "Ferrovia Mesolcinese" Castione–Grono–Cama section of the old Bellinzona to Mesocco RhB line. In 2014 the line was supposed to close completely to make way for a bypass but instead it was cut back. Its future was unsure at the time of writing. All stock is in the depot at Grono.

3 railcars.

Stiftung Museumsbahn SEHR&RS

SEHR&RS

www.etzwilen-singen.ch

This group's aim is to see trains running regularly all the way from Etzwilen to Singen.

Swiss Classic Train

(SCT)

www.swissclassictrain.ch

Former SNCF 141 R 568 is based in Schaffhausen and owned by William Cook Rail. After offering excursion trains around Switzerland in impeccably restored Swiss rolling stock, the French loco is now for sale. The company continues to hire its train with other classic traction.

Swisstrain

www.swisstrain.ch

Swisstrain is a preservation organisation with a very large number of locos and a few other items of stock at several sites around the country, mainly in store, at Le Locle and Payerne depots. The organisation is linked to dealer Classic Rail AG and it is not often clear who owns what!

Schynige Platte Bahn   SPB

www.jungfraubahn.ch

The Schynige Platte Bahn (see main section) has one steam locomotive available for charter at Wilderswil and in the summer period June to August it sees regular use on alternate Sundays.

Dampfzug Sursee-Triengen   ST

www.dampfzug.ch

The Sursee Triengen Bahn has one steam locomotive, based at Triengen, available for charter but public excursions are operated two or three times a year.

Train Nostalgique Du Trient   TNT

www.trainostalgique-trient.ch

This is the preservation section of the former Martigny-Châtelard, now part of RegionAlps, and also known as the Mont Blanc Express. The TNT has its own depot near Martigny station.

2 electric railcars.

Train Touristique D'Emosson   TTE

www.chatelard.net

The Parc d'Attractions du Châtelard runs a most unusual line, originally built to provide access to a hydroelectric scheme. A funicular operates from Le Châtelard VS station on the Mont Blanc Express (TMR, former MC) line to Château d'Eau then a 600 mm gauge line runs from there to Emosson. From Emosson a second funicular continues to Barrage (the dam). Operates daily late May to late October.

2 diesel, 5 battery electric.

Tramverein Bern   TVB

www.trittbrett.ch

In principle, devoted to preserving trams but also has other stock – many Swiss light railways were inter-urban tramways.

Verein 241.A.65

www.241a65.ch

This club looks after Europe's biggest (ex SNCF 4-8-2) steam loco at Militärmuseum Full. The club also has other stock.

Verein Dampfzug Waldenburgbahn

www.waldenburgerli.ch

The Waldenburgerbahn has one steam locomotive used on public excursions on the last Sunday of the month (June to September) between Liestal and Waldenburg (see Waldenburgerbahn WB). The association involved is trying to save the service as the stock is 750 mm gauge, unique in Switzerland, but there is a project to convert the line to metre gauge.

Verein Dampflok Muni VDM

www.muni-dampflok.ch

A club which now bases its former industrial steam loco "MUNI" at the Militärmusuem in Full.

Verein Dampfgruppe Zürich VDZ

www.dampfgruppe-zuerich.ch

A group based in Zürich looking after three steam locomotives, usually found at Brugg.

Verein Historische Eisenbahn Emmental VHE

www.historische-eisenbahn-emmental.ch

Verein Historische Eisenbahn Emmental is based in the old depot at Huttwil and runs public excursions May–October.

3 steam, 2 EMUs, 2 tractors.

Verein Historische Mittel-Thurgau Bahn VHMThB

www.mthb.ch

A group which preserves former MThB stock. This is usually housed at Locorama.

1 steam, 1 railcar, 5 tractors.

Verein Pacific 01 202

www.dampflok.ch

The Verein Pacific 01 202 looks after former DB 01 202, is based ay Lyss and works several public excursions each year.

Verkehrshaus VHS

www.verkehrshaus.ch

The National Transport Museum (Verkehrshaus) is located in Luzern on the north side of the Vierwaldstättersee, and now has its own station. The lake steamers also call at a pier adjacent to the museum. Some of the exhibits are changed from time to time, so not all are on display.

9 steam, 11 electric, 9 EMUs

Verein Pendelzug Mirage VPM

www.pendelzug-mirage.ch

A club looking after former EBT railcar BDe 4/4 82.

Vapeur Val-de-Travers VVT

www.vvt.ch

Les Eterpilles, CH 2123 St Sulpice.

Vapeur Val-de-Travers, with a depot at St Sulpice, operate steam services on certain weekends over the TransN line from Travers to Buttes plus the normally freight-only St. Sulpice–Fleurier section. This is claimed to be the biggest collection of steam locos in Switzerland. The depot is open on Saturdays, except during holidays.

11 steam, 6 diesel.

Verein ZB Historic   ZB Historic

See BNB above.

Züger Depot Technikgeschichte   ZDT

www.zdt.ch

A museum in Zug which displays all types of vehicles, the ESZ tram – an electric railcar – being somewhat hidden.

Zürcher Museums-Bahn   ZMB

www.museumsbahn.ch

The Sihltal Zürich Uetliberg Bahn has one steam locomotive at Sihlwald available for charter plus other vintage stock which is now under the Zürcher Museums-Bahn. Operates on the last Sunday of the month April to October.

2 steam, 1 electric, 2 diesel, 2 EMUs.

▲ RVT Historic's ex SBB electric shunter TEM^{III} 292 is seen at Fleurier with the club's 1945-vintage railcar ABDe 102 on 14 March 2015. **Mario Stefani**

7. PADDLE STEAMERS

Details of these beautiful ships are covered in this book since most can be used free by holders of a Swiss Travel Pass, and can be easily combined with railway visits. Routes, days of operation, timetables and prices can be found by referring to the websites shown. With the exception of the NEUCHÂTEL, all are shown in the SBB timetable. There are numerous non-steam ships on these lakes and substitutions sometimes take place.

BRIENZERSEE

www.bls.ch

Ship: LÖTSCHBERG   Escher, Wyss   1914

LAC LÉMAN (Lake Geneva)

www.cgn.ch

Ships:	MONTREUX	Sulzer	1904
	LA SUISSE	Sulzer	1910
	SAVOIE	Sulzer	1914
	SIMPLON	Sulzer	1920
	RHÔNE	Sulzer	1927
	VEVEY (diesel)	Sulzer	1907
	ITALIE (diesel)	Sulzer	1908
	HELVETIE (diesel)	Sulzer	1926

ITALIE and HELVETIE were laid up "long term" in 2014 awaiting major rebuilding

LAC DU NEUCHÂTEL

www.trivapor.ch

Ship: NEUCHÂTEL   Escher, Wyss   1912

THUNERSEE

www.bls.ch

Ship: BLÜMLISALP   Escher, Wyss   1906

VIERWALDSTÄTTERSEE (Lake Lucerne)

www.lakelucerne.ch

Ships:	URI	Sulzer	1901 (out of use after fire in 2014)
	UNTERWALDEN	Escher, Wyss	1902
	SCHILLER	Sulzer	1906
	GALLIA	Escher, Wyss	1913
	STADT LUZERN	Sachsenburg	1928

ZÜRICHSEE

www.zsg.ch

Ships:	STADT ZÜRICH	Escher, Wyss	1909
	STADT RAPPERSWIL	Escher, Wyss	1914

In addition to the above the HOHENTWIEL, based in Austria, runs excursions on the Bodensee (Lake Constance) to Swiss and German piers. www.hohentwiel.com

The PIEMONTE on Lake Maggiore sees occasional use in the Locarno area mainly operating charters. www.navlagh.it

There is also a small screw ship, the GREIF, on the Greifensee at Uster. www.sgg-greifensee.ch

Further information on Swiss and Italian paddle steamers can be found at www.swissitalianpaddlesteamers.com

Richard Franklin / John Bird

▲ 1913-vintage paddle steamer "GALLIA" leaves Fluëlen for Luzern on 3 July 2015.   **Brian Denton**

APPENDIX I. ABBREVIATIONS

RAILWAY COMPANIES NOW ABSORBED INTO LARGER GROUPS OR NO LONGER OPERATING

Many of the companies merged or absorbed in the recent past are still known by their original names.

AG	Altstätten–Gais, later SGA, now AB
AL	Aigle–Leysin, now TPC
AOMC	Aigle–Ollon–Monthey–Champéry, now TPC
ASD	Aigle–Sépey–Diablerets, now TPC
BA	Biasca–Acquarossa, closed 1973
BAM	Bière–Apples–Morges, now MBC
BD	Bremgarten–Dietikon, now BDWM
BN	Bern–Neuchâtel, now BLS
	Brünigbahn (SBB), now ZB
BSB	Bern–Schwarzenburg Bahn, later GBS, now BLS
BT	Bodensee–Toggenburg, now SOB
BTB	Burgdorf–Thun Bahn (standard gauge), later EBT, RM, now BLS
BTB	Birsigtalbahn (metre gauge), now BLT
BTI	Biel–Täuffelen–Ins, now ASm
BVB	Bex–Villars–Bretaye, now TPC
BVZ	Brig–Visp–Zermatt, now MGB
CEG	Chemins de fer Electriques de la Gruyère, later GFM, now TPF
CEV	Chemins de Fer Electriques Veveysans, now MVR
CMN	Chemins de Fer des Montagnes Neuchâteloises, later TRN, now transN
EB	Emmenthalbahn, later EBT, RM, now BLS
EBT	Emmental–Burgdorf–Thun, later RM, now BLS
ESZ	Elektrische Strassenbahnen im Kanton Zug
EZB	Erlenbach–Zweisimmen Bahn, now ZVB
FMG	Ferrovia Monte Generoso, now MG
FO	Furka–Oberalp, now MGB
GB	Gotthardbahn, now SBB
GBS	Gürbetalbahn–Bern–Schwarzenburg, now BLS
GFM	Gruyère–Fribourg–Morat, now TPF
GTB	Gürbetalbahn, later GBS, now BLS
HWB	Huttwil–Wolhusen Bahn, later VHB, RM, now BLS
JS	Jura–Simplon, now SBB
KLB	Kriens–Luzern Bahn, now closed
LCD	Lugano–Cadrio–Dino, now closed
LG	Lausanne–Gare, now part of TL metro Line 2
LHB	Langenthal–Huttwil Bahn, later VHB, RM, now BLS
LJB	Langenthal–Jura Bahn, later OJB, RVO, now ASm
LLB	Leuk–Leukerbad, closed 1967
LMB	Langenthal–Melchnau Bahn, later OJB, RVO, now ASm
LO	Lausanne–Ouchy, now part of TL metro Line 2
LSE	Luzern–Stans–Engelberg, now ZB
MC	Martigny–Châtelard, later Mont Blanc Express, now TMR
MCM	Monthey–Champéry–Morgins, later AOMC, now TPC
MO	Martigny–Orsières, later Saint-Bernard Express, now TMR
MThB	Mittelthurgau Bahn, now SBB
MTGN	Montreux–Territet–Glion–Naye, now MVR
NOB	Schweizerische Nordostbahn, now SBB
OC	Orbe–Chavornay, now Travys
OJB	Oberaargau–Jura Bahn, later RVO, now ASm
OSST	Oberaargau Solothurn Seeland Transport, now ASm
PBr	Chemin de Fer de Pont-Brassus, now Travys
RdB	Regional des Brenets, later CMN, TRN, now transN
RHB	Rorschach–Heiden Bergbahn, now AB

RhW	Rheineck–Walzenhausen, now AB
RM	Regionalverkehr Mittelland, now BLS
RSG	Régional Saignelégier–Glovelier, now CJ
RVO	Regionalverkehr Oberaargau, now ASm
RVT	Régional du Val-de-Travers, later TRN, now transN
SCB	Schweizerische Centralbahn, now SBB
SeTB	Sernftalbahn. Closed 1969
SEZ	Spiez–Erlenbach–Zweisimmen, now BLS
SGA	St Gallen–Gais–Appenzell, now AB
SiTB	Sihltalbahn, now SZU
SMB	Solothurn–Münster Bahn, later RM, now BLS
SNB	Solothurn–Niederbipp Bahn, now ASm
SSB	Städtische Strassenbahnen Bern, now SVB (Bernmobil)
STB	Seethalbahn, now SBB
StEB	Stansstad–Engelberg Bahn, later LSE, now ZB
SZB	Solothurn–Zollikofen–Bern, now RBS
TB	Trogenerbahn, now AB
TRN	Transports Régionaux Neuchâtelois, now transN
TSOL	Transports du Soud Ouest Lausannois, now TL
UeBB	Uerikon–Bauma Bahn, now SBB
VBW	Vereinigte Bern–Worb Bahn, now RBS
VHB	Vereinigte Huttwil Bahn, later RM, now BLS
VRB	Vitznau–Rigi Bahn, now RB
VZ	Visp–Zermatt, later BVZ, now MGB
WM	Wohlen–Meisterschwanden, now BDWM
WMB	Wetzikon–Meilen Bahn, closed 1950
WSB	Wynental and Suhrentalbahn, now AAR bus+bahn
WT	Worblentalbahn, later VBW, now RBS
YSteC	Yverdon–Ste Croix, now Travys

TRAIN OPERATORS FROM OTHER COUNTRIES

BDZ	Balgarski Darzhavni Zehleznitsi (Bulgarian State railways)
CP	Caminhos de Ferro Portugueses (Portuguese Railways)
DB	Deutsche Bahn, formerly Deutsche Bundesbahn
DR	Deutsche Reichsbahn
FKE	Frankfurt–Königstein Eisenbahn (DE)
FNM	Ferrovie Nord Milano (Italy)
FS	Ferrovie della Stato (Italian Railways)
HFHJ	Hillerød-Frederiksværk-Hundested Jernbane (DK)
HGK	Häfen- und Güterverkehr Köln, now Rheincargo (DE)
HP	Hjørring Privatbaner (DK)
ISC	Interporto Servizi Cargo (IT)
LTE	LTE Logistik und Transport (A)
MWB	Mittel Weser Bahn (DE)
NS	Nederlandse Spoorwegen (NL)
ÖBB	Österreichische Bundesbahnen
PKP	Polskie Koleje Padstwowe
RhV	Rheintalische Verkehrsbetriebe
RSR	Royal State Railway (Siam, now Thailand)
SAR	South African Railways
SNCF	Société Nationale des Chemins de fer Français
SWEG	Südwestdeutsche Verkehrs AG (DE)
TXL	TX Logistics (DE)
VHJ	Västervik Hultsfreds Järnväg (DE)
VHX	Vietnam Hoa Xa
VPS	Verkehrsbetriebe Peine-Salzgitter (DE)
WLC	Wiener Lokalbahn Cargo (A)

COUNTRIES

A   Austria
DE   Germany
DK   Denmark
IT   Italy
NL   Netherlands

APPENDIX II. BUILDERS

The following builder codes are used in this publication (all are in Switzerland, unless stated):

ABB	ASEA Brown Boveri, Baden & Zürich Oerlikon (now Bombardier).
ACEC	Ateliers de Constructions Électriques de Charleroi, Belgium.
ACMV	Ateliers de Constructions Mécaniques de Vevey SA, Villeneuve (now Bombardier).
AD	ADtranz (ABB Daimler-Benz Transportation Systems), Oerlikon & Pratteln (now Bombardier).
AEG	Allgemeine Elektrizitätsgesellschaft, Berlin, Germany (now Bombardier).
ALIOTH	Elektrizitätsgesellschaft Alioth, Münchenstein.
ALSTOM	Alstom, several plants.
ASPER	Viktor Asper AG Maschinenbau, Küsnacht.
BBC	AG Brown Boveri & Cie, Baden, Münchenstein, Oerlikon (now Bombardier).
BBC (M)	AG Brown Boveri & Cie, Mannheim, Germany (now Bombardier).
BEIL	Martin Beilhack Maschinenfabrik, Rosenheim, Germany.
BIBUS	Bibus Hydraulik AG, Zumikon.
BL	Anciens Établissements Brissonneau & Lotz, Creil, France.
BOMB	Bombardier (numerous plants).
BREDA	SA Ernesto Breda, Milano, Italy.
BüH	Bühler SA, Taverne.
BüS	Büssing Fahrzeug und Motorenbau, Braunschweig, Germany.
CAT	Caterpillar, Peoria, Illinois, USA.
CEG	Chemins de Fer Électriques de la Gruyère (predecessor of GFM).
CEM	Compagnie Électro-Mécanique, France.
CET	Carminati e Toselli, Milano, Italy.
CFD	Chemins de Fer Départementaux, Montmirail, France.
CGV	Compagnie Générale de Villefranche sur Saône, France.
CMR	Constructions Mécaniques SA, Renens.
CUM	Cummins Engine Corporation, Columbus, Indiana, USA.
DBZ	Daimler Benz AG, Stuttgart, Germany.
DIEMA	Diepholzer Maschinenfabrik (Fr. Schöttler GmbH), Diepholz, Germany.
DMG	Daimler Motoren Gesellschaft, Stuttgart, Germany.
DUEWAG	Düsseldorfer Waggonfabrik (now Siemens).
DZ	Klöckner Humboldt Deutz AG, Köln, Germany.
DWA	Deutsche Waggonbau AG, Ammendorf, Bautzen, Görlitz, Germany (now Bombardier).
FFA	Flug- und Fahrzeugwerke AG, Altenrhein (later SWA).
FIAT-SIG	Fiat-SIG Schienenfahrzeuge, Neuhausen am Rheinfall (now Alstom).
FORD	Ford Motor Company, Detroit, Michigan, USA.
FUCHS	H. Fuchs Waggonfabrik AG, Heidelberg, Germany.
GANG	Carrosserie Gangloff AG, Bern.
GEC-A	GEC-Alsthom, several plants (now Alstom).
Gm	Gmeinder & Co GmbH, Maschinenfabrik Mosbach, Germany.
GM	General Motors AG, Biel.
GSEG	Gewerkschaft Schalker-Eisenhütte, Gelsenkirchen, Germany.
HEN	Henschel Werke AG, Kassel, Germany (now part of Bombardier).
HESS	Hess AG, Carrosserien, Bellach SO.
HÜR	H. Hürlimann Tractorenwerke, Wil SG.
IEG	Compagnie de l'Industrie Électrique, Genève.
JMR	J. Meyer AG, Rheinfelden.
JUNG	A. Jung Lokomotivfabrik GmbH, Jungenthal bei Kirchberg an der Sieg, Germany.
Kaeble	Kaeble-Gmeinder, Mosbach, Germany.

KM	Krauss Maffei AG, München, Germany (now Siemens).
KRON	L. Kronenberger & Söhne, Luzern.
KRUPP	Fried. Krupp Maschinenfabriken, Essen, Germany.
LEW	Lokomotivbau-Elektrotechnische Werke, Hennigsdorf, Germany (now Bombardier).
LISTER	R & A Lister & Co Ltd., Dursley, Glos., UK.
LMG	Lübecker Maschinenbau AG, Werk Dorstfeld, Germany.
LÜTHI	Eduard Lüthi, Worb.
MaK	Maschinenbau Kiel GmbH, Kiel, Germany (now Vossloh).
MAN	Maschinenfabrik Augsburg-Nürnberg AG, Germany.
MAYBACH	Maybach Motorenbau, Friedrichshafen, Germany.
MB	Mercedes Benz, Berlin Marienfeld, Germany.
MFO	Maschinenfabrik Oerlikon, Zürich Oerlikon (now part of Bombardier).
MOY	Établissement Gaston Moyse, La Courneuve, France.
MTU	Motoren- und Turbinen-Union GmbH, Friedrichshafen, Germany.
MWM	Motorenwerke Mannheim, Germany.
NEN	Martin Nencki AG, Fahrzeugbau und Hydraulik, Langenthal.
OK	Orenstein & Koppel AG, Dortmund, Germany.
PER	Perkins Engines Ltd., Peterborough, UK.
PETER	Konrad Peter, Maschinenfabrik, Liestal.
PFING	Pfingstweid AG, Zürich.
PLEI	Paul Pleiger Maschinenfabrik, Blankenstein, Germany.
POY	Moteurs Poyaud, Surgères, France.
Puch	Puch Werke.
RACO	Robert Aebi & Co AG, Regensdorf (later SLM).
RC	Regazzoni Costruzioni, Lugano.
REG	Officine Meccaniche Italiane Reggiane, Reggio Emilia, Italy.
REN	Régie Nationale des Usines Renault, Billancourt, France.
RIET	AG vormals J. J. Rieter, Winterthur.
RING	F. Ringhoffer Werke AG, Waggon & Tenderfabrik, Smichow, Czech Republic (later CKD, then Siemens).
ROBEL	Robel Maschinenfabrik, München, Germany.
RUHR	Ruhrthaler Maschinenfabrik, Mülheim, Germany.
SAAS	SA des Ateliers de Sécheron, Genève (later BBC, now part of Bombardier).
SAU	AG Adolf Saurer, Arbon.
SCH	Christoph Schöttler Maschinenfabrik GmbH, Diepholz, Germany (trade name Schöma).
SCIN	Scintilla AG, Zuchwil.
SE	Siemens AG, Werk Erlangen, Germany.
SIG	Schweizerische Industrie-Gesellschaft, Neuhausen am Rheinfall (now Alstom).
SLM	Schweizerische Lokomotiv- und Maschinenfabrik, Winterthur (now Bombardier and Stadler).
SSW	Siemens Schuckert Werke, Berlin, Germany.
STAD	Ernst Stadler AG, Fahrzeugbau, Bussnang.
STECK	Ferdinand Steck, Maschinenfabrik, Bowil.
SWA	Schindler Waggon, Altenrhein (now Stadler).
SWP	Schindler Waggon AG, Pratteln (now Bombardier).
SWS	Schweizerische Wagons- und Aufzügefabrik AG, Schlieren.
SZ	Gebrüder Sulzer AG, Winterthur.
TIBB	Tecnomasio Italiano Brown Boveri, Milano, Italy (now Bombardier).
TUCH	Gebrüder Tuchschmid AG, Frauenfeld.
U23A	Uzinele 23 August, Bucuresti, Romania.
VBZ	Verkehrsbetriebe der Stadt Zürich (Zürich Tramways).
VM	Stabilimenti Meccanici VM SpA, Cento Ferrara, Italy.
VOITH	J. M. Voith GmbH, Heidenheim, Germany.
VOSS	Vossloh Locomotives GmbH, Kiel, Germany.
VR	Von Rollsche Eisenwerke, Gerlafingen.
VW	Volkswagenwerke, Wolfsburg, Germany.
WIND	Rheiner Maschinenfabrik Windhoff AG, Rheine, Germany.
WINPRO	Winpro AG, Winterthur (formerly SLM, now Stadler).
ZÜR	Zürcher & Cie SA, St. Aubin.

Other initials used for builders are the railway companies which built or rebuilt stock.

APPENDIX III. COMMON TERMS IN ENGLISH, FRENCH and GERMAN

English	French	German
railway	le chemin de fer	Die Eisenbahn
train	le train	Der Zug
locomotive	la locomotive	Die Lokomotive (Lok)
electric loco	la locomotive électrique	Die Elllok
steam loco	la locomotive à vapeur	Die Dampflok
shunter	la locomotive de manoeuvre	Die Kleinlok
passenger coach	la voiture	Der Reisezugwagen
couchette	la couchette	Der Liegewagen
restaurant car	la voiture-restaurant	Der Speisewagen
electric multiple unit	l'automotrice éléctrique	Der Elektrotriebwagen
trailer car	la remorque	Der Beiwagen
freight train	le train de marchandises	Der Güterzug
sleeping car	la voiture-lits	Der Schlafwagen
class (of vehicles)	la série	Baureihe
wheel	la roue	Das Rad
station	la gare	Der Bahnhof (Bhf)
main station	la gare principale	Der Hauptbahnhof (HB)
platform	le quai	Der Bahnsteig
rail	le rail	Die Schiene
track	la ligne/la voie	Der Gleis
(narrow) gauge	voie (étroite)	Das Spurweite (schmalspur)
goods depot	la gare de marchandiises	Der Guterbahnhof
marshalling yard	(la gare de) triage	Der Rangierbahnhof (abbreviated to Rbf)
loco depot	le dépôt	Der Bahnbetriebswerke (abbreviated to Bw)
stabling point	la remise	
works	le dépôt	Ausbesserungswerke (abbreviated to AW)
passenger	le voyageur	Der Reisender (m), Die Reisende (f)
ticket	le billet	Die Fahrkarte
single	aller simple	einfache Fahrt
return	aller-retour	hin-und-rück Fahrt
first class	la première classe	Erste Klasse
second class	la deuxième classe	Zweite Klasse
to change (trains)	changer (de train)	umsteigen
late	en retard	haben Verspätung
driver	le conducteur	Der Lokführer
guard, conductor	le chef de train/controleur	Der Zugführer (m)/Die Zugführerin (f)
strike	la grève	Das Streik
timetable	les horaires	Der Fahrplan, das Kursbuch
	l'indicateur (on paper)	

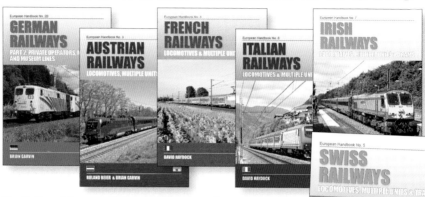